JOURNAL FOR THE STUDY OF THE OLD TESTAMENT
SUPPLEMENT SERIES
178

Sheffield Academic Press
Sheffield

Between Sheol and Temple

Motif Structure and Function
in the I-Psalms

Martin Ravndal Hauge

Journal for the Study of the Old Testament
Supplement Series 178

In memory of Professor Arvid Schou Kapelrud

Copyright © 1995 Sheffield Academic Press

Published by Sheffield Academic Press Ltd
Mansion House
19 Kingfield Road
Sheffield, S11 9AS
England

Typeset by Sheffield Academic Press
and
Printed on acid-free paper in Great Britain
by Bookcraft
Midsomer Norton, Somerset

British Library Cataloguing in Publication Data

A catalogue record for this book is available
from the British Library

ISBN 1-85075-491-8

CONTENTS

ABBREVIATIONS

AB	Anchor Bible
AnBib	Analecta biblica
ATANT	Abhandlungen zur Theologie des Alten und Neuen Testaments
ATD	Das Alte Testament Deutsch
BETL	Bibliotheca ephemeridum theologicarum lovaniensium
Bib	*Biblica*
BKAT	Biblischer Kommentar: Altes Testament
BWANT	Beiträge zur Wissenschaft vom Alten und Neuen Testament
BZAW	Beihefte zur *ZAW*
CBQ	*Catholic Biblical Quarterly*
CBQMS	*Catholic Biblical Quarterly* Monograph Series
ConBOT	Coniectanea biblica, Old Testament
FRLANT	Forschungen zur Religion und Literatur des Alten und Neuen Testaments
HAT	Handbuch zum Alten Testament
HSM	Harvard Semitic Monographs
HUCA	*Hebrew Union College Annual*
IB	*Interpreter's Bible*
Int	*Interpretation*
JBL	*Journal of Biblical Literature*
JSS	*Journal of Semitic Studies*
OBO	Orbis biblicus et orientalis
OTL	Old Testament Library
SBLDS	SBL Dissertation Series
SBM	Stuttgarter biblische Monographien
SBS	Stuttgarter Bibelstudien
ST	*Studia theologica*
TBü	Theologische Bücherei
TLZ	*Theologischer Literaturzeitung*
TZ	*Theologische Zeitschrift*
VT	*Vetus Testamentum*
VTSup	*Vetus Testamentum*, Supplements
WMANT	Wissenschaftliche Monographien zum Alten und Neuen Testament
ZAW	*Zeitschrift für die alttestamentliche Wissenschaft*
ZTK	*Zeitschrift für Theologie und Kirche*

ACKNOWLEDGMENTS

The first draft of this book was set out at King's College London during the academic year of 1989-90. It was possible to stay for so long and in such good working conditions at the Department of Theology and Religious Studies thanks to the intercession of Professor Michael A. Knibb. For his help and steady encouragement I am deeply indebted.

During this year I was supported by the The Norwegian Research Council for Science and the Humanities, which was brought about, I believe, by my colleague Professor Halvor Moxnes.

My colleague Professor Hans M. Barstad has provided cheerful companionship and invaluable help in surmounting the intricacies of technical 'word processing'.

The initial delight in having my manuscript accepted for the JSOT Supplement series was great indeed. It has been added to by the care and effort put into the publication by Sheffield Academic Press.

Chapter 1

PSALM 140: INTRODUCTION

Deliver me, Yahweh, from the evil man,
from the man of violence preserve me!
Those who plot evil in the heart,
every day they provoke battle.
They sharpen their tongue like a serpent,
the viper's poison is under their lips.
Guard me, Yahweh, from the hands of the unjust,
from the man of violence preserve me!—
Those who plot to 'push my steps'.
The proud have hidden a trap for me,
with cords they spread a net,
by the wayside they set snares for me.
I say to Yahweh: You are my God!
Give ear, Yahweh, to the sound of my supplications!
Yahweh my Lord, my powerful salvation!
you covered my head on the day of battle.
Grant not, Yahweh, the desires of the unjust,
do not prosper his plans!
Those who surround me lift up their heads.
Let the mischief of their lips overwhelm them!
Let burning coals fall upon them.
Let them fall into pits and never stand up.
The man of tongue shall not stand firm in the land.
The man of violence—let evil hunt him speedily down!
I know that Yahweh shall judge the afflicted,
shall execute justice for the poor.
Yes, the righteous shall praise your name,
the upright shall dwell in your presence.

1. Basic Questions

Psalm 140 makes a good starting point for an inquiry into the characteristics of the I-psalms. As one of the less popular texts,[1] it has invited
stereotyped treatment as an expression of a certain genre, and thus
serves as a good illustration of the traditional models of interpretation.

The understanding of the psalm is traditionally sought in connection
with the I of the text as related to his enemies. Three motif groups which
describe the enemies have been distinguished: the motifs of war (vv. 3b,
8b), of the hunt (v. 6, cf. also v. 12b), and of words (vv. 4, 10, 12a). In
addition, the judicial motifs of v. 13, usually combined with the word
motifs and/or the first sentence of v. 12, can be emphasized as significant.

When motifs of war are stressed,[2] the I is seen as a king or national
leader, under attack by national enemies, in the appropriate ritual situation before battle. Thus war motifs are understood as literal references to
the actual historical and ritual situation. The other motif groups are subordinated to the one understood in the literal sense. This subordination is
different for the different motif groups. The word motifs, as referring to
a situation of planning or cursing, can express aspects of the actual situation. But motifs of hunt[3] or of judgment[4] are separated from any
immediate connection with the actual situation, and are given some
figurative function.

When word motifs are stressed as the most literal expression for the
Sitz im Leben, the I is usually regarded as a private individual with private
problems. Motifs of war and hunt then have some figurative function.[5]

1.	The psalm is 'one of the less pleasing examples' without any 'high spiritual
aspirations or sense of personal frailty' according to Taylor in W. Stewart McCullough
and W.R. Taylor, *The Book of Psalms* (IB 4; New York: Abingdon Press, 1955),
p. 718.
2.	H. Birkeland, *Die Feinde des Individuums in der israelitischen Psalmen-
literatur. Ein Beitrag zur Kenntnis der semitischen Literatur- und Religionsgeschichte*
(Oslo: Grøndahl & Søns Forlag, 1933), pp. 228ff.; S. Mowinckel, *Salmeboken*
(Skriftene 1. Del, Det gamle testamente oversatt av Michelet, Mowinckel og Messel,
IV; Oslo: H. Aschehoug, 1955), p. 279; S.J.L. Croft, *The Identity of the Individual in
the Psalms* (JSOTSup 44; Sheffield: JSOT Press, 1987), p. 32.
3.	Mowinckel, *Salmeboken*, p. 279.
4.	Birkeland, *Die Feinde*, p. 230 on war 'als ein Rechtsstreit dargegestellt'.
5.	Cf. H. Gunkel, *Die Psalmen* (Göttingen: Vandenhoeck & Ruprecht, 5th edn,
1968), p. 594 on the war motifs as 'eine dichterliche Übertreibung', based on material
from Royal psalms. According to Taylor, *Psalms*, p. 718, the author is 'comparing'

The enemies' words can refer to curses, to which the present psalm forms a contra-curse,[6] or to some kind of slander.[7] When related to a national figure, the motif group can be seen to reflect the special situation of the king beset by internal opponents in addition to his national enemies.[8]

When judicial forms and motifs—usually combined with the word motifs—are stressed, the dominant situation of the psalm becomes one of judicial procedure. According to the classic theory of H. Schmidt, the enemies are the prosecution versus the I as defendant, appealing to the ultimate divine judgment.[9]

For the judicial approach also, the text is seen as a reflection of some actual life situation. Features relevant to this situation form the centre of gravity for understanding the psalm, and are treated as more or less literal expressions. Other features which are less directly connected with a situation of judicial procedure are given some kind of metaphorical function. Thus motifs of war and hunt are seen as metaphorical pictures within the dominant interpretational framework.[10]

---

the enemies to warriors and hunters. M. Dahood (*Psalms III. 101–150* [AB; New York: Doubleday, 1970], p. 301) uses the term 'liken'. E.S. Gerstenberger (*Der bittende Mensch. Bittritual und Klagelied des Einzelnen im Alten Testament* [WMANT 51; Neukirchen-Vluyn: Neukirchener Verlag, 1980], pp. 145-46) finds 'dem Kriegs- und Jagdleben entliehenen Bilder'.

6.   Gunkel, *Psalmen*, p. 594; cf. also Gerstenberger, *Der bittende Mensch*, p. 146 who resumes Mowinckel's hypothesis from 1921 on black magic.

7.   Taylor, *Psalms*, p. 718; Dahood, *Psalms III*, p. 301; L. Ruppert *Der leidende Gerechte. Eine motiv-geschichtliche Untersuchung zum Alten Testament und zwischentestamentlichen Judentum* (FB 5; Würzburg: Echter Verlag, 1972), p. 183.

8.   Croft, *The Identity of the Individual*, p. 32.

9.   H. Schmidt, *Die Psalmen* (HAT 15; Tübingen: Mohr, 1934), p. 246; A. Weiser, *Die Psalmen* (ATD 14/15; Göttingen: Vandenhoeck & Ruprecht, 1955), pp. 559-60; H.-J. Kraus, *Psalmen* (BKAT XV/1 and 2; Neukirchen-Vluyn: Neukirchener Verlag, 1961), pp. 924ff.; W. Beyerlin, *Die Rettung der Bedrängten in den Feindpsalmen der Einzelnen auf institutionelle Zusammenhänge untersucht* (FRLANT 99; Göttingen: Vandenhoeck & Ruprecht, 1970), p. 33; L. Delekat, *Asylie und Schutzorakel am Zionheiligtum. Eine Untersuchung zu den privaten Feindpsalmen* (Leiden: Brill, 1967), pp. 216-19; L. Ruppert, 'Klagelieder in Israel und Babylonien—verschiedene Deutungen der Gewalt', in N. Lohfink (ed.), *Gewalt und Gewaltlosigkeit im Alten Testament* (Quaestiones Disputatae 96; Freiburg. Herder, 1983), pp. 151-52.

10.   Cf. Schmidt, *Psalmen*, and Kraus *Psalmen*, on 'der bildlichen Veranschaulichung', also Beyerlin, *Rettung*, on v. 11 and Delekat, *Asylie*, on v. 4 as 'Bilder'.

While the underlying text-theory seems to be the same, the judicial approach varies somewhat from the other models in the understanding of what constitutes the dominant situation. Those who find the I to represent the king or a private figure beset by individual enemies tend to stress the text as some reflection of the actual life situation of the I. All presuppose the text to reflect some kind of ritual. But in understanding this ritual, commentators use the text mainly as a reservoir of data on the character of the life crisis of the I. When judicial motifs are stressed, the text is analysed mainly as a reflection of the agenda of the ritual ordeal.[11]

This short survey of the basic models of approach to the psalm refers to the monumental effort of interpretation since Gunkel. The basic models are mutually exclusive. The either/or character of the positions involved veils the fundamental affinity of these approaches. What I find most remarkable is not the differences, but the similarity of a given mind-set again and again turning to solutions originally stated by the scholars of Gunkel's generation. Thus, Gerstenberger's *Der bittende Mensch* of 1980 is remarkably similar to the 'pre-Birkeland' *Psalmenstudien I* of Mowinckel from 1921 with regard to results and to methodology. This is extraordinary, especially as Gerstenberger's work does not represent any deliberate reference to the 'old ways', but relates to the scholarly efforts of the whole period both negatively and positively.

The close affinity of given mind-sets together with the exclusivity of the single position taken has led to a very repetitive situation, with each new approach to the old problem striking out for a new beginning,[12] cut down to size by the next.[13] Given this background, it is extremely important to describe the common denominator of these approaches, which has proved itself so extremely hard-wearing and which must be so fundamental for the traditional exegetical procedures.

The most striking characteristic of these approaches is their methodological simplicity. Complex and ambiguous sets of textual data are sifted and labelled as they relate to some fundamental question on some specific

11. Especially detailed by Schmidt *Psalmen*, and Beyerlin *Rettung*, and very concretely by Delekat, *Asylie*, pp. 218-19, 235.

12. E.g. Delekat, *Asylie*, pp. 1-11; Gerstenberger, *Bittende Mensch*, pp. 3-11, 165ff.

13. On Delekat see, for example, Beyerlin, *Rettung*, pp. 15-16; on Delekat and Beyerlin see Ruppert, 'Der leidende Gerechte', pp. 7ff.; on Gerstenberger see Ruppert, 'Klagelieder', pp. 113-14.

social grouping or some specific institutional background. The resulting basic positions are of a peculiarly exclusive character, confronting and negating what exegetical practice has established as, at least possible, alternative positions. The exegetical practice of the last seventy years should fully have demonstrated the necessity of more inclusive sets of criteria. Referring to this experience, P.D. Miller[14] asserts 'open' and 'openness' as key words when suggesting a better approach to the text. The 'language of the psalms is open', with 'an openness to varieties of application and actualization'.

In the second place, and probably even more importantly, the simplicity of the basic positions is combined with an extremely subtle exegetical approach. By the established practice, the exegete is free immediately to describe the text as the expression of multidimensional reality or sometimes 'realities', with the text treated as a combination of elements which refer to different sets of reality. In terms of method, this represents an ambitious undertaking indeed!

The different positions on Psalm 140 can serve for a demonstration of this basic attitude. Independent of the different positions, there is a general agreement that the textual elements broadly fall into two categories.

1. There are elements which can be treated as relatively literal expressions for the original function of the psalm, to be paraphrased into the exegete's chosen vocabulary. As the psalm is usually transcribed into some kind of biographical categories, these elements are seen to describe the historical situation of the I. This 'situation' refers to the actual life situation of the person described in the first person, and/or the ritual situation of the I when some actual life problem is related to the appropriate rite. These elements are thought to reflect directly the actual situation of the I. The war, word and judicial motifs of Psalm 140 exemplify elements of this type. As only one motif type can be given this function of 'literalness', the exegete's task becomes very much a quest for elements of this type.

2. The other type of element has a more indirect connection with the dominant situation. Compared to the literal elements, this second type is given some kind of figurative function, suggested by terms like 'Bild', 'bildliche Veranschaulichung', 'liken', 'compare'. These terms cover a number of interpretative possibilities, dealing with what critics of non-biblical literature would describe by a number of terms (e.g. pleonasms,

14. P.D. Miller, 'Trouble and Woe (Interpreting the Biblical Laments)', *Int* 37 (1983), p. 35.

similes, metaphors, symbols). Only rarely is the precise function of these elements discussed, usually in confrontational connections.[15] This rather relaxed treatment of this type of element must be due to its supposed secondary value in the description of the character of the text. The elements defined as figurative usually represent elements rejected as literal and thus as really important for the understanding of the psalm.[16]

In this way, the different positions with regard to the understanding of Psalm 140 are manifested as different sets of 'literal' and 'figurative' elements. What is one scholar's literal element becomes the other scholar's metaphor, and vice versa.

To discriminate between elements with different functions in a text, as for example dominant and subordinate elements, represents a rather natural operation. That the discrimination outlined above has been so problematical must be due to the special interests which made it necessary. Its practice is determined by the historical interests of the interpreters: one type of element has significance for the dominating interest, the other not.

Both for a historical as well as for any type of interpretative approach to the psalms this method of interpretation is problematical. One suspects that the remarkable consistency which has resulted in the same questions and the same answers being pondered over and over again is an indicator of the similar cultural mind-set of the exegetes.

Due to the autobiographical form of these texts, the separation between literal and figurative elements and the possibility of culturally biased attitudes could be related to materially important aspects. The separation presupposes set opinions on what constitutes meaningful historical and biographical data, and excludes other phenomena as meaningful. Thus, the crisis of the I is usually related to some version of the basic crises of sickness, war or some judicial process. These crises

15. E.g. royal concepts as 'übernommen' or 'demokratisiert' Kraus, *Psalmen*, p. 925: As 'democratisized', the elements describe the I within a royal typology as 'king', which make the War motifs significant for the understanding of the psalm. When 'übernommen', the War motifs are rejected to secondary status as similes.

16. This description could seem unjustified when applied to e.g. Gerstenberger, *Bittende Mensch*, who in principle regards the text as 'Chiffren', decodable only through its setting (pp. 163ff., 118). The practical application of the theory, however, presupposes the traditional categories with certain text-elements (pp. 144ff.) forming the basis for observations on setting (pp. 130, 132, 135, 138, 140ff., 148ff., 152-53) and even on the character of the personal crisis (pp. 144ff., 132, 140), while the term 'Bilder' is applied to a certain type of element (pp. 145-46).

obviously represent meaningful types of personal crisis to the modern
reader, aside from representing highly possible transcriptions of some
important motif groups. On the other hand, the strong emphasis on
these and similarly concrete social or physical types of problem as
expressions for what the crisis 'really' is about, could lead to very lop-
sided representations of the texts.

The possible lopsidedness could be illustrated by the attention given to
elements which describe the relationship to Yahweh as essential to the
crisis. Such elements are usually given a rather subordinate function in
relation to the 'real' problem. In special texts like Psalms 84 and 42–43,
the distance between the motifs emphasized within the composition and
the modern transcription of what the texts are all about is quite remarkable. In these texts, 'God' is obviously not only described as some mir-
acle-producing *deus ex machina*, but as the object of intense longing.
The relationship to this 'God'—especially as made concrete by temple
motifs—forms a significant part of the motif development. These motif
groups could be expected to be reflected in the scholarly descriptions of
the 'real' problem. Instead the resonant sentences on this relationship
are obviously only seen as meaningful to the modern reader when
related to a concrete material frame of pilgrimage to some special festival; to rites of Thanksgiving presupposing the 'real' problem as solved;
or to a stay in the temple linked to some concrete cultic profession or to
protection in a specific life crisis. The very few and notable exceptions
only underline the peculiar tendency to treat motifs on 'God' as consistently figurative and ornamental with regard to the 'real' interests. The
transcription of the motifs into social, material, or physical categories
suggests that only certain types of phenomenon qualify as historically
meaningful, while elements which could reflect other categories—
potentially just as 'historical'—are virtually ignored. In this way, modern
notions of what constitutes real life problems and how real life problems
are related to 'religious' categories could exclude vital parts of what
constituted 'historical reality' to the psalm composers.[17]

This certainly should not be taken to mean that the transcription necessarily would have to define the 'real' crisis of, for example, Psalm 42
as somehow 'spiritual', with the implication of social and physical
categories as 'unspiritual'.[18] What should be avoided is the accepted

17. Cf. below to recent proposals to extend the definition of *Sitz im Leben* to
include a wider frame of reality.
18. With modern notions on 'spirituality' as equally fatal, cf. the difficulties

analytical habit of separation between elements understood to reflect directly the historical situation, and figurative elements.

The problem is confounded by this apparently two-levelled approach really being three-levelled. This is due to the special character of these texts as supposedly referring to ritual practice. The historical interest can be applied both to the actual life situation of the I or to the ritual situation in which the I is supposed to play a part. This three-levelled approach can be illustrated by the automatic identification of the literary figure 'the I'[19] with the 'worshipper' on whose behalf the psalm is applied in the cultic situation, and often with the 'author' too, either literally or in the sense that the text represents actual biographical references.[20] In this way, textual elements are related to three main types of reality:

1. Elements which reflect the actual life situation of the I.
2. Elements which reflect the ritual situation.
3. Subordinate elements with a literary, figurative function.

To undertake an analysis of contemporary literary texts for arriving at such subtle results would be ambitious. Indeed, literary critics, having traditionally tormented themselves only with two of these types of elements, left such an undertaking decades ago. When related to ancient

in defining the term *Spiritualisierung* without implications of spirituality and non-spiritualized phenomena illustrated by H.J. Hermisson, *Sprache und Ritus im altisraelitischen Kult. Zur 'Spiritualisierung' der Kultbegriffe im Alten Testament* (WMANT 19; Neukirchen-Vluyn: Neukirchener Verlag, 1965), pp. 24ff., 147ff.

19. The problems involved with the traditional identification of the author/user and the literary figure of the I is well illustrated by the discussion of N.H. Ridderbos arguing for the traditional position 'Response', *JSOT* 1 (1976), p. 17, and L. Alonso Schökel, 'Psalms 42–43. A Response to Ridderbos and Kessler (JSOT 1 [1976], pp. 12-21)', *JSOT* 3 (1977), pp. 62-63. To Alonso Schökel it is necessary to understand the I as a literary figure apart from the author: 'To simply make such an inference appears to me illegitimate, since it operates on an unproven and uncritical supposition: that the author has been making a personal confession'.

20. Usually taken for granted as a presupposition, this identification is precisely described by C.C. Broyles, *The Conflict of Faith and Experience in the Psalms. A Form Critical and Theological Study* (JSOTSup 52; Sheffield: JSOT Press, 1989), pp. 16-17. He employs the term 'psalmist', aware that the term can 'signify either the composer of the psalm or the worshipper using the psalm. By and large I will be referring to the composer.' Both 'composer' and 'worshipper' are assumed to 'have passed through each phase that a lament psalm represents: a distress, and an interpretation of it, and an appeal from it'.

texts, the results of such an undertaking must necessarily be haphazard.[21]

One suspects that the remarkable consistency of interpretation since Gunkel must be due (aside from the common mind-set of the exegetes) to the fact that the form-historical approach as applied in practice has left the materials with little or no possibility of resistance to manipulation. With the presupposed connectedness of ritual and actual life situation and the corresponding possibility of adapting the dominating elements to the most suitable reality, the freedom of the exegete is quite unrestricted. With the possibility of denouncing the most difficult elements as figurative, it is absolute!

With this background it could be tempting to leave the traditional quest as altogether too subjective. The original function and the original meaning of the laments in I-form could prove as elusive, illusory even, as the *ipsissima verba* of the prophet or the original shape of the Pentateuch traditions. Types of 'later' applications and actualizations of the texts could provide more tangible settings for interpretation, and could even have repercussions for the understanding of the 'original' character of psalm language. Such applications could be connected both to literary[22] and more general 'functional'[23] categories.

---

21. The basic form-historical model can be elaborated into an even more compli-cated version; cf. D.A. Knight, 'The Understanding of "Sitz im Leben" in Form Criticism', in G. MacRae (ed.), *SBL 1974 Seminar Papers I* (Missoula, MT: Scholars Press, 1974), pp. 105-25; and R. Knierim, 'Old Testament Form Criticism Reconsidered', *Int* 27 (1973), pp. 435-68, with Broyles, *Conflict of Faith*, for a con-crete application of their viewpoints. Referring to the unsatisfactory methodological situation outlined above, they have argued that the concept of 'setting' should be extended. Also, for example, historical, ideological-theological, literary and linguistic aspects should be included. In his application of these views, Broyles sets out to 'trace each lament psalm through its stages of composition: from the distress to the interpretation of the distress to the appeal'. The exegete should be taken 'step by step through the whole process of experience that a lament psalm reflects' (*Conflict of Faith*, p. 16). Such an extension of the *Sitz im Leben*-category represents an ironic twist of methodological development. Originally, form-criticism represented very much a reaction against the traditional emphasis on individual, rational and theological categories as important for Hebrew religion, with a new emphasis on social acts and social experience connected with institutions and cult. A strong expression for this reaction is represented by Mowinckel in *Norsk Kirkeblad 1921*, pp. 142-147, 164-168, presented in English in M.R. Hauge 'Sigmund Mowinckel and the Psalms—a Query into his Concern', *SJOT* 2 (1988), pp. 59ff.

22. Cf. especially T. Collins, 'Decoding the Psalms: A Structural Approach to the Psalter', *JSOT* 37 (1987), pp. 41-60. The structuralist model of Greimas is applied

On the other hand, the tenacity of the ever-recurring themes of analysis since Gunkel is a strong testimonial to the significance of historical questions. As nobody could believe that the texts fell down from heaven without some decisive relationship to some contemporary form of activity, this activity must have had consequences for the form and the meaning of the texts. Even if the texts should represent metaphorical systems, the significance of this type of language must be connected to meaning and thus to original background, to function and literary interest—intention[24] even—and also to the original reception and application. There must be some connection to the character of the environment in which such a remarkable language was created and experienced as meaningful. Even if later usages are 'intentionally' close to the

---

for the analysis of the psalms in their present literary setting in a book, with 'individual psalms...viewed as segments of the whole' (p. 41). Also to Collins, the psalms are originally a 'combination of both religious activity and literary production. In their original setting they were part of cultic ritual...' (p. 48). But with the emphasis on the texts as parts of a book, his understanding marks a radical change in viewpoint compared with the traditional approaches.

23. W. Brueggemann, 'Psalms and the Life of Faith: A Suggested Typology of Function', *JSOT* 17 (1980), pp. 3-32 (with a concrete example of application in 'A Response to "The Song of Miriam" by Bernhard Anderson' in E.R. Follis [ed.], *Directions in Biblical Hebrew Poetry* [JSOTSup 40; Sheffield: JSOT Press, 1987], pp. 297-302). He refers to the literary models of Ricoeur for fresh suggestions, with the emphasis on the function of the psalms. This includes also contemporary devotional use, which share with the ancient use 'a common intent and function even though other matters such as setting and institution may be different' (pp. 4-5). The wording suggests that 'setting' and 'institution' are of secondary significance, while 'intent' and 'function' refer to phenomena which are really important for the interpretation. Also to Miller, 'Trouble and Woe', pp. 32-45, the importance of later usages is stressed. The language of the psalms is 'open and metaphorical' (p. 35), with e.g. the enemies not to be pinned 'down to one particular category, group or type of person' (p. 34), open to varieties of application and actualization continued into the present. If one is interested in 'earlier actualizations of the psalms', this will 'be more usefully and helpfully done by relating the laments to narrative and historical context than by simply examining in as exhaustive a fashion as possible the language of the laments themselves...a step in that direction has already been made by the historical superscriptions to the psalms' (p. 36). With the emphasis on function and actualization as the important categories of interpretation, also these types of approach mark a radical change of viewpoint.

24. J. Barton, *Reading the Old Testament. Method in Biblical Study* (London: Darton, Longman & Todd, 1984), pp. 147ff.

'original' function, the prime intention/function must represent the prime point of attraction.

So, if we confess to the historical interest, the most immediate lesson from traditional exegetical practice consists in the warning against the methodological optimism which expresses itself in the immediate transition from text to historical considerations. If the criticism voiced above is valid, this optimism has traditionally manifested itself in the three- or two-dimensional treatment of the textual phenomena. New ways must be found to relate the text to the underlying religious activity. And while such new ways very much need to be found through trial and error, at least some beginning could be suggested from the traditional practice so obviously leading into perdition: the necessity practically to separate the historical interest from the actual textual analysis.[25] One practical way to start, then, could simply consist in keeping faithfully to the 'one-dimensionality' of the text.

Practically, keeping to this 'one-dimensionality' would mean valuing textual phenomena as *textual*, that is 'literary' phenomena, defined within the frame of the written text and related to other 'literary' phenomena of other texts. With the figure of the I as the focal point of investigation, this would mean valuing the I as a 'literary' phenomenon, his 'identity' given by the data contained within the frame of the text. Thus, the 'individual' of the text can neither be the author nor the 'user' /'worshipper', but must simply be designated 'the I'. This certainly should not be taken to mean that questions on authorship and original function are held irrelevant. But as exegetical practice has amply demonstrated, these basic questions cannot be answered directly from isolated I-elements within the texts.

Nor should 'one-dimensionality' mean that all textual data are to be treated as equal. Formal and rhetorical considerations—that is, considerations based on textual data—make it necessary to distinguish between 'central', or 'dominant', and 'subordinate' elements, as of course between different types of saying. Moreover, phenomena within the text might refer to phenomena 'outside' the usual I-situation (cf. below to 27.14 as related to 42.6, 12, 43.5 and to 62.9ff., 131.3). Intimately connected with such considerations are questions of function which will

---

25. The form-historical past could of course also invite some further finger-wagging at the dangers of projecting one's own ideas of historical reality into the past—but hardly with any practical consequences save pure passivity for the methodological presence.

sooner or later disturb any striving for a methodically neat and easy data collection. Indeed, while the term 'one-dimensionality' can serve as a useful rallying cry with regard to traditional exegetical practice, its usefulness soon exhausts itself when faced with textual reality. The list of possible sets of reference is frighteningly rich.[26] On the other hand, the very richness of interpretative possibilities stresses the necessity of the textual frame and *sensus literalis* as basic points of reference,[27] especially if one hopes to arrive at points of relevance for the historical interest.

This approach could also of course result in very unsatisfactory positions. In disregarding the accepted expressions for religious activity or allusions to contemporary *Sitz im Leben*, however speculative, we might isolate ourselves from the only means by which we could give the text any kind of meaning. The carefully assembled data might only results sets of *chiffres*, neatly arranged for the methodical purist, completely meaningless as the expression of a literary code.

On the other hand, recent models suggest that the texts could be meaningful also as literary codes. When later actualization and application is emphasized, the texts are implicitly understood as established and meaningful language systems also as separated from the experiences of the original author or 'user'.[28]

26. E.g. Broyles, *Conflict of Faith*, p. 13 on these texts as multidimensional: 'A lament psalm relates an experience, so it conveys a narrative. It presents this within a metrical structure, so it is poetry. It asks for something from God, so it is prayer. It pleads a case, so it is argument. It expresses a faith, so it is theology.' This list is only the beginning of the diverse dimensions of the text. 'The experience itself that a lament describes has its own set of dimensions. It may be historical, it may be cultic, but it is certainly psychological and social.'

27. Cf. Childs urging the return to the *sensus literalis* of scripture as opposed to the 'historical' or 'original' sense in connection with 'the present confusion in the discipline of biblical interpretation'; 'The Sensus Literalis of Scripture; an Ancient and Modern Problem', in H. Donner, R. Hanhart and R. Smend (eds.), *Beiträge zur Alttestamentlichen Theologie. Festschrift für Walther Zimmerli zum 70.Geburtstag* (Göttingen: Vandenhoeck & Ruprecht, 1977), p. 13. Whereas his arguments refer to the whole range of hermeneutical endeavour (cf. the critical remarks by J. Barr, 'The Literal, the Allegorical, and Modern Biblical Scholarship', *JSOT* 44 [1989], pp. 3-17), his categories might well be applied as catchwords for a proper practical approach. The disdain of Childs for the 'historical' and 'original' sense could result from a misplaced application of the historical interest. This interest might ultimately be linked with a methodically more relevant application of the *sensus literalis*.

28. Cf. notes 22 and especially 23 aside from the general presentation Barton,

When the texts are valued as 'literary' phenomena, in opposition to other types of approach, single-minded study of the single text might be the natural consequence. After so many years of emphasis on the single text as the individual expression of some *Gattung*, the individual character of the texts could deserve more attention.[29] In my opinion, Alonso Schökel's short study of Psalms 42–43,[30] compared to traditional approaches, is a remarkable suggestion of the richness contained within a text allowed to 'speak for itself'—at least to some minimum degree of self-expression—and not as an unhappy representative for the assumed typical nature of some genre.

On the other hand—especially with 'original meaning' linked to the figure(s) of the I as the ultimate question—so many texts are so hauntingly 'similar' in certain respects. Behind the singular formal-rhetorical frame of the single composition, we immediately note many central phenomena which link to other texts. What is immediately experienced as a singular whole could just as well be described as an individual compilation of stereotypes.[31] 'Stereotypes' could refer to phenomena of a formal nature, for example, with regard to subunits, certain types of phrase, and certain formal structures.[32] But also, and above all when linked to questions of the figure of the I, with regard to more material categories there is a link with certain sets of motifs and concepts arrayed in certain structures. When such aspects are stressed, the frame, not only of the single text, but also of the genre as a whole, has to be widened to include texts of different literary genres as parallel reflections of given phenomena. A search for parallel texts, and thus for comparable phenomena, could also result in a better ability to appreciate the singular character of the single text.[33] This is especially the case when we pay

Reading the Old Testament, pp. 140ff.

29. M. Weiss, 'Die Methode der "Total-Interpretation"', in *Uppsala Congress Volume 1971* (VTSup 22; Leiden: Brill, 1972), pp. 88-112.

30. 'The Poetic Structure of Psalm 42–43', *JSOT* 1 (1976), pp. 4-11.

31. R. Alter, *The Art of Biblical Poetry* (New York: Basic Books, 1985), pp. 112-13.

32. Cf. especially R.C. Culley, *Oral Formulaic Language in the Biblical Psalms* (Near and Middle East Series 4; Toronto: University of Toronto Press, 1967); further I. Ljung, *Tradition and Interpretation. A Study of the Use and Application of Formulaic Language in the so-called Ebed YHWH-psalms* (ConBOT 12; Lund: Liber Läromedel/Gleerup, 1978); W.R. Watters, *Formula Criticism and the Poetry of the Old Testament* (BZAW 138; Berlin: de Gruyter, 1976).

33. Cf. Alonso Schökel, 'The Poetic Structure', p. 4: 'Identification of the

attention to the inherent uncertainties in the registration and interpretation of rhetorical effects in an ancient and specialized language system.

A situation of fundamental methodological uncertainty must also be emphasized with regard to the current trend to use terms like 'literature', 'literary' , and 'author' as catchwords to signal a special understanding of the character of the texts.[34] Such terms can be useful when opposed to traditional and 'non-literary' approaches. With this confessional function, emphasizing the significance of data contained within the textual frame above and instead of the traditional historical speculations, such terms are both subjectively necessary and also meaningful. But as expressions of some analytical categories, they may at best prove meaningless, at worst quite disastrous. With our basic ignorance of the character and function of ancient 'literature' and the ancient 'literary' genres, the terms cannot but channel modern notions of 'authors' and 'literary' activity.[35]

To conclude: a 'literary' approach in the present study is intended to avoid historical speculations in preference to textual data. The analysis of these data is meant to lead in the direction of 'original' meaning and function—so far as this aim can be linked to phenomena within the textual frame. Ultimately, this means that one could be stuck with the texts as sets of *chiffres* or as metaphor systems. In view of the attraction of these *chiffres*, such a fate ought to be preferable to the traditional exegetical practice of historical projection.

For practical reasons, the figure of the I represents the point of reference for the registration and relating of textual data. And finally, the obvious connections between certain texts together with our basic ignorance of the meaning of the single textual datum make comparable data

"form" of a psalm should serve to advance understanding of an individual poem, and not to dissolve it in general categories'.

34. For illustrations of the dramatic methodological changes that have taken place in Pentateuch criticism, cf. especially R.N. Whybray, *The Making of the Pentateuch. A Methodological Study* (JSOTSup 53; Sheffield: JSOT Press, 1987); further D.J.A. Clines, *The Theme of the Pentateuch* (JSOTSup 10; Sheffield: JSOT Press, 1982), pp. 7-15; and H.C. Brichto 'The Worship of the Golden Calf: A Literary Analysis of a Fable on Idolatry' *HUCA 54* (1983), pp. 1-44. On the other hand, the current trend invites the timely warning that also 'the literary character of the Old Testament historical narratives' has historical consequences: N.P. Lemche, *The Canaanites and Their Land. The Tradition of the Canaanites* (JSOTSup 110; Sheffield: JSOT Press, 1991), pp. 151-52.

35. Barton, *Reading the Old Testament*, pp. 166ff.

from other texts essential for any interpretative effort. Practically, this would mean that the figure of the I could be seen as a concept embracing a number of I's contained within the individual texts.

With the emphasis on the figure of the I as the central phenomenon, this study will immediately be connected with the biographical categories of the form-critical approach. As related to the situation of the I as the basic question, the texts are primarily analysed as compilations of motifs and interrelated motif groups, with the formal structure seen as an expression for the relationships between motifs. Moreover, the motifs are immediately translated into biographical categories, and understood as expressions for acts or events or aspects of a 'situation', with the I acting in a situation or series of situations. The main difference would be that the biographical data are limited to the textual frame, so that 'situations' refer to literary categories. Thus, the I related to Yahweh, to the circle of enemies in human or animal form, or to the circle of the righteous, or to temple activities, refers to situations equally 'real' as consecutive or related events within the one dimension of textual reality. Practically, this will also mean that it is possible to relate to and profit from the enormous mass of observations and insights of interpretation since Gunkel.

The emphasis on the significance of parallel expressions for the figure of the I could also be referred to traditional methodological positions. With the I as king, or sick, or involved in judicial procedures, data of *typicalness* have been stressed, with the text mainly valued as an individual expression for a superior socio-historical or ritual situation.[36] With the one-dimensionality of the situation stressed, the typicalness of the particular text could consist in some basic system of religious ideology connected to a set of concepts expressed in a series of motifs. And given the difficulties in translating directly from the literary reality of the texts to some concrete situation of socio-historical or ritual reality which is demonstrated by the form-critical efforts, the basic series or sets of motifs could well reflect a system of religious meta-language. Related to biographical categories connected with the I, this could imply the I as the typical or ideal or paradigmatic figure.

36. Cf. especially the general model of Mowinckel expressed by the terminological triad of 'cult-act', 'cult-myth', and 'cult-drama' as the basic aspects of what is typical for the concrete text, 'Det kultiske synspunkt som forskningsprincip i den gammeltestamentlige videnskap', *NTT* 25 (1924), pp. 10ff.; further *The Psalms in Israel's Worship I* (Oxford: Basil Blackwell, 1962), pp. 15ff.

24   *Between Sheol and Temple*

Such a position could be related to traditional models. The idea of democratization[37] of the so-called 'Uppsala School' implies royal ideology as an established set of concepts and motifs of religious interpretation, transferable in nature: whatever the particular life problem, the individual figure to whom the pattern is applied stands forth as the royal I, ideologically, and thus really described in the situation of the royal sufferer. Also, von Rad's idea of 'spiritualization'[38] would presuppose the idea—at least in certain central aspects—of the text as an expression of super-individual categories. With the text as 'kultisch-agendarisch gebundene Rede', the personal experience is expressed 'nur stark gebrochen in einem kultisch konventionierten Vorstellungs- und Phrasengut'.[39]

With this background, different sets of terminology could be applicable to describe the character of what is common for a number of texts. 'Mythical', 'ideological', 'metaphorical', recently also 'symbolical'[40] in connection with modern sociological categories[41]—related both to a primarily ritual or to a conceptual background—could all represent relevant terminological approaches to the common 'something'. Whatever term seems best suited to describe some concrete aspect, the number of individual expressions for the biography of the I indicates it to be supremely applicable for forever new actualizations. This would also indicate that religious activity and experience form an important part of the development and transmission of this biography.

Perhaps simply 'religious language' is the most flexible and un-biased term for what is common to these texts. In one respect, however, this

37. G. Widengren, *Sakrales Königtum im Alten Testament und im Judentum* (Stuttgart: Kohlhammer, 1955), p. 41.

38. E.g. *Theologie des Alten Testaments I. Die Theologie der geschichtlichen Überlieferungen Israels* (Munich: C. Kaiser, 1961), pp. 394ff., and further Hermisson, *Sprache und Ritus.*

39. *Theologie I*, pp. 397-98; cf. also other terms on the individual as related 'zum Typischen' (p. 397) and described as 'die paradigmatisch Leidenden' expressing 'das Urleiden der Gottverlassenheit' (p. 398). A parallel expression for the I as 'typical' and related to ritual categories is represented by Mowinckel, *Psalms II*, p. 133 (cf. also Gerstenberger, *Der bittende Mensch*, p. 139) on the I as cult-participant, defined according to the character of the special rite.

40. B.C. Ollenburger, *Zion the City of the Great King. A Theological Symbol of the Jerusalem Cult* (JSOTSup 41; Sheffield: JSOT Press, 1987) with a presentation of the terminology, pp. 19-22.

41. As especially influential C. Geertz, *The Interpretation of Cultures. Selected Essays* (New York: Basic Books, 1973).

term is not flexible—and properly so: the common denominator is profoundly religious. The use of the texts may indeed ultimately reflect the type of interest suggested by the traditional models. As solemn prayers or even as magical incantations, the ultimate interest of the texts might really consist in their forming part of some activity aimed at the production of some wish-fulfilment, with good health or success in some civil or national strife as the end-result. Even so, this interest is expressed in a type of language which, in its formal character, must be qualified as 'religious', centred in motifs which define the I as a being related to the divine reality.

On the other hand, it should be acknowledged at the outset that the solemn undertaking of some methodological purity as outlined above need not be sufficient to avoid the reader's bored feeling of *déjà vu* when facing any new study on the I-psalms. A boring interpretation of texts which are very much alive might not be related to the methodologically correct procedure within the established exegetical tradition, but to the need for some fundamentally new hermeneutical model encompassing cultural experiences since World War I.

In my opinion, this dilemma is well illustrated by the impression of the theories of René Girard.[42] Rejected as too subjective when related to the texts, his ideas on violence and victims—dealing with central Old Testament themes whose theological implications[43] are usually avoided—linger with the reader. Even if an impossible model of interpretation, they remain a haunting reminder of the possible existence of strata of meaning in the texts, left undisturbed by the traditional approaches. Moreover, his ideas could be especially helpful in connection with the I-psalms, where a new perspective is sorely needed, especially one based on ideas of collective violence directed towards the scapegoat. This is demonstrated by the self-professed non-specialist Raymund Schwager,[44] stressing the enemy constellation as the central situation for the description of the crisis. The I surrounded by the evil is an expression for 'eine urtypische Situation—und eine universale Erfahrung'.[45]

---

42. E.g. *La route antique des hommes pervers* (Paris: Grasset, 1985).

43. N. Lohfink, '"Gewalt" als Thema alttestamentlicher Forschung', in Lohfink (ed.), *Gewalt und Gewaltlosigkeit*, pp. 15-50 and especially pp. 39-40, 49-50.

44. *Brauchen wir einen Sündenbock? Gewalt und Erlösung in den biblischen Schriften* (Munich: Kösel Verlag, 1978) and also 'Eindrücke von einer Begegnung', in Lohfink (ed.), *Gewalt und Gewaltlosigkeit*, pp. 214-24.

45. *Sündenbock*, p. 105.

The enemy constellation applied to a private or royal or collective situation refers to the same type of experience. As objects for the enemies' banding together, the private I, the king, Israel, the just, the prophet, Zion, God even, all reflect this 'urtypische' situation of collective violence, the description of which express 'eine grundsätzliche theologische Aussage'.[46]

This type of understanding could also illustrate the possible implications of the term 'religious language', especially when related to how the traditional models of understanding transcribe the 'real' problem of the I in crisis into social, material, or physical categories. The problem of the scapegoat in Girard's universe is intensely physical. But the experience and interpretation of this problem—both by the collective's mythical projections and the victim's unmasking of the violence—transcend categories of social and personal 'success', dealing with the ultimate conditions of human existence. The recurrent attraction of such ideas is remarkable.[47] Even as rejected, they are lively demonstrations of the texts as possible reflections of more profound human experiences than usually suspected.[48] This could also imply that they reflect levels of textual reality which transcend the normal application of, for example, 'historical' and 'literary' categories—especially when applied as opposites. The very number and repetitiveness of studies on the I in the Psalms could witness the fundamental attraction of something important still unnamed.

46. *Sündenbock*, pp. 111ff. It is to be noted, however, that Schwager in his application of Girard's ideas on the concrete texts differs considerably from Girard's treatment of Old Testament texts demonstrated in *la route antique* .

47. The influence of the basic ideas of James Frazer must be considerable upon this model (e.g. H.J. Lundager Jensen, 'Efterskrift', in R. Girard, *Job—Idol og syndebuk* [Fredriksberg: Forlaget ANIS, 1990], p. 179). The so-called 'Uppsala School' marks a parallel application of these ideas, especially as represented by Ivan Engnell. The line from the Suffering King in the I-psalms to the suffering of Christ in the New Testament (e.g. the article on suffering, 'Lidande', in I. Engnell and A. Fridrichsen [eds.], *Svenskt Bibliskt Uppslagsverk. Andra bandet* [Gävle: Skolförlaget, 1952], pp. 69-78) corresponds closely to that of Girard, linking the fundamental character of Job as scapegoat to Christ.

48. Cf. also the efforts to refer a number of I-texts to categories of theological and personal conflict related to experience, represented by W. Brueggemann, 'Shape for Old Testament Theology I: Structure Legitimation', *CBQ* 47 (1985), pp. 28-46 and 'Shape for Old Testament Theology II: Embrace of Pain', *CBQ* 47 (1985), pp. 395-415; and Broyles, *Conflict of Faith*.

2. *The Basic Motifs*

The formal structure of Psalm 140 can be connected to the introductory elements 'I say' v. 7 and 'I know' v. 13. Accordingly there are two sections of prayers (vv. 2-6 and 7-12). The second prayer section begins with a confession to Yahweh (vv. 7a-8) and contains a gradual transition from prayers addressed to Yahweh to 'wishes' in the third person (vv. 10b-11), ending with the special v. 12. Finally, vv. 13-14 form some kind of concluding statement of belief.

Within this structure, the situation of the I is relatively clear. He is related to somebody 'evil' as his enemies and to Yahweh as his God. The qualification of the enemies as evil forms an important aspect for the text as whole. This is most easily seen in the stylized composition of the first part, with a repeated sentence structure in vv. 2-4 and 5-6. An introductory prayer with the verb related to a complement based on negatively qualifying nouns ('the evil man' 2a, 'the guilty' in 5a) is repeated in the reversed order ('the man of violence' 2b and in 5a). This is followed by descriptive sentences introduced by *'ašær* (3-4, 5b-6). The descriptive sentences are dominated by verbs which describe the evil as related to the I by hostile acts (except the general nominal qualification 'the proud' of 6a).

The return to negative nominal qualifications in the concluding v. 12, which correspond to those of vv. 2 and 5a ('man of tongue', 'man of violence'), stresses the essential significance of the qualification of the enemies as evil for the psalm as a whole (cf. also the element 'the guilty', v. 9a in the first enemy prayer in the second part vv. 7-12).

In this context it is interesting that we do not find corresponding positive qualifications of the I as 'non-evil'. Verse 14, introduced by 13, forms a positive contrast to v. 12. The terms 'afflicted', 'poor', 'righteous', and 'upright' immediately contrast the negative terms of qualification used on the enemies. The meticulous composition of vv. 2-6 concluded by v. 12 could lead us to expect a similar relationship between vv. 13-14 and the I-elements in the rest of the psalm. But compared to the enemy descriptions, the situation of the I is described only indirectly. He is the object of the evil enemies' violence, and in this situation is praying for divine help. The significance of these—seemingly self-evident—aspects is stressed by the parallel 'I say' of v. 7 and 'I know' of v. 13.

The first element introduces a new series of prayers related to the

enemy situation. Similar to the pattern of prayer and enemy qualification
vv. 2ff., vv. 7ff. extend the prayers by qualifications of Yahweh as 'my
God', with nominal constructions (vv. 7a-8a) and a verbal sentence on
Yahweh's acts (v. 8b). Introduced by the 'I say', this suggests that the
material significance of the prayer situation is a situation of confession
and trust. Surrounded by terrible enemies, the turning to Yahweh for
help marks an act of confession, with trust in 'my God' as the contrast
to the active enmity of the evil. According to this indirect qualification,
the I presents himself as confessor in crisis.

This is supported by the second element 'I know' introducing the
final confession of vv. 13-14.

> I know that Yahweh shall judge the afflicted
> shall execute justice for the poor.
> Yes, the righteous shall praise your name,
> the upright shall dwell in your presence.

These verses are traditionally understood to have a function as expressions of confidence. Thus, the motifs of v. 14 are usually found to refer
to a ritual situation of thanksgiving. Most often this rite is placed in the
future, depending on the happy outcome of the crisis.[49] But the verse—
with the function of expression of confidence—can also be thought to
refer to a concluding ritual act within the present agenda in which the
psalm is originally set.[50]

On the other hand, v. 14 has also been more directly related to the
context. It can be seen as a contrast to v. 12:

> The man of tongue shall not stand firm in the land.
> The man of violence—let evil hunt him speedily down!

This verse can refer to a situation of 'Ausscheidung der Frevler aus der
Kultgemeinschaft' and from possession of the land, while v. 14 refers to
a contrast situation of participation 'in der Gemeinde'.[51] Or v. 14b is

49. E.g. Gunkel, *Psalmen*, p. 594; Taylor, *Psalms*, p. 721; Kraus, *Psalmen*, p. 924;
Mowinckel, *Salmeboken*, p. 279 (for the latter, v. 14 is a promise of future
thanksgiving in response to an oracle of salvation inferred to have taken place between
the ritual situations expressed in vv. 2-12 and 13-14).

50. To Schmidt, *Psalmen*, p. 246, the final situation concluding the judicial process
(cf. also Kraus, *Psalmen*, pp. 924, 926), by Gerstenberger, *Der bittende Mensch*,
p. 142 connected to the ritual 'des Bittgottesdienstes'.

51. Weiser, *Psalmen*, p. 560 in connection with the first sentence of v. 12 as 'ein
allgemeiner Grundsatz des Sakralrechts'; cf. also Kraus, *Psalmen*, pp. 925-26 on the
separate vv. 12a, 14b.

thought to refer to a special judicial act immediately connected with the acts referred to in the preceding verses, in which the asylum seeker is granted protection against extradition.[52] Or v. 14 refers to a situation of the 'just in heaven' in 'eternal union with God in the afterlife', contrasted to the fate of the slanderers in 'Hell' v. 12.[53]

It is to be noted that to both of the two types of understanding, the immediate identification of the I with the righteous and the upright of v. 14 is taken for granted.[54] Especially in contexts understood as expres–sions of confidence, 'I' and 'righteous' are evidently found as inter–changeable designations in this as in comparable texts. It is natural to suppose some kind of connection between the situation described vv. 13-14 and the situation of the I. But in view of the direct qualification of the I's enemies as evil, the determined use of third-person forms in the statements introduced by 'I know' should not be disregarded.

The significance of vv. 13-14 as statements in the third-person is evident when their formal background is taken into consideration. This is most easily seen for v. 14. This verse can be referred to a number of stylized sayings on the *ṣaddîq* in the Psalms. A group of such sayings is constructed with *ṣaddîq* in singular or plural for subject, linked with verbs or nominal constructions, and often related to parallel constructions with corresponding subjects, with nominal terms of religious qualification.[55] Similar to the relationship of vv. 14 and 13, a *ṣaddîq* saying can be extended by corresponding sentences with Yahweh for subject, related to human objects designated by corresponding qualifying terms.[56] Usually such sayings are statements on the fate of the qualified

52. Delekat, *Asylie*, pp. 157-58
53. Dahood, *Psalms III*, pp. 306-307.
54. Cf. generally Ruppert, *Der leidende Gerechte*, pp. 22, 39.
55. With *šāmaḥ* for verb 58.11, 64.11, 68.4 and further 52.8-9, 118.15-16, in imperative 97.12, 32.11, and with a corresponding verb 33.1. Similar sentence types on the fate of the righteous are found 37.29 (cf. also 25-26), 92.13ff., 112.6; cf. also 75.11b, 72.7a and 125.3. Nominal constructions on the fate of the righteous 55.23 and 58.12a, 97.11 and also 37.16.
56. Aside from the compilations of contrasted sayings on the plus- and minus-group in Pss. 34 and 37 cf. 32.10b related to v. 11, in 97.10a.b related to v. 11, 146.7-9b related to 8b and also 68.4, 6-7. Such sentence types with Yahweh for subject are also found as *ṣaddîq* sayings, as in the participle constructions 1.6a, 37.17b, 146.8b and also 34.21a; with the verb in impf. 5.13, in 7.10, in 11.5a and also 34.20b, 37.33, 40; in nominal constructions 14.5b, 34.16, 37.39a.

person. Moreover, their character as third-person statements must be significant.[57] Their formal characteristics and usage seem to indicate that they basically refer to proverbial sayings, stating—perhaps even citing—religious truths. In a number of cases, the saying might even represent a traditional, 'proverbial' statement of religious truth being applied as a citation to a new situation. But they could also represent individual *ad hoc* constructions, with a formal character which defines them as statements of a certain character and function.

Such a background corresponds to the concluding position of vv. 13-14, introduced by the element 'I know', with the 'yes' of v. 14 for further emphasis. This element could be related to some ritual event as its cause, with the 'I know' meaning 'I have experienced' or 'I have been assured of'.[58] But the formal character of vv. 13-14 points to a more general situation of confession.[59] Here, the 'I know' is to be related to the 'I say' followed by confessions and prayers in vv. 7ff., thus concluding a structural development with the emphasis on the I as confessor.

This background would also stress the significance of third-person forms in vv. 13-14. The situation of the I is clearly one of crisis, its solution the result of the prayers as responded to by Yahweh. And the description of the blessed fate of vv. 13-14 markedly refers to divine intervention.[60] The desired outcome cannot be taken for granted.[61] With

57. Cf. especially when connected to admonishments in the second person, 55.23 and 97.11 related to v. 10, and further 34.16-23 as related to vv. 12-15, and within Ps. 37. Due to the function of the beatitude, 1.3-6 and 112.2-10 must have a similar function of motivation. A corresponding pattern could also be seen in the connection between statement and challenge to praise, as in 97.12 related to v. 10, and 68.5 related to v. 4. In this context, 58.11-12 and 52.8-9 within compositions of warning and threat addressed to the evil, and also 14.5 as related to the rhetorical challenge of v. 6, could demonstrate a parallel negative use.

58. Cf. especially the reference to Mowinckel, *Salmeboken*, p. 279.

59. For comparison cf. 58.12, especially as related to v. 11, with a similar introduction as confession, here dependant on the divine intervention, and further 64.11 as related to v. 10 and the *śāmaḥ*-sentences in indicative form referred to above. 62.12 has a corresponding introduction to a saying with a similar function. These forms could provide a background for the understanding of the similarly introduced Isa. 3.10-11.

60. Cf. also the concept of *ṣaddîq*-hood connected to a special ritual examination and verdict with regard to the religious status of the cult seeker as part of special entrance rites; G. von Rad, 'Die Anrechnung des Glaubens zur Gerechtigkeit', in *Gesammelte Studien zum Alten Testament* (TB 8; Munich: C. Kaiser, 1971),

the term of *saddîq* in v. 14, it is natural to relate *saddîq*-hood and its consequences of a special fate to the divine act of judgment described in v. 13, that is a motif connection which can be related to the judicial categories of the terms illustrated by Deut. 25.1ff. While the divine intervention and the fate of the *saddîq* cannot be taken for granted, the I confesses his belief in Yahweh and a special fate for those 'judged' by Yahweh. The objective character of these confessions corresponds to and concludes the subjective first-person forms of the confessions in vv. 7a, 8.

Moreover, v. 14 can be related to v. 12 as a contrast statement on the negative fate of the evil. Formally the two verses correspond, with qualifying nouns dominant in the sentence construction. The first sentence of v. 12a especially, with the qualifying noun as subject, is stylistically close to v. 14. Equally stressed, 'man of tongue' and 'man of violence' correspond to the 'righteous' and 'upright'. The two verses are linked by their formal relationship to their context. Both verses represent a formal rupture with regard to the preceding sentences. This is most marked for v. 12. Verses 7-11 are dominated by verbal sentences, the evil-doers referred to as objects of the wished-for acts. Dominated by nominal qualifications, v. 12 stands out with a special formal character. Isolated from the context, v. 12 would naturally be read as a statement.[62] Verse 14 has a similar relationship to v. 13. While nominal qualifications are important to both types of construction, they do not have the commanding position within v. 13 as objects for the divine acts.

Such an antithetical relationship between vv. 12 and 14 corresponds to a typical usage for the *saddîq* sayings in the Psalms.[63] The formal

---

pp. 130-35; *idem*, '"Gerechtigkeit" und "Leben" in der Kultsprache der Psalmen', in *Gesammelte Studien*, pp. 225-47; W. Zimmerli, 'Die Eigenart der prophetischen Rede des Ezechiel', *ZAW* 66 (1954), pp. 1-26; *idem*, '"Leben" und "Tod" im Buche des Propheten Ezechiel', *TZ* 13 (1957), pp. 494-508; and also M.R. Hauge, 'Some Aspects of the Motif "The City facing Death" of Ps 68,21', *SJOT* 1 (1988), pp. 1-29.

61. It must be important that we do not find any formula in the first person which corresponds to the construction *saddîq hû / 'attâ* (cf. the references to von Rad and Zimmerli in the preceding note). Only in the case of Job could a self-description of this kind be construed, but then as blasphemy (32.1)!

62. Its verbs are usually read as subjunctives, but as indicatives by Weiser, *Psalmen*, p. 559.

63. Aside from the repeated contrast sayings of Pss. 34 and 37 cf. especially 1.6, 7.10, 11.5; 92.13-15 with the antithetical v. 8; 32.11 as related to v. 10; 68.4 as related to vv. 2-3; and also 55.23 followed by v. 24, 14.5a and b, 75.11, in addition to the

relationship of the two verses and their concluding location in the text suggest that they form parts of one antithetical saying. Their basic elements could reflect an independent literary past as proverbial statements, now being cited. Or they represent *ad hoc* constructions, given a form which qualifies them as contrasted statements of religious truth. In either case, they refer to each other as descriptions of the fate of contrasted positive and negative groups.

This function corresponds to their present use in the context. In this psalm, the negative and positive parts are split, with v. 12 concluding the prayers introduced by 'I say', v. 14 enlarged by 13 as the expression of the 'knowledge' of the I. The special function of v. 12 within vv. 7ff. is also suggested by the compositional development. In vv. 7-12 we find a gradual transition from prayers based on sentences with a divine subject to 'wishes' with different third-person subjects. The final sentence of v. 11b has the enemies for subjects. This development forms a natural transition to v. 12. Also, the motifs of the two final sentences of v. 11 correspond to those of 12a, with the enemies 'fallen' and 'not-rising', foreshadowing the 'man of tongue' as 'not-firmly standing in the land'. This development stresses the significance of v. 12 as concluding vv. 7-12. Introduced by 'I say', this part concluded by v. 12 prepares for and contrasts with the final statement introduced by 'I know'.

In addition, the conclusion of v. 12 also relates to the first part vv. 2-6. In this part, the meticulous composition stresses the significance of the enemies qualified as evil, with nominal qualifications (vv. 2-5, cf. above) which correspond to those of v. 12 and the contrasting qualifications of vv. 13-14. This reflects an interest which corresponds to the concluding statements.

With this background, and given the special character of the sentence type of vv. 12-14, it is possible to understand Psalm 140 as constructed upon the ground of a traditional contrast saying. But either as ground or as conclusion of the literary development, the final verses are central to the psalm. As objects of 'I say' and 'I know', these statements stress the impression of the I in this psalm as the confessor. Also, it is essential to this type of confession that it is expressed in third-person form, referring to the special fate of some specially qualified group, and without any explicit link to the situation of the I.

elaborate constructions 112.5-9 related to v. 10, and 146.7-9a related to 9b. In this context 58.11 reflects the contents of an antithetical saying, contracting the plus and minus-fate into one scene.

But even as a confession referring to some religious truth, vv. 13-14 must have a meaning applicable to the situation of the I. This is given by the relationship to the contrast saying v. 12. As conclusion of the prayers vv. 7ff. and connected with the nominal qualifications vv. 2ff., it is obvious that the enemies of the I are identified with the negative group of v. 12. Implicitly, the fate of the contrasted positive group should have a corresponding relationship to the fate of the I. But while the ideological qualification of the I's enemies is immediate, the corresponding description of the I is much more circumspect and indirect.

This reticence is natural with regard to the categories implied. The assignation of *ṣaddîq*-hood and its corresponding fate is impossible as a self-qualification, and refers to a divine subject. Moreover, the use of third-person statements corresponds to a situation of confession: surrounded by evil enemies, the I stands forward with sublime trust in Yahweh. The confession to the divine judgment and the blessed fate of the righteous as opposed to the negative fate, forms the basic expression of this trust. On the other side, this implies that the situation described in vv. 13-14 is also relevant for the I as the wished-for outcome of the crisis, dependant on the divine intervention.

The compositional development must be important for our understanding of the motif usage as related to the situation of the I. The motifs of v. 12 and especially v. 14 are the central expressions for the 'good' and 'bad' fate as linked to the contrasted positive and negative groups. 'Praising the divine name' and 'dwelling in the divine presence' contrast with the opposite fate of 'not-firmly standing in the land' and 'being hunted down'. These motifs do not refer unambiguously to one type of situation. Implicitly, the 'firmly standing in the land' of v. 12 is to be added to the 'praising and dwelling' of v. 14 as expressions for the positive fate.[64] Seen together, vv. 12 and 14 could well be abstracted into a contrast of 'life' and 'death'.[65] Especially for the negative fate, stressed when v. 12 is related to the rest of the psalm, 'death' might seem a

64. Cf. above and concretely Kraus, *Psalmen*, p. 926 on v. 14 referring to 'bleibende Aufenthalt im Lande Jahwes' or to 'Bleiben im Heiligtum'.

65. Cf. the references above to von Rad and Zimmerli, both stressing the significance of life for the concept of the *ṣaddîq* as admitted into the temple; on the other side Dahood, *Psalms III*, pp. 301ff. and N.J. Tromp, *Primitive Conceptions of Death and the Nether World in the Old Testament* (Biblica et Orientalia 21; Rome: Pontifical Biblical Institute, 1969), pp. 54, 94, 175, 191 on the negative motifs of Ps. 140 as allegorical expressions for death.

reasonable transcription of the different motifs. The use of 'firmly standing' and 'dwelling' contrasts some kinds of permanency and impermanency.[66] The motifs of v. 14 refer immediately to temple categories, alluding to a special type of 'remaining in the temple'. This 'remaining' is defined as a permanent relationship to the divine presence. Thus, at the very least, v. 12 would describe the opposite of staying in the temple, and indirectly stress the lasting character of the special temple abiding alluded to in v. 14.[67]

But in the present composition, the contrasted statements on the plus- and minus-fates are differently applied. The negative statement concludes the prayers on the enemies. The positive states the assurance of the I, as a confession of trust. On the other hand, the qualification of the I's enemies as evil and thus as qualified for the negative fate indirectly suggests that the blessed fate of permanent relationship to Yahweh also represents the possible outcome of the I's crisis. Dependent on divine intervention, the state of dwelling and praising, implicitly also of firmly standing in the land, must describe the blessed fate as possible also for the I, while the contrasting fate of v. 12 represents the negative outcome.

This connection is also suggested by the motifs which describe the crisis of the I in vv. 2-6. In the hands of his enemies, he is clearly on the verge of suffering the negative fate.

The rhetorical point of the concrete motifs—as for example motifs of war, hunt, poisonous words, 'pushing my steps'—obviously cannot be found in any effort to describe a typical life situation. The mixture of motif groups adds to the depiction of a completely hopeless situation, with the I given to defeat and destruction without divine help.

The most important aspect of the function of these motifs must be sought in the emphasis on the I as confessor within the psalm as a whole. As stereotyped visualizations of the 'very worst which could happen' to a human being, they make the confessions of vv. 7-8 and 13-14 stand out in relief. Such a pleonastic effect could be typical for this type of motif usage (cf. below especially with regard to Psalm 27).

---

66. E.g. Ps 37.9b, 11, 22a, 27b, 29, 34a on the plus group as somehow permanently related to the 'land', contrasted with sayings on the evil as somehow 'removed'.

67. For the connection of land and temple motifs cf. especially the use of the expression 'land of the living/life' Ps. 52.7 as contrasted with the temple motifs of vv. 10-11; and further land and motifs on the special relationship with Yahweh as contracted 116.9, Isa. 38.11; in both cases related to motifs of death.

But in addition, we also note the motif connection between the situation of the I in vv. 2-6 and of the evil in v. 12. The concluding description in vv. 5b-6 combines 'pushing my steps' with hunt motifs, corresponding in v. 12 with 'non-firmly standing' combined with a parallel visualization of hunt. Surrounded by more violent motif types, the enemies' 'pushing' would seem rather tame. But as related with v. 12, a general motif of 'falling' or 'causing to fall' could form a special and important motif group for the description of the negative outcome.[68]

Also v. 11b could be connected to these motifs. The enemies 'made to fall into pits...never to stand up' [69] represent parallels to the I as pushed and surrounded by traps. And v. 12 would be immediately connected with v. 11b, with 'firmly standing in the land' as opposed to 'falling into pits'.[70]

This motif connection suggests the negative outcome as identical for the contenders. Either the I is 'made to fall' by his enemies, or the enemies are 'made to fall' by Yahweh.[71] Contrasting with the fate of defeat, the special stay in the temple with a lasting relationship to Yahweh signifies the fate of victory.

---

68. Dahood stresses the significance of *dāḥâ* not in connection with this psalm, but as used 118.13 related to 5.11, 35.5, 36.13, 56.14, 116.8 'specifically to describe casting someone into the infernal abyss', *Psalms III*, p. 158; cf. Tromp, *Conceptions of Death*, pp. 172, 93, and further below to Pss. 36.13, 62.4, 118.13. The usage in Ps. 118 is especially interesting due to vv. 5, 13 and 18 as parallel narrative forms; cf. F. Crüsemann, *Studien zur Formgeschichte von Hymnus und Danklied in Israel* (WMANT 32; Neukirchen-Vluyn: Neukirchener Verlag, 1969), p. 219 on vv. 5, 13 and 17-18. The past crisis is described in parallel motif groups as confinement, as 'being pushed into falling', and as being chastened by Yahweh. The special significance of the 'pushing' is stressed by the form of v. 13 as an address to the enemy You.

69. Or read alternatively by relating the *bā'ēš*-element to the following verb, e.g. Kraus, *Psalmen*, p. 923: 'stürze sie ins Feuer, in Gruben, dass-'; also Dahood, *Psalms III*, p. 300.

70. The motif connection for the psalm as a whole is especially stressed by Dahood, *Psalms III*, pp. 301ff., who understands the motifs as metaphorical and allegorical expressions for 'death the hunter' and 'hell'.

71. Also, the pleonastic character of the descriptions of the enemy fate corresponds to the descriptions of the I as persecuted. In both cases, any literal connection to any actual life situation cannot be intended. The stereotyped character of v. 11 for example is illustrated by a similar combination of motifs of fire and hunt Ps. 11.6 and of fire and descent into Sheol in the present composition of Num. 16.

In this way, the composition of Psalm 140 is determined by the relationship of first-person forms and third-person statements. The crisis of the I is described as related to religious 'truths' on the fates of two contrasted types of human being. The 'personal' situation is interpreted as a concrete representation of aspects of the 'ideological' situation. The partial identification of the two types of situation is demonstrated by the enemies' qualification as evil, and thus as representatives for the minus group. The I is described as object for the evil's persecution and as confessor. For the situation of the I, the divine intervention is essential.

For the character of such a relationship between 'individual' and 'ideological'[72] situations, Pss. 55.23, 97.10-11 and Gen. 18.16ff. are good illustrations. In the two psalms, different types of admonishments in the second person are related to third-person statements on the blessed fate of the positive group. The relationship clearly presupposes some connection between the admonished you and the positive group. The blessed fate of the righteous must also be relevant for the You. On the other hand, the address as admonishment demonstrates that inclusion into the group of the righteous cannot be taken for granted. This is illustrated by the narrative of Gen. 18.16ff. Verses 23-25 allude to dogmatic statements in the third person on the fate of the righteous, the truth of which even Yahweh has to acknowledge.[73] And the statements are related to a concrete situation with regard to the cities' fate. But to find concrete representatives for the ideological figure of vv. 23-25[74] is obviously quite another matter. The haggling of Abraham in Genesis 18, leaving the verdict to the divine judge, and the rare application of the term *ṣaddîq* (6.9, 7.1)—the rarity surprising in a series of stories given to the fathers as paradigmatic figures—could suggest that the religious qualification of *ṣaddîq* is reserved for extraordinary phenomena.

---

72. The concepts involved do not only refer to religious ideals of abstract nature, but also to concrete representatives for the ideal figure. This is suggested by the righteous addressed in the hymnic challenges 97.12, 32.11, 33.1, and especially by the righteous referred to as a group (in e.g. 125.3 and also 52.8, 118.15-16) to which the I can be related (141.4-5, 142.8 and especially 118.19-20) and from which the evil are excluded (1.5, 69.28-29).

73. Also the concrete situation Gen 20.4 alludes to the term as connected with given truths.

74. Cf. the singular form of *ṣaddîq* and the contrast term *rāšā'* vv. 23, 25, while v. 24, referring to concrete representatives for the concept, has the term in plural form. It is natural to relate the difference to vv. 23, 25 as allusions to given sayings, while v. 24 represents the concrete application.

In this way, the third-person statements on the fate of the righteous as related to the crisis of the I in Psalm 140, to an admonished you, and to concrete figures in the Genesis narratives, form parallel applications of the concept of the righteous. Also, the applications of Gen. 18.23ff., 20.4 and of 6.9 and 7.1 provide an immediate illustration of the significance of the concept for the fate of those qualified: the *ṣaddîq* is spared from being killed by the divine judge. This corresponds to the descriptions of the I in crisis and the fate of the evil in Psalm 140 (cf. above to v. 12).

On the other hand, Psalm 140 suggests that the concept of the *ṣaddîq* as spared from death is connected with the idea of some special stay in the temple. Also with regard to the relationship to the evil, the motif structure in Psalm 140 differs from the Genesis narratives. In Genesis, the characters are related to the divine judge as righteous or evil, to be destroyed or spared by divine intervention. In Psalm 140, the relationship of the actors is more complicated. Here, the divine judge is related to contending parties, the victory of the evil meaning death for the I. By the logic of the motifs as they are used, the divine verdict as negative for the I would consist in letting the enemies have their way. But victory for the I, resulting from divine intervention, means death for the evil at the hands of the divine judge.

The different consequences of divine judgment could reflect different applications of the concepts. Compared to the richer motif structure of Psalm 140, the Genesis applications would centre on the divine intervention in its negative mode. The differences could also reflect historical development, with the two types of application representing a succession of different types of usage.[75] For now, the Genesis applications can serve for illustrations of important aspects of the concepts developed in Psalm 140.

---

75. Cf. e.g. Kraus, *Psalmen*, pp. 928-29 with separation between 'older' and 'younger' laments, the conflict accordingly related to original social categories of 'Anklage und Verfolgung', in younger texts related to religious categories of 'Verführung' connected with law observance; cf. also p. 851. For the texts analysed below, this distinction seems rather speculative.

Chapter 2

PSALMS 84 AND 36: THE PARADIGM

For the composition of Psalm 140, we found the relationship of I-forms
to third-person forms to be important. And for the third-person statements, motifs on dwelling in the temple express the fate of the positive
paradigmatic figures. The significance of these aspects can be illustrated
by Pss. 84.5-8 and 36.8-13.

1. *Psalm 84*

This psalm has traditionally been connected with a situation of pilgrimage. The connection is usually found to be quite substantial, with the text
giving expression to the pilgrims' subjective sentiments[1] on finally
arriving at the holy city.[2] The pilgrims' arrival is usually connected with
some central festival, most often some version of the 'Autumn festival'.

Only the prayers in vv. 9-10 could disturb the supposed atmosphere
of festivity and yearnings fulfilled. But they are usually given a function
subordinate to the situation of festivity.[3] On the other hand, the occur-
rence of prayers should be an important pointer to the function of a text.

---

1. This 'privatisierende Stimmung' is refused by Gerstenberger, *Bittende
Mensch*, pp. 152-53, to whom the yearnings reflect the I as excluded from the official
cult due to sickness.

2. With v. 7 seen as expression for the concrete physical hardships involved in
the pilgrimage, the 'Baka-valley' even found to refer to a concrete spot on the road to
Jerusalem, e.g. Kraus, *Psalmen*, pp. 585-86; McCullough, *Psalms*, p. 455; or to Dan,
M.D. Goulder, *The Psalms of the Sons of Korah* (JSOTSup 20; Sheffield: JSOT
Press, 1982), p. 40.

3. E.g. by stressing the king's position as a central concern in connection with
the supposed festival, A.R. Johnson, *Sacral Kingship in Ancient Israel* (Cardiff:
University of Wales Press, 1967), pp. 104-105; Kraus, *Psalmen*, pp. 585-86. Or the
prayers can be seen as later additions, Gunkel, *Psalmen*, pp. 369-97; McCullough,
Psalms, p. 456; Gerstenberger, *Bittende Mensch*, p. 152 on the royal intercession.

Thus, both to Gerstenberger[4] and Delekat,[5] the prayer is decisive for the understanding of the psalm as a whole. Given the introductory invocation vv. 9-10 must express a concern of vital interest to the I:

> Yahweh God Zebaoth—hear my prayer!
> give ear, God of Jacob!
> God our Shield, look!
> behold the face of your anointed!

If we not are to conclude that the verses are so badly localized that they must be regarded as additional to the original text, the context suggests that they are connected with gaining entrance to the sanctuary.[6] Framed by v. 8 on the triumphant entrance of the blessed, and v. 11 on staying in the temple as the sublime good, the prayer introduced by the I-forms of v. 9 must be related to the I having his yearnings of vv. 2-4 fulfilled.

There is no indication of the function of verses 9-10 in the context. Somehow the I as related to the temple is connected with an act of intercessionary prayer or with Yahweh's looking favourably on the king. The character of the 'somehow' must be surmised from ideas not stated explicitly in the text. Thus, Delekat's ingenious hypothesis does justice to many phenomena in the text. Alternatively, the connection between the admittance of the I and Yahweh's favour towards the king could reflect some situation of entrance, in which the admittance of a group depends upon the admittance of a supreme 'enterer'.[7] Or the riddle could be

---

4. As an Individual Lament, *Bittende Mensch*, pp. 125-26, 'fern vom Heiligtum gesprochen' (p. 153), with the royal intercession secondarily added to the original prayer v. 9 (p. 152).

5. To Delekat, *Asylie*, pp. 242ff., the royal intercession v. 10 and the I's interest in the royal well-being represents the very interest of the psalm: vv. 2-4 express a retrospect on the past when the I was waiting for acceptance as 'Asylschützling' in connection with judicial proceedings. Verses 5-8 are a description of the life of the 'Asylschützling', also this seen from a rather remote point of view. First vv. 9ff. express 'das eigentliche Anliegen des Dichters': his period of asylum depends on the length of the life of the king during whose reign he was accepted to a permanent stay.

6. Cf. especially the similar composition of I-forms related to temple motifs and comparable third-person forms on the king in Ps. 61.

7. For a parallel cf. especially Ps. 118 with a We-group vv. 22-27 related to the entering of the I vv. 19ff. Also this psalm is characterized by an urgent prayer v. 25 which seemingly disrupts a context of praise and thanksgiving. The context relates the prayer to the situation of the I entering the special 'Gates of the Just'; M.R. Hauge, 'Salme 118—initiasjon av en Rettferdig', *NTT* 82 (1983), pp. 101-17.

solved by the king of v. 10 being identical with the I of the psalm.[8] Or simply, the I as described in the psalm might reflect a special cultic function[9] or religious position[10] where his intercession in favour of the king is relevant. Whatever the relationship between vv. 9 and 10, the prayer must be meaningful within a context of the I describing his relationship to the temple.

As in Psalm 140, temple motifs are expressed in special third-person statements:

> Blessed those who dwell in your house!
> ever in praise of you.
> Blessed the man whose strength is in you!
> their heart set on the highways.
> Going through the valley of Baka (?)
> they make it into a spring
> enwrapped in blessings by the early rain (?)
> They go from might to might,
> he appears before God on Zion.[11]

The understanding of these verses is usually sought in connection with the supposed ritual situation. Related to the yearnings of vv. 2ff., vv. 5ff.

8. Mowinckel, *Salmeboken*, p. 181. In this case, however, it should be noted that the entrance is connected with general religious criteria, cf. below to vv. 5-8 together with 13b.

9. The high-priest of Dan, or his deputy, according to Goulder, *Sons of Korah*, pp. 37-38, identical with the I of Pss. 42–43.

10. The relationship between the entering I and the We-group of Ps. 118 could also be relevant for this type of constellation—the We obviously understanding the fate of the entering I to be of communal significance. A parallel expression for such a relationship could also be expressed by the connection of I-forms and admonishment Pss. 62 and 131 (cf. Chapter 6), and also by the peculiar constellation in the present composition Exod. 33.12–34.9 setting the 'beatific vision' of Moses in a frame of intercession (cf. Chapter 5). Cf. also the ideas of D. Eichhorn, *Gott als Fels, Burg und Zuflucht. Eine Untersuchung zum Gebet des Mittlers in den Psalmen* (Europäische Hochschulschriften, 23.4; Frankfurt: Lang, 1972), pp. 123-24 on the I in a special group of psalms as a cultic servant responsible for a certain type of intercessionary and oracular functions.

11. Starting from the ancient translations, these verses have been objects to different shapings, especially vv. 7 and 8b. But the MT is understandable and reasonable as a rendering of poetic stereotypes. The transition from plural to singular from vv. 8a to b—usually corrected—corresponds to the transition from vv. 5 to 6. With the connection between 6a and the concluding 13b, it is more natural to suppose these transitions to reflect an artful composition than repeated editorial clumsiness.

are understood to refer to different groups of participants. Thus, reflecting the emotions of the arriving pilgrim, v. 5 refers to the privileged class of permanent temple dwellers.[12] Verses 6-8 refer to the general[13] pilgrim whose stay is limited. With this function, vv. 6-8 are seen to reflect the 'self-comfort' of the ordinary pilgrim[14] or the comforting blessing from the privileged cult servants.[15]

These kinds of interpretation rest rather heavily on a foundation of cultic suppositions. The motifs of v. 5 seen in isolation could point to a function of blessing.[16] But within the context, vv. 5-8 are linked as a series of beatitudes, dominated by forms in the third person, in contrast to vv. 2-4 and 9-11 dominated by first-person forms. The connection between vv. 5 and 6-8 is also stressed by the frame of 'Yahweh Zebaoth'—elements in v. 4 and in 9a. Within the context, vv. 5-8 should clearly be seen as a subunit. As such, vv. 5-8 should be related to the concluding beatitude 13b:

Blessed the man who trusts in you!

Aside from the *'ašrê*-form itself, vv. 5, 6, and 13b are formally linked by the form of the introductory sentences 5a, 6a, and 13b, with a concluding second-person element relating the blessed to the divine you: 'who dwell in your house', 'whose strength is in you', 'who trusts in you'. And also 13b is introduced by the appellation 'Yahweh Zebaoth', corresponding to the frame of vv. 5-8.

12. With special emphasis on the priestly group, Schmidt, *Psalmen*, p. 159; Weiser, *Psalmen*, p. 386; McCullough, *Psalms*, p. 454; M. Dahood, *Psalms II. 51–100* (AB; New York: Doubleday, 1968), p. 278; Goulder, *Sons of Korah*, p. 42; Croft, *The Identity of the Individual*, p. 173; the king in addition to the priests, Mowinckel, *Salmeboken*, p. 182; Johnson, *Sacral Kingship*, p. 103; or the group of the *saddiqim* added to the priests Kraus, *Psalmen*, p. 584. To Gunkel, *Psalmen*, p. 369, the elect group, contrasted with the I, consists of those able to visit the temple regularly.

13. To Gunkel, *Psalmen*, p. 369, vv. 6ff. represent a somewhat more heroic type, namely the pilgrims with an especially long travel; to Kraus, *Psalmen*, p. 584, the asylum-seeker.

14. Cf. esp. Weiser, *Psalmen*, p. 386; Johnson, *Sacral Kingship*, p. 104; McCullough, *Psalms*, p. 455.

15. Schmidt, *Psalmen*, pp. 159-60; Croft, *The Identity of the Individual*, p. 173 According to Croft, 'three categories of men associated with temple worship' are blessed, namely the priests, the pilgrims, and the king—the latter in the form of a prayer. The composer of the psalm belongs to the first group, whose being mentioned first is held to be significant for the interpretation of the psalm.

16. Cf. especially Mowinckel, *Psalms I*, p. 47.

This connection could also be reflected in the interplay of plural and singular third-person forms in vv. 5-8. The singular form of v. 6a corresponds to v. 13b, both with the unusual construction *'ašrê 'āḏām*. The plural form v. 6b corresponds to the continuation vv. 7-8a and to the first beatitude v. 5. And the concluding singular v. 8b corresponds to the introductory v. 6a and v. 13b.

The relationship could well be the result of a meticulous composition[17] of traditional sayings forming the backbone of the psalm (cf. below on v. 5 as related to Ps. 140.14). Their significance for the structure of the psalm as a whole is stressed by the use of the repeated 'Yahweh Zebaoth' elements in vv. 2, 4, 9 and 13. Probably with an introductory function of appeal as suggested by v. 13a and v. 9a related to the following sentences, these elements point to a composition of four parts: vv. 2-4 (2 line MT), vv. 4 (3 line)-8, vv. 9-12, and v. 13. This would suggest a formal structure of I-forms, beatitudes, I-forms, beatitude (with the third-person statement v. 12 preparing the final beatitude).

In any case, this relationship shows that vv. 5 and 6ff. do not refer to sociological phenomena of different groups of people. The two beatitudes are materially parallel, referring to the same type of blessed person. Given a connection with v. 13, the function of vv. 5-8 should also be related to the didactic function of the beatitude. Certain qualities are stressed as religiously positive, the persons of such qualities related to a certain fate.[18]

The special qualities are described primarily in vv. 6 and 13b. Materially v. 6a and v. 13b correspond, with the ideal figure defined by a special relationship to Yahweh as object of trust. The way motifs of v. 6b correspond to the motifs of vv. 7-8, the ideal figure defined as pilgrim 'at heart',[19] in a fundamental relationship to the temple.

The motifs on the fate of the blessed in vv. 7-8 are usually related to the supposed cultic setting of the psalm and correspondingly understood as a reflection of the actual experiences of the pilgrims on their journey.[20] But the motif usage points to a more general language of sacred

17. For the formal relationship of vv. 5 and 6 with *'ašrê* followed by a participle form and by a construction introduced by *'āḏām* cf. Ps. 32.1-2 as a parallel example.

18. E.g. Sæbø, *THAT* 1, pp. 259-60, and the compilation of forms W. Käser, 'Beobachtungen zum alttestamentlichen Makarismus', *ZAW* 82 (1970), pp. 225ff.

19. Cf. especially Goulder, *Sons of Korah*, p. 44.

20. With Goulder, *Sons of Korah*, p. 39 for an extreme representation, with statistics on the probable rainfall for the contrasted Zion and Dan pilgrimages.

journey. Verse 7 reflects a general structure of crisis and divine intervention on the way. Parallel types of motif in similarly stereotypical
descriptions can be illustrated by, for example, Pss. 66.10-12 (cf. the
following I-forms on temple entrance) and 126.5-6 (related to the return
to Zion). Ps. 68.8-11, Isa. 35.5-10 and the Deutero-Isaiah versions of
water motifs[21] form obvious parallels as expressions of crisis and intervention to the rain motifs and the probable contrast of dryness on the
way.

The general character of vv. 7-8 is stressed by the relationship to the
religious qualities of the ideal figure of v. 6. The aspirations of the heart
given to the sacred journey (v. 6b) are realized by the journey of miracles
ending on Zion. And the relationship to Yahweh as the repository of
man's 'strength' (v. 6a) corresponds to v. 8 by the miraculous journey
from 'might' *'æl* 'might' ending with the appearance *'æl* God on Zion.
In this way, v. 8 combines the parallel relationship to God and to temple
in v. 6 in the image of temple entrance. The qualities of the ideal figure
of v. 6 denoting inner and volitional acts of religious attitude correspond
to a series of outer events of successful pilgrimage: the pilgrim at heart
has realized his aspiration in a story of miracles.

Verse 5 can be related to this motif development. The motifs
of dwelling in the temple and praise correspond to those of v. 8. As
an expression of a series of events, v. 5 would immediately continue
v. 7. But as a stereotyped expression for the religious *summum bonum*
(cf. for example, Ps. 140.14),[22] it is here used as a parallel form

---

21. E.g. H.M. Barstad, *A Way in the Wilderness. The 'Second Exodus' in the
Message of Second Isaiah* (JSS Monograph 12; Manchester: Manchester University
Press, 1989), pp. 21-36, who opposes the category of 'Exodus' and 'Exodus tradition' for the automatic labelling of such phenomena. Based especially on Ps. 107.33ff.
(pp. 27-28), ancient Canaanite creation mythology is seen as the background for
Deutero-Isaiah's use of Water in the Desert—the motifs seen as 'purely metaphorical'
language (p. 37). On the other hand, a number of usages connects these and parallel
motif types (cf. the references above) to a situation of some kind of sacred
'movement' related to divine guidance or intervention. Thus, also the 'Exodus
tradition' could be seen as an individual application of a given tradition of 'pilgrimage'.

22. This implies that v. 5a is here understood as a statement on fate, parallel to b,
and not as a qualification of religious 'virtue' as could be expected from the normal
beatitude. But the motif of dwelling in the temple in 5a might have the sense of its
application in Ps. 62 (cf. Chapter 6) and thus function as a qualification of 'virtue'. In
this way, a and b would form a normal beatitude, the sense of *'ôd* corresponding to its
use in the refrain of Pss. 42–43. But due to its location in the context, concluding

to introduce the motif execution of vv. 6-8.[23]

Given this background it is natural to stress the general character of vv. 5 and 7-8 as description of the blessed fate of the ideal figure. In correspondence with the function of the beatitude, motifs of pilgrimage and dwelling in the temple are used as categories for the description of the 'successful' religious life.

This also suggests that the function of the beatitudes of Psalm 84 is comparable to Ps. 140.13-14. Both types of third-person statement express religious truths about the ideal fate of the ideal person. Moreover, 84.12 which bridges the I-forms of 9ff. and the concluding beatitude v. 13, is formally close to 140.13-14: sentences of stating form relate Yahweh by verbs or nominal constructions as somehow benevolent to objects defined by qualifying nouns.[24] The connection of 84.12 and 13 reflects the functional connection between the statements of 140.13-14 and the beatitudes of Psalm 84.

The parallel application of the proverbial statements supposedly cited in Psalm 140 and the beatitudes of Psalm 84 is important in illustrating the significance of religious qualities connected to 'religious fate'. The nominal qualifications 'righteous' and 'upright' parallel to 'afflicted' and 'poor' (140.13-14) correspond to the qualifications of relationship to Yahweh as 'strength' (84.6a) or as 'trusted' (v. 13) or by motifs of 'way' (v. 6b) and 'perfect walking' (v. 12b) as comprehensive descriptions of the religious ideal. As such, the ideal figure is related to the ideal fate of a special relationship to Yahweh in the temple.

For our understanding of this special relationship, 84.6-8 is interesting as related to v. 5 and 140.14. The parallel motifs of dwelling and praise in formally independent sayings suggest that 84.5 and 140.14 reflect stereotyped forms and concepts.[25] Staying in the temple, praising God, represents the model 'good fate'. But through the meticulous

vv. 2-4 and introducing the following beatitude with related temple motifs, it is difficult to understand 5a to refer to a critical situation!

23. In addition, the motif of temple dwelling also formally links the introductory I-forms, vv. 2ff., to the beatitude, the former ending with the imagery of the swallow as the lucky 'temple-dweller'. The relationship of v. 5 as a comprehensive motif application and vv. 7-8 as a detailed one, can be compared to 27.4 as a relatively independent saying followed by vv. 5-6.

24. Cf. Chapter 1, note 56.

25. This could also be reflected in the formal influence of 84.5 for vv. 6-8 as dominated by plural forms in spite of the singular form in the introduction 6a and the conclusion 8b.

composition of 84.5 and 6-8 the stereotypical expression of the ideal fate is linked with motifs of pilgrimage and temple entrance. The model situation of temple stay presupposes a more extensive model story, encompassing a journey which ends before God on Zion, moreover a miraculous journey which includes events of crisis and crisis overcome.

The parallel function of the statements 140.13-14 and the beatitudes of Psalm 84 is stressed by the parallel relationship to I-forms. In Psalm 84 the relationship is more direct, due to the use of Temple motifs in vv. 2-4 and v. 11:

> How lovely are your dwellings, Yahweh Zebaoth!
> My soul is longing, even pining for the courts of Yahweh.
> My heart and my flesh are crying towards the living God.
> Even the birds have found a home,
> for the swallow there is a nest
> to place her young at your altars,
> Yahweh Zebaoth, my King, my God.
>
> For a day in your courts is better than a thousand![26]
> I choose standing at the threshold of God's house
> before dwelling in the tents of evil!

As in Psalm 140, the third-person forms on the ideological situation are formally kept separate from the description of the I-situation, as separate types of statement. The I is not identified with the blessed group of temple-dwellers nor the blessed pilgrims on their miraculous journey.

On the other hand, the composition as determined by the relationship of first-person forms and third-person statements is more easily seen in this psalm. The repeated appeal to 'Yahweh Zebaoth' vv. 2, 4, 9, and 13 links the four subunits functionally as parts within one address. But above all, the temple motifs immediately link the two types of situation. With single-minded concentration, the I is defined by his yearning to stay in the dwelling of Yahweh. In this way, the description of the I represents a concrete application of aspects of the model situation of vv. 5-8. As 'longing' (vv. 2ff.) and 'choosing' (v. 11) the I represents a situation on the 'outside' compared to the happy birds of v. 4 and the

---

26. With regard to the construction *ṭôb-yôm* cf. especially Goulder, *Sons of Korah*, pp. 46ff., who equates it with *yôm-ṭôb* as a technical expression for 'feast day'. But the similar elliptical construction *ṭôb-me'aṭ* with the preposition *min* (Ps. 37.16-17) supports the traditional understanding of the first sentence of v. 11 as a stereotyped saying. Here the elliptical form prepares the more concrete following statement in v. 11.

blessed dwellers vv. 5-8. Corresponding to the use of 140.13-14, the
blessed fate of vv. 5-8 depends on divine intervention, here connected
with the miraculous journey.

Only with regard to the qualification of the blessed in vv. 6 and 13b
(cf. also 12b) can a more direct linkage be found by the motifs on the
temple and the relationship to God. As he is described in vv. 2ff. and 11,
the I certainly comes across as someone with 'highways in his heart'.
That these self-descriptions not do represent sentimental outpourings,
but an individual application of a religious ideal, is seen by the contrast
of 'a day' and 'thousand' which prepare the contrasting of a humble
relationship to the temple to 'dwelling in the tents of evil'. We find a
similar contrast in the self-qualification Ps. 26.3-8 (cf. below).
Corresponding to the contrast of temple and sheol in Psalm 140, temple
and evilness are related as two contrasted localities for the I's 'dwelling'.
By 'choosing' the temple as the object of his aspirations, rejecting the
negative ideal of evilness, the I stands forth as the confessor.

The relationship of an objective religious ideal and the I as an individual representation of aspects of this ideal is also expressed by the
localization of v. 12 in the context:

> For Yahweh God is Sun and Shield.
> Yahweh gives grace and glory,
> no good is withheld for those who walk in sincerity.

On the one hand, this verse corresponds to the objective statements of
Psalm 140.13-14 on the fate of the ideal figures, here designated by the
element 'who walk in sincerity'. Thus, as to form, v. 12 is immediately
linked to the following beatitude on the ideal figure, here designated by
the element 'who trusts in you'. On the other hand, v. 12 is related to
the I-forms in vv. 9ff. The introductory *kî* links it to the preceding v. 11
which is similarly introduced. Followed by the Yahweh Zebaoth-element
in v. 13, the verse concludes vv. 9-12. With this function, the element
'who walk in sincerity' corresponds to 'dwelling in the tents of evil'
(v. 11b) as stereotyped contrasts for the negative and positive ideals. As
in Psalm 140, the I is related to two contrasted types of being. In Psalm
140, this contrast is expressed by the I, persecuted by his enemies, as
related to two opposed groups of the righteous and the evil. In 84.11-12,
the situation of the I is qualified by the contrast of the positive group of
'walkers' and the negative 'dwelling'. Formally linking the I-forms of
v. 11 and the beatitude v. 13, the function of v. 12 is thus comparable to
that of Ps. 140.13 in the context.

The meticulous composition of vv. 11-13 also stresses the impression of the I in this psalm as confessor. While the I of Psalm 140 is related to the evil as enemies, the relationship to the negative ideal in Psalm 84 is described by the I 'choosing' between the positive and negative ideal. With temple and the 'tents of evil' as two contrasted localizations for the I's 'staying', and the significance of the temple stressed by the rest of the psalm, the act of choosing represents an important act of confession.

This could explain also the reticence in identifying the I of this psalm and Psalm 140 with the positive ideal group. Compared to the blessed dwellers, the I represents a being 'in between'; orientated towards the temple, but still on the outside in a state of yearning. In both psalms, the difference between outside and inside is connected with the divine intervention. The divine intervention as related to the I is expressed in the form of the enemy prayer in Psalm 140, while the function of Ps. 84.9-10 is more uncertain. In both psalms, the intervention as stated is connected with the third-person statements. Thus the beatitudes of Psalm 84 as cited by the I in connection with his own situation must have the function of confessions (as in Ps. 140.13-14). This is most clearly seen in v. 12 bridging the I-forms and the beatitudes, with the statements about Yahweh's acts with regard to the 'walkers' cited as a motivation for the I's choice of orientation.

With this background, vv. 2-4 represent an individual application of the religious ideal, with the I as confessor as the actualization of the model figure. This does not mean that we should disregard the aspects of subjective feeling expressed in these very moving sentences. On the contrary, as described in these powerful verses the I represents a truly remarkable figure of religious experience and feeling. Verse 11 demonstrates that the inner commitment also includes choice and exclusion of a negative ideal. The intense subjectivity of the I-forms connected with the objective forms of given religious truth must be important for the character of the confession. Indirectly, this must also have repercussions for our valuation of the religious *milieu* in which such descriptions were created.

This is also illustrated by the relationship of vv. 5 and 6-8. In this composition, the stereotypical allusion to dwelling in the temple in v. 5 (cf. Ps. 140.14) is extended by motifs of a sacred journey of crisis and miraculous intervention, ending with the triumphant entrance on Zion. The motifs suggest a series of successive events in a model story of pilgrimage, the inner attitude of the blessed man with the 'highways in his heart' (cf. 'walking in sincerity', v. 12b) connected to a story of divine intervention, with temple entrance and dwelling for the final events of the story.

This motif development also suggests that the temple motifs have a special function. Connected with the motifs of inner commitment and miraculous pilgrimage, and contrasted to the 'tents of evil' as the alternative localization for the I's 'staying', the significance of temple in this text should not be related to an actual journey to some ritual event for its immediate meaningful reference. This, of course, does not exclude a background of ritual language, nor could one deny ritual application for the text once created. The type of language represented by Psalm 84 could be as applicable to rites of temple procession as it is to an institutional situation of admonishment or of individual/communal contemplation. For such types of later application, the I-form would function as a literary vehicle for a process of identification by the cult participants or 'users'. Fundamentally, the way and temple motifs must be understood as a reference to religious orientation and total life commitment, with the relationship to the temple signifying some comprehensive type of *via religiosa*.

2. *Psalm 36*

While there is a general agreement on the formal character of the main parts of this psalm, the coherence and the genre of the composition as a whole has been much debated. The main problem concerns the relationship between the description of the evil in vv. 2-5 and the hymn in vv. 6-10. These uncertainties are added to by the hymn being connected to the prayers of vv. 11-12 and to the final description of the destruction of the evil v. 13.

An original coherence can be refuted[27] or sought by derivation from a supposed cultic setting.[28] When more literary categories decide the

---

27. Schmidt, *Psalmen*, pp. 67-68; Taylor, *Psalms*, p. 187.

28. As connected with enemy motifs, the hymn and the prayer are characteristic for a 'Psalm of Protection' connected with the 'Enthronement Festival' (Mowinckel, *Psalms I*, pp. 164, 220), or connected with a 'Covenant Festival' (Weiser, *Psalmen*, pp. 205-206; Croft, *The Identity of the Individual*, p. 159 [the latter attributing a function of warning to the I as a cultic prophet]). According to Delekat, *Asylie*, pp. 239ff., vv. 2-5 cites the original 'Aufnahmeorakel' accepting the I into asylum, the psalm as a whole understood as a prayer for a prolonged stay as 'Asylschützling'

analysis, the prayer elements of vv. 11-12 are usually found to be decisive. Thus, the psalm is described as an individual lament, usually found to be influenced by forms of Wisdom.[29]

In the context of Psalms 140 and 84, vv. 8-10 are of special interest:

> How glorious is your grace!
> Gods and men seek refuge in the shadow of your wings.
> They saturate themselves with the fat of your house.
> From the torrents of your delights you water them.
> For with you is the fountain of life.
> In your light do we see light.

Comparably to Pss. 140.13-14 and 84.5-8, 12-13, these verses state general religious truths on the favourable fate for a group mentioned in the third person. As in Pss. 140.14 and 84.5-8, the blessed fate is expressed by motifs of entrance to and dwelling in the temple. Also in Psalm 36, these assertions are related to the situation of the I in crisis through the connection with the prayers of vv. 11-12:

> Prolong your grace for those who know you!
> your righteousness for the upright of heart.
> Let not the foot of pride come upon me!
> nor the hand of the unjust make me flee!

And, comparably to 140.12-14, with contrast statements ending the prayers, these forms are concluded by v. 13 on the negative fate related to a contrast negative group described by qualifying nomina:

> There[2] they fall, those who do evil,
> they are pushed down, they can not rise.

(literally expressed by v. 11!), after the death of 'des Asylherrn' normally should have ended the period of asylum. Also Kraus, *Psalmen*, p. 284 stresses the connection between the temple as asylum and the prayer, with the 'fleeing' of v. 12 as a 'fleeing' away from the sanctuary.

29. Cf. especially N.H. Ridderbos, *Die Psalmen. Stilistische Verfahren und Aufbau. Mit besonderer Berücksichtigung von Ps. 1–41* (BZAW 117; Berlin: de Gruyter, 1972), pp. 260ff.; further Kraus, *Psalmen*, p. 281; Gerstenberger, *Der bittende Mensch*, p. 118. Also to Mowinckel (cf. the preceding note), vv. 2-5 has the function normally expressed by enemy complaints. To M. Dahood, *Psalms I.1–50* (AB; New York: Doubleday, 1966), p. 218, 'the coexistence of these literary types' (Wisdom elements, hymn, lament) 'points up the limitations of the form-critical approach'.

30. Weiser, *Psalmen*, p. 205, while 'there' usually is found to be meaningless in the context and most often emended according to Gunkel's proposal *šāmemû*, while Dahood, *Psalms I*, p. 224 equals the word with El Amarna *šumma* 'behold!'.

The common structure must be important for the understanding of these texts. This seems the more the case as the expressions for the common structure vary. Thus, in 140.13-14, the religious truths are in the form of statements introduced by 'I know', and in 84.5-10 in the form of beatitudes. In Psalm 36, the third-person statements are addressed to the divine you, framed by the hymnic introduction on the divine grace and concluded by the we-forms of v. 10.[31] On the other hand, v. 13 as a saying on the fate of the negative group, which contrasts with the positive vv. 8-10, has a general stating form corresponding to 140.12, 13-14.

But the group related to the temple blessings in vv. 8-10 is not, seemingly,[32] described by general religious qualifications corresponding to the terms of 140.13-14 or the elements 84.6, 12b, 13b. 'Gods and men' are here the favoured ones, parallel to the equally comprehensive 'man and beast' in v. 7b. Instead, we find the expected religious qualifications in the immediate context. In the introductory prayer v. 11, the nominal terms 'those who know you' and 'the upright in heart' correspond to the qualifications of Psalms 140 and 84. In the present context of prayer and the preceding hymn (cf. below), the sentences are closely related. And the relationship is stressed by the concluding sentence v. 13, where the term 'those who do evil' corresponds negatively to the nominal qualifications of v. 11.

Given this background, we can conclude that the individual forms represent some common basic material. At the very least, the common phenomena are discernible as a set of common concepts and motifs which describe the fate of qualified persons. For this description, temple motifs seem to be basic. Moreover, the three psalms suggest some kind of relationship between two parallel sets of religious qualification and

According to *BDB* (1979), p. 1027, the usage here and Ps. 14.5 represents the poetic 'pointing to a spot in which a scene is localized vividly in the imagination'. Due to the motif connection between vv. 12 and 13, the word could in the present composition have the meaning as when preceded by the relative *'ašær*, i.e. 'where', 'there where'.

31. On v. 10 as concluding the hymn as a whole and preparing the transition to the following prayers see Ridderbos, *Psalmen*, p. 265.

32. 'Man' and 'beast' with an immediate function as the first pair of concrete illustrations of the divine justice and grace spanning the highest and lowest, could also play upon special connotations. Thus, Ps. 73 which is relevant also for the understanding of Ps. 36 (cf. below), qualifies the I without the miraculous 'knowledge' as an 'animal' (v. 21, cf. also Ps. 49.13, 21). With such a function, also the second pair of 'gods' and 'men' might have a secondary alluding function, referring to stages of religious development.

fate: Psalms 140 and 36 describing two sharply opposed groups of religious being, Psalm 84 two opposing modes. Thus, the three psalms seem to represent individual applications of the common material. The differences do not only refer to formal characteristics, but also to more material aspects. Thus, Psalm 84 is given to the positive aspects of the motif structure, while Psalm 36 is dominated by the negative aspects (cf. below).

In addition, the relationship between Pss. 140.12-14 and 36.8-10, 13 also suggests that the common material of concepts and motifs could be related to some basic types of form. The differences of individual application seen together with common elements and formal structures stress the importance of the sentence types of 140.12-14, with simple statements based on nominal qualifications and verbs describing the fate of the qualified. The formal development of these forms in the context—supported by the third-person statements of Psalm 84—suggests the sentence type where the nominal qualification has subject-function to be especially important.[33]

Finally, the usages in the three texts are also suggestive with regard to the function of the common material. The common context of third-person statements and prayers in the I-form must express some kind of application of the religious truths to the situation of the I. The prayers represent the I relating his fate—in subjunctive form—to the given pattern.

For such a connection between prayers and stating forms, Psalm 36 is of special interest. Here, the parallel 'your grace' and 'your righteousness' of v. 11 immediately link the theme of the prayer to the theme of the hymn (cf. vv. 6-7, 8).[34]

The formal relationship between the prayers of vv. 11 and 12 is comparable to 84.9-10, with I-forms related to third-person forms. 36.11 could also have a rather independent function as a special intercession.[35] But due to the general character of v. 11 in addition to the special

33. In 36.7b (cf. also the prayer of v. 11) we find the other sentence type with a divine subject, corresponding to 140.13. The two applications of this sentence type are remarkably similar. In both cases they make parallel statements, formally separated (cf. the 'Yes' of 140.14 and the introductory hymnic exclamation of 36.8) from the other sentence type.

34. Cf. especially Ridderbos, *Psalmen*, pp. 266-67.

35. E.g. Kraus, *Psalmen*, p. 284, to whom the I 'fraglos' understands himself as part of the special group referred to.

significance of the qualifying terms of v. 11 in this sort of context, it is
natural to understand v. 12 as the concrete prayer. As an introductory
prayer, v. 11 connects the theme of the hymn and the real prayer.[36] In
addition, the we-forms of v. 10 which conclude the hymn probably have
a similar preparatory function, as a link between the third- and first-
person forms.

In this way, the relationship between hymn and prayer provides a
concrete illustration of how the general truths are applied to the situation
of the I. Related to the divine intervention, it obviously is not 'done' to
apply the third-person statements directly to the concrete situation. The I
cannot be immediately identified with the blessed group. Only divine
intervention makes this identification possible. Thus, the prayer represents
the indirect application—in subjunctive form—of the religious truths
confessed in the hymn.

The use of the nominal qualifications—which 'really' belong to the
stating sentences in the third person—in the introductory prayer v. 11 is
a concrete expression for the material connection between the paradigmatic situation as stated in vv. 8-10 and the individual situation of the I
in v. 12. Within this compositional development, the prayer represents
an application in subjunctive form; the I asking for the fate of the
paradigmatic figures. This also means that the prayer ultimately must be
related to the kind of temple dwelling which describes the blessed fate in
vv. 8-10. The crisis of the I must—at least as related to the paradigm—
have been a crisis connected with admittance to or dwelling in the
temple.

But on the other hand, when we turn to the motifs of the prayer, they
are exclusively enemy motifs. According to these motifs, the crisis of the
I consists in his being attacked by evil and superior enemies. And the
divine intervention must consist in the enemies being restrained.[37]

For this and comparable texts, the traditional understanding has given
priority to the enemy motifs as the most concrete indication of the situation of the I. Only in connection with the asylum theme—explored

36. Cf. Ridderbos, *Psalmen*, p. 266 on v. 11 as 'Übergang'.
37. It is difficult to relate the concrete enemy motifs of v. 12 to any concrete
situation. For Kraus, *Psalmen*, p. 284, v. 12a represents the royal motif of Ps. 110.1;
for Dahood, *Psalms I*, p. 224, the imagery of the chase as in Ps. 35.8. Thus, neither
Birkeland, *Die Feinde*, pp. 140-41, stressing national enemies or Delekat, *Asylie*,
p. 240, stressing individual enemies of an I in financial trouble, invoke the concrete
motif usage as basic for their understanding.

primarily by Delekat[38]—has a model been expressed which could combine both aspects: on the one hand the gravity of the enemy situation, on the other hand this situation related to the special significance of staying in the temple as an expression of a special wished-for state.[39]

The meticulous composition of vv. 8-10 and 11ff. suggest that enemy and temple motifs are related in this text. This could also be expressed in the prayer of v. 12 as concluded by v. 13:

> Let not the foot of pride come upon me!
> nor the hand of the unjust make me flee!
> There they fall, those who do evil,
> they are pushed down, they can not rise.

'Making me flee' in v. 12b could simply be an expression for 'defeat', in immediate continuation of 12a. On the other hand, due to the connection with motifs of locality in vv. 8ff., it is noteworthy that the motifs of v. 12b taken literally describe a negative movement from a given place. This literal sense is supported by the special form of v. 13. As we have seen, v. 13 represents basically a contrast statement, negatively related to the stating sentences of vv. 7b, 8-9. Sentences of this kind can be differently applied within the individual composition. In this case, the introductory 'there' makes the statement meaningless unless a special place is referred to. And with the local categories of v. 12b preceding v. 13, the 'there' makes v. 13 an immediately meaningful part of the prayer.[40] Left alone to the superior enemies, the I would flee to a place of 'falling' and 'pushing' and 'no rising'.

Such a use of *nûd* could be compared to Ps. 11.1. There also the 'fleeing' is related to the attack of the unjust (v. 2). Further, the situation of the I in Psalm 11 is also related to general statements on the fate of the two contrasted types of religious being (vv. 4-7). Given this background, it is significant that the challenge to 'flee' is sharply contrasted to the confessional statement 'With Yahweh I take refuge!' in v. 1. Such a motif contrast of 'taking refuge' and 'fleeing' corresponds to the motifs of 36.8-10, 12 (cf. the use of *ḥāsâ* in the introductory statement

---

38. Cf. also below to Eichhorn, *Gott als Fels*.

39. To the latter aspect Delekat, *Asylie*, pp. 194-256 on the asylum-seekers as cultic servants of lower rank ('Schwellenhüter und Tempelsänger').

40. The localization of v. 13 corresponds to the contrast statement 140.12 which also concludes preceding prayers, cf. above.

v. 8). The I as fleeing suggests a situation opposite to the blessed fate of dwelling in the temple.[41]

The description of the negative fate in Ps. 36.13 corresponds to the statements of Ps. 140.12 (and also partly v. 11, cf. above), with *nāpal* and non-*qûm* corresponding to *nāpal* in hiph. form, non-*qûm* and non-*kûn*. Moreover, both the motifs of 'falling' and 'being pushed' (36.13) link to the description of the I under attack in 140.5.[42] It is evident that these texts—especially with regard to the stating sentences in the third person—reflect given sets of concepts and motifs.

With this background, it is especially interesting that Ps. 36.11-13 suggests that the negative fate also can be described in categories of locality. Connected to the immediately preceding third-person statements, the I is thus related to the two contrasted localities of temple and a 'place' of falling. The significance of the two localities is illustrated. The temple is qualified as a place of life (v. 10a), while the motifs of v. 13 ultimately must qualify the negative 'there' as a place of death. Moreover, the implied contrast of localities corresponds to Ps. 84.11. Here the I is related to two types of dwelling, either 'in the house of my God' or 'in the tents of evil'. The motif of the 'negative locality' is differently used in the two texts. In Ps. 36.12-13 the motif refers to fate connected to the enemy situation. In Ps. 84.11 the motif refers to 'volitional' categories of confession, the I choosing between and preferring the one place before the other. But ultimately, the two types of use refer to different aspects of the same concept.[43]

---

41. Cf. the comparable contrasts of Kraus and Delekat, who both understand the 'fleeing' concretely, related to the state of asylum in the sanctuary. For similar usages cf. also Jer. 49.30, 50.3 with *nûd* contrasted with *yāšab*. For the motif relationship of Ps. 36.12 and 13, Gen. 4.12, 14 could represent an interesting parallel. There being *nā' wānād*, 'on the earth', expanded by 'being driven away from the soil' and 'hiding from your presence', leads to a situation where the 'fleer' is under constant threat of being killed. Moreover, here the negative situation is directly described as relationship to a locality, the land Nod arrived at after leaving the divine presence (v. 16). The hints of Ps. 11.1 and 36.12-13 together with the elaborate story of Gen. 4 could point to a common religious 'topography'!

42. Both for 140.11-12 and 36.13, Dahood, *Psalms I*, p. 224, finds given motifs of death: *dāḥâ* has a 'special reference to Sheol', and *qûm* means rising from Sheol (cf. also *Psalms III*, pp. 304ff. and further Tromp, *Conceptions of Death*, pp. 93-94).

43. The parallel imagery of the 'Alien woman's house' of Prov. 2.16ff., 5.3ff., 7.5ff. could provide a good visualization of the two aspects of the negative locality, with the 'house' as a place of temptation and as opening into Sheol.

The relationship between the motifs of vv. 8-10 and 12-13 also immediately connects the temple and enemy motifs as parts of the same motif-development. They do not refer to separate aspects of reality, with for example the enemy motifs as the more concrete expressions for the 'real' siuation of the I, but refer to the same 'reality': The I longs to dwell in the temple, the enemies drive him away from the temple to the negative place, and the divine miracle is the solution to the crisis.

In detail, the negative fate as caused by the enemies is differently described in Psalms 36 and 140. In 140, the effect of the enemies is direct, as for example 'pushing' and 'setting bait by the wayside'. In Psalm 36 the effect is more indirect: the enemies causing the I to flee to the place of 'pushing'. The difference could depend on individual exposi-tions of the same basic motifs, or on different types of event within the given motif structure.

In any case, the similarities between the two texts point to a common basis.[44] As related to a common set of concepts, the I of this psalm is clearly described as a being 'in between', confessing the blessed fate of dwelling in the temple, but given to the negative fate save for the divine intervention. This also corresponds to the peculiar relationship between first- and third-person forms of this text and Psalm 140 (cf. also in Psalm 84), and explains why the I cannot be directly identified with the blessed group of temple dwellers. Within the motif execution of these texts, the I related to his enemies is given to doom. The prayer, relating the I to divine grace, represents the possible positive fate. The motif of 'fleeing' is especially interesting in this connection. While Psalm 84 is given to the motif of pilgrimage, the I confessing the paradigm of the blessed on the way to the temple, 36.12-13 represents an opposite movement of defeat, from temple orientation towards a 'place' of falling.

The I as a being 'in between' could, in this text, also be related to the peculiar introduction vv. 2-5:

> A saying of sin to the unrighteous
> is in the middle of my heart.
> No fear of God is before his eyes.
> For in his eyes, one deals smoothly with him
> on finding his iniquity hateful (?)

44. Cf. also below to a third type of motif execution Ps. 26.9, with a divine subject for the negative fate described as 'togetherness' with the evil, and further the 'together'-formula of Pss. 28.1; 88.5; 143.7; Ezek. 26.20; 31.16; 32.18, 24, 25, 29, 30; and also 31.14.

> The words of his mouth are mischief and deceit,
> he has ceased to consider to do good.
> Mischief does he ponder in his bed,
> he stands himself on a road which is not good,
> evil does he not reject.

In a context where lively complaints on the enemies are to be expected, vv. 2b-5[45] give a general description of the characteristics of the *rāšā'*. Aside from the introductory, and usually emended, 'in the middle of my heart' in 2a (cf. below), the acts of the unrighteous are not related to the I, but are presented as a general catalogue of vices. The hymn on the divine grace in vv. 6-10 seems rather abruptly added to this description.

Psalm 52 could serve for a parallel to the structure of 36.2-5 and vv. 6-10.[46] Save for the second-person forms, the statements on the character and fate of the mighty 52.2-7 (with 8-9) correspond to the description of 36.2-5, 13.[47] The contrasting self-description of the I followed by forms of praise 52.10-11 could have a function corresponding to the hymn of 36.6-10.[48]

The two texts clearly are related. But in comparison, Psalm 36 has a special character as not concluded by the hymn, but by forms which reflect the I in crisis.

Related to the motif structure of Psalms 140 and 84, however, the complicated composition with description of the unrighteous (vv. 2-5), hymnic elements (6-10) and prayers (11-13) could be meaningful. The third-person description of the unrighteous contrasts with the third-person description of the blessed group of vv. 7b and 8-10.[49] Thus, they describe the two contrasted paradigmatic types of religious being, which are relevant to the present situation of the I. Similarly to the application of the negative paradigm in Psalm 140, the nominal qualifications in the I-forms (v. 12) directly identify the enemies of the I with the negative

45. Usually understood to have the function of the normal enemy complaint.

46. Croft, *The Identity of the Individual*, p. 158, stresses the connection between 36 and 52.

47. The immediate connection between vv. 2-5 and 13 is illustrated by Schmidt, *Psalmen*, p. 67, who understands these verses as an original unit '36 B', cf. also Taylor, *Psalms*, p. 187.

48. Cf. also concretely the introductory challenge 52.2 connected with a reference to the divine grace, corresponding to the theme of 36.6ff.

49. Cf. especially Taylor, *Psalms*, p. 187, on the text as composed of two originally independent units, the present composition setting forth 'in bold relief the two conflicting ways of life'.

ideal. In this respect, the formal character of vv. 2-5 with its detailed description underlines the formal difference between enemy-descriptions contained within first-person forms and the third-person qualifications of the evil. The third-person statements obviously express the negative paradigm, while the negative qualifications of 'my enemies' represent concrete applications or actualizations of the negative ideal as related to the situation of the I.

Similarly, the third-person descriptions of the positive group must represent the contrasting positive paradigm. This is also applied to the individual situation. We have earlier found reason to stress that religious truths as stated by the I have a confessional function. Related to two types of religious being, the I separates himself from the negative ideal, orientating himself towards the positive ideal of the blessed temple dwellers. The prayer is the concrete expression for this orientation. With the enemies of the I qualified as evil, the qualification of the I as related to the positive ideal is stressed.

The composition of Psalm 36 underlines the probability of such an understanding. The formal independence of the description of the evil in vv. 2-5 within the composition stresses the significance of the enemies qualified as evil. And the description of the positive paradigm in the literary frame of hymnic address corresponds to the third-person statements as confessions in Psalms 140 and 84.

Compared to Psalm 84, Psalms 140 and 36 represent both the positive and negative figures of paradigm. On the other hand, Psalm 36 being formally dominated by expressions for the negative aspect, could form an application which reversely corresponds to the beatitudes of Psalm 84. Thus, the psalm is characterized by the frame of statements on the qualities and fate of the evil in vv. 2-5 and 13. Conceptually closely related, as connected statements on the religious character and fate of the evil, their introductory and concluding location must be significant for the composition. Moreover, this 'negative' character corresponds to the motifs of the prayer in v. 12, with the I threatened by the negative movement towards the evil-doers' place of falling.

This could also be related to the much-discussed introductory line of v. 2a. Starting with the ancient translations, the special form of 2a has invited rather differing renderings. Given this uncertainty as to meaning, it must be important that we find corresponding uses of *ne'um* in other texts. With its introductory locality, the construction *ne'um - pæša' lārāšā'* of 2a corresponds immediately to the similar constructions in

Ps. 110.1a[50] and Prov. 30.1. Formally, this could even characterize 2a as an introduction to an oracle cited in what follows. And as a nomen qualified by the proposition *le*, the parallel constructions would suggest the *rāšā'* as the addressee of the oracle, given 'to the unrighteous'. Accordingly, instead of the usual proper name, 'sin' as *nomen rectum* to *ne'um* would designate the source of inspiration.[51] And the concluding first-person forms of the MT could even reflect the mediator of revelation.[52]

According to this understanding, the following verses would express the cited oracle. On the other hand, vv. 2b-5 together with 6-13 as an oracle, with its very proper contents, could hardly have 'sin' for source. Thus, for the introductory construct *ne'um - pæša'*, it has been proposed that the *nomen rectum* designates the object of the oracle, as an 'oracle on sin'. This is possible, although rather unsatisfactory in view of the formal connection with the similar constructions of Ps. 110.1 and Prov. 30.1. Thus, the usual understanding of the *nomen rectum* as the source of inspiration seems more reasonable. Another possibility which retains a more immediate relationship to the parallel forms, is obtained if the *nomen rectum* has a qualifying function, describing the 'oracle' as 'sinful'[53] Understood in this way, the MT could be rendered:

> A sinful saying to the unrighteous is in the middle of my heart.

This, however, makes it difficult to understand v. 2a as an introduction to a following citation, corresponding to the similar constructions of Ps. 110.1 and Prov. 30.1. Moreover, the element 'in the middle of my heart' could not refer to the I as mediator. As is witnessed by the usual emendations into third-person forms, the 'middle of the heart' is naturally associated with pondering and mental activity. Given this, and if MT is adhered to, v. 2a is a statement of the I, which refers to mental

---

50. Delekat, *Asylie*, p. 239, with 'sin' understood as a correction for an original *ba'al* as the source of inspiration.

51. As is the usual understanding, e.g. the precise rendering of Dahood, *Psalms I*, p. 217: perversity inspires the wicked man.

52. Schmidt, *Psalmen*, p. 67; Ridderbos, *Psalmen*, p. 260; Croft, *The Identity of the Individual*, p. 159.

53. Cf. corresponding constructions with *dābār* in sg. and pl. Ps. 52.6; 35.20b; 119.43a; Prov. 13.5a; 29.12; Qoh. 12.10. Especially in the latter case, with 'words' qualified by the categories of vv. 9 and 11, the usage with *ne'um* is relevant for the construction of 2a introducing forms of wisdom (cf. also 2 Sam. 23.1-3a and Prov. 30.1).

anguish and struggle, the 'sinful saying' rooted in his own heart.

This tentative rendering of v. 2a would explain the peculiar composition of Psalm 36, with its extended description of the evilness of the evil in the introduction (vv. 2b-5) and the concluding statement on the fate of the evil (v. 13) immediately connected with the preceding prayer. The negative mode of the psalm—especially when compared with Psalm 84 as the positive exposition of the motif structure—would correspond to the I in such a situation.

Such a psychological state could be compared to the anguish of the I in Psalm 73. The unhappy I of Psalm 73 is obviously on the very brink of succumbing to the negative ideal as described within the third-person statements of vv. 4-12 concluded by 13-14, nearly uttering the 'deceitful' confession (v. 15).

The relationship of the heroes of Psalms 36 and 73 is the more interesting as the two texts also have formal characteristics in common. The composition of Ps. 73.1-14 forms an interesting parallel to the composition of 36.2-5 followed by the hymnic vv. 6ff. The psalm is introduced by I-forms which describe the situation of the I as related to representatives for the negative ideal (73.2-3, corresponding to 36.2a). The retrospective I-forms of v. 15 and especially vv. 21-22 attest to the importance of the subjective state of anguish and near apostasy described in the introduction.

The introductory I-forms are followed by third-person descriptions of the evil (73.4-12). Verses 6-11, describing the qualities of the evil, are parallel to 36.2b-5. In both cases the description of the evil is immediately connected with forms of 'confession': in Psalm 36, by the hymnic description of the fate of the temple-dwellers (vv. 6-10), in Psalm 73 by the almost said 'confession' on the fate of the evil (v. 12) together with the contrasting I-forms (vv. 13-14—cf. also the immediately following 'proper' statements on the fate of the evil, vv. 18-20, 27 connected with confessing I-forms). Against this background,[54] Psalms 36 and 73 must reflect a common dependence on basic formal elements and also a certain formal structure. Moreover, Psalm 73 with its more complicated application of the common material, attests to the importance of the I as confessor in a situation of confrontation with the evil as the negative paradigm.

Given this, the third-person qualifications of the evil in these texts

54. Cf. the more detailed discussion in Ps. 73 in connection with Ps. 62.

must have a significance beyond that of qualifying the enemies of the I.
That function surely is important, as witnessed by Psalms 36 and 140
where the prayers are immediately given to the danger from the evil
enemies. For the application of the paradigm to the situation of the I, the
enemies identified as evil obviously are important. But the extended
form of the qualification in 36.2b-5 together with the possible understanding of v. 2a and the special form of the prayer (vv. 12-13), also
connects to the situation of 84.11, with the evil relevant as paradigmatic
figures for the I.

In this way, the qualifications of the evil also must have a confessionary function as renunciations of the negative paradigm. Pss. 84.11
together with 52 and 73 as entities would be expressions for different
aspects of such a function. In this respect Psalm 36 is interesting as a
combination of the two aspects. The enemies of the I are very much evil,
but, the evil paradigm is also relevant for the I.

A fundamental link between the two aspects could also be found in
the motif development. In Psalm 36, the threat of the enemies is immediately connected with the temple motifs, the I being forced to 'flee' to
the contrast locality of 'falling'. A corresponding contrast is alluded to in
Ps. 84.11, and is also relevant for Psalm 140 with the more immediate
contrast of the I being killed as opposed to dwelling in the temple
described as the positive fate. Within the composition of Psalms 36 and
140, enemy motifs and temple motifs are not separated from each other
as referring to separate levels of reality (cf. the traditional understanding
of the enemies connected with a 'real', historical crisis 'out in life', the
temple motifs with cultic events taking place after the 'real' problem has
been solved). The two types of motifs are related to each other as parts
of the same motif development, referring to the same level of reality.
With dwelling in the temple as the ultimate event of the religious pattern,
the enemies as evil represent the immediate danger to the I's attainment.
Thus, the special composition of Psalm 36 with the introduction of vv. 2-
5 and the conclusion of vv. 12-13 suggests that the concrete expression
of the 'foot of pride' and 'hand of the unrighteous' would consist in the
I succumbing to the 'saying of sin' in his 'heart'!

3. *Conclusions from Psalms 36, 84 and 140: The Paradigm*

a. *The Third-person Statements*
For these texts, the relationship between third-person statements and I-
forms is essential. The form of the third-person statements vary. But

basic to them is the connection of religious qualification—usually by nominal terms—and statement on fate. Both aspects can be extended into relatively independent forms. Thus, in Psalm 36, vv. 2b-5 are given to a description of the character of the negative figure, but vv. (7b), 8-10 describe the fate of the positive figures. But basically, the sentence types of Ps. 140.12-14 seem central for the different types of statement. This type of construction can be related to a group of '*saddiq*-sayings'— especially as used in the Psalms. These sayings, as well as the general concepts of the *ṣaddîq* and the contrast term *rāšā'*, could be important for our understanding of the traditional background of the third-person statements.

The statements express given truths on the fate of the qualified beings. Temple motifs, contrasted with motifs which could be abstracted as motifs of 'death' or 'sheol', signify the two types of fate. Psalm 36 elaborates the stereotypical temple motifs of Psalm 140, adding to the significance of the concept of dwelling in the temple by motifs of 'refuge' and 'meal' in addition to deepening the category of 'life'. In addition, Psalm 84 extends the temple motifs with motifs of 'pilgrimage' / 'way' leading to the temple. The motif exposition connects this way with crisis and miraculous intervention. The 'topographical' impression of these motifs is added to by Psalm 36 with suggestions of the I also in negative movement towards Sheol.

But it could be important that the localities are referred to by many instances of motifs. Obviously the expression of the basic concepts is not confined to some stereotypical terms. The allusions to the negative fate are of markedly individual character, the transcription of them as motifs of 'death' or 'sheol' representing an abstraction. Also, the expression for 'the evil as localized' could refer to different aspects. Thus, in Ps. 84.11 the 'tents of evil' which contrast temple as the place for dwelling, must refer to an alternative for longing and aspiration, and thus as a place of wrong orientation and temptation. But neither is the positive fate in 140.12 confined to temple categories, but it is described as 'firmly standing in the land' (cf. also below to Isa. 38.10ff.). And when the 'good state' is described as dwelling in the temple, Pss. 140.14, 84.8 and 36.8b 10 provide a number of motifs, applied as comprehensive and probably alluding terms.

But motifs of temple-sheol-way seem basic to the motif use. They need not represent the prime or original expression for the basic concepts involved.[55] But at the very least they are observable as suggestions for what 'it is all about'. And their use in these texts defines them at least as an important expression of the central concepts. They allude to some basic topography, with the religious reality defined by relationship to some decisive places.

This also suggests that the motifs as well as the statements reflect a religious meta-language of ideological nature. This language can have a cultic background and could also refer to actual ritual practice. But for the statements—especially as seen isolated from their application in the texts—human reality defined by contrasted types of humanity related to contrasts of temple and sheol would point to an ideological type of language.

b. *The Relationship between Third-person Statements and I-forms*
The formal separation between the third-person statements of religious truth and the I-forms of these texts must be important for the under-standing of the I-psalms. The separation obviously implies that the I cannot be identified with the figures of the positive statements. However, the statements just as obviously express a situation highly rel-evant for the I. The relationship seems to represent an expression of paradigm and actualization. The situation of the I seems to represent a concrete application of the paradigmatic situation of the third-person statements. The form of beatitude in Psalm 84 is an expression of such a relationship between statements and I-forms. The other types of state-ment refer to ideal figures which represent the religious laws, while the I is described as an actualization of (aspects of) the ideal figures.

To a certain degree, this application is expressed by parallelism between the I-forms and the third-person forms. Especially in Psalm 140, the contrast of statements on the negative and positive fate corresponds to the implications of the conflict between the I and his enemies. The qualification of the enemies as somehow 'evil', thus identified with the negative paradigm, most directly connects the paradigmatic and the indi-vidual situation.

This type of parallelism does not mean that we find motifs and con-cepts which refer to two separate types of situation. On the contrary, the

---

55. Cf. e.g. the parallel 'short-forms' 84.13b and 36.7b with 'trust' and 'salvation' as comprehensive expressions for the paradigmatic quality and fate.

central motifs of the two situations correspond.[56] The I stands forth as the potential actualization of the blessed fate.

Divine intervention is presented as the decisive factor for this actualization. In Psalms 36 and 140, while 84 is more uncertain in this respect, the prayer is central for the fate of the I. Divine intervention must represent the direct expression of the I identified with the religious ideal as for example *ṣaddîq*. Thus, these texts represent partial actualizations of the paradigm as linked with some decisive crisis. But also as partial, this application is related to the central motifs of the paradigm. Compared to, for example, Psalms 73 and 52, the I of the three psalms seems to represent the initial stages of the story, a being on the outside of the temple—while dwelling inside represents the sacred goal.

This connection could be related to the I not only as supplicant, but also as confessor within these texts. The blessed fate—in parallel to statements on the negative fate—is confessed, with the prayer as an important expression of the confession. The importance of this act of confession is stressed by the I as related not only to the positive paradigm, but also to the negative. As enemies/negative paradigms, the evil represent the concrete threat to the I's orientation. Against this background, the I is very much a being in between—renouncing the negative ideal, professing the positive. Both in Psalms 36 and 140—by inference probably also in 84—the I is in a most desperate situation, doomed to defeat unless saved by divine intervention. In this respect, the application in Psalm 36—stressed in Psalm 73—is important in relating the possibility of doom not only to the threat of the evil enemies, but also to the relevance of the negative ideal.

In this way, the relationship between third-person statements and I-forms in these texts suggests a background of religious practice. While the third-person statements are ideological in character, the psalms seem to express a practice of actualization and identification. The paradigm is embodied by the fate of the I. As prayed for, the decisive form of embodiment is dependent on divine intervention. But it is also partly actualized in the I attacked by the evil enemies or by the I threatened by the fate of the evil. Thus, the paradigm seems to imply some sort of role embodied by the I. Also as confessed, the paradigm obviously is relevant also for the presence of the I. Thus, the categories of actualization and

---

56. The exception might be the puzzling royal theme of the prayer 84.10, cf. above.

identification also seem to include aspects of concrete 'religious behaviour' and practice.

Aspects of this practice are illustrated by Psalms 84 and 36 especially. In Psalm 84, the central concepts of the paradigm are expressed in I-form, in an intensely personal and emotional way. As orientated towards the temple, the I represents a person totally defined within the categories of the paradigm. Connected to forms of beatitude, the I-forms clearly present a (potentially) blessed man. The blessedness is here connected to internalized attitudes of religious feeling. The hymn of Psalm 36 can be related to this exuberance of actualization. But in addition this psalm could represent other aspects of internalization, with a hero split between two contrasted modes of religious being, in danger of succumbing to the negative ideal. The personal aspects of actualization as connected to a situation of anguish are also illustrated by Psalm 140, here connected to an external situation of having enemies. On the other hand, Psalm 36 can represent an immediate connection between the enemy situation and the anguish of internal actualization. In this way, the seemingly bland and objective character of the third-person statements presented in a literary context of I-forms must reflect a biographical background of intense mental and emotional distress in addition to the probably physical aspects of the crisis.

This could also be reflected by the relationship of the three psalms. Their immediate literary relationship must express a background of traditional, even stereotypical expositions of the main concepts. At the same time, they are highly individual expressions for the given concepts and motifs. The exposition—both with regard to the composition as a whole and to the detailed motif use—is characterized by literary freedom of application. Also as we have seen, they represent different aspects of the I as a being on the outside. The formal differences could, at least partly, be related to a background of religious practice and experience, with the texts reflecting different modes in the application of the religious ideal to the personal fate. Psalm 36 related to 73 could even suggest that the differences of some texts could reflect different stages of religious development.

Such a background would have repercussions for our understanding of the use of I-forms. The 'I' seems to be rooted in autobiography, reflecting the religious experiences of a group of individuals or more probably an individual. The I-form could immediately reflect an interest in religious autobiography as a vehicle for transmitting a certain type of religious experience.

But the use of the I-form could also be related to other functions. The texts as transmitted—probably also as created—point not only to the very fact of original experience, but also to a *milieu* where the texts were appreciated and used. Whatever the original form of this use, later users have somehow participated in the story of the original experience. That this experience has been presented in I-form and re-experienced as the story of 'I' could mean that the participants were invited to identify with the experience. Such a process would be natural in a *milieu* characterized by a practice connected to categories of paradigm and actualization. This would imply that the I of the single text, presented as a concrete embodiment of the religious ideal, would have functioned as a paradigmatic figure. Parallel to the I related to the paradigm of the third-person statements, the participants are somehow reliving the experience and have related the experiences of the I to their own reality. This would also imply that the texts as transmitted—possibly also as created—represented a means of teaching and admonishment.

c. *The Application of the Paradigm in Psalm 118 related to 2 Kings 20 and Isaiah 38*

An illustration of the relationship between third-person statements and I-forms is found in Ps. 118.19-21:[57]

> Open for me the Gates of Righteousness!
> that I may enter through them,
> that I may praise Yah.
> This is the gate of Yahweh.
> The Righteous may enter through it.
> I will praise you, for you answered me.
> You became my salvation.

Verse 20 represents a description of the gates mentioned in v. 19, qualifying them as '*le* Yahweh' and reserved for the group of the Saddiqim.

A similar structure of sentences and motifs as appears in these two verses can be found in Ezek. 44.1-3. Here we also find a precise specification of the gate in question, with the presentation of the gate (v. 1) followed by the repetitive 'this gate', in v. 2. This corresponds to the introductory 'Gates of Righteousness' followed by 'this gate', 118.19-20. In the regulations of Ezek. 44.2 we note two parallel sentences using

---

57. Hauge, 'The City facing Death', pp. 7ff.

the verbs *pātaḥ* and *bô be*. This corresponds to the verb structure of
Ps. 118.19ab.[58] The regulations in Ezek. 44.2a αb are in aß motivated
by the special act of Yahweh's *bô be* the gates. This corresponds to the
qualification of the gates in 118.20a.

Following the motivation which relates the gates to Yahweh, special
sentences (Ezek. 44.3 and Ps. 118.20b) describe those who may use the
special gate. In both cases this is done by introductory *nomina* which are
of a character to qualify the special status of those permitted to enter.
And finally, the entrance motifs are extended by forms which describe
the significance of entry. The prince may enter 'to eat bread before
Yahweh', corresponding to the 'I will praise' of 118.19b, 21a.

In this way, the two texts reflect a common structure of sentences
given to presentation of the gates in question, a qualification of the gates
as very special due to some relationship with Yahweh, and finally regulations on the proper use of the gates in connection with rights of entry.
This structure of sentences and motifs must point to a common origin,
probably in sacred regulations of admittance. Given this background, the
specially qualified gates and qualified entrants stress the significance of
the very act of entry.

The connection with Ezek. 44.1-3 shows that the function of the
description of the gates in Ps. 118.20 is to confine the special entry to
the sanctuary to some special type of enterer. Whoever is 'righteous'
may enter. The plea for admission of v. 19—with the verbs *pātaḥ* and
bô be in first-person forms—means that the I presents himself as potentially representing this ideal. Moreover, the hymnic introduction of
v. 15a also refers to the Saddiqim as a group, localized to their 'tents',
corresponding to the 'tents of evil' of Ps. 84.11. If the I is permitted to
enter, he is accepted as a *saddiq*, representing the ideal, included in the
group of *saddiqim*.[59]

Compared to the other texts, the relationship of v. 19 to v. 20 indicates a much more immediate relationship of third-person statements
and I-forms. But in this case, some distance is kept by the parallelism of
the two sets of forms. The paradigm is applied to an individual situation.[60]

---

58. Cf. also these verbs in the closely related Isa. 26.2 and also Ezek. 46.1b
and 2a.

59. Cf. the similar scene of Ps. 142.8 with the I liberated from 'constriction' and
afterwards surrounded by the Saddiqim, and also a corresponding concept in Ps. 1.5
of 'standing in the congregation of the Saddiqim'.

60. Ps. 24.6 might reflect a parallel application of the paradigmatic third-person

Moreover, *saddiq*-hood is solidly connected with temple motifs, here in the form of temple entry. This corresponds to the other texts, reserving dwelling in the temple for a special group. Also, the act of entering the temple is connected to a situation of crisis. In Psalm 118, the crisis is described as a crisis of the past, expressed by the narrative forms of vv, 5, 13 and 18,[61] in addition to the more general v. 14b and in v. 21:

> From constriction I called on Yah
> Yah answered me with open space.
>
> You pushed me hard that I should fall.
> But Yahweh helped me.
>
> Yah chastened me hard.
> But into death he did not hand me.

The stereotypical sentence structure of these narrative forms points to their parallel function in the composition: an introductory statement on the crisis, contrasted with a corresponding description of Yahweh's help. In addition, the three descriptions can be related. The crisis described by the I in supplication, as tormented by the hostile you, and as chastened by Yahweh, would reflect the basic aspects of the situation. On the other hand, the relatively independent character of the three descriptions,[62] depicting three different types of scene, also illustrates the literary freedom for individual expression.

In this way, this psalm reflects the basic motif structure common to Psalms 36, 84 and 140, with the I in a situation of crisis and suffering,

---

forms (vv. 3-5) on a concrete group. The transition from Yahweh mentioned in the third person to being addressed in the second person, following the third-person statements (vv. 3ff.), corresponds to the similar transition in 118.19-21. In connection with Pss. 15 and 24 understood as gate liturgies, von Rad argues for special rites of priestly examination conducted in the temple gates, ending in a verdict expressed by the 'deklaratorische Formel' of *ṣaddîq hû ḥāyô yiḥyæ*, 'Die Anrechnung des Glaubens', p. 133 and ' "Gerechtigkeit" und "Leben" ', p. 227, followed by W. Zimmerli, *Ezekiel 1. A Commentary on the Book of the Prophet Ezekiel, Ch. 1–24* (Hermeneia; Philadelphia: Fortress Press, 1979), pp. 375ff., '"Leben" und "Tod"', pp. 494ff.

61. Verses 17-18 together with 5 and 13 as narration according to Crüsemann, *Hymnus und Danklied*, p. 219, cf. Hauge, 'The City facing Death', p. 10.

62. Illustrated by H. Schmidt, *Psalmen*, p. 212, who finds the narrative forms to express the personal fates of three different figures, and also by the usual difficulties of the commentators to pinpoint the concrete figure of the I in this psalm.

praying for the divine intervention, with dwelling in the temple reserved for the ideal figures as the ultimate goal. The connection between the texts must reflect that they are individual expressions for one basic type of application of super-individual character. In this respect Psalm 118 related to the other texts is of special importance in connecting the motif structure to the categories of successive events. The different texts are centred round different events of a story. Psalms 36, 84, and 140 are given to the situation of suffering and prayer. To the I of Psalm 118 (cf. also above to Psalm 73), the crisis belongs to the past, while the literary 'now' is given to the ultimate events of the I-story, namely the triumphant entry into the temple, which also means the I qualified as a *saddiq*, identified with the group of blessed temple dwellers.

Thus, to these texts seen together, a situation of crisis and suffering and supplication seems to represent the initial events of a story ending in the temple. Also in Psalm 118, the character of the crisis is connected with motifs of death (cf. the contrast of praise and death—v. 17 in addition to v. 18—and the motifs of 'pushing' and 'falling' v. 13). Basically, the story seems to reflect two main types of situation, one characterized by crisis and ultimate death outside the temple, and a contrast situation inside the temple. Also in Psalm 118, the narrative in you-form (v. 13) together with the motifs in the forms of confidence (vv. 10-12) indicate that the enemy motifs are significant for the crisis on the outside. On the other hand, vv. 5 and 18 as parallel narrative expressions for the crisis use other motif types as valid descriptions of the same situation.

For the understanding of the religious significance of the motif structure, it could also be important that the praise of the divine *hæsæd* frames the I-story of Psalm 118 (vv. 1-4, 29). This corresponds to the use of this motif in Psalm 36, and could further be related to the significance of the I as supplicant in the versions of the I-story in Psalms 36, 84 and 140.

For this psalm, the traditional cultic understanding could seem rather obvious. The character of the temple motifs of vv. 19-21—stressed by Ezek. 44.1-4—could even suggest an immediate connection between literary expression and ritual practice. Even if Jer. 7.2ff. presupposes a rather loose and ideologically undramatic *bô be* (v. 2) the temple gates as normal (cf. in Chapter 5), it is natural somehow to relate the language of 118.19-21 to concrete ritual experience. This could also have consequences for the other expressions for the I-story.

On the other hand, Psalm 118 also entails the Babylonian poem 'I will praise the Lord of Wisdom'[63] as relevant. This is often referred to in connection with Psalm 118,[64] reflecting a comparable structure of events. Told in I-form, the poem describes a series of events of a man dying and being brought to life by divine intervention. The story is concluded by the triumphant entry through the temple gates, the significance of which is stressed by each gate being given a name and described by its effect on the I. The connection between the two poems could hardly be coincidental.

Also the structure of the Babylonian text could naturally be related to a background of ritual practice. But for Psalm 118 as well as for the other I-psalms with a common motif structure, the existence of the Babylonian text at the very least introduces some ancient literary tradition as influential.

The story of Hezekiah's healing in 2 Kings 20 and Isaiah 38[65] could have some relevance for this problem. The complicated traditio- and redactio-historical problems represented by the two texts individually and especially as related,[66] warn against making them the basis for any sure conclusions. But they are interesting in this connection as stories centred round a particular 'life crisis' connected with ritual language. If we stress the significance of their final form, they can at the very least illustrate possible types of application for the I-story.

In both versions we find a motif 'ascent to the temple' (2 Kgs 20.5, 8; Isa. 38.22) connected with a story of an individual's sickness and healing. As the events are unfolded, the ascension is presented as the final and a most important event. The exposition of the events in the two versions is peculiar.

In 2 Kgs 20.5 the king is promised healing, connected with ascension to the temple on the third day. To this is added a promise of his lifetime being extended by 15 years and, moreover, of help against the Assyrians. After the promise, a concrete act of healing is described (v. 7). After this, the king refers to the divine promise and asks for a corroborative miracle. It is to be noted that the promise of 15 years of life and victory

---

63. J.B. Pritchard (ed.), *Ancient Near Eastern Texts Relating to the Old Testament* (Princeton: Princeton University Press, 1969), pp. 596-601.

64. E.g. Kraus, *Psalmen*, p. 983.

65. Hauge, 'The City facing Death', pp. 23-29.

66. E.g. H. Wildberger, *Jesaja*. III. *Jesaja 28–39* (BKAT 10.3; Neukirchen-Vluyn: Neukirchener Verlag, 1982), pp. 1439-68; to Isa. 38.10ff. Crüsemann, *Hymnus und Danklied*, pp. 239ff.

over the foes is ignored by the king who concentrates on the healing and the ascension.[67]

Now this order of events, as witnessed by modern commentators, is rather illogical; quite apart from the astonishing fact that the healing itself should be overshadowed by a rather unnecessary corroborative sign. The story ends with a detailed description of the corroborative sign, while nothing is told of the solution to what modern readers would perceive as the real problem of the story, namely the healing. However illogical, the present composition in this way stresses the significance of healing as connected with ascent to the temple. The actual medical treatment of vv. 7-8 could have marked a happy ending to the story.[68] But the present composition defines the healing as connected with ascent to the temple as the real matter of the story.

This seeming illogicality and the resulting weight on the ascension motif is even more concretely demonstrated by the Isaiah-version. Here, only the promises of 15 years of life and salvation from the Assyrians are given (vv. 5-6). In the Kings version the number of promises is reduced by the king to healing and ascension. The Isaiah version is even more singleminded in defining what is important in this story, as the promises in v. 22 are boiled down to the question of ascending to the temple.

Also in Isaiah 38 the request for a sign is located after the description of the medical treatment (v. 21), which by itself could be expected to form a natural ending of the story. But in this version, the king has already been given a corroborative sign by the prophet (vv. 7-8). Concluded by the psalm of thanksgiving, the story could also have been ended very satisfactorily in v. 20, as v. 9 presupposes the healing to have taken place. Most logically, the original story could be seen as comprising vv. 1, 2-3, 4-5 (+6), 7-8 and 21.[69] Instead, the story is concluded— formally completely unmotivated by the present composition—by the

---

67. To Snaith, *Kings*, p. 306, the political promise is secondary, added by the Deuteronomic compiler; while to Wildberger, *Jesaja*, p. 1446 the promise of healing and ascension is secondary, adding to the miraculous character of the story.

68. Cf. Wildberger, *Jesaja*, p. 1446, on the function of the parallel Isa. 38.21.

69. Proposed by Wildberger, *Jesaja*, p. 1447, with the 'höchst deplazierte Frage' of v. 22 as due to some ancient reader's reaction on the absence of the ascension motif in the Isaiah-version as compared with the Kings-version, noted down somewhere in the margin of the manuscript and later inserted into the text and in a very unsuitable location.

king's question regarding his ascension.

But this peculiar composition corresponds to the tendency of 2 Kings in stressing the ascension to the temple as the decisive event of the story. That this interest is differently expressed in the two versions of the same traditions—with Isaiah 38 even supposed to be literarily dependant on the Kings version—adds to the material significance of the illogicalities. The common tendency and its different expressions make it more natural to assume a common interest in the ascension motif as expression for the really significant event than two independent expressions of aimless editorial clumsiness.

Such a compositional interest would correspond to the applications of the temple motifs in Psalms 84 and 36 especially. The I as totally related to the temple, described as full of longing or 'wholeheartedly' walking, and, in this state, embodying the religious paradigm, corresponds to the two versions of the story. The king must embody the ideal of piety. The description of the king's request in 2 Kgs 20.8 after the promises (vv. 5-6) and the prophet's ministrations (v. 7) and especially in Isa. 38.22 after the promises of vv. 5-6 and the corroborative sign in v. 8, could be seen as expressions of the king's embodiment of a religious ideal.

In connection with this, it is interesting that the versions are centred round the situation of crisis as a situation of relatively independent character, related to a series of other events. Within the literary presence of the two versions, the ascension motifs refer to events of the future. Also, the relatively independent character of these 'situations' is connected to categories of locality. The events of crisis are connected to the king 'at home', with sickness, prayer, and visits by the prophet ending with the miraculous healing, taking place outside the temple.[70] The ascension motif alludes to other types of events, localized to the temple.

So, at the very least there is a difference between—if not non-ritual and ritual, then—'non-temple' and 'temple' events. It is of course possible that the ascension to the temple refers to rites of thanksgiving with the function normally envisaged as centred round the solution of the 'life

---

70. Stressed by Gerstenberger, *Der bittende Mensch*, pp. 135ff. on the significance of 'rituals of prayer' taking place outside the sacred compound, as 'vom offiziellen Kultus getrennte Heilungs- und Scutzzeremonien für einen Einzelmenschen'. For example Pss. 27, 42/43 and 84 are seen as expressions for 'Bittzeremonien im ausserkultischen Bereich'.

crisis'.[71] Even so, it is interesting that instances of the life problem of sickness, described in the two texts, are presented within a second set of categories, the problem of sickness transcribed as the problem of ascension to the temple. As linked, the life situation and the temple situation obviously refer to each other, the latter presupposing the first. But as to significance, they differ; the latter representing the implications of the life situation as related to categories of temple.

The complexity of description is added to by the psalm of thanksgiving in Isa. 38.10-20. The psalm may very well be related to the assumed rites of thanksgiving as the authors' representation of the text cited during these rites.[72] But it is very loosely related to the context (cf. above), especially as introduced v. 9 by a normal psalm superscription which presents the king as psalm composer.

In the psalm the king—in v. 9, presented as the I of the psalm—is related to the temple. But here the temple relationship is described as staying in the temple, this situation further qualified as 'playing all the days of our life' (v. 20). Similar categories of locality are referred to v. 11 with the I related to the land of life, connected with the motif 'Look upon Yahweh'. This connection of dwelling in the temple and life (cf. above to 140.12, 14) is also applied v. 19 to 'the living, the living' as praising Yahweh.

The locality of the temple/land of life and the state of the I as living/praising is contrasted by a relationship to death, mostly described by categories of locality.[73] The I is walking through the gates of Sheol (v. 10b), is 'together with those dwelling in the Underworld' (11b),[74] related to 'those descending to the pit' (18b), and finally brought ('lovebound' by Yahweh!) 'from the grave of destruction' (17b).

Within these verses 'temple' and 'dwelling in the temple' clearly do not refer to some isolated ritual event, nor to some locality having the sick-bed for contrast. With a lasting stay of praise, connected with the state of life, and contrasted with stay and non-praise in Sheol, the motifs refer to rather abstract categories of reality visualized as localities of life/relationship with Yahweh and death/non-relationship with Yahweh. Obviously presented as a description connected with the concrete life

71. Cf. the preceding note and further Crüsemann, *Hymnus and Danklied*, pp. 270ff.
72. Crüsemann, *Hymnus und Danklied*, pp. 241, 270ff.
73. Tromp, *Conceptions of Death*, pp. 129ff.
74. Tromp, *Conceptions of Death*, p. 84.

crisis of mortal sickness and healing, the language of the psalm expresses an ideological interpretation of the life events, the biography of the king transcribed by the categories of the I-biography.

In this way, these texts could basically refer to three levels of reality, all of them of 'religious' character:

1. The actual life situation of the king, centred round sickness and healing connected with extended life-time.
2. Some ritual situation of thanksgiving in the temple. Due to the special literary character of the two texts, this situation can only hypothetically be identified with the ascension motifs, which as well could refer to ideological categories.
3. Temple and dwelling in the temple as central expressions for some—at least in this context—rather abstract categories of interpretative, ideological character.

Basically, the character of the two compositions seems to reflect that the different levels are linked to one language system. This is suggested by the transition from one aspect to the other within the story and especially clearly by the insertion of the thanksgiving poem of Isaiah 38 as given to the ideological description of 'what really happened'. More concretely, the basic concepts of God and temple must be common to the three levels.

1. Yahweh is the miraculous healer and giver of extended life-time, while ascension to the temple represents the final event of the life crisis.
2. The proper rites would be related to Yahweh in the temple by the cult participant.
3. Yahweh is the presence in the temple to be seen and praised by the living temple dweller, with non-praise in Sheol for contrast.

This type of language with a linkage of the levels is basic to the two stories. However, their peculiar composition also demonstrates that one level can be stressed as the more relevant for a particular interest.

These possibilities are interesting with regard to the understanding of Psalm 118 in connection with Psalms 36, 84 and 140. The language of these texts corresponds to that of the thanksgiving poem Isa. 38.10ff. In this way they directly express the ideological level and the ideological interest of the language system. On the other hand, the linkage of the levels in the Hezekiah-story suggests that the psalms—at least at the time of composition of 2 Kings 20 and Isaiah 38—are applicable also as expressions of a normal life crisis, linked to the problems and solutions of the life crisis, as well as to cultic situations.

The possibility of different applications could be expressed by Ps. 118.19ff. The ideological level must reflect the prime interest of the composition. Against this background, these verses, and the psalm as a whole, can be related to some literary-religious tradition of the I-story; and can be linked with other Old Testament expressions in this literary tradition as well as the Babylonian 'I will praise the Lord of Wisdom'. On the other hand, the linkage to the traditions of Ezek. 44.1ff. and ritual practice is also relevant. Finally, the Hezekiah-story also suggests that the 'users' of Psalm 118—whatever they used it for—also could identify with this 'I-story', even from a background of some ideologically rather commonplace life crisis.

With God and temple as equally relevant categories for any level of application, the language of these texts must allude to immensely rich possibilities of understanding and application. Even with the ideological level predominant, the language would constantly call forth criss-crossing connotations of life crises, ritual practices, and literary applications, together making the I of the text a vehicle for religious interpretation of the most diverse materials of human experience. And finally, in spite of the uncertainties in making any inferences from the two versions of the king's sickness, they firmly demonstrate the linkage of the I-story with biographical experience.

Chapter 3

PSALMS 42–43: THE SACRED JOURNEY

1. *The Psalm as a Whole*

The different types of motif have led to the traditional solutions as to the crisis of the I in this psalm.[1] Usually they are connected to the basic three types of suffering, with the I as sick, as a king confronting national enemies, or as accused in a judicial process.[2] But in this psalm, the geographical references of v. 7 have necessitated special adaptations. When not emended,[3] these references could mean that physical separation from the homeland is added to the main problem of sickness,[4] or of warfare.[5] Connected to such models, the temple motifs of 42.1ff. are taken to refer to the subjective emotional reactions of the I, while the temple motifs of 43.3-4 would refer to the concluding rites of thanksgiving after the 'real' problem has been solved.

Solutions of this kind present a rather weak reflection of the function of the temple motifs in this psalm. Other suggestions do more justice to the significance of these motifs in the composition. The crisis could

---

1.   To Beyerlin, *Die Rettung*, p. 11, the relationship of enemy motifs and the other motifs of suffering in this psalm is too uncertain to give priority to one special motif type, cf. also P.C. Craigie, *Psalms 1–50* (Word Biblical Commentary 19; Waco: Word Books, 1983), p. 325 naming some kind of exile or sickness as the possible causes which could limit the poet's possibility of going to Jerusalem.

2.   To the latter cf. Ruppert, *Der leidende Gerechte*, pp. 182-83, in addition to the references below.

3.   By Schmidt, *Psalmen*, p. 79; cf. also Taylor, *Psalms*, p. 220; and Dahood, *Psalms I*, p. 258. To Dahood, v. 7 refers to the land of Sheol in connection with the 'Foe' (v. 10, 43.2) and the 'Assassin' (v. 10) on death residing in the body of the sick person; cf. also Tromp, *Primitive Conceptions*, pp. 91 and 145-46.

4.   Gunkel, *Psalmen*, p. 178; Kraus, *Psalmen*, p. 321.

5.   Birkeland, *Die Feinde*, pp. 169-70; Mowinckel, *Salmeboken*, p. 100.

consist in banishment or exile, with the emotional significance of the separation from the temple due to the role of the I as a cultic servant.[6] Or the physical separation could reflect exclusion from the official temple cult due to the uncleanliness of sickness.[7] Or the motifs could refer to the asylum-function of the temple.[8] Or the temple motifs could be related to a ritual situation of festival procession.[9]

But for Psalms 42–43, in part due to the influence of Alonso Schökel's studies,[10] new solutions have been proposed, with the main motifs

6. Weiser, *Psalmen*, p. 234; Ridderbos, 'Response', *JSOT* 1 (1976), p. 17; Eichhorn, *Gott als Fels*, pp. 93-94; Croft, *The Identity of the Individual*, p. 174; cf. also below to Alonso Schökel.

7. To Gerstenberger, *Der bittende Mensch*, p. 152, this psalm together with 27 and 84 exemplify 'Bittzeremonien im ausserkultischen Bereich'.

8. Delekat, *Asylie*, pp. 148ff.: the I is in a sanctuary situated on the sources of Jordan, and is now searching an oracle for 'Schutzbrief' to be accepted into the home-sanctuary.

9. To Eaton, *Kingship and the Psalms*, pp. 130-31, the royal psalm is evoked by a crisis of warfare, but reflects ritual stereotypes of the Autumn Festival with the king 'installed as mediator of Yahweh's kingship and established by sacramental scenes of promise, suffering and exaltation'. The concrete local setting is some station off the temple hill 'such as the Gihon spring and caves in the Kidron Valley'. First when the divine favour is manifested, the worshippers can ascend the processional way to the temple (p. 70). To Goulder, *Sons of Korah*, p. 17, Ps. 42 is a song of the pilgrims on arriving at the sanctuary of Dan, Ps. 43 somewhat separate as used before dawn the following morning. As in Ps. 84, the motifs of longing and thirst refer to a most concrete situation, namely the pilgrims' panting after water and rest after days of strenuous walking and climbing on the way to Dan. The waters of v. 8 refer to the pilgrims' hope of abundantly slaking their thirst (pp. 28ff.).

10. Cf. especially 'The Poetic Structure', *JSOT* 1 (1976), pp. 4-11; and 'Response to Ridderbos and Kessler', *JSOT* 3 (1977), pp. 61-65; the former discussed by M. Kessler, 'Response', *JSOT* 1 (1976), pp. 12-15; and Ridderbos, 'Response', *JSOT* 1 (1976), pp. 16-21. For the valid analysis of the text, Alonso Schökel stresses the necessity of confinement to the literary 'I' of the poem. On the other hand, 'at a secondary stage it may become possible to make the jump from the poem to the author'. Thus, the literary I will have a relation, 'probably close relations', to the cult, he is finding himself exiled in a heathen country, he is 'probably' suffering persecution for his devotion to God etc. ('Response to Ridderbos and Kessler', *JSOT* 3 [1977], p. 63; cf. also a similar 'hypothetical reconstruction ' The Poetic Structure', *JSOT* 1 [1976], pp. 4-5). It is to be noted that 'jumps' of this kind—however hypothetical—severely limit the possibilities of understanding the imagery. Thus, a

detached from an immediate relationship to ritual and the traditional biographical-social categories. As connected with life-death categories, the central motifs could mean that 'the psalmist needs to obtain access to the temple, his source of life'.[11] Or the spatial language could have a metaphorical or symbolic function.[12] Even the temple motifs could be used with a symbolic function.[13]

Against the background of such a new orientation for the under-standing of the function of the basic motifs, this psalm is of special importance. Its formal character is traditionally linked to the repeated refrain of vv. 6, 12 and 43.5 which separates vv. 2-5, 7-11 and 43.1-4 as relatively independent subunits. This impression is supported by similar repetitions which link two and two parts. Verses 2ff. and 7ff. are linked by the taunting question 'Where is your God?' (vv. 4b and 11b); verses 7ff. and 43.1ff. by the parallel questions of v. 10 and 43.2, addressed by the I to God, who is related to the I by nominal qualifica-tions as 'my rock' and 'my fortress': 'Why have you forgotten/ rejected

biographical frame seems to be presupposed as the sole basis for the imagery. This would leave us with the traditional socio-biographical categories in addition to the subjective 'inner' experiences of the poet as the given categories for the analysis of the connotations of the motifs, with textual data as the means for arriving at the experiences of the poet.

11. Broyles, *Conflict and Faith*, pp. 201-202; this situation described as 'primarily religious' with God as the 'primary source of distress' and the enemies as a 'secondary source of distress'. This corresponds to Broyles's understanding of the enemy motifs for the whole group of the laments of the individual. For this group of texts, the enemies are 'not the explicit cause of distress (except perhaps for Pss. 22 and 35). They simply harass and mock the psalmist' (p. 218). Due to the uncertain-ties of 42.11a, this understanding may be valid for 42 seen in isolation. But the prayer of 43.1 suggests that the enemy motifs reflect a situation of real conflict.

12. As 'symbolic' for the psalmist's feeling of separation from God, according to J.W. Rogerson and J.W. McKay, *Psalms 1–50* (The Cambridge Bible Commentary; Cambridge: Cambridge University Press, 1977), p. 201; cf. also G. Wanke, *Die Zionstheologie der Korachiten* (BZAW 97; Berlin: Topelmann, 1966), p. 9. To the latter, 'die Verbindung Jahwe-Jerusalem', with Jerusalem's 'Ausschliesslich-keitsanspruch' for the divine presence, is a special characteristic of 'die Theologıe der Korachiten' (p. 33).

13. According to E.S. Gerstenberger, *Psalms Part I with an Introduction to Cultic Poetry* (FOTL 14; Grand Rapids: Eerdmans, 1988), p. 182, this psalm together with 84 and 102.13-23 reflect 'early Jewish community, where the Jerusalem temple had become a central symbol even for the personal faith'.

me? Why do I walk/walk around mourning from the oppression of my enemy?'.

Moreover, the first and the last part are linked by temple motifs, with an especially close relationship between v. 3 second line MT and 43.3b, 4.[14] The first and the second part also are linked by introductory descriptions of the soul as suffering, vv. 2-3, in addition to the contrasted water motifs, vv. 2-3 and 8. Also, the I 'remembering' linked to the soul's plight, v. 5 first line MT, is repeated in v. 7. Given this background, the day and night references of vv. 4 and 9 must be linked.[15] Finally, the descriptions of v. 5 and v. 8 somehow relate the festival procession and the terrible waters.

In addition to these obvious phenomena, the psalm is characterized by a subtle development of water and mountain motifs. Water motifs are important for the first part in vv. 2ff.;[16] water and mountain motifs are peculiarly combined for the second part vv. 7ff., while the temple in 43.3b is qualified as a mountain.

Held together, these characteristics suggest a meticulous composition. The motif development clearly relates this psalm to the texts analysed above. It is dominated by forms which describe the I as related to the temple (vv. 2-5 and 43.3-4, in addition to vv. 7-8 as a negative temple motif). According to the dominant motifs, the crisis of the I clearly consists in separation from and 'coming to' (v. 3a, 43.3b, 4) the temple.

On the other hand, the character of the crisis is as clearly linked to the enemies as constituting a similarly central problem. This is demonstrated by the laments and especially the parallel prayers in 43.1-2, 3-4. This linkage of temple and enemy motifs corresponds to Psalms 140 and 36, while the character of the crisis is more uncertain in Psalm 84. If one wishes to avoid the rather subjective choice of which motif set should be regarded as less metaphorical than the other—as witnessed by the different models of understanding, with probably only Delekat's model fully embracing both—this psalm with the parallel prayers 43.1ff. should be significant for the understanding of the given motif structure. If the

14. Kessler, 'Response', p. 14.
15. Kessler 'Response', p. 14.
16. According to Alonso Schökel, 'The Poetic Structure', *JSOT* 1 (1976), p. 4, the psalm as a whole is dominated by the two images of water as life and water as death in the two first parts.

temple motifs should represent, for example, metaphorical or symbolical language, the enemy motifs must form a part of such a language system.

It must be important that the given motifs are here presented in first-person forms, in contrast to those Psalms analysed above. The relationship between third-person statements and the I-forms in the other psalms suggests a relationship between paradigm and actualization. Such a relationship is expressed by types of parallelism between third-person statements and I-forms, which suggests the I as identifying himself and his situation with the paradigmatic figures, with the divine intervention as the ultimate act of identification. Psalms 42–43 reflect a much more immediate relationship between paradigm and actualization. Here, the basic motifs are presented in first-person forms. Within this composition the I is an immediate expression of certain aspects of the paradigmatic fate.

The introductory subjective expressions of the I as longing, comparable to 84.2-4, and the linkage of the crisis with admittance to the temple in the prayer 43.3-4, corresponding to the introduction of the psalm, stress the I of this psalm as representative of the ideal figure in crisis.

This can also be related to the special refrain vv. 6, 12 and 43.5:

> Why are you cast down, my soul?
> you did sound within me.
> Wait for God!
> for yet I shall praise him for saving acts from his face

According to MT, the versions of v. 12 and 43.5 are slightly different. The motif of the divine face is stressed: 'from my Face, from my God'. In addition, the motif of the soul's 'sounding' is formed as a parallel question: 'Why do you sound within me?'

The refrain certainly should not be read as a monotonous repetition, but must as to meaning reflect the dynamic development of each of the preceding three parts.[17] But, on the other hand, it remains a fact that the structural dynamic is not expressed by differing conclusions, but by the refrain again and again referring to one basic situation of the I talking to his soul.

The relationship between the address to the soul and the rest of the psalm is peculiar. While the two first parts (vv. 2-5 and 7-11) have the

---

17. Alonso Schökel, 'The Poetic Structure', pp. 8ff; Kessler, 'Response', pp. 12-13; Ridderbos, 'Response', p. 20.

character of self-description, 43.1-4 are addressed to God as prayer. It is natural to stress the compositional significance of the prayers for the psalm as a whole, with the two first parts preparing for and motivating the address to God. But the refrain disturbs this function by the introduction of a second level of communication, now with the soul as the addressee.

Within a psalm of this character, to stress the significance of the first level is obvious—its literary present connected to a situation of prayer. But the second level should not be disregarded as solely ornamental.[18] This is demonstrated in Psalm 131. Here is depicted a parallel situation of an I related to his soul as the weaker part; the soul even having undergone educational development and change for the better (vv. 1-2).[19] And here also, this situation is connected with waiting for God in the form of an admonishment, now addressed to Israel (v. 3). Obviously, the situation of the human in inner dialogue between a stronger and weaker part, the latter represented by the soul, must refer to some traditional situation.[20] Thus, the two I-descriptions as related to the admonishment to wait correspond with the 'soul' and 'Israel' in a parallel addressee relationship. The main difference between the two Is seems to consist in Psalm 131 as expression of a more advanced stage of soul-soothing.

In this way, the composition of Psalm 131 stresses the significance of the refrain to the composition as a whole. The literary now is not only concentrated into a situation of prayer addressed to God, but also into an inner dialogue addressed 'downwards'. With Psalm 131 as an independent composition consisting of I-description and admonishment,

18. Alonso Schökel's sensitive efforts of analysis of the 'Dialogue structure' and the 'Dynamic structure' of this psalm in 'The Poetic Structure', pp. 8ff, are marred by far too optimistic expectations as to the possibilities of immediately transcribing the literary expressions into descriptions of the poet's inner drama; cf. also Kessler, 'Response', p. 13

19. To this psalm cf. the detailed analysis of W. Beyerlin, *Wider die Hybris des Geistes. Studien zum 131.Psalm* (SBS 108; Stuttgart: Katholisches Bibelwerk, 1982).

20. Cf. a comparable situation of address also in Pss. 62.6 and 116.7 together with 35.3 and the negative message Ps. 11.1 (confronted with the dogmatic statements vv. 4ff.) in addition to 77.3 and the hymnic challenges 146.1 and 103.1ff., 22; 104.1, 35. 'I' as acting with regard to the soul cf. also 35.13 and 69.11 and further 25.1; 86.4; 143.8 (24.4).

Psalms 42–43 as a whole could be characterized as an admonishment motivated by the I-forms.

On the other hand, both the first and the second part are introduced by descriptions of the soul's plight addressed to God (vv. 2-3 first line, v. 7 first line). While these forms add to the significance of the soul motifs, they stress the importance of the prayer situation as relevant also for the admonishment. Within the psalm as a whole, the I represents some kind of mediation between God and soul, reminding God of the soul's plight, reminding the soul of God's help.

The background for such a situation could be related to the understanding of these texts as applications of a religious ideal. The relationship between third-person and first-person forms of the psalms analysed above characterizes the I as a being in between, seeking identification with the religious paradigm, but still on the outside with regard to dwelling in the temple, in danger of succumbing to the enemies and thus to a negative fate. Moreover, the texts seem to reflect a level of application where the ideological paradigm is rather closely connected with the biographical experience. For this type of usage, the I described with the characteristics of the ideological figure not only represents an ideological level of what really takes place in a life crisis, but seems quite directly to reflect a personal biography of immediate application of the religious ideal.

The idea of the paradigm not only applied as an external frame of ideological interpretation but as an ideal embodied by the personal fate is supported by the I of Psalms 42–43 split into supplicant confessor and the anguished soul. In this constellation, the I, representing the religious ideal, is applying the dogmatic truths in admonishment as relevant to the soul's suffering, while the soul's suffering is presented to God in the prayers.

The significance of such a situation as representing the literary now of the psalm is stressed by Psalm 131. Here the motifs depict a more mature I, with a still soul as the result of a history of the I 'making still'. The parallel motif development of the two texts could show that the inner cleavage of Psalms 42–43 represents an intermediate stage of some person enacting the religious ideal. Moreover, Ps. 131.3 with the I-description applied in the admonishment of Israel even suggests that an I of such personal achievements represents a paradigmatic figure.

Given the subjective and emotional character of the composition as a whole, it is the more interesting that the motif development of the three parts vv. 2-5, 7-11 and 43.1-4 applies the super-personal, objective stereotypes of the given motif structure for the description of the I.

2. Verses 2-5

> As the hart longs for flowing waters,
> so my soul longs for you, God.
> My soul thirsts for God, for the living God.
> When can I come and be seen before God?
> My tears have become my food by day and night
> as they say to me all day long: Where is your God?
> This I shall remember as I pour out my soul within me:
> How I went by in a throng and made them go (?) to the house of God
> to the noise of joy and thanksgiving, a mass of sound and feast.

The composition of these verses is centred round the three questions in vv. 3, 4 and 6. The first question relates the I as 'coming' to God and the second implies God as absent in relationship to the I. The address to the soul (v. 6) is connected with these basic motifs, with 'waiting for God' implying God as 'coming', while the motifs of praise connect to the situation of 3b.

The suggested connection between vv. 2-3, 4 and 5-6 as subunits corresponds to the motif development. The first is given to motifs of water and thirst in addition to the motifs of temple entrance. Verse 4 continues the motif of water and implied drinking,[21] but now with tears for food. Corresponding with the negative form of the 'water' motif contrasting the longed-for drinking, the question in this subunit is in the form of a taunt.

In this way, vv. 2-3 and 4 connect to the same basic motifs, describing the same situation by contrasted use of the motifs. Materially, both stress the problem of relationship to God by categories of locality.

Verse 5 stands more apart within the composition. But the motifs correspond to the implied temple motifs of the preceding verses, now as probably describing similar occasions of temple relationship in the past. Due to the play on water motifs in vv. 2-3, it is natural to stress the special ending of v. 5 as a parallel reference to these categories.[22] In this

---

21. Craigie, *Psalms 1–50*, p. 326.

22. Cf. *'ābar* and *qôl* used for both the procession (v. 5) and the terrible water falls (v. 8). The soul's *hāmâ*, v. 6, and as 'poured out' in v. 5 suggests that also for this concept water categories are applied.

context, the surging throng described as moving masses of water must refer to the imagery of vv. 2-4 and also to the imagery of the soul as poured out, v. 5. The water richness of the past contrasts both the present aridity in the preceding verses and must prepare the negative water motifs in the new description of the present situation of v. 8; the 'remembering' of past 'waters' in festival movement is contrasted by the present 'remembering', v. 7, to the sounds of the terrible waters, v. 8.[23]

This supports Alonso Schökel's assertion that water motifs dominate the psalm,[24] at least vv. 2-8. On the other hand, the richness and variety of application warns against too hasty an identification of their function.[25] The thirst of the hart for water and the thirst of the soul for God, the tears of the I and the outpouring of the soul, the sound of the festival throng and the sounding of the soul and finally the terrible call of the deep can not be easily abstracted into one set of imagery. Within the first part the different water motifs could reflect some contrast of 'much water as good', 'lack of water as bad'—corresponding to the (probable) contrast of aridity and rains in Psalm 84 and also the 'torrents' of Psalm 36. But this simple contrast effect of the first part is broken by v. 8, posing the I flooded by the deep as the parallel to the thirst for 'flowing waters'.

On the other hand, the concept of the temple is a common denominator for the separate images. Temple ideology with traditions of 'Cosmic' or 'holy mountain' could explain some aspects, including the deep motifs of v. 8.[26]

But for the motif execution of vv. 2-4, a background of a sacrificial meal must be relevant (cf. especially the imagery of 36.9-10). Thus, their

23. Craigie, *Psalms 1–50*, p. 326 stresses the connection of *zākar* vv. 5 and 7.

24. 'The Poetic Structure', p. 4; cf. Kessler's contrasting assertion, 'Response', p. 12, that the water as a 'simile' is 'strictly subordinate to the relationship of the poet to his God' and Alonso Schökel's 'Response to Ridderbos and Kessler', pp. 64-65, on the meaning of an image with 'symbolic value' as understood within the literary categories of Ricoeur.

25. Cf. Alonso Schökel, 'Response to Ridderbos and Kessler', p. 65 on the water motifs of vv. 2ff. and 8 as God appearing 'in the poem in two symbols, from one semantic field, but mutually antithetical', which reflects the 'the polarity within the experience of God as a *mysterium fascinans et tremendum*'.

26. Tromp, *Conceptions of Death*, pp. 205ff.; R.J. Clifford, *The Cosmic Mountain in Canaan and the Old Testament* (HSM 4; Cambridge MA: Harvard University Press, 1972), pp. 158ff., 177ff.; Hauge, 'The City facing Death', pp. 1-29.

connection with motifs on the divine presence corresponds to the concluding description of the temple in 43.3-4, qualified as the altar and the
divine presence. These applications—especially compared with 36.9-
10—illustrate how freely this background can be alluded to. The simile
of the hart of v. 2 and v. 4 presupposes a rather close relationship to
some concrete eating and drinking. Subjectively, the crisis of the I is
comparable to the thirst of the hart, juxtaposed to the I's present diet of
tears. But fundamentally, the imagery of vv. 2-3 is determined by a
more distant relationship, by the implication of 'drinking God' which is
deflected by the traditional motifs of v. 3 second line 'come and appear
before God'. A similar application is found Ps. 17.15. The I as 'sated by
God' reflects a more direct application. But also here this is mitigated by
the more acceptable form of intimate communion with God through
seeing. On the other hand, the parallel applications must reflect that the
connection of eating/drinking and seeing/being seen must reflect a traditional language of some special communion between God and worshipper in some special place.[27]

The water motifs of v. 5 break the implied sacramental frame by their
connection with the mythic concepts of the deep in v. 8. But as
qualification of the temple procession, they also here refer to temple
relationship. And also the seeming break with regard to the preceding
applications could be traditional. The 'torrents of your delights' and the
'fountain of life' in 36.9-10—especially when related to the temple
description of Ezekiel 47—suggest that the sacramental drinking need

---

27. Cf. also the sacred meal of, for example, Exod. 24.11 combining eating and
seeing, corresponding to Ps. 17.15. Isa. 25.6-7 is of special interest in connection
with Pss. 42-43 and 36.9-10 with a motif structure of eating, seeing and death/life
motifs in a context of dwelling in the temple and connected with the divine
intervention. The 'covering' of v. 7 is now usually understood to refer to rites of
sorrow, H. Wildberger, *Jesaja. II. Jesaja 13–27* (BKAT 10.2; Neukirchen-Vluyn:
Neukirchener Verlag, 1978), p. 966, and O. Kaiser, *Isaiah 13–39* (OTL; London:
SCM Press, 1980), p. 201; both pointing to 2 Sam. 15.30; 19.5; Jer. 14.3-4;
Est. 6.12. On the other hand, the concrete use of *lôṭ* 1 Kgs 19.13 provides good
support for the older understanding however 'mystical'. In a context of critical valuation of the theophanic tradition (J. Jeremias, *Theophanie. Die Geschichte einer
alttestamentlichen Gattung* [WMANT 10; Neukirchen-Vluyn: Neukirchener Verlag,
1965], pp. 112ff.; Eichhorn, *Gott als Fels*, pp. 84ff.), the prophet's covering his face
could illustrate the significance of the theophanic vision as traditionally an 'unveiling'.
On the other hand, the veil motif could allude to more than one connotation; cf. the I
of Ps. 42 in v. 10, 43.2 and also in 30.8, 12-13.

not be confined to the cups of Pss. 23.6 and 116.13!

In this way, the water motifs of the first part demonstrate the central function of the temple concept. The flexibility of these applications, with a pronounced literary freedom for allusions and *pars pro toto* representations, demonstrate that the verses refer to a wide range of connotations not easily accessible to our analytical tools and not easily abstracted into one type of language usage. But even if we miss many of the aspects communicated, it is evident that the temple represents the frame of reference for these verses; with vv. 2-3 describing the temple as longed for, v. 4 describing the present by a negative form of temple relationship, v. 5 referring to a past temple relationship, the refrain referring to a future one.

Basic for these motif groups is the temple qualified by the divine presence, in addition to motifs which describe a special relationship to the divine presence. This corresponds to the parallel qualifications of the psalms analysed above. The subjective types of motif in first-person forms in Psalms 42 and 84 stress especially the connectedness of some special relationship to God and to temple: longing for God means longing for the temple (Ps. 42), while longing for the temple means longing for God (Ps. 84).

At first hand, this would seem a rather obvious and even superfluous observation. But in view of the traditional models of understanding, it is necessary to stress this obvious fact. Thus, both with regard to this text and especially to texts like Psalm 140 with less prominent temple motifs, the traditional approach links divine intervention not to these categories, but to the 'real' problem of the I. With sickness or war or some judicial process or other types of socio-historically probable difficulties as the real problem of the I, in this text added to by geographical distance and homesickness, motifs on the relationship to God and temple are subordinated to the real problem. Save for the function of miracle-maker, and thus connected to some real cultic setting of prayer and thanksgiving, the motif of God is given a purely ornamental function compared to what is understood as the reality of the I.[28] Given the culturally

28. A good illustration of the tendency to treat the God motif as the ultimate metaphor is provided by Goulder, *Sons of Korah*, pp. 13-14, 27ff. To Goulder, v. 7 is of crucial importance in precisely locating the original sanctuary of the Korah-psalms to Dan on the river Jordan. The waterfalls of v. 8 are identified with the local spring of the river and mean to the exhausted throng that the thirst described in vv. 2-3 soon is to be slaked. The longing and thirst for God of this psalm, as well as Ps. 84, refer to a

conditioned preconceptions as to what constitutes real reality and how this is expressed in language, even the categories of 'symbol' and 'symbolic' of more recent models of understanding should be avoided as analytical tools. Such terms will be relevant to questions of function in connection with original and later applications of the texts, and thus ultimately to questions of meaning. But in analysis of the language, their function could be doubtful. This is demonstrated by the composition of 42.2-6. On the one hand we find a clear motif consistency, centred around water motifs. On the other hand, this consistency is coupled with an almost playful series of motif applications. Linking this series is a single-minded concentration on temple motifs. The relationship to God, connected to temple motifs, both represents the object of the I's longing and of the divine intervention (43.3-4). Here the crisis of the I clearly consists in separation from God and temple.

3. *Verses 7-11*

My God!
My soul is cast down within me! therefore I shall remember you
from the land of Jordan and Hermon, from the little mountain.
Deep calls to deep, to the noise of your torrents.
All your breakers and waves fall over me.
By day Yahweh calls forth his grace.
By night his song is with me, a prayer to God my life.
I say to God my rock: Why have you forgotten me?
Why do I go mourning from the oppression of my enemy?
With murder in my bones (?) the adversaries taunt me
when they say to me all day long: Where is your God?

This part also is formally dominated by the composition of two questions, that of the I and of the enemies' taunt. Here the two questions are connected as a conclusion for the two first parts, immediately preparing the prayers of 43.1ff. The introductory *'āmar* of vv. 10 and 11b link the two questions as a contrast: 'When they say to me, I say to you'. Such a connection is also suggested by the enemy motifs in the I's question v. 10 and the elaborated version of the taunting question in v. 11 compared to 4b. In this way, the I's saying would stress the I as turning

most concrete situation, namely to the throng's panting after many days' strenuous walking and climbing. The parallel deep motifs of 88.6-7 are given the opposite function, reflecting a special rite of the Dan sanctuary, in which a priest is placed in a dark and watery pit for the optimum of spiritual concentration (pp. 198-99).

towards God in his situation of distress. This orientation qualifies the I as confessor (cf. below to a similar motif development in Ps. 27.1-4). And it corresponds to a self-description introduced as a 'remembering of God' in v. 7.

Such an interest is also stressed by the qualifications of God as 'my God' (v. 7), 'God my life' (v. 9) and 'God my rock' (v. 10), which correspond to the concluding 'God my God' of 43.4 and above all by the similar forms of the refrain. In the first part, such constructions are only found in the enemies' taunt 'your God', v. 4.[29]

The use of day and night motifs in v. 9, connected to the enemies' taunt in vv. 4b.11b, could also have a similar function.[30] In this way, v. 4 and v. 9 would function as parallel central expressions of the I in crisis, representing different aspects of the crisis with the I as sufferer (v. 4 as connected with vv. 2-3) and the I as the suffering confessor in vv. 9-11. The verses are not primarily subjective outpourings, but expressions of the I 'remembering God' in his distress.[31]

The I's distress is clearly linked to the oppression by the enemies, concentrated by the taunt. Thus, while the first part (vv. 2-5) is dominated by motifs on the I related to God and to temple, the second part (vv. 7-11) is correspondingly dominated by the I as related to his enemies. This composition, which stresses the significance of the enemy motifs for the second part, corresponds to the composition of the prayers 43.1ff., the

29. Alonso Schökel stresses the insistent repetition of the name of God, though asserting that is has no 'clear structural value', 'The Poetic Structure', p. 9.

30. The riddle of the function of v. 9 in the context could be solved by the imperfect-forms understood as referring to the past, and thus with a function similar to v. 5 in the context, Ridderbos, 'Response', pp. 16f.; Broyles, *Conflict of Faith*, p. 204. On the other side, the relationship of vv. 4 and 9 must be important. Thus, to Alonso Schökel, 'The Poetic Structure', pp. 10-11, in v. 9 'at the exact centre of the strophe' 'speaks the voice of hope' which transforms the painful continuity of day and night into an 'alternating rhythm of grace and of praise'. The change reflects 'an emotional transformation' due to an inner voice of self-encouragement.

31. Cf. especially Gerstenberger, *Psalms Part I*, pp. 179-80 stressing the I in this psalm not as the subjectively emotional sufferer, but with the complaint linked to the affirmation of confidence. This assertion could also negatively be related to W. Brueggemann, 'Shape for Old Testament Theology I: Structure Legitimation', *CBQ* 47 (1985), pp. 28-46, and 'Shape for Old Testament Theology II: Embrace of Pain', *CBQ* 47 (1985), pp. 395-415; and to Broyles, *Conflict of Faith* (e.g. pp. 51ff.). To the latter, the complaint category is important with its implications of protest and argument, to Brueggemann as implying confrontation with the traditionally accepted theological structure.

first of which (vv. 1-2) reverts to the immediately preceding enemy motifs.

Against this background, the motifs of vv. 7-8 pose a special riddle. The geographical references of v. 7 have, when not emended, led to many peculiar historical suppositions on the situation of the I. Verse 8 seen for itself would immediately suggest the I to be in a situation described by the more elaborate motifs of Psalm 88.[32] And v. 7 seen for itself could be related to, for example, Psalm 120 with similar geographical references in v. 5.[33] The present location of the two verses, without any expression of rupture, would suggest that the description of the I's locality in v. 7 is immediately continued by v. 8, in a combination of motifs of mountain and the deep of Sheol.[34]

As to the function of vv. 7-8, the often referred to Pss. 61.3 and 9.14 could serve for parallels. In addition, the similar riddle of the 'Baka-valley', 84.7—with a corresponding function as a place of crisis and related to temple motifs—should be connected to the problem. But with the precise geographical references, Ps. 120.5 is of special interest. Here, the I is located in a 'bad place', the locality characterized by enemy motifs and by a situation of prayer given to the enemy problem—that is, a situation which corresponds closely to that of the I in 42.7ff.

A possible background for such 'topographies' could be found in, for example, Pss. 76.5 and especially 68.16-17 and 46.3-7. In the two first, we find Zion contrasted to rival mountains, especially vividly and in mythical terms in 68.16-17. With the following procession motifs (vv. 25ff.), the context of 68.16-17 is also of special interest as a parallel to 42.7-8. Ps. 46.3-7 adds to such an ideological 'topography' of contrasted mountains by combining motifs of mountain and sea, that is, a motif combination which corresponds to that of Ps. 42.7 followed by v. 8. In Psalm 46, the 'tottering mountains' are contrasted to the

32. Cf. especially Dahood, *Psalms I*, p. 258 and Tromp, *Conceptions of Death*, pp. 91, 145-46.

33. Rogerson and McKay, *Psalms 1–50*, p. 203, qualifying the spatial language of Ps. 42 as 'symbolical', that of 120 as 'metaphorical' (p. 114); cf. also Gerstenberger, *Psalms Part I*, p. 180 '—separation from Yahweh and his temple is expressed by employing the imagery of the wild regions of the northern mountains'.

34. While v. 8 as a qualification or immediate continuation of v. 7 represents the traditional view on the un-emended text, Craigie, *Psalms 1–50*, p. 325 finds the two verses to express contrasts of experience. Verse 7 reflects the poet's effort to mentally call forth places where he experienced the presence of God. But the effort is unsuccessful; only 'springs of chaos and despair are released in his mind'.

'non-tottering' God's city (vv. 3, 6). And the contrast mountains, described as 'mountains in the heart of the sea', combine in one image what in 42.7-8 is described by two added images.

The immediate linkage of the two motif sets in Ps. 68.23 could even suggest that such a combination is traditional. With Bashan qualified as a rival mountain in vv. 16-17, the combined motifs in v. 23 can hardly have the usually supposed function as a vivid simile for 'everywhere',[35] but must have more sinister connotations. This corresponds to the context of v. 23, which refers to a situation of enemies and divine retribution.[36] So there is a motif cluster of contrasted mountain, sea, enemies and divine intervention which corresponds to Psalms 42–43, especially as connected to a frame of procession and temple motifs. Such a motif cluster is also demonstrated by Psalm 46, by the application of the mountain and sea imagery in v. 7.

In this way, the connection between 42.7 and 8, followed by motifs which qualify the 'bad place' as a place of enemies, can be understood as an expression for a traditional set of motifs. The different expressions demonstrate that the motifs can be differently applied. What, for example, in 46.3 and also 68.23 is combined in one image, is in 42.7-8 executed as two related motif sets of relatively independent character (cf. on the one hand Psalm 88, on the other hand 120.5 together with 76.5 and 68.16-17).

When we also take expressions like Pss. 61.3 and 9.14 into consideration, the concept of the contrast or negative locality must be connected with extremely rich and varied motif groups, used with a remarkable literary freedom for individual application. The 'contrast locality' is obviously peopled, in, for example, Psalm 120 by the enemies of the I, and in Ps. 88 by the dead. This would correspond to the combination of 42.7-8 with the enemy motifs of vv. 10-11.

Moreover, Psalm 46 even suggests that 42.2ff. as related to vv. 7ff. could represent a traditional motif connection. The 'pleasing waters' of the holy city completes the image of the non-tottering God's city as the contrast to the tottering mountains in the sea. This would correspond to the imagery of Psalm 42, with the I located in the watery hell of v. 8, thirsting for the waters of the divine presence (cf. also Ps. 68.7ff. with a

35. Cf. e.g. 36.6-7 demonstrating a more abstracted usage.
36. Hauge, 'The City facing Death', pp. 22-23.

similar contrast of dryness connected to the evil and a miracle of rain in the desert).[37]

Such a connection between two contrasted localities of water could be stressed by the composition of vv. 5 and 7-8. The motif of *zākar* links the two verses, especially as connected with parallel soul motifs. In v. 5 the description of the procession is coloured by concluding water motifs. The 'sound' of the throng in procession qualified as waves of the sea subtly connects the two situations of v. 5 and v. 8. The watery past of the I in procession to the temple is thus contrasted to the watery hell of the present locality. Also, the temple motifs concluded by the image of the I surrounded by people would correspond to the categories of the contrast locality of rival mountains and the deep as peopled with the enemies.[38] The formal composition of vv. 7-11 stresses the enemy motifs as the most significant characteristic of the contrast locality. As the conclusion of the second part, immediately preparing the enemy prayer of 43.1, the enemy motifs of vv. 10-11 dominate the expression of the I's 'remembering' in vv. 9-11. In this way, the concluding procession and enemy motifs stress the contrast relationship of the two first parts.

The relationship of vv. 2-5 and 7-11 suggests a meticulous composition which contrasts the two localities. The I is located to a place which in every respect is qualified as 'not temple'. Such a contrast could also characterize the composition of Psalms 42–43 as a whole. In vv. 7-8 the

37. Ultimately, this motif connection might be related to Alonso Schökel's assertion of the contrasted water motifs as expressions for 'the polarity within the experience of God'. If so, such an understanding could be related to the cosmological categories of Ps. 74.13-14 followed by v. 15 and 104.6-9 followed by vv. 10-11, which suggest some kind of connection between the waters of the sea and the sweet water of fountains. Such a connection could also be reflected in the present composition of Gen. 1 and 2ff. This could also be related to the 'water' motifs of Isa. 40–55, with the many versions of Yahweh as connected with water/fertility (41.17-20; 44.2-4; 45.8; 48.18, 20-21; 49.9-11; 50.3; 55.1-2, 10-13) and as somehow negatively related as e.g. 'drying out' (42.14-17; 43.2; 44.26-27; 50.2-3; 51.9-10; 54.9-10), combined 43.16-21 and also 51.15-16; cf. Barstad, *Way in the Wilderness*, pp. 21-36 on their possible background and function.

38. Cf. also the parallel motif constellation of temple, rival mountains and enemies, the latter as dead expressed by motifs of sleep (T.H. McAlpine, *Sleep, Divine & Human, in the Old Testament* [JSOTSup 38; Sheffield: JSOT Press, 1987], p. 68) in Ps. 76.2-7; in addition to the startling possibilities for free application of 'water' motifs in connection with temple and enemy motifs illustrated by Ps. 48.8 and Isa. 33.16, 21, 23 in their present contexts.

contrast locality is qualified by the peculiar constellation of mountain and deep motifs. This corresponds to the temple of the first part, vv. 2-5, qualified as watery place, and thus juxtaposed to v. 8. In the third part, 43.1-4, the temple is qualified as a mountain in v. 3, corresponding to the qualification of the contrast locality as a place of mountains in v. 7.

This compositional development would also emphasize the significance of the mountain and deep motifs as combined in vv. 7-8. The startling imagery of the I as located both in the mountains and in the deep could play on the connotations of the two motif types. Thus Pss. 68.16-17 and 76.5 both refer to rival mountains. And the second-person forms of 42.8 suggest the watery hell as a place of divine punishment and retribution. This would correspond to the deep as described in, for example, Psalm 88. Connotations of this kind would correspond to the repeated questions of 42.10 and 43.2, where the suffering of the I as related to his enemies is described as ultimately due to the divine 'forgetting' and 'rejecting' of the I.

This adds to our understanding of the contrast place and could have significant implications. With the deep as a place of retribution connected with the divine activity, it also qualifies God in a 'negative mode', ultimately the subject of the I's suffering, with waters and enemies for parallel means of retribution (cf. above to the narrative elements of Ps. 118.5, 13 and 18 as parallel expressions for three aspects of the I's suffering). But in addition to God's being connected with retribution, the I's remembering also qualifies God as positively active through his 'grace' (v. 9). The day and night motifs of v. 9, corresponding to v. 4, must connect this divine activity to the present situation in the negative place.

This seemingly contrasts with the imagery of vv. 2-5. Here the motif execution is only meaningful with God understood as terribly absent relative to the I, with the divine absence connected with the I's absence from the temple. But obviously also stay in the contrast place is characterized by some kind of relationship to God. With God qualified both as negative and as 'summoning his grace', the contrast place includes some kind of, if not divine presence, then activity through the mediums of sea and enemies and 'his grace'.

This must be linked to the contrast locality as the place of *zākar,* with the confession on the presence of 'grace' (v. 9 first line) and the nightly 'his song' and 'prayer' of vv. 10-11 as the concrete expression for the 'remembering'. Thus, also dwelling in the contrast place implies some

relationship to God, as suggested by the terms of 'remembering', 'song'
and 'prayer' in addition to the motif of waiting in the admonishments to
the soul. The two latter motifs also implicitly qualify the contrast locality
as the place for the miraculous divine intervention.

These qualifications could suggest important aspects of the motif
structure. But the compositional development of the second part concluded by vv. 10-11 stresses the presence of the enemies as the most
important characteristic of the contrast place. In addition, the I is
qualified as the 'rememberer' from the contrast place, that is, as the suffering confessor.

4. Psalm 43.1-4

> Judge me, God! and struggle my struggle!
> against a people without grace.
> From a man of deceit and wrongness—deliver me!
> For you—God my fortress—why have you rejected me?
> Why do I walk around mourning from the oppression of my enemy?
> Send your light and your truth—they lead me!
> They make me come to your holy mountain, to your dwelling!
> So I can come to the altar of God, to God the joy of my rejoicing,
> so I can praise you with the lyre, God my God.

The two prayers, separated by the *kî*-sentence of v. 2 which repeats
elements of the address 42.10-11, conclude the motif development of the
two first parts. The introductory enemy prayer of vv. 1-2 immediately
continues 42.7-11, with the enemy situation as the central characteristic
of the contrast locality, while vv. 3-4 reverts to the temple motifs which
dominate 42.2-5. The parallel composition of the prayers, stressed by the
meticulous composition of Ps. 42, demonstrate that enemy and temple
motifs are closely connected as expressions for the one crisis of the I.

It is interesting that the motifs of vv. 1-2 qualify the enemy problem
as a situation of struggle and conflict, from which the I is to be
'delivered' by divine intervention. In Psalm 42, the enemy motifs refer
mainly to a situation of taunting, in connection with a situation of suffering, related to the I as absent from the temple and confined to the
contrast place. Connected with this imagery, the divine intervention, also
with regard to the enemy situation, would consist in the prayer of vv. 3-
4 as fulfilled. God leading the I to the temple would have silenced
the taunting enemies. Thus, the prayer of Ps. 43.1-2 reverts to the
enemy situation of the other texts, which must represent the traditional
expression for the crisis caused by the enemies. Such a relationship to

given traditions is also suggested by the form of the enemy prayer. Verse 1 corresponds to 140.2ff., 5-6 and 36.12, with verbs related to objects of qualifying nouns, in a chiliastic structure. Obviously, the basic enemy situation consists in the I being related to figures of 'evil' in a situation of conflict and 'struggle', from which he is to be 'delivered'. The I as separate from the evil—not only connected to a situation of conflict, but with regard to 'volitional' life orientation—is stressed by 84.11b.

Such a parallel relationship between the execution of the enemy motifs in Ps. 42 and 43.1-2, the first representing a more individual expression, the latter reverting to traditional forms and motifs, is comparable to the relationship of first-person forms and third-person statements of the texts analysed above. We found that this relationship could be explained as expressions for individual applications of the given motif structure, with the paradigm of the *saddiq* applied to some singular situation. While the motif pattern in Psalms 42–43 is expressed in first-person forms, the specific character of the two expressions for the crisis of the I in Psalms 42 and 43 could reflect the same type of relationship between traditional forms and individual application.[39]

The second prayer, 43.3-4, reverts to the crisis as it is described in the first part, 42.2-5, with the I separated from the temple. The significance of the temple as the place of relationship with God is vividly expressed by the nouns of locality in vv. 3b, 4 first line. Split two and two between forms of *bô*, the arrangement depicts the I's coming as a gradual coming near to God: 'to your holy mountain, to your dwelling', 'to the altar of God, to God the joy of my rejoicing'. The final address 'God my God' concludes this gradual heightening of intensity connected with the categories of locality.

The motif connection with Ps. 42.2-5 is expressed thus, with the elements of 3b and the first line of v. 4 as an extended version of the motifs of 42.3 second line, with *bô* for the central verb. In addition, the qualification of the temple as mountain in v. 3 concludes the composition of the psalm as a whole. The contrast place of the second part, 42.7-11, described as a place of mountains and deep in vv. 7-8, corresponds to the qualification of the temple in the first part, 42.2-5, as a place of

---

39. This also suggests a relationship between external and internalized categories, the enemy situation as relevantly described by, for example, motifs of war or persecution as by motifs which refer to inner mental and emotional categories (cf. also above on Ps. 36).

water, and in the third part of Psalm 43 as mountain.

These indications of a meticulous composition, which connects the three parts as expression of the situation of the I, is important with regard to the motifs of the second prayer as a prayer to be led to the temple, to the divine presence. For the psalms analysed above, we found that the relationship of the motifs suggested that the I's being 'on the outside' of the temple constituted the crisis, and that the divine intervention was related to temple admittance and dwelling as the 'real' problem of the I. On the other hand, in these texts the I as related to dwelling in the temple is mainly expressed in the application of third-person statements. Given this background, it must be significant that in Psalms 42–43, with the given motifs consistently expressed in first-person forms, not only are motifs of longing and subjective orientation related to the I, but also the divine intervention is directly qualified as 'making come' the I to the temple. Moreover, this definition is stressed by the I localized to a contrast place consistently defined as anti-temple in the second part, Ps. 42.7-11. With the reversion to the traditional enemy motifs in the parallel prayer 43.1-2, it is clear that the motif development of Psalms 42–43 is relevant to the other texts.

The temple prayer introduces a special set of motifs, in addition to those of Ps. 42.3. The motif on the I as 'coming' to the temple is extended by motifs on 'light' and 'truth' 'sent out' by God to 'lead' the I and 'make him come'. The idea of movement relative to the temple represents a natural extension of the imagery of the first two parts. With the I localized in the negative place, longing to come to the temple, motifs which describe the I in movement from one place to the other represent a making explicit of the imagery implicit to the first two motif groups. Also, this corresponds to the way motifs of Psalms 140 and, especially, 84, the latter with a qualification of the journey related to God and temple as pilgrimage. Also, the use of the procession motifs of Ps. 42.5 must be relevant as an expression of this idea.

As well as alluding to the motifs of temple and of the contrast locality, Ps. 43.3-4 could refer to a third set of relatively independent motifs. As in Ps. 84.6-9, the way motifs refer to miraculous categories. The special character of this motif group could also be reflected by the concrete motifs which express divine intervention. God is not acting directly, but guides the I by the substitutes of 'your light' and 'your truth'.[40] This

---

40. E.g. Gerstenberger, *Psalms Part I*, p. 181.

suggestion of a special divine mode of acting in connection with way motifs would correspond to the different descriptions of God and relationship with God in connection with the contrast localities. The relationship with God in the temple in these texts obviously represents something special. Within Psalms 42-43, the motif development seems consistently to presuppose God as localized to the temple, with absence from the temple meaning absence from God. But also, Ps. 42.7ff. suggests a special relationship to God in a negative mode, with the contrast place as a place of retribution, in addition to the divine 'summoning of his grace', and the I as 'remembering', 'praying', and exhorting his soul to 'wait'.

5. *Conclusions*

a. *The Motif Structure*

Given this background, the meticulous composition and motif development of Psalms 42–43 is of special significance for the understanding of Psalms 36, 84, and 140. The four texts could represent singular expressions of a given motif structure based on some 'sacred topography'. The composition of Psalms 42–43 expresses an especially clear motif representation, with 'reality' defined by motif sets of two contrasted localities. In addition, a third motif set connected with movement, by divine guidance, between the two localities complements the motif structure. It is clear that the topography of this and the other texts is of ideological character. It gives a religious description of man as a being located somewhere in a sacred landscape of temple, contrast locality, and way.

The negative locality obviously has the characteristics of Sheol, with death as the opposite of relationship with God (42.8, 36.13, 140.11b-12). In this respect, it could be significant that Ps. 42.7-8 qualifies the negative place as a place of divine retribution, connected with revolt and rivalry. This corresponds to the category of 'evil' related not only to the enemies, but also to the I (36.12-13, 84.11 and further as general statements on the negative fate 140.11b-12). The local category of the negative place seems to encompass two aspects immediately linked, one volitional aspect of revolt and evil, another of retribution and defeat and suffering and death.

Some special type of relationship with God characterizes the temple. While motifs of praise and joy are basic for motifs of dwelling in the temple, Psalms 42–43 together with 36 and 84 refer to a tradition of some special communion with the divine presence, connected with motifs of meal linked with seeing/being seen. In Psalm 36 the meal is connected to life and seeing light, in Psalm 42 connected to the motif of the soul's thirst for God.

While the contrast place is related to the evil, the temple is inhabited by some special beings. In Ps. 140.14 the special character of the positive group is suggested by the terms 'righteous' and 'upright of heart'—the significance of the term *ṣaddîq* emphasized by Psalm 118. But motifs of positive qualification of the ideal figure are peculiarly scarce in the four texts (cf. 84.6) compared with the richness of negative motifs. The situation of the I and the stereotyped self-descriptions of the I as the suffering confessor, orientated towards the temple and relationship with God, with the solution of the crisis dependent on the divine intervention, could serve as the most concrete illustration of the characteristics of the blessed temple dwellers.

For motifs of the way, miraculous categories are characteristic according to Pss. 84.7-8 and 43.3-4. Psalm 43.3 qualifies the movement of the I by motifs of divine guidance 'making come' the I to the temple, the significance of which is emphasized by the motif development of Psalm 23 centred round the concept of the divine shepherd.

In this way, Psalms 42–43 are of special importance as a clear representation of the three motif groups which form the basis of the applications of the motif structure in the other texts.

As related to the three motif sets, the I is described in a consistently passive mode. While the motif groups also can be used with the I as active (cf. below on Psalm 26), the I in these texts—both as related to the torments of the enemies/the negative place and to the temple—is completely in the hands of external forces. The motif of waiting for God of the refrain in 42–43 seems the suitable response to a situation of suffering heightened by the qualification of the I in these texts as confessor. Left to himself, the I is doomed. On the other hand, this stresses the importance of the miraculous categories for these psalms as a whole.

The I of this sacred landscape of Temple, Sheol and Way, is a being of transformation and change—with change, corresponding to the local categories, expressed most clearly as movement. Compared with the inhabitants of the two localities, the I is in between, a being very much in movement related to one of the localities. The third-person statements relating to the temple and the expressions of longing in Psalms 42 and 84 obviously qualify the I as basically orientated towards the temple. But the descriptions of the crises—save for the uncertainties of Psalm 84—

demonstrate that only divine intervention can save the I from the negative fate of 'falling'.

The negative fate is consistently connected with categories of 'evil', usually connected with the motif of the evil enemies. But the expressions of the enemies' threat differ from text to text. They are actively pursuing the life of the I (Psalm 140). Connected with the local categories of Psalm 36, the enemies are 'making the I flee' to the place of 'falling'. Also Psalm 43.1 presents the evil as active enemies. But other types of description—connected to the externalized types of imagery—refer to internalized categories, the threat of the evil related to mental and emotional phenomena. Thus, in Psalm 84, the 'tents of evil' represent the alternative to the I's temple orientation and thus must represent localities of subjective attraction (cf. below on Psalm 26). The elaboration of the negative paradigm 36.2ff. could refer to the same categories of attraction and temptation. And finally, in Psalms 42–43 the motif development of 42.7-11 together with v. 4 suggests the enemies as co-inhabitants of Sheol, taunting the I in the same manner as the dead of, for example, Isa. 14.9ff. In this psalm, the threat of the enemies could be related to the dejection of the soul (cf. especially 42.4a and b).

The motif execution within each particular psalm demonstrates the literary freedom of application. Different motif types are even combined within one psalm, with 36.2-5 related to vv. 12-13; and, especially, the taunting of 42.4, 10-11 connected to the normal motifs of conflict 43.1-2. Obviously, the motif application in all cases presupposes the evil enemies to be somehow related to death/Sheol, and to represent the basic motif for the threat of death. But the fluidity of motif application—demonstrated by the competing exegetical models which have been based mainly on the analysis of the enemy motifs—suggests the motifs carry a wealth of connotations not immediately recognized.

This is also demonstrated by the evil in relation to the contrast place. In Psalms 140 and 36, the enemies, very much alive and seeking the death of the I, are obviously candidates for the place of falling (cf. the qualification of evil in connection with the general statements of 36.13 and 140.12 concluding v. 11). Here, the enemies and the I seem to be involved in a conflict of 'who shall die?' In Psalm 42, the I and the enemies seem to be co-inhabitants in Sheol. And finally, the 'tents of evil' (cf. below to Psalm 26) must, as contrasting the temple, be connected with the fate of death. But alluding to places of attraction, the motif application could suggest a relationship between the tent motif and

Sheol similar to that of the house of the foreign woman and Sheol of Prov. 2.16ff., 7.6ff.

Perhaps the most important point of reference for the understanding of the differing applications of the basic motifs could be represented by the situation of the I in relation to the motif structure. In this respect, the topographical categories of Psalms 42–43 are especially helpful. In the sacred landscape, the I can be located to Sheol, while the way motifs of Psalms 84 and 140 locate the I to some place between the two localities. And while Psalms 84 and 43 presuppose the way as movement towards the temple, Psalm 36 suggests the I is in danger of a negative movement towards Sheol. The significance of the latter is supported by Psalm 42 with the I located to Sheol qualified as a place of retribution, contrasted to a happier past of temple relationship (v. 5). Finally, the individual psalm must reflect subtler differences within these broad categories. This could be illustrated by the different applications of the motifs of longing for the temple in Psalms 84 and 42.

In these cases, the different applications of the given motifs could be related to the basic situation of the I as stationed 'somewhere' in the sacred landscape. Moreover, and especially in connection with the intensely personal expressions of Psalms 42–43, it is difficult to avoid the impression that this 'somewhere' ultimately must reflect personal experience. This personal experience seems not to reflect experiences separate from the basic motifs, as some ideological meta-language ornamenting the real problem, but to be identical with the motif structure as the language of personal experience.

Furthermore, Psalms 42–43 related to the other texts justify some tentative remarks on aspects of the language of these texts. Characteristic of this language are sets of basic components which we could describe as motifs of temple, way, Sheol/death, enemies, the I. Viewed from this angle, each text represents a very limited number of stereotypical material units. On the other hand, the execution of these stereotypes is characterized by a remarkable degree of literary freedom of particular expression, making each compilation of the limited number of stereotypes into a singular literary achievement.

The combination of these two characteristics is peculiar. In view of the usual exegetical approach (and this one) looking for some common denominator and thus emphasizing real or asserted common factors, the mental flexibility, if not fluidity, represented by these applications of some given language must be stressed. This flexibility makes possible the free combination and application of the basic motifs (cf. above on the enemy motifs). Also, it permits the combination of phenomena which to a modern mind would represent types of language which refer to different levels of reality.

Ps. 42.2ff. is good illustration of this type of combination. Verse 2a could satisfactorily be labelled as a simile. The application in 2b, 3 first line could represent metaphorical language, while its associations of sacred meal would tempt labels like sacramental or mystical or 'spiritualization of ritual usage'. Verses 3 and 5 second line could be called cultic language of 'cultic experiences'. But v. 3 second line is obviously related to the preceding verses, while v. 5 is influenced by mythical concepts probably used metaphorically. Verse 4 refers to real experiences of sorrow in metaphorical language, but must also be related to the thirst motifs of vv. 2-3 with their possible labels. And the carefree adding of vv. 7 to 8 place mythical or cosmological motifs in continuation of the geographical references of v. 7, which, on the other hand, combines the geography with subtle mythical overtones. All these references are combined in relation to each other and to the temple and I motifs of the rest of the psalm, encompassing these many-sourced torrents of connotations.

Obviously none of the usual labels does justice to this special type of language. While terms like poetical or symbolical are readily available, their application entails too many culturally conditioned implications and would primarily demonstrate the exegetical lack of suitable categories. Traditionally, the emphasis on some cultic or institutional setting has provided some frame of reference for the valuation of the literary phenomena. But with the uncertainties pertaining to such an approach, an adequate understanding of the language used is the more necessary.

At least some aspects of this language can be appreciated when the flexibility of the motif use is seen together with the stereotypical nature of the basic motifs. The combination of stereotypes and literary freedom suggests some rather fixed background of structurally given connotations. While problems of origins are too uncertain, the connection with certain basic terms and motifs suggests that this structure is of a conceptual nature. In this way, the language of these texts could have a markedly referential or allusive function, with the single motif execution having some *pars pro toto* function.

Thus, individual pieces could be characterized by their relationship to some basic point of interest. The differences between Psalms 36, 42–43,

84 and 140 would reflect them as parallel expressions of one motif
structure, dominated by some special interest. Thus, while, for example,
Psalm 84 has a short reference to the evil and is dominated by temple
motifs, Psalm 140 is given to the motifs of evil enemies and only alludes
to the temple in the conclusion. Obviously, the two psalms are reflections
of the same basic motif structure, while the compositional development
is centred around different aspects of meaning which come about by the
elaboration of a certain motif group. Other motifs are alluded to only as
points of reference, hinting at the more comprehensive frame of
connotations.

Psalm 23 is good illustration of the alluding character of the texts. The
two motif sets of vv. 1-4 and v. 5 create a plastic expression of the way
and guidance motifs used in 43.3-4, with the transition to You-forms and
the special motifs on Yahweh as host stressing the special relationship to
Yahweh after the arrival in the temple (cf. below to Psalm 27). In this
way, the composition is given to aspects of the motif structure as a
whole. This clearly is connected with an interest of confession, with the I
as recipient of the divine blessings connected to way and temple motifs.
On the other hand, the peculiar application of enemy motifs in v. 5
demonstrates the dependence on the given motif structure. Instead of
the normal connection with crisis and suffering, the function of this motif
group in this psalm is connected to dwelling in the temple, with the envy
of the enemies spicing the blessed meal. While such a motif application
can not directly reflect any cultic or real-life situation, it must express
the interest of the psalm as a whole and demonstrates the literary freedom of application. But also, the motif alludes to the connotations of the
traditional situation, the sweetness of the pastoral enhanced by the
despair and darkness of the associated frame. Against this background,
Psalms 42–43 are of special importance both as expressions of a
remarkable degree of literary creativity and as faithful reflections of the
traditional motif structure.

This understanding of the texts as expressions of given motifs connected with a basic point of interest could be taken one step further if
the texts are linked with categories of personal experience and development. The I of Psalms 23 and of 42–43 evidently are very differently
described in their relationship to the motif structure, especially within the
local categories as located somewhere in the sacred landscape.
Connected with the situation of the I in Psalm 36 under threat of some
negative movement towards the place of falling, the psalms obviously

3. *Psalms 42–43: The Sacred Journey*   101

reflect experiences of different stations of reality. The personal and psychological categories of Psalms 42–43 suggest that these stations also, perhaps even primarily, could refer to stages of inner development.

While the function and application of the texts remain uncertain, the motif development of Psalms 42–43, connected with the basic events of dwelling in Sheol, guidance on the way, and the ultimate arrival at the temple, at the very least suggests categories of change. Especially, the temple motifs hinting at some relationship of special intimacy with God connected with dwelling in the temple could even relate this change to personal transformation, connected with a special level of religious attainment. On the other hand, Psalms 42 and 36 illustrate that these categories of change and transformation also can be related to some negative development.

b. *The Motif Structure as Narrative in 1 Kings 19.1-18*
(Exodus 33.18ff.) and Exodus 14 and 15
i. *1 Kings 19 (Exodus 33.18ff.).* A connection between the motif structure and 1 Kgs 19.1ff., seen together with the closely related Exod. 33.18ff.[41] is the more interesting as these stories are understood as critical comments upon traditional ideas of a special relationship to Yahweh, usually connected with the theophanic vision in the temple. According to this understanding, both the material and the compositional interest of these stories could be connected with the I-Psalms as more traditional expressions of these themes.[42] The critical reflection of the two stories would be centred round the same situation which, in the above analysed psalms, forms the concluding and decisive event of the motif structure.

The compilation of motifs, especially in 1 Kgs 19.3ff., corresponds to the basic motifs of the psalms, especially as expressed in Psalms 42-43.

41. Usually with the central elements of 1 Kgs 19 seen as dependent on Exod. 33.18ff., e.g. Jeremias, *Theophanie*, pp. 112ff.; cf. also 1 Kgs 17–19 on Elijah as 'ein zweiter und neuer Mose' with the Horeb-story as the original; G. Fohrer, *Elia* (ATANT 53; Zürich: Zwingli Verlag, 1968), pp. 55ff.; G.W. Coats, *Moses. Heroic Man, Man of God* (JSOTSup 57; Sheffield: JSOT Press, 1988), p. 206. On the other hand, E. Aurelius, *Der Fürbitter Israels. Eine Studie zum Mosebild im Alten Testament* (CBOTS 27; Stockholm: Almqvist & Wiksell, 1988), p. 104 denies any connection between the two texts.
42. Cf. concretely Eichhorn, *Gott als Fels*, p. 86 on the connection between Pss. 27.5, 61.3 and Exod. 33.18ff.

The structure of the story is expressed in a series of situations related to localities of a special character, with the development of the story related to movement from one place to the other. The character of the localities as well as the movement can be related to the corresponding motifs of the I-psalms.

In contrast to the mountain of God, the first locality corresponds to the negative place of Psalm 42. The prophet is located in the desert, qualified by the broom motif. This can be related to the description of the negative place of Ps. 120.4 and also Job 30.4 in a description of the terrible land of the outcasts.[43] Moreover, the place is also qualified by death motifs, here in the form of the prophet in despair surrendering his soul. This adds to the death motif of the biographical frame (vv. 1-3, cf. in the prophet's complaint vv. 10b, 14b), with the prophet fleeing to save his life. While the prophet clearly is in a state of despair similar to the I of Psalm 42, the different applications of the death motifs together with the parallel descriptions suggest that the expression of a state of despair and personal crisis is linked to dwelling in a place of special character.

The movement from the one place to the other is dependent here also on divine intervention. While Ps. 43.3 refers to the divine substitutes of 'light' and 'truth', Yahweh is here represented by the Angel. The journey's connection with miraculous categories is here expressed by a meal which gives strength for the special effort (vv. 6-8, cf. the activities of the divine shepherd of Psalm 23 connected with grazing and water vv. 1-3a). The repeated commands to 'stand up and eat', emphasized by the prophet's lying down again (v. 6) stresses the divine initiative and the passivity of the pilgrim. The journey is started and maintained from above. In addition, the qualification of a walk of forty nights and days adds to the special character of the journey to the mountain.

The mountain of God is clearly defined as a place of meeting for God and man. It is the place of Yahweh manifesting himself in a special way as 'passing' for somebody specially chosen to witness the divine manifestation. The manifestation is related to some special place on the

43. The broom fixture could refer to given connotations. Its roots as food in Job 30.4—with a function comparable to tears as food in Ps. 42.4—could correspond to the connection of broom and miraculous meal in vv 5-6. Cf. also Gen. 21.14-19 and 16.5-14 reflecting a stereotyped motif compilation of (bush related to dying 21.15-16) thirst, water, seeing/being seen and miraculous intervention by the divine messenger.

mountain[44] where the chosen is standing[45] (vv. 11a, 13a, cf. also Exod. 33.21-22) to experience the divine 'passing'. The mountain is the place both for some special type of divine presence and for some special relationship to this presence.

The negations of the traditional experience of the theophany in the two stories (vv. 11-12, 13; Exod. 33.20, 22-23), in addition to the positive expressions for the chosen witness as experiencing the divine presence (v. 13; Exod. 33.23), stress the category of 'sensory' experience for this kind of event. The emphasis on the eyes as 'covered' by the prophet's veil or the divine hand qualifies the traditional experience as being primarily connected with seeing. The deliberate reflection and critical examination of traditional beliefs which characterize the two stories make the theophanic descriptions the more interesting with regard to the stereotyped temple motifs of the psalms analysed above. Obviously, the motifs of dwelling in the temple must refer to very special states of relationship to and experience of the divine presence. Close encounters of this kind, qualified by such motifs of experience and moreover related as the sublime experience of such elevated persons as Moses and Elijah (cf. also the traditional version in Isa. 6.1ff.), clearly cannot refer to ordinary events. In this way, these stories have repercussions on our understanding of the psalms in question. The reality they reflect must refer to the sublime experience of the very few.[46]

In 1 Kings 19 the sacred journey is connected to the motif of the evil enemies (vv. 1-3, 10, 14). Here, the enemy motifs are not directly

---

44. According to Eichhorn, *Gott als Fels*, p. 86 this reflects Zion traditions of the holy rock 'unter dem Debir des Tempels', standing upon which cultic servants could see the divine face, while Jeremias, *Theophanie*, pp. 107, 112 stresses the literary dependence on Exod. 33.18ff.

45. M.R. Hauge, 'On the Sacred Spot. The Concept of the Proper Localization before God', *SJOT* 1 (1990), pp. 30ff.

46. Cf. Eichhorn, *Gott als Fels*, pp. 85ff., where the understanding of the exceptional character of these phenomena is connected to categories of profession. The theophanic experience is limited to cultic servants (p. 85), 'vermutlich wohl levititische Tempelsänger und Kultpropheten' 'die ihr Amt als Mittleramt in der Tradition des Mose verstehen' (p. 87). This curtailment to a certain profession is rather uncertain with regard to the poetic material, and also ignores the special character of Exod. 33.18ff. (cf. the transition from vv. 17 to 18 as a classical *crux*, B.S. Childs, *Exodus. A Critical, Theological Commentary* [OTL; Philadelphia: Westminster Press, 1974], pp. 595ff.). But on the other hand, it is a concrete illustration of the extraordinary character of the experiences in question.

connected with the way and temple motifs, but form the background for the prophet's flight into the desert. Within the frame of the biographical introduction in vv. 1-3 and the application of the traditions in vv. 19ff., the events in the desert are of special character.[47] Separate from the events of everyday life, the journey from a place of despair and death to the mountain of God takes place in some special landscape of miraculous manifestations.

Within the present composition of Exodus 33–34, the separation from normal reality is connected with motifs of ascent and descent related to the mountain. With relationship to God meticulously connected to categories of locality relative to the mountain,[48] the description of the descent of Moses and the reaction of the people in Exod. 34.29ff. reflects the experience as something outside normal reality. But on the other hand, the enemy motifs of 1 Kings 19 lay particular stress on the material connection between normal biographical reality and the events on the mountain of God (vv. 10b, 14b and especially vv. 15-18).

This can be related to our discussion on the character of the language of the I-Psalms. The texts express a special religious meta-language of ideological character, with reality defined by man located to a mythical landscape. On the other hand, the religious description seems to reflect personal experience. Especially for the latter aspect, the Moses and Elijah stories are important. As applied to these figures of attainment, the language describes events of 'real' character, not only referring to an ideological level of religious interpretation, but to a level of personal experience.

The literal aspects of the motif structure as the vehicle of some personal experience of extraordinary character might even, tentatively, be related to ideas of different levels of religious reality. This could be reflected by the formal structure of vv. 4ff. Within the present composition, the prophet is related to the divine reality as a peculiar combination of angel (vv. 5, 7), word of Yahweh (v. 9) and the special

47. The special character of the motif development of the 'desert events' could also be related to traditio- or redactio-historical categories, for example, Jeremias, *Theophanie*, p. 65 on vv. 1-3a as 'überlieferungsgeschichtlich sekundären Verse'. To Fohrer, *Elia*, pp. 38ff., vv. 3b-18 reflect an originally independent story 'sehr geschickt' connected to other stories. The present combination with its peculiar change from triumph in ch. 18 to despondency in 19 is explained as due to a special Hebrew psychology of emotional versatility (p. 20).

48. Hauge, 'On the Sacred Spot', pp. 46ff.

manifestation as 'the fine-grained stillness'. The parallelism of vv. 9b-10 and 13b-14[49] suggests the 'word' to be seen as an independent manifestation, as recipient of the prophet's complaint and as preparing the prophet for the ultimate manifestation. The parallel relationship between three different types of divine manifestation is stressed by the composition.

In the three cases, preceded by narrative sentences on the prophet's acts, the manifestation is presented by an introductory *hinnê*, followed by a nominal sentence relating the manifestation to the prophet, followed by the narrative 'he said' introducing a message centred round imperative forms (vv. 5b, 9bff., 13bff., in the two last cases introduced by a question and the prophet's complaint). In addition, the last manifestation is introduced by a participle construction introduced by *hinnê* (v. 11), giving special emphasis to the concluding event.

This composition both stresses the parallel relationship of the three manifestations as representing the extraordinary, and at the same time suggests a hierarchical order of closeness relative to Yahweh. This order is also connected to local categories, with the prophet differently located under the broom, in the cave, and finally 'going out and standing' 'on the mountain'/'at the opening of the cave'.

The hierarchical order of divine manifestation—with a corresponding hierarchy of localities—could be related to the fundamental separation in the I-psalms, the religious reality connected with a being 'outside' and 'inside' the temple. Especially as presented in Psalms 42–43, the temple motifs are used for a special relationship to God. But the I as located in Sheol and described by motifs of way is also related to God. At the same time, the three 'stations of reality' are differently qualified.

In this way, the basic motifs of the story of 1 Kings 19 correspond to the motif structure of the I-psalms, with a specially close relationship to the motif elaboration of Psalms 42–43 centred round the contrast localities and the concept of a sacred journey. This composition, together with that of Exodus 33, is characterized by its combination of typicality and singularity; on the one hand a compilation of stereotyped motifs in a given structure, on the other hand demonstrating a vividly individual motif elaboration. And also in this case, the execution of the motif structure is characterized by a certain point of interest which is seen in the

49. According to Fohrer, *Elia*, p. 21, vv. 9b-11aα is added as an dogmatic effort to reduce the effect of the theophany description (cf. also pp. 38-39 on the tendency to elaborate the miraculous motifs by repetition).

emphasis on a certain motif set. Above all, however, the applications illustrate the significance of the motif structure as contained in the I-psalms. For our understanding of the psalms, it must be important that the two texts apply the motif structure as a structure of events connected to biographical experience, and that the central event of this biographical experience is concentrated on the ecstatic experience on the 'mountain'. The two stories of Exodus 33 and 1 Kings 19 demonstrate that the motif structure reflects a history of transmission and interpretation, also including critical examination of its material significance. Whatever the age of the psalms in question, it is reasonable to suppose that these psalms represent the traditional application of the motif structure. This not only adds to the venerability of the motif structure of the psalms in question as 'old', but also to its material significance as the suitable literary vehicle to express the sublime experiences of such singular figures as Moses and Elijah.

Such figures as the embodiments of the I-role of the motif structure also add to our understanding of the relevant psalms. Obviously, these texts must reflect personal experiences of heights and depths comparable to those of 1 Kings 19 and Exodus 33. Moreover, if this is relevant for the texts in question, it must also be relevant for a milieu of literary creativity and transmission and application, connected with some type of religious practice centred round the ecstatic experience of sensory character related to the divine presence.

Also, these texts considerably widen the scope of literary application of the motif structure. The mountain of God traditions, relating to Moses, reflect an immense body of material. And further, this relationship opens up the possibility of relating the grand story of Egypt, wilderness and land traditions to the basic motif sets of the I-psalms.

The dramatic changes in Pentateuchal criticism which have taken place during the last decades invite new questions on the coherency of the composition of the complex traditions. More or less disassociated from the traditional categories of historicity,[50] the understanding of this composition is linked to literary categories. In recent studies, the rather loose and anecdotal character of the final composition has been stressed.[51] Thus, to Van Seters and Whybray, the composition reflects a

---

50. E.g. T.L. Thompson, *The Historicity of the Patriarchal Narratives: The Quest for the Historical Abraham* (BZAW 133; Berlin: de Gruyter, 1974), pp. 11-40, 194ff.; Lemche, *The Canaanites*, pp. 151-52.

51. Aside from the significance of R. Alter, *The Art of Biblical Narrative* (New

compilation of traditions by an author employing literary techniques comparable to those of Herodotus; to Whybray a considerable and unidentifiable part of the materials represent literary fiction.[52] In examining the given traditions, Thompson finds 'blocks of narrative', described as five or six 'traditional complex chain narratives' compiled into 'a unifying historiography' resulting from 'a very late editorial work whose ideological centre is probably to be found in the prophetic reforms some time close to the reign of Josiah'.[53]

The emphasis on the editorial looseness of the composition is understandable as a reaction to traditional Pentateuchal criticism, especially as the observation of these phenomena forms the basis for the gradual dissolution of the documentary hypotheses.[54] On the other hand, the compilation of diverse materials, within one literary frame and with obvious ideological significance, invites investigation into questions of coherency for literary materials which to modern readers' notions of thematic logicality seem rather haphazardly put together. In this respect, the present uncertainty with regard to materials of such theological significance represents an exciting challenge for new models of understanding.[55]

Against this background, the motif structure of the I-psalms might represent an interesting possibility as a formative structure in the present composition of the Pentateuch traditions. The ideological significance of the basic motifs, together with the combination of basic stereotypes and freedom of individual expression which characterizes their literary application, would make them suitable also as focal points for a vast agglomeration of diverse traditions. The significance of biography as the

York: Basic Books, 1981), cf. concretely J. Van Seters, *In Search of History. Historiography in the Ancient World and the Origins of Biblical History* (New Haven: Yale University Press, 1983) and especially Whybray, *The Making of the Pentateuch*, pp. 232ff.

52. Whybray, *The Making of the Pentateuch*, pp. 238ff., with the book of Job for a parallel to the compositional frame of the Patriarchal narratives.

53. T.L. Thompson, *The Origin Tradition of Ancient Israel. I. The Literary Formation of Genesis and Exodus 1–23* (JSOTSup 55; Sheffield: JSOT Press, 1987), p. 156.

54. R. Rendtorff, *Das überlieferungsgeschichtliche Problem des Pentateuch* (BZAW 147; Berlin: de Gruyter, 1977).

55. E.g. the different types of approach by Clines, *The Theme of the Pentateuch*; G.W. Coats, 'A Structural Transition in Exodus', *VT* 22 (1972), pp. 129-42, M.R. Hauge 'The Struggles of the Blessed in Estrangement', *ST* 29 (1975), pp. 1-30, 113-46.

compositional frame for the compilation and formal coherence of the Pentateuch materials would correspond to the biographical interest of the I-psalms.

ii. *Exodus 15.* A possible connection between the motif structure of the I-psalms and the Pentateuch traditions can be illustrated by Exod. 15.1-21. Verses 1b-18 consist of a pattern of more general hymnic elements: 1bα; 2 (in the first person); 3; 6-7; 11; and 18. These are immediately connected with narrative elements: 1bß; 4-5; 8-10; 12-17. While vv. 6-17 are addressed to Yahweh, the introductory and concluding third-person forms on Yahweh (vv. 1-5, 18) frame the poem.

A satisfactory label for the genre is hard to come by. The first-person forms in vv. 1b-2 reflect elements of thanksgiving in the I-form. The narrative forms, especially as related to the situation described vv. 19ff., could suggest that the poem is influenced by the genre of thanksgiving.[56]

Within the narrative forms, the divine acts are related to the enemies (vv. 1bß; 4-5; 8-10; 12, cf. also in the hymnic elements vv. 3; 6-7) and to the people (vv. 12-17, with the reaction of the peoples 14-16a subordinate to the events of vv. 13 and 16b).[57] The two groups of human actors are related to Yahweh by contrast qualifications. The relative clauses in vv. 13a and in 16bß qualify the positive group as the people 'redeemed' and 'acquired' by Yahweh, in addition to the element 'your people' in v. 16bα. And due to the pattern of hymnic and narrative elements, the negative group is qualified as representative of 'the enemy' and 'your adversaries' of vv. 6-7.

Given this background, the motif sets which describe the divine intervention are interesting. Related to the people, the divine act of grace is seen as guidance into the temple, qualified as 'your holy abode' (v. 13) and as 'the mountain of your inheritance', 'the site you made for your dwelling', 'the sanctuary your hands established' (v. 17).

This corresponds to the divine intervention of, for example, Ps. 43.3-4.

56.　Cf. especially the discussion of Crüsemann, *Hymnus und Danklied*, pp. 191ff. Disregarding the third-person narrative elements of vv. 4-5, he finds the second person elements in the 'Hauptteil' (vv. 6-17) as 'Jahwe-anredende Bericht-stil' to qualify the poem as a hymn. Both the genres of collective Thanksgiving and also Victory song (pp. 206ff.) are refused as expressions for 'einer festen Gattung'.

57.　On the suggestions of parallelism between the two descriptions of the enemies and the peoples cf. Childs, *Exodus*, p. 252.

The sentence construction of v. 17 with an introductory *bô* hiph followed by three parallel qualifications of the place of destination as 'mountain', 'site' and 'sanctuary' can be compared to Ps. 43.3b, 4. Whatever the literary relationship between the two texts, the parallel conclusion with its suggestions of heightened intensity and climax[58] adds to the significance of dwelling in the temple. The sacred journey has the temple for goal, with relationship to the locality qualified as relationship to the divine presence. In Exod. 15.17 this aspect is added to by the motif of planting parallel to the motif of guidance. Corresponding to the application of tree motifs in Pss. 52.10-11 and 92.13ff., dwelling in the temple is qualified as lasting 'for ever'.

Corresponding to aspects of the contrast locality in Psalm 42, the divine intervention in its negative mode consists in the enemies as lastingly related to the deep. The different motifs of Yahweh's negative acts in the hymnic vv. 6-7 and especially the narrative v. 12[59] suggests that the sea/deep here primarily functions with the connotations of Sheol/death.[60]

In this way, the basic motifs of Exod. 15.1ff. correspond to the sacred world of Psalms 42–43, with a negative fate/place of death contrasted to dwelling in the temple with a relationship to the divine presence. The deep is the place of retribution, while dwelling in the temple is attained through divine guidance. The motifs define the plus group as passive, helpless with regard to the enemies, dependent on divine grace.

The main differences can be related to the two texts as reflections of different events of the motif structure, the I of 42–43 praying for the divine intervention which in Exodus 15 has taken place. Another difference is connected with the relationship of the positive group to the negative locality. In Psalm 42 the I in the act of praying is located in the

58. Such suggestions of climax can also be illustrated by Mowinckel's assertion that v. 17 together with v. 18 reflect the culmination of the enthronement festival myth with the foundation of the temple and the Enthronement of Yahweh, *Psalms I*, p. 126.

59. According to Crüsemann, *Hymnus und Danklied*, p. 193, v. 12 cannot refer to the destruction of the Egyptians as a 'völlig singuläres Verständnis dieses Geschehens', but must as a part of the assumed subunit vv. 11-17 refer to later events as e.g. Num. 16.

60. The amazing freedom of application of the motifs of the 'sea tradition', with the corresponding difficulty of fixing any original or historically more reasonable version (e.g. the examples by G.W. Coats, 'History and Theology in the Sea Tradition', *ST* 29 [1975], pp. 53ff. and also B.S. Childs, 'A Traditio-historical Study of the Reed Sea Tradition', *VT* 20 [1970], pp. 406-407) could be explained as due to a special connotative background, the richness of which amply demonstrated by Ps. 42.

deep, while only the enemies in Exodus 15 are directly related to the negative place. While v. 8 is usually understood to allude to Israel in the midst of the sea, it is primarily the literary frame of v. 1a connecting to 14.30-31 and vv. 19-21, which directly locate Israel in crisis and the divine intervention to the deep, with way and guidance motifs immediately connected to the negative place. Through this redactional 'adding' to the situation of crisis described in the poem, the application of the basic motifs corresponds closely to Psalms 42–43; by a miraculous intervention Israel is led on the way from the deep to the temple.

The relationship of Exod. 15.1b-18 to the frame of vv. 1a and especially 19-21, and thus to ch. 14, makes an interesting and much-discussed traditio-historical and redactio-historical problem. The present redactional frame connects the Song of the Sea and ch. 14 as literary expressions for the one event. At the same time, the two texts are markedly different and the differences not immediately reducible to the stylistic characteristics inherent to narrative and poetry.[61] If the differences should be related to traditio-historical categories, the Song of the Sea must be seen as the expression of a special development of tradition.[62]

Conversely, the character of the discussion could demonstrate that traditio-historical considerations are used too sweepingly to give answers to complex problems which should involve other types of methodological approach. Thus, important aspects of the problems of the connection between chs. 14 and 15 could be related to the two versions as

61. To Thompson, *The Origin Tradition*, pp. 146ff. the song is a poetic version of the narrative, reflecting both the 'base narrative' and the redactional expansion of ch. 14, the song relatively late in the development of the Exodus tradition. The special character of vv. 12-18 is due to the events interpreted 'in the theological terms of salvation history' within the historiographical framework of the Pentateuch. Also for the song of Miriam, often thought of as a surviving fragment of an earliest form of tradition, the narrative context of ch. 14 form 'the original Sitz im Leben' (pp. 147-48).

62. As, for example, a parallel development of a common tradition or originally an independent tradition secondarily related to dominant traditions, cf. on the one hand Childs, 'The Reed Sea Tradition', p. 412 on a 'common tradition being shared by the early prose account of J and the early poetic tradition of Ex.xv'; on the other hand Coats, *Moses*, pp. 114ff. who separates between Moses traditions and wilderness traditions with occasions of salvation without reference to any contribution from Moses, and finds nothing of the Moses tradition in the Song of Miriam or the Song of the Sea (cf. 'The Traditio-historical Character of the Reed Sea Motif', *VT* 17 (1967), pp. 253-65.

parallel applications of the given motif structure represented by, for example, Psalms 42–43.

Some of the difference could reflect the one application as narrative, the other as a psalm of praise and thanksgiving. In addition, the two versions are centred round different parts of the motif structure. The Song of the Sea is the more immediate application of the structure as a whole, with the literary present connected to the decisive divine intervention as it happened and as it is reflected in the human response of thanksgiving. The narrative is centred round the introductory events of the motif structure, with the divine intervention related to the enemy crisis. The motifs which describe the human actors are related to the enemy situation, given to reactions of fear and despondency connected with the salvation oracle[63] and contrasted with the figure of Moses as the paradigmatic confessor, and concluded with the experience of the crisis as overcome.

Given this background it is interesting that motifs of way and divine guidance link the two applications. In ch. 14 the way leads through, implicitly 'from', the deep; in ch. 15 to the temple. Usually related to traditio-historical categories for the exact fixation of the original setting of tradition,[64] the way motifs could link Exodus 14 and 15 as expressions of one motif structure, similarly to the motif exposition of Psalms 42–43 which implies a sacred journey taking the I from Sheol to temple.

In this respect, the two versions of chs. 14 and 15 are significant for the understanding of the motif expositions in the I-psalms. Especially in Psalms 36 and 140, the crisis of the I can be referred to two motif sets. The crisis is due to the threat of the enemies as the mortal foes, or can be related to gaining entrance into the temple inferred as the ultimate goal. The prayers relate the divine intervention to the enemy crisis. In Psalm 84, the motif execution stresses the importance of the temple motifs. This is also the case for Psalm 42 seen for itself, while 43 combines the two aspects as parallel manifestations of the divine intervention. And in 1 Kings 19 the motif structure is concentrated on the 'temple'

---

63. E.W. Conrad, *Fear Not Warrior: A Study of 'al tira' Pericopes in the Hebrew Scriptures* (Brown Judaic Studies 75; Chico, CA: Scholars Press, 1985); Coats, *Moses*, pp. 117ff. and also below to Ps. 27, in addition to the different aspects of the experience of the crisis in the other I-psalms.

64. While the Jordan crossing earlier was thought to reflect the sea crossing, the ranking of the traditions has been reversed, Coats, 'The Reed Sea Motif', pp. 259ff., Childs, 'The Reed Sea Tradition', pp. 414-15.

motifs, the enemy motifs kept apart as the biographical background to the exposition of the sacred story. The applications of Exodus 14 and 15 as two parallel versions of the same event—with motifs of the way as the common denominator—illustrate that the enemy crisis and the 'admittance to the temple'-crisis, while aspects of the same story, can be independently developed. Within the present literary frame they are presented as introductory and concluding events of the one story.[65] Also, the parallel versions demonstrate the literary and religious applicability of the motifs, the first version connecting the miracle to human reactions of despondency and faith corresponding to the dialogue of Psalms 42–43, the second to a situation of praise and confession.

Such a background could illustrate the redactional importance of chs. 14 and 15 for the literary development of the 'Egypt', 'wilderness' and 'conquest' traditions. While immediately connected to the context and usually understood to form some kind of climax with regard to the preceding chapters,[66] the sea traditions stand out with a character of their own, forming a traditio-historical puzzle.[67] Their special character combined with the contextual connection could reflect some special function with regard to the rest of the materials. Given the materials of the Pentateuch as originally disparate traditions, the redactional function of Exodus 14–15 could be important. In the present location, chs. 14–15 could provide a concrete linkage between two types of tradition connected with Egypt and wilderness.[68] Chapter 14 is an immediate continuation of the themes in the preceding chapters, centred on the enmity of the Egyptians and the divine retribution as the final plague destroying Pharaoh himself and setting Israel totally free. In this way, chs. 14–15 forms the climax of the literary development of chs. 1–13.

---

65. Cf. also the enemy motifs as 'split' between the mortal foes left in death in chs. 14, 15.1ff. and the terror-stricken witnesses to the triumphant passing of the people, 15.14ff. This can be compared to the motif execution of Ps. 23: while v. 4 alludes to the way leading through death, the enemy motif is reserved for the situation of dwelling in the temple, the enemies the witnesses to the triumph of the I.

66. E.g. O. Kaiser, *Die mythische Bedeutung des Meeres in Ägypten, Ugarit und Israel* (BZAW 78; Berlin: Topelmann, 1959), p. 156; G. Fohrer, *Überlieferung und Geschichte des Exodus* (BZAW 91; Berlin: Topelmann, 1964), pp. 97ff.

67. E.g. M. Noth, *Das zweite Buch Mose. Exodus* (ATD 5; Göttingen: Vandenhoeck & Ruprecht, 1959), p. 82 on 13.17–14.31 as both a 'Nachspiel' and as 'Höhepunkt' in the context.

68. Cf. Coats, 'The Reed Sea Motif', pp. 262ff. on the redactional significance of ch. 15, developed further by Childs, 'The Reed Sea Tradition', pp. 416ff.

Chapter 15 continues this interest with the Song as the human response to the miraculous events of Exodus, providing a pause in the narrative development of events. On the other hand, the divine intervention understood as guidance related to the ultimate goal of conquest, introduces the main themes of the following exposition as events within one story started in Egypt and ended with the conquest of the land.

A redactional function of this kind would also be linked with the character of the motif structure. Applied in the I-psalms, the motif structure seems to have an ideological, interpretative function, providing a pattern for the religious definition of humanity. In the exposition in Psalms 42–43, man related to God is a being related to the localities of Sheol and Temple linked by the concept of the way. The relationship to the enemies is the central motif connecting the I to Sheol, while the divine intervention represents the sole possibility of salvation from the enemies and dwelling in the temple.

The motif exposition of the Song of the Sea seems a striking parallel to this version of the motif structure. Here the wilderness- and conquest-traditions are interpreted as parts of a sacred journey under divine guidance from Egypt/sea/Sheol to Cana'an, with stay in the land of Cana'an interpreted in the categories of dwelling in the temple. But the application could also have a similar interpretative function with regard to the preceding events. With the connotations of the motifs, the events of the sea form a parallel to the events of ch. 12.[69] The first-born of Egypt killed by the terrible divine intervention in the Paschal night—especially as prepared by 1.15ff.—has the same connotations of meaning as the sea miracle, the latter however extending the scope to include Pharaoh and all the Egyptians contrasted with all of Israel confined to Sheol.

On the other hand, this interpretative frame provided by chs. 14–15 would also considerably broaden the significance of the Exodus-wilderness-conquest traditions. Interpreted as one story of divine guidance bringing Israel from Egypt/Sheol to the temple, the story would have the general connotations of the motif structure, as an application parallel to and with religious implications comparable to, for example, the story of the I in Psalms 42–43.

---

69. Cf. also D. McCarthy, 'Plagues and Sea of Reeds: Exodus 5–14', *JBL* 85 (1966), pp. 137-58; and especially J. Pedersen, *Israel, Its Life and Culture III–IV* (London: Oxford University Press, 1940), pp. 728-37 on the events of the Paschal night and of the sea as parallel expressions for Israel's victory over the enemies of the one cultic legend of Passover.

The Song of the Sea, in isolation, could rather directly reflect such an interpretation with its implications of a given religious pattern overlaying existing traditions. In its present form, isolated from the frame of vv. 1a and 19-21, it could be disassociated from the present historiographical context and regarded as a very general application of the pure motif structure, as a collective version closely parallel to the I-version of Psalms 42–43 and also 1 Kgs 19.4ff. With this character, the present composition set in the frame of vv. 1a and 19ff. can be compared to, for example, Psalm 114 with a setting given by the historiographical commentary vv. 1-2 and 77.14ff. by v. 21. Compared to, for example, Pss. 76.6ff.[70] and 66.10ff., and for that matter to Pss. 46 and 42.8, it is primarily the historiographical notes which define the one version of divine intervention as reflection of Exodus and the other as not. As to meaning, the connection with Exodus, Jordan, Zion or I motifs would ultimately refer to the same sets of connotations.

Such a connection could also be linked to the first-person forms 15.1b-2, which are formally peculiar within a composition where the objects of divine salvation are described in third-person forms.[71] According to the historiographical frame, the 'I' refers to ' Moses and the sons of Israel'. Related to the I-psalms, this compilation of I-forms and third-person descriptions can be compared to the pattern of I-forms and third-person statements in, for example, Psalms 36, 84 and 140. In the psalms, the statements express religious truths being professed by the I as applicable to his own fate. Such a connection could also be reflected by the present composition of Exodus 15. Either from an original text being cited or composed by 'Ex',[72] the I-forms suggest that the Exodus events also could be connected to a personal confession. And with the Exodus events representing one type of application of the motif structure, parallel to those of the I-psalms and closely related as to religious significance, such a connection would be rather natural. Especially with regard to function, connected to the intended use of the story, the I-forms would express an invitation to the listeners to identify

---

70. Cf. Jeremias, *Theophanie*, pp. 160-61, 139ff. on these texts as expressions for 'die Gattung der Theophanieschilderungen'.

71. Cf. Crüsemann, *Hymnus und Danklied*, p. 193, who ignores vv. 1b-5 as significant for the understanding of the formal character of the poem defined by its 'Hauptteil', vv. 6-17.

72. G.A.F. Knight, *Theology as Narration. A Commentary on the Book of Exodus* (Edinburgh: Handsel Press, 1976), p. XI.

with the sacred story as expression of the 'I-story'.[73]

Thus, the present composition of I-forms and third-person statements can be compared to the use of the Exodus motifs in Psalms 77 and 66. In 77.12ff. the Exodus events are confessed in a lament in I-form. And in 66.10-12, which are connected through the we-forms with v. 6, the Exodus events are transcribed into a more generalized version of God's typical dealings with 'us'. In vv. 13ff., this version of the Exodus/we-story is linked with forms of thanksgiving, thus suggesting an immediate connection between the narrative elements of I-story and the response of praise and the preceding collective story of divine intervention. In this way, the two psalms suggests that the I both in crisis and in triumph can identify his own fate with the collective story of Exodus. Usually, the connection has been thought to reflect late compositions mixing traditional genres,[74] or that the I in these psalms is a corporate personality, representing the collective.[75] But it could also—especially when related to the general problem of collective/individual categories in I-psalms[76]— be the result of the fundamental connotative connection between different versions of a common motif structure.

With Exodus 14–15 seen as an expression of a given motif structure, the scope of possible actualizations for the I-figure in the Psalms has been considerably widened. Moses and Elijah as representatives for the figure demonstrate its applicability as an expression for personal experience and exalted religious states. This can be related to special motif sets and also to the expressions of intense personal, emotional involvement of the I-psalms. The connection between 1 Kgs 19.3ff. with Exod. 32.18ff. and the I-psalms is the more significant as the narratives not only are orientated towards isolated biographical experiences of exalted figures, but relate the concrete biographical experience to a given tradition of ecstatic experience.

But Exodus 14–15 demonstrates that mere ordinary mortals can also represent the positive figure of the sacred story. In ch. 14, this role is split between Moses as the paradigmatic confessor and the very unheroic

73. Cf. also—from a different view-point—Brueggemann, 'A Response to "The Song of Miriam" by Bernhard Anderson', in E.R. Follis (ed.), *Directions in Biblical Hebrew Poetry* (JSOTSup 40; Sheffield: JSOT Press, 1987), pp. 298ff.

74. E.g. Kraus, *Psalmen*, p. 456 on Ps. 66, p. 530 on Ps. 77.

75. Esp. Mowinckel, *Salmeboken*, pp. 140-41, 164-65 and generally *Psalms I*, pp. 42ff.

76. E.g. Mowinckel, *Psalms I*, pp. 42-80.

'sons of Israel'. The constellation of the admonishing Moses and the murmuring people in 14.11ff. can even be compared to the actor of Psalms 42–43 split into an admonishing I and the downcast soul. In the psalm, this constellation could reflect ideas of religious development and inner change, connected with situations of crisis and suffering. This aspect could be relevant for the execution of the motif structure in ch. 14, as well as for the following exposition of the wilderness themes, with both Moses and the 'sons of Israel' as paradigmatic examples for later generations relating to the story of the Exodus.[77]

In this way, Exodus 14–15 together with 1 Kings 19 and Exod. 33.18ff. could illustrate important aspects of the motif usage. The interpretative function seems rather obvious, with the motif structure as an ideological frame of religious meaning. Exodus 14–15, in particular, could illustrate such a function, with a set of ideological motifs related to given traditions. But also the two stories of the 'beatific vision'—especially the story of 1 Kings 19 read in this context—reflect that the motif structure refers to a special level of reality,[78] not identical with the level of normal experiences in every-day life. Thus, these stories can immediately be added to the impression of the ideological function of the motif structure in Psalms 36, 84 , and 140.

But on the other hand, these stories also illustrate that the ideological level of reality refers to very concrete sensory experience. The events from Israel's past and the experiences of Moses and Elijah demonstrate that certain events with specific actors are presented as expositions of the sacred story. Moreover, the special interest of 1 Kings 19 and Exod. 33.18ff. demonstrates that Elijah and Moses embody the mythical role not as ideological entities, but as representatives of normal humanity. Also the number of singular I-psalms can be seen in this connection as expressions of the motif structure constantly related to new, concrete experience.

In addition, the examples above, referring to the use of the Exodus-events, illustrate a third type of application of the ideological pattern. In Psalms 66 and 77, an individual I is related to the collective story of the past with that past being relevant for his own fate. This relationship is especially close in Psalm 77, where the collective experience is confessed

---

77. Cf. Coats, *Moses*, pp. 109-24

78. Posing the same problems of interpretation as the motifs of the I-psalms, cf. Fohrer, *Elia*, pp. 67-68 with the story valued as 'bildhafte Ausdruck für theologische Aussagen' with the concrete materials as a 'Mose-parallelle'.

in the I-story. The very fact of the literary exposition of the Exodus traditions could also be connected to this type of application, with future generations related to the paradigmatic experiences of Moses and the children of Israel.

These seemingly very different types of application—further complicated if we pay attention to questions of cultic/personal application—make it difficult to find a single formula for the definition of the function of the motif structure. At least some aspects of the riddle might be connected to the stories of 1 Kings 19 and Exod. 33.18ff. related to their traditional background. These stories put a special emphasis on the ecstatic[79] or mystical experience as central for the motif structure and, moreover, connect this experience to a certain tradition. This suggests some milieu of religious practice centred round such experiences as a possible setting for the development of a religious language of this kind.

A *milieu* of such characteristics could even be connected to the prophetic tradition—especially when linked to ideas of institutions of cultic prophecy.[80] On the other hand, the I-psalms seem to represent the traditional expressions of the motif structure. So far, nothing in these psalms seems to refer to specific categories which would necessitate a label of 'prophetic experience'. The I is qualified as the confessor in crisis, the divine intervention as deliverance from the crisis. And the crisis is linked to a goal of special communion with God in the temple, connected with motifs of praise and of the relationship to God and temple. Such a situation could very well have been part of the normal prophetic experience (Isa. 6.1-4). But motifs of a connection with a professional crisis of failing revelation, the I beseeching Yahweh for a good message to communicate to a suffering people,[81] cannot be found. Labels such as ecstatic or mystical are relevant to emphasize the extraordinary character of the experience. But compared to a situation of prophetic reception of oracles and the literary forms where such a reception is described, the motifs of the I-psalms refer to a more general situation of intimate communion with Yahweh in the temple. Thus, while it would be rather high-handed to exclude prophets and for that matter

79. That is, categories especially relevant for Eichhorn, *Gott als Fels*, cf. the following notes.

80. Aside from Eichhorn, *Gott als Fels*, p. 87, cf. especially Mowinckel, *Psalms II*, pp. 55ff., 92ff. on the direct connection between the institutions of cult prophecy and temple singers.

81. Eichhorn, *Gott als Fels*, pp. 123ff.

other cultic servants[82] from the experience of such a sacred communion the I-story should not be confined to the traditional categories of ritual function.

Moreover, in Exodus 14–15 and 2 Kings 20/Isaiah 38, 'the sons of Israel' and a very human king are presented as actualizations of the I-figure. This suggests that the motif structure as a vehicle of religious interpretation is applicable to a wide range of human experience. While the usual applications of the motif structure primarily would reflect the experiences of some religious élite, the character of these experiences and the aspirations of the élite must have been common also to more humble people.

The rich possibilities of application must be connected to the type of religious practice which is involved. Even as connected to a religious interest of ecstatic experience, the motif structure of the language describing this experience demonstrates that the extraordinary happenings of dwelling in the temple—as well as the preparatory events—have been connected to some events, of a nature to be expressed in a series of literary stereotypes as the dogmatically given paradigm; to be repeated as confessed and reactualized or as re-applied for theological description and equally relevant for the élite few as the many. Some relationship to normal ritual language and practice could, at least partly, explain the traditional character of this language.

Seen together, the types of application illustrated by the texts of this chapter have important implications for our understanding of the language of the I-psalms. Dependent on the type of application, the textual 'I' can as well be related to an interpretative frame of ideological, of biographical and of paradigmatic categories.

---

82. Cf. von Rad, '"Gerechtigkeit" und "Leben"', pp. 239-40 suggesting an 'inneren Kreis von Riten, Weihen und Erlebnissen' reserved for special cult servants.

Chapter 4

PSALMS 27 AND 26: THE I AS ACTUALIZATION OF THE PARADIGM

1. *Psalm 27*

a. *The Psalm as a Whole*
In the analysis of Psalm 27, the traditional models of understanding have
been related to the impression of the text as consisting of different
genres.[1] When some kind of original connection for vv. 1-6 and 7-14 has
been found, the unity is usually[2] sought from the supposition of the text
as reflecting a given cultic situation.

Thus, dominated by expressions of confidence and by prayers connected with enemy motifs, the psalm could reflect the king under threat
of war, seeking protection through rites connected with the genre of
psalms of protection.[3] With a royal I, the psalm could also be related to a
series of succeeding events within a ritual of enthronement or renewal of
kingship.[4]

---

1. Cf. Taylor, *Psalms*, p. 144 and Delekat, *Asylie*, pp. 103, 197 on 1-6 and 7-14
as originally independent units.
2. On the other hand, Dahood, *Psalms I*, pp. 166-67 stresses the literary integrity
of the composition as a 'psalm of confidence' related to this life and the next, while
Rogerson and McKay, *Psalms 1–50*, p. 122 find the formal structure to correspond to
Ps. 22, but with reversed order of supplication and confidence. Verse 14 represents a
priestly word of encouragement or the psalmist exhorting himself (p. 125).
3. Birkeland, *Die Feinde*, p. 186; Mowinckel, *The Psalms I*, pp. 219-20;
J.H. Eaton, *Kingship and the Psalms* (Sheffield: JSOT Press, 1986), p. 39. Here,
v. 14 naturally represents the responding oracle or cultic encouragement (or also the
king's encouragement to Israel, Eaton, *Kingship*, p. 39).
4. To Ridderbos, *Psalmen*, pp. 211-12, vv. 1-6 reflect the ascension which ended
with sacrifices of thanksgiving, followed by rites of prayer, vv. 7-13, which were
answered by the admonishment, v. 14. Similarly Craigie, *Psalms 1–50*, pp. 230-31,
with the anniversary of coronation for setting (with the king's departure for battle as a
less probable possibility): the psalm represents a liturgy of three relatively independent
parts. Verses 1-6 are a public declaration of faith addressed to the congregation and

When judicial motifs are found to be central,[5] some kind of event connected with a situation of ordeal[6] or asylum-seeking[7] is sought. The latter understanding would reflect the significance of the temple motifs in this psalm.

But the motifs could also form the basis for other models of understanding. Thus, the temple motifs of vv. 4ff. should not too easily be subordinated to other motif groups. The acts of entering and continued stay in the temple must somehow be important in their own right[8] and

---

followed by sacrifices, vv. 7-13 a prayer addressed to God and followed by rites to determine or receive the oracle, v. 14 the oracle. Paying more attention to the enemy motifs, Croft, *The Identity of the Individual*, pp. 101-102, sees vv. 1ff. as the king's response to divine promises, while vv. 7ff. serve as a final prayer before the ritual battle.

5.   Cf. especially the 'false witnesses' of v. 12b, although this motif is ambiguous in this respect, e.g. Birkeland, *Die Feinde*, pp. 312ff., on the vassal king accused at the court of the great king. On the other hand, Beyerlin, *Die Rettung*, p. 124, claims that military motifs are more reasonably functioning as metaphors ('Bildern', 'bildhaft umgescrieben') for judicial matters than vice versa!

6.   To Schmidt, *Psalmen*, pp. 49ff., vv. 1ff. expresses the confidence of the falsely accused uttered before entering the sanctuary, while vv. 7ff. is orientated towards the immediately expected divine judgment. Similarly Kraus, *Psalmen*, pp. 222-23, with emphasis on distance in time and space: vv. 1ff. as psalm of confidence used 'fern von Jerusalem' (cf. also the sick person of Gunkel, *Psalmen*, p. 114, 'in der Diaspora'), the lament vv. 7-13 used on arrival in the temple, v. 14 representing the divine answer. To Beyerlin, *Die Rettung*, pp. 127ff., v. 14 cannot represent the decisive oracle. Verses 1ff. as '*tôdâ*-Teil' reflects the psalmist accepted into temple protection, dependent on v. 14 representing 'vorlaüfigen Orakelbescheiden', vv. 7ff. is 'Bittgebet' expecting the ordeal theophany.

7.   Aa. Bentzen, *Jahves Gæst. Studier i israelittisk salmedigtning* (København: P. Haase, 1926) and especially Delekat, *Asylie*, pp. 197ff. on Psalm v. 27 A as 'Erhörungsbekenntnis' reflecting the I as admitted into asylum, while B is a prayer for a divine oracle admitting the asylum-seeker (pp. 103ff.).

8.   Esp. E. Vogt, 'Psalm 26, ein Pilgergebet', *Bib* 43 (1962), p. 335, referring the temple motifs to a ritual setting of examination outside the temple; M.S. Smith, 'Setting and Rhetoric in Psalm 23', *JSOT* 41 (1988), pp. 61-66, to rites of pilgrimage in connection with Temple Festivals, and also Gerstenberger, *Der bittende Mensch*, p. 152, who relates the psalm to penitential rites connected with sickness and taking place outside the sanctuary. Dahood, *Psalms I*, pp. 166-67, finds vv. 4 and 13 to refer to eternal bliss with Yahweh in heaven. Referring to categories of 'spiritualization', von Rad, *Theologie I* (1961), p. 401, asserts the psalm to reflect a 'fast mystischen Spiritualismus', followed by Hermisson, *Sprache und Ritus*, pp. 114ff.

could be taken to suggest the I as, for example, a cultic servant.[9]

Seen together, these models illustrate the richness of the materials and demonstrate the necessity of a more comprehensive and less speculative approach. When the psalm is related to the texts analysed above, the motif connection is obvious: the I is in a situation of crisis, with enemy, temple and way motifs for basic components. Especially, the end of the psalm corresponds closely to Psalms 42–43. The combination of way and enemy motifs in the concluding prayers (vv. 11-12), followed by the exhortative form (v. 14), corresponds to 43.1-4 followed by vv. 5.

But for the understanding of the use of these motifs within the psalm, the relationship between vv. 1ff. and 7ff. is obviously crucial.

b. *Verses 1-6*

> Yahweh is my light and my salvation! Whom should I fear?
> Yahweh is the stronghold of my life! Of whom should I be afraid?
> When the evil approach against me to eat my flesh,
> those who are my adversaries and my enemies—they stumble and fall.
> If a host encamp against me, my heart is not afraid.
> If war arise against me, then I am confident.
> Only one thing do I ask from Yahweh, this do I seek:
> My stay in the house of Yahweh all the days of my life
> to behold the beauty of Yahweh, to contemplate[10] in his temple.

---

9. Eichhorn, *Gott als Fels*, pp. 116-17, on the I as cultic servant with 'Schaufunktion' (related to v. 4b cf. the following note). Also to Delekat, the admitted asylum-seeker becomes a cultic servant of lower order, *Asylie*, p. 198.

10. *biqqer* is often understood as a technical term for divination, referring to 'Opferschau', S. Mowinckel, *Psalmenstudien*. I. *Åwæn und die individuellen Klagesalmen* (Videnskapsselskapets skrifter. II, Hist.-filos. klasse; Kristiania: Jacob Dybwad, 1921), p. 146; Eichhorn, *Gott als Fels*, p. 117; cf. also the discussion in Delekat, *Asylie*, p. 198. With the verb parallel to *ḥāzâ*, Lev. 13.36 is of special importance for a parallel usage. Here *rā'â* is used for the immediate visual impression, *biqqer* for a continued visual examination. This corresponds to the usages in Lev. 27.33 and Ezek. 34.11-12, while Prov. 20.25 refers to mental examination. In addition, 2 Kgs 16.15 refers to the copper-altar reserved for the royal *biqqer*. While other royal rites take place at the other altar and with a priestly officiant (v. 15a), the language of 15b suggests that *biqqer* refers to the king's own activities. These activities must be related to the qualification of the copper-altar in v. 14 as located *lifnê* Yahweh. This qualification together with the use of *biqqer* could correspond to the language of Ps. 27.4 seen together with the special relationship to Yahweh and his face in these texts. Whatever the possible connotations of *biqqer* it must in this context be connected with the 'seeing' of the divine 'beauty' and thus also with the relationship to the divine face, vv. 8-9, and probably also the concluding 'seeing' of the

> For he will conceal me in the shelter on the evil day,
> he will hide me in the hiding-place of his tent,
> he will lift me upon the rock.
> And then my head is lifted up above my enemies around me.
> I shall offer in his tent sacrifices of joy.
> I shall sing and play for Yahweh.

The subunit poses problems of composition similar to those of the psalm as a whole. The relationship between vv. 1-3 and 4ff., and within the latter, between vv. 5 and 6, can be differently described. This ambiguity can be related to the verbal forms of the subunit, the translation of which is necessarily tentative.

But these verses could hardly reflect a structure of thanksgiving. Even with the introductory perfect form, v. 4, the imperfect forms of v. 5 are unsatisfactory expressions of the narrative when followed by v. 6 pointing to sacrifices of thanksgiving. For v. 2 seen in isolation, a narrative function could be possible.[11] But the conditional form of v. 3 must link to the rhetorical questions of v. 1. Thus, it is natural to follow the common understanding of vv. 1-3 as a whole, as a declaration of confidence.

For the understanding of v. 4ff., the basic observation must be that these verses immediately continue the preceding verses as a series of self-descriptive statements in the I-form, with Yahweh referred to in the third person.[12] This formal connection is added to by the motif usage. The application of the enemy motifs in vv. 5-6 links the two situations of the I as related to his enemies in vv. 1-3 and as related to the temple in vv. 4-6. With this linkage, vv. 4ff. continue the self-description of vv. 1ff.: in mortal crisis, the response of the I is to ask for temple admittance.

In this way, vv. 4-6 can be compared to the self-descriptive statements in 42.2-3 and 84.2-4. The introductory element 'Only one thing do I ask—do I seek' corresponds to the expressions of longing for the temple of the other texts. In all the three texts, the expressions of longing are

divine 'goodness', v. 13. The relationship between the parallel verbs of 'seeing' in 4b (cf. Lev. 13.36) can be compared to Ps. 17.15. Moreover, ended by the motifs of v. 6, the contents of v. 4b should be related to 43.4 and thus to the other expressions for the intimate relationship to Yahweh in the temple in Ps. 42 and the other texts. Motifs connected with visual impressions of the divine presence seem to be central for this relationship.

11. Craigie, *Psalms 1-50*, p. 232.

12. According to Kraus, *Psalmen*, p. 223, v. 4 cites a concrete prayer uttered in the past.

connected with motifs of entrance (27.4-6 and 42.3 in I-form, 84.5ff. by third-person forms.). And with these texts, the third-person forms of 36.6-10 and 140.14 are also relevant as parallel expressions. In these cases, the I is qualified as confessor, with temple motifs as the expression of the confession.

Aside from the basic temple motifs, the confessions are individually expressed. Characteristic of Psalm 27 are the introductory vv. 1-3 which link to enemy motifs, in this way stressing the I as wholeheartedly turned towards communion with God whatever the crisis. To a certain degree, this linkage can be compared to the formal structure of 36.2-5 on the evil and 6-10 on temple relationship. Correspondingly, 36.8 qualifies the temple as a place of refuge.

These texts represent parallel examples of the connection of confession and crisis, with prayer for expression, and thus underline the connection between vv. 1-6 and 7ff. Formally, the relationship between Psalms 27, 36 and 84 is especially close through a parallel structure of a subunit of prayers following statements on the temple relationship. And in all the texts, aside from Psalm 84, enemy motifs are used to describe the crisis.

In addition to these parallels, the relationship of 27.1-6 to Psalm 118 can demonstrate that these texts represent individual literary applications of a given motif structure. On the one hand, 27.1-3 corresponds to 118.6-9 and probably also 10-12[13] as an expression of the sublime confession of confidence. And the relationship between 27.1-3 and the *šā'al* for temple admittance corresponds to that of 118.6ff. and the plea for admittance in vv. 19-20. On the other hand, Psalm 27 presents these forms and motifs with a preparatory function related to a situation of crisis (vv. 7ff.), while in Psalm 118 these motifs are connected to a crisis of the past narrated in vv. 5, 13 and 18 (cf. vv. 14b and in 21) and given function within a literary frame of collective praise (vv. 1-4, 29). Both texts have a parallel relationship between the motifs of the confession and of the crisis. The hypothetical enemies of the confessions have representatives in the crises of the present (27.11-12) and the past (118.13). In these texts, the basic motifs seem to function as some material nucleus, alluding to given situations which are connected as a series of events,

---

13. Usually seen as a problematic reference to the past (e.g. Crüsemann, *Hymnus und Danklied*, pp. 217-18), vv. 10-12 could in the same way as 27.1-3 (cf. the perfect-forms of 27.2b corresponding to 118.10a, 11a, 12a) be understood as expression for the somewhat pleonastic style of confession. With such a function for vv. 10-12, the character of v. 13 as narration addressed to the hostile You would not be disturbed.

and which can be given individual literary expressions and applied in different types of genre.

This can be illustrated also by Psalm 23. As series of stating sentences in I-form, concluded by temple motifs, the two texts are closely related. And comparably to the transition from 27.1-3 to 4-6, also in Psalm 23 the compositional development is formally broken by the transition vv. 4-5 into Yahweh's being addressed and by the change from shepherd to host motifs. In addition, v. 4 repeats the sentence types of v. 1 (cf. below). This could suggest some type of parallel relationship between two parts, with Yahweh related to the I as food-giver forming some abstract thematic link between the motifs of the first and the second part.

At the same time there is an obvious connection between the two parts, illustrated by the shepherd motif retained in v. 4 which, formally considered, introduces the second part addressed to Yahweh. The motif structure of the psalm as a whole demonstrates a compositional development of pilgrimage motifs, the I in movement under divine guidance (1-4) and ultimately in the temple (5-6).[14] This corresponds to the motif structure of the texts analysed above, with the allusion of v. 4 to the dangers on the way especially close to the motif development of 84.5-8.

The close relationship between Pss. 23 and 27.1-6 is also demonstrated by the sentence types of 23.1, 4 and 27.1 together with 118.6-7. Introductory nominal statements on Yahweh related to the I are followed by stating sentences on the I related to some type of crisis. Of the motifs in the I-statements, the fear motif is of special significance.[15] Both in 27.1-3 and 118.6-7, this motif is connected with the enemy situation.[16] The significance of this situation is also underlined by Psalm 23. While the situation of crisis in v. 4 is expressed in topographical terms similarly to 84.7, the combination of temple and enemy motifs in 23.5, similarly to 27.5-6, stresses the enemy situation as the central expression for the

14. Smith, 'Psalm 23', pp. 61-66, with the psalm understood on a background of rites of pilgrimage. Verses 1-4, parallel to Pss. 42–43 and 84, draws on the language of the journey to Jerusalem, while vv. 5-6, parallel to Pss. 27 and 63, echoes the celebration in the temple precincts.

15. With an obvious connection between these forms and 'the priestly oracle of salvation', J. Begrich, 'Das priesterliche Heilsorakel', *ZAW* 52 (1934), pp. 81-92, reprinted in *Gesammelte Studien zum Alten Testament* (TB 21; Munich: C. Kaiser, 1964), pp. 226ff.; and *Studien zu Deuterojesaja* (TB 20; Munich: C. Kaiser, repr. 1963 [1938]), pp. 20-21.

16. On the connection of the '*al tirâ*-saying and holy war-traditions with special emphasis on the king as the recipient, see Conrad, *Fear Not Warrior*.

crisis prior to dwelling in the temple.

Given this background, the parallel formal rupture within 27.1-6 and Psalm 23 is worth noting, especially as it is of different character. Clearly the two texts reflect dependence on a connected series of motifs which ultimately could be expressed as a series of succeeding events. The execution of the motifs can have the same function as statements of confidence. On the other hand, the different exposition of way and enemy motifs compared to the temple motifs is suggestive. When we pay attention to 118.19ff. with a situation of entrance into the temple following a situation of crisis and connected to a situation of confession, the formal character of Psalms 23 and 27 in presenting the temple motif must be significant. The two motif groups refer to different types of situation, connected to the I as outside and inside the temple.

This is important with regard to the application of the enemy motifs in Psalms 23 and 27. In both texts, the enemy motifs are connected with the situation of the I in the temple. In 23.5 the enemies are witnessing the sacred meal. And in 27.1-6, the connection is made logical by the temple in vv. 5-6 being defined as the I's place of protection, with Yahweh 'hiding' him and 'making (him) high on the Rock' so the I's 'head is high' above the enemies surrounding him. This corresponds to Yahweh defined as 'my stronghold' (1b).

Here, the enemy and temple situations are closely linked. The temple is related to the enemy situation; the literary expositions of 23.5 and 27.6 even presenting the enemies as inside (cf. the traditional models of understanding of the temple as asylum/refuge or as the place of ordeal). On the other side, the other temple motifs should not be subordinated to the enemy motifs. Corresponding to the other texts, staying in the temple refers to a series of events of special character, with a special relationship to Yahweh as central (in 27.1-6 with the beatific vision qualifying dwelling in the temple in v. 4, in addition to motifs of praise and sacrifice, the importance of the latter stressed by the sacred meal motifs of Psalm 23). Here, as in the other texts, it is obvious that the temple motifs refer to experiences not sufficiently described as salvation from the enemy situation.[17] The singular motif applications of 23.5 and 27.6, with the presence of the enemies underlining the triumph of the I in the temple, could be related to the character of the two texts as confessions.

---

17. This is also illustrated by on the one hand Dahood referring to heavenly bliss, on the other hand von Rad and Hermisson to 'almost mystical' states.

In this way, Pss. 23 and 27.1-6, together with 118.6-12, can be understood as reflections of the motif structure as confessed in I-form. The close relationship of the texts makes the individual differences the more distinctive, demonstrating the literary freedom of application. While Psalm 23 is given to motifs of way and guidance, aside from the temple motifs, 27.1-6 (as also 118.6ff.) is dominated by enemy motifs. And while 23.5 alludes to the enemy situation, way and guidance motifs are found in the prayer part (v. 11) of Psalm 27. At the same time, the development towards dwelling in the temple as the concluding climax of the I-story and the other parallel phenomena stress the common dependency of some formative basis. Obviously, these types of usage must reflect the motif structure as traditional, both as given and as the object of literary applications.

At the same time, the three applications are characterized by a common function. The I-forms present the I as confessor, representing a model figure of *bāṭaḥ*. This aspect can also be illustrated by the third-person forms of Ps. 112.5ff. Here we find the basic motifs of these texts in the form of an extended beatitude extolling the virtues of the merciful money-lender. The repeated non-fear vv. 7 and 8 connected with *bāṭaḥ* corresponds to these texts. The fate of the model is linked to categories of judgment (v. 5) and framed by the relationship to the evil enemies (8b, 10). The stereotypical use of motifs of 'firmly standing' (6a, 7b, in 9a) and also of *rûm* (9b) in an expression similar to that of the first sentence in 27.6 demonstrates the traditional language of the beatitude. Whereas the connection with virtues of money-lending suggests a rather late application of the motifs compared with the other texts, this connection stresses the stereotypical character of the figure as the expression of a religious paradigm. Also the I-forms of Pss. 23, 27.1-6 and 118.6-12 must present the I as an actualization of the ideal figure.

c. *Verses 7-14*

> Listen Yahweh! I cry aloud. Be gracious to me and answer me!
> My heart speaks to you: Seek (?) my face!
> Your face, Yahweh, do I seek. Do not hide your face from me!
> Do not turn away in anger your servant—my help have you been.
> Abandon me not! Leave me not—God my salvation.
> For my father and my mother have left me—but Yahweh will gather me.
> Teach me, Yahweh your way!
> Lead me on the level path because of those who spy me out!
> Deliver me not to the will of my adversaries!

For false witnesses have risen against me, snorting (?) violence.
Oh—if I did not believe that I shall see the goodness of Yahweh
in the Land of the Living!
Wait for Yahweh! Be firm and your heart be strong! Wait for Yahweh!

Separated by v. 10, the prayers in vv. 7-12 fall into two parts. The pattern of two sets of prayer, separated by a *kî*-sentence, and the concluding exhortation of v. 14 corresponds to the formal structure of 43.1-5. The formal relationship between the two texts corresponds to the motif usage. This could suggest a common dependence on a rhetorical figure. But the formal structure of Psalm 27 is more complicated. The second prayer is ended by a *kî*-sentence v. 12b. The formal relationship could be expected to point to a common function for vv. 10 and 12b. But while 12b is given to enemy description and thus could be labelled a complaint, the parallel description v. 10a prepares negatively the confessionary 10b. In this way v. 10 should be related to the elements 'my help have you been' in 9a and 'God my salvation' in 9b as concluding the pattern of prayers and confessionary forms stressing the relationship to Yahweh.

On the other hand, the relationship between 12b and the exclamation v. 13 could correspond to the two sentences of v. 10. Formally, v. 13 represents an unfinished construction, but must have the function of confession.[18] Then v. 12b would correspond to 10a as negatively preparing the exclamation of ultimate trust during a terrible situation. In this way, both sets of prayer would be linked to the I as confident. This would connect the prayer part of the psalm to the dominating interest of the first part vv. 1-6. It is even possible that v. 14 asyndetically completes the unfinished construction of v. 13, with the imperatives repeating and underlining the exclamation.[19]

The open character of the exhortation in v. 14 makes the identity of the addressee uncertain. Traditionally, it has been seen as expression or reflection of the oracle given for the ritual setting of the text. On the other hand, the relationship to 43.1ff. would suggest v. 14 as self-exhortation similar to the refrain of 42-43. In any case, it is natural to see the addressee as identical with the I of the psalm. Formally, the pattern of elements in v. 14 can be connected to the structure of vv. 1-3. Verse

18. Usually emended, e.g., Craigie, *Psalms 1–50*, p. 230, while Kraus, *Psalmen*, p. 221, stresses the significance of the present form as 'Gewissheitsaussage'.

19. For a comparable relationship between exhortation and confessionary I-forms cf. Ps. 55.23-24 with the elements in reversed order.

14 has two imperatives and a special element with 'your heart' for subject before the last imperative. This corresponds to the I-forms of vv. 1-3, with three sentences in the first person, the second last with 'my heart' for subject. In v. 14, the subtle difference between imperatives addressed to 'you' and the jussive related to 'your heart'[20] can also be compared to the I of Psalms 42–43, split between the confessing I and the soul for the weaker part of his totality.

With the I for addressee, v. 14 can be seen as self-exhortation or as a literary device of encouragement, mitigating the subjective tension of the exclamation in v. 13 and concluding its confession. This can be compared to the exhortation of 55.23, following forms of confession in vv. 17ff. and connected with descriptions of the evil enemy (vv. 19b; 20 second line MT; 21-22). In the context, the concluding I-form addressed to Yahweh in v. 24 is naturally understood as the final confession of the I of the psalm.

On the other hand, the open character of the exhortation in 27.14 could make its function more open-ended. While the context of the psalm points to the I as the natural addressee, the exhortation could reflect the psalm as applied to a secondary situation of users in some way relating their fates to the fate of I of the psalm. Either as identifying themselves with the literary I or as otherwise partaking in the fate of the I-figure, the users, addressed as 'you', could be included in the exhortation. This possibility is supported by the formally close exhortation of Ps. 31.25. Part of the conclusion of vv. 24-25, the exhortation is related to I-forms of praise in vv. 22-23 connected to general third-person forms (vv. 20-21). Verses 22-23 allude to a situation of suffering (v. 23 first line MT) which contrasts with the present situation of relationship to Yahweh. Connected to a wider context of prayers and descriptions of the I as suffering, the function of 31.24-25 is comparable to that of 27.14. Against this background, it is interesting that the second-person plural forms of the concluding exhortation explicitly include a second layer of actors textually present. The abrupt introduction, concluding a context given to the story of the I, must reflect that the fate of the I, as expressed in the psalm, is relevant to the fate of the 'You'.

The composition of the prayers in vv. 7-12 stresses the function of the I as an actualization of the ideal figure. The prayers correspond to the confessions of vv. 1-6.

---

20. Cf. also Ps. 31.25 with a similar construction.

In the introductory prayer in vv. 7-10, the invocation of v. 7 is elaborated by motifs on the I's relationship to Yahweh. Of special importance are motifs connected with 'the divine face' (v. 8b and the first sentence 9a)—with a parallel relationship to 'my face' (8a) corresponding to the basic motifs of seeing/being seen. This corresponds to the qualification of dwelling in the temple (4b). The connection is the more evident as v. 4 describes the I related to the temple by the verbs of *šā'al* and *biqqeš*. The prayer for relationship to Yahweh (cf. also the use of *biqqeš* v. 8) makes the I of vv. 7-10 an expression of the professed attitude of v. 4. Surrounded by enemies (12b), the I seeks the 'one thing' from the Lord. The confessionary elements in vv. 9a, 9b and 10 stress this connection with vv. 1-6.

The prayer in vv. 11-12 consists of way and enemy motifs. But the enemy motifs are clearly dominating. Not only is the *kî*-sentence v. 12b, concluding vv. 11-12, given to these motifs, as is 12a, but also the way-motifs in 11a are connected to enemy motifs in 11b. This special combination corresponds to the confessions of 1-6. In vv. 1-3, the confession is related to the enemy situation. And in vv. 5 and 6, admittance and dwelling in the temple are connected with the I as confronted by enemies.

In this way, with prayer both for a special relationship to Yahweh and for salvation from the enemies, vv. 7-12 correspond closely to vv. 1-6. What is stated in the first part in self-descriptive sentences, is in the second part connected to forms of prayer. The I as supplicant is another expression of the I as confessor.

This relationship between the two parts can especially be demonstrated by the enemy situation as confessed and as object of prayer. As elaborations of the rhetorical 'whom should I fear?', the enemies of vv. 2-3 represent stereotypes of frightfulness (2a) and hyperbolical might (3a). Contrasting with the I as confident and praying for the 'one thing' of Yahweh-relationship, the enemies are hypothetical illustrations of 'come whatever may come'. But as 'false witnesses' in 12b, the enemies of the prayers are cut down to human size, aside from their basic character as 'evil'.[21] The I of v. 14 remains confessor in crisis. But the exclamation, presupposing a situation of utmost despair save for the basic hope, strikes a subjective posture far removed from the heroic stance of vv. 1-3.

---

21. Cf. especially the relationship between the enemies of the confession Ps. 118.6-12 and the more modestly 'pushing' You of the narrative v. 13.

In this way, the parallel relationship between the two parts must reflect vv. 7-12 as an actualization of the I as confessor, linked to a particular situation. Thus, the relationship between the two sets of I-forms can be compared to the relationship of the confessed third-person statements of religious truth and the I-forms of Psalms 36, 84 and 140. The I of vv. 1-6 represents the ideological pattern of religious behaviour, vv. 7-13 the pattern as actualized.

That vv. 7-13 with the concluding v. 14 basically represent the given pattern can be illustrated not only by the parallel relationship to the motifs of vv. 1-6, but also by their relationship to 43.1-5. Aside from the concluding exhortation 43.5, the prayers are of special significance. Separated by a *kî*-sentence, these prayers fall into two parts. As to contents, they more or less correspond to the relationship between 27.7-10 and 11-12, with 43.1-2 given to the enemy situation, vv. 3-4 to the relationship with God on the holy mountain.

However, the expressions for this basic correspondence differ. The closely related prayers for divine guidance in 27.11a and 43.3 are in 27 related to the enemy situation by the context and the loosely added 11b; in 43 to the special relationship to God. Also, in Ps. 43 the way and temple motifs are connected in a logical development: divine guidance brings the I to the dwelling-place of God. Moreover, with the I located in Sheol, the way motifs are implicitly connected also with movement from the negative locality. While the introductory enemy prayer is parallel and without any formal relationship to the prayer for guidance, the motifs of Psalm 42 suggest that the enemy situation is linked to stay in Sheol. Thus, the I in movement from Sheol to temple could also be linked to the enemy situation. Compared to this type of motif connection, the application of the way motif in 27.11 seems rather loose with a very uncertain relationship between 11a and 11b.

On the other hand, the differences of the two sets of prayers correspond to their contexts. The conclusion of 42–43, with the concentration on temple motifs, corresponds to the introductory vv. 1-3. Similarly the emphasis on the enemy situation of the concluding prayer in 27.11-12 corresponds to the introductory confession vv. 1-3; both connected with the threat from enemies.

In this way, the differences between the prayers characterize them as individual expressions of a common set of motifs linked to given concepts of enemy, way, and the divine presence in the temple—the latter in Psalm 27 also occurs as a separate motif group without reference to dwelling in the temple. The application and combination of the stereo-typical motifs is characterized by literary freedom for individual expression. The close relationship of 27.7-14 and 43.1-5 indicates that these prayers—and thus also the function of the motifs—must have a close relationship with regard to contents and function. They—and probably also the enemy prayers in 140.2, 5, 9ff. and 36.12, together with the pleas for a special divine attention in 140.7, 84.9, 36.11—could have a primary function as referential allusions to a given situation of the I in crisis.

d. *Conclusions*

i. *The I as confessor.* The basic elements of the given motif structure are represented in Psalm 27. 'Reality' is described by local categories, here by temple and way motifs. While Psalms 42–43 are important in linking the crisis to stay in a negative contrast locality in addition to the usual enemy motifs, Psalm 27 describes the crisis by reference to enemy motifs. But when the way of v. 11 is linked to enemy motifs, and the entrance into the temple in v. 5 described as 'hiding' and 'concealing', the crisis in this psalm is connected also to a situation outside—the negative character of the outside stressed by the fervour of the wish to be inside. In this way, Psalm 27, together with 42–43, is important for the under-standing of the other texts analysed above, with its clear connection between the enemy situation as *the* crisis and dwelling in the temple with relationship to God as *the summum bonum*.

What is special about the application of the motifs in Psalm 27 is the repetition of the basic pattern. The way in which this repetition is executed stresses the allusive and referential character of the central motifs. The communicative significance of the single motif is not limited to the particular application, but depends also on a *pars pro toto* function as a reference to a more comprehensive situation. In addition, the relation-ship between the two applications of the motif structure demonstrates the literary freedom of exposition in relation to the particular interest of the single composition.[22]

22. Cf. also above to the use of the enemy motifs in Ps. 23. Also the applications in Pss. 15, 24, and Isa. 33.14ff. are interesting in this respect. Orientated towards criteria of admittance, the basic enemy relationship can only be inferred from certain motifs which describe dwelling in the temple; cf. 15.5b and especially 33.16 with the temple indirectly qualified as a fortress.

The repetition of the motif structure is important in stressing the character of the I as confessor in these psalms. This is illustrated by the relationship of 27.1-6 to Psalms 23 and 118. In Psalm 23, a parallel confession forms an independent composition. In Psalm 118, similar forms are connected to a situation of enmity narrated as having taken place in the past. Correspondingly, in Psalm 27 the confession is linked to prayers for Yahweh's intervention in a situation of enmity. In Psalms 118 and 27 the enemy situation and what we might term an 'ideal' enemy situation, linked to the confession, are differently described.

The repetition of the basic pattern could be helpful with regard to the understanding of the other texts. As related to prayers, the confession in the I-form of Psalm 27 corresponds functionally to the third-person confessional statements of Psalms 140, 36 and 84. The relationship of the I of the confession and the I of the prayer corresponds to that of the I to the righteous or the blessed or of 'men' in the other texts. With regard to Psalms 140, 36 and 84, this correspondence stresses the connection between the dogmatic statements and the situation of the I as that of paradigm and actualization. With regard to Psalm 27, it would stress that the I of the confession represents a paradigmatic figure. In both cases, the third-person and first-person confessions stress the ideological ideal as relevant also to an actual situation of crisis.

This would have consequences for the understanding of the enemy motifs of these texts. The ideological situation clearly encompasses the model figure in mortal crisis due to enemies. So the application of the enemy motifs in these texts should not primarily be related to real life experiences or to contemporary social life in general, but to the requirements of the paradigm. The religious paradigm as expressed in the motif structure presupposes the model figure in mortal conflict, the enemies an integral part of the ideal story. The enemies' being basically mythical figures would explain the indifference of the texts towards consistency and biographical accuracy with regard to the nature of the crisis. Just as the male hero of the typical Norwegian folk-tale must confront the trolls or giants, the paradigmatic figure must face the evil enemies.

On the other hand, the parallel relationship of the enemy motifs in the two parts of confession and prayer in Psalm 27 suggests that the I of the psalm—and probably also the other texts—not only is described according to a given pattern of ideological nature, but that the description has a background in some actual crisis. The relationship of mythical and actual enemies could reflect a relationship of paradigm and actualization.[23] This would add to the significance of the I in a situation of prayer. The I of vv. 7ff. represents the actualization of the I in the self-description of vv. 1ff. In this way, the complaints and the prayer should not be understood as primarily emotional outpourings of distress intended to mollify the *deus ex machina* to produce a happy ending. To modern readers, the composition of laments, prayers and expressions of sublime confidence are bewildering because these elements seem to express psychical reactions/ritual situations of different nature. This modern attitude is well demonstrated by the difficulties of commentators with regard to the composition of Psalm 27. Prayers which express total helplessness and descriptions of the terrible situation of the I are naturally found to express a subjective situation greatly different from that of the fearless confessor of vv. 1-3. But as related to the given pattern, a situation of suffering with the I confronted by evil enemies would represent '*die positiven Merkmale des ṣaddîq*'.[24] And the act of prayer especially would characterize the I as conforming to the ideal of vv. 1ff., with *šā'al* (v. 4) as the expression of the I as *bôṭēaḥ*. In this way, the I as supplicant in a situation of suffering defines the I as the embodiment of the model figure. Verses 7ff. are thus of special importance in expressing the I as verily the confessor of vv. 1ff.

This could be related to the peculiar lack of a positive qualification of the I in these texts which could have the function of contrast relative to the negative qualifications of the enemies. The negative figures are consistently qualified as somehow 'evil', described in categories which have the qualifications of, for example, righteous and upright in the contrast statements of Ps. 140.12-14 for opposites. But the texts analysed so far (cf. below to Psalm 26) underline that such positive contrast descriptions are not necessary for the qualification of the I as embodiment of the positive ideal. The situation of attack by evil enemies and the I turning to God/relating himself to the temple is the necessary qualification.

Such a significance attached to the prayer as the sublime confession

23. A relationship of this kind would also be relevant for the understanding of the connection between these texts and other literary genres as parallel reflections of the motif structure, such as the prophet legend of Elijah and the collective story of the Exodus (cf. Chapter 3, above).

24. Von Rad, *Theologie I*, p. 379 on the righteous characterized by his relationship to the Torah.

could also be related to the utter passivity of the I in these texts. The enemies are the active attackers—the attacked obviously helpless. Given the Holy War associations of the *'al tîrâ*-oracle, we might expect references to some type of active participation in the confrontation. But the I is consistently passive, with the act of supplication as the one expression of the active mode.

This puts a corresponding emphasis on the significance of the miraculous category of the motif structure, the prayer calling forth the decisive action of the events. With regard to divine intervention, the I is utterly passive, with the force from the other level of reality breaking up the impasse, saving the I, revealing the way and bringing him to the temple. In this way, the I as paradigm could also have a theological function as a demonstration of the conditions in which the divine force manifests itself, the situation representing some sacred magic channelling the divine forces.[25]

And finally, the relationship of vv. 1ff. and 7ff. in Psalm 27 could have repercussions for our understanding of some apparent ambiguities of language. The analysis suggests that vv. 1ff. as confession express the religious paradigm in I-form, while vv. 7ff. reflect the I as embodiment of the paradigm in a concrete situation. As we have seen, the different types of enemy-description in, for example, vv. 2-3 and 12b could reflect such a difference between ideological and actual reality.

Such a difference could also be reflected in vv. 4 and 13. The construction in v. 13 'to see the goodness of Yahweh in the land of life/the living' corresponds, both in basic motifs and form, to that of 4b 'to behold the beauty of Yahweh, to contemplate in his temple'. 'The land of life/the living' as expression for the positive locality corresponds to Isa. 38.11 in the context and also to the motif 'firmly standing in the land' in 140.12, in both cases connected with motifs of death and dwelling in the temple.

Thus, the I is related to two types of positive locality within the one text, to the 'land of life' with Sheol for the obvious contrast, and to the temple. While the temple motif in these texts also has Sheol for the con-

---

25. This aspect could especially be demonstrated when actors such as Moses and Elijah are the heroes of the sacred story. Their function is clearly to bridge heaven and earth as channels for the divine forces. But the hero as a figure of 'magic' could also be related to the peculiar collective application of a number of I-psalms (e.g. Pss. 51.20-21, 69.36-37), as well as to the traditional models of understanding which interpret the individual as some kind of 'representative' figure.

trast locality (cf. above all Psalm 42), it must in addition have associations of ritual locality and practice. And for the I as 'seeing', v. 4b refers to states of mystical exaltation, while v. 13 presents the much humbler, however attractive, goal of experiencing the divine goodness as alive.

The two qualifications of the positive fate must be significantly related. Thus, in this psalm, the state of intimate relationship to the divine presence is related to the enemy situation, with the exaltation of the I (v. 5, cf. especially Ps. 63.3-4) as an exaltation of the head above the surrounding enemies (v. 6). But even with a function of saying the same thing, the two motif sets are basically different and must allude to different sets of connotations. This is demonstrated by the one motif set extended into descriptions of the exalted experiences of Moses and Elijah on the sacred mountain, as contrasted with the motifs used for the description of the healing of Hezekiah.

Given this background, the localization of the two types of motif in the two parts of Psalm 27 could hardly be coincidental. On the one hand, with regard to function, the qualifications of the good fate must be identical. On the other hand, it is natural to understand the two types of motifs to refer to the different levels of reality relevant for the language of these texts. In this case, v. 4 would reflect the language of the paradigm, immediately connected with ritual practice and ideology, while v. 13 more directly reflects the biographical reality of the I.

This certainly should not imply that the materials of any text of this type could easily be separated into parts giving ideological and biographical information, corresponding to the traditional exegetical operations. As to composition, Psalm 27 is rather special. Within the ideological vv. 1ff., the temple is not only the place of mystical contemplation, but also a place of protection; that is, it is given a function subordinate to the enemy motifs. In addition, the very interest of the composition would be centred round the ideological aspects. But at the same time, the special composition of Psalm 27 could be used to suggest the different levels of reality relevant for the language of these texts and thus of different possibilities of original application.

This could also be illustrated by the traditional qualification of Yahweh as the 'stronghold of my life' in the initial confession in v. 1, stressed by the rock motifs of vv. 5-6.[26] While the traditional application in vv. 4ff. expresses Yahweh as being *in* the temple as his place of dwelling, the I

---

26. Eichhorn, *Gott als Fels*, pp. 30-91.

brought into the temple to see the divine dweller, the qualification of vv. 1-2 implies Yahweh as the locality which contains the life of the I.[27] The two types of motif application could reflect an immediate and unproblematical mixing of two sets of language, one reflecting a background of ritual practice and experience, the other ancient divine epithets.[28] But even with some background of this type, the actual motif usage reflects that the ancient traditions not only are repeated as traditional sacred language, but also applied creatively in new types of usage. The compilation of the two types of motif in, for example, Pss. 27 and 61.3-5 must presuppose some connection as to meaning. The numerous elaborations on Yahweh as rock, fortress and so on could be qualified as similes or metaphors or simply as poetic elaborations of ancient terminology. Even so, they must reflect some type of ideological application of temple motifs, the language expressing some experience of relationship with Yahweh.[29] At the very least, the meaning of inside and outside the temple cannot be confined to physical categories of presence in the local sanctuary.

In this way, the composition of Psalm 27 suggests that the text from its very origin is open to more than one type of interpretation and application. In addition, the beatitude of Ps. 112.5-10 is an interesting illustration of the implications of 27.1 and v. 13. Here, the traditional language of enemy crisis and dwelling in the temple is connected to the fate of the money-lender, even internalized with 'his heart' and 'his righteousness' as 'firmly' or 'eternally' 'standing'. The no-fear and trust motifs are not connected to any terrors comparable to Ps. 27.3, but to bad tidings. Even in a rather young text, the application of the traditional language of Ps. 112.5ff. is comparable to that of 27.1 with Yahweh for temple and in v. 13 with the beatific vision connected to normal experiences of the I as alive.

---

27. These applications are immediately connected in Ps. 61.3-4, with Yahweh (v. 3b) guiding the I unto the rock, motivated (v. 4) by Yahweh as the refuge and tower of the I, and followed (v. 5) on the I as eternal guest in Yahweh's tent, seeking refuge under his wings.

28. Eichhorn, *Gott als Fels*, pp. 83-88, on 'Yahweh as rock' reflecting an old Jebusite sacral tradition on a Jerusalem divinity which reveals itself on a special holy rock. With such a background, one could expect motifs which both reflect the concrete cultic usage centred round the holy rock and the ancient epithets.

29. The special type of motif usage in vv. 1 and 13 could also be related to their location in the psalm as introducing and concluding the I-forms, in addition to their special formal character. In addition, the two verses are connected by the life motif.

Thus, many possible actors could have identified with the literary I of Psalm 27. The soldiers of Deuteronomy 20 and the bourgeois money-lender of Psalm 112 can be added to the Israel of the Exodus and the sick Hezekiah in addition to exalted figures on the levels of Moses and Elijah.

But whatever the application, the textual I is presented as an actualiza-tion of the ideal confessor. In the line of events connected with the basic motif structure, the textual situation is centred round the situation of crisis, dominated by prayer and thus orientated towards the divine mani-festation as the decisive event.

With this function, Psalm 27 is significant as an illustration of the con-nection between ideological language and some biographical reality. This is expressed by the separation of the text into two parts, the one given to an I representing the typical model figure, the other to an I in a situa-tion of conflict, interpreted as an actualization of the religious paradigm. This connection also points to the literal connection between ideology and biography. The I of this psalm represents an embodiment of the paradigm, the personal fate an expression of the paradigmatic fate. Connected to a frame of religious development, the I both of the first and second part of Psalm 27 represents a being of extraordinary attainment.

ii. *The Address to the 'You'*. This conclusion could be complicated by the possible intrusion of a secondary situation of application. The con-cluding exhortation of v. 14 could reflect an application with users relating/being related to the fate of the I. This understanding of v. 14 is not certain. But as we find other texts with a more determined transition to You-forms, Ps. 27.14 raises an important problem for the under-standing of the function of the I-psalms. This secondary situation of application might even represent the prime—perhaps even the sole!—interest of the composition.

An interest of admonishment would stress the superpersonal, ideolo-gical character of these texts. As for the relationship between the I and the users, the character of these texts implies a relationship of paradigm and imitation/identification. Especially in the case of the normal I-psalm without any explicit expression for any secondary situation of application, such a process of identification would be immediate, due to the use of first-person forms.

On the other hand, this raises the possibility that the use of first-person forms in these texts represents a literary device, the textual I made concrete by the single user identifying with the paradigmatic fate, or related to it in admonishment when addressed as 'You'.

138   *Between Sheol and Temple*

This would represent the simplest model of application for these psalms. The textual situation of an I turned to Yahweh in prayer would correspond to the situation of application, with living figures enacting the role of the I.

But as we have seen, Psalms 130 and 131[30] suggest a more complex relationship, with an I presented as an example figure to be imitated by a new set of 'waiters for Yahweh'. From texts like Psalms 31 and 130, 131 connected to Psalms 42–43, 27, and 55 in addition to 62 (cf. below), it is natural to surmise this second layer of actors to be relevant also for the other I-texts. In the case of Psalms 130, 131 and 62, the descriptions of the I-figure and the form of the address to the You make it difficult to understand the I as a literary projection materially identical with the addressed. The 'I' and 'You' of these texts must represent different actors.

In addition, the composition of the psalms analysed above stresses the importance of a given I-figure as actualization of the paradigm. This is expressed by the compilation of I-forms related to 'objective' forms which reflect the paradigm, usually in the form of third-person statements in addition to the I-forms of Psalm 27 and probably also 42. Thus, the late redactional superscriptions which connect a particular I-psalm to some biographical event in David's life could be regarded as a reflection of this original understanding of the textual I as giving expression to some lived experience.

In this way, Psalms 130 and 131 together with 31, 62, and possibly also 27 and 55, which show an explicit transition from I-forms to an addressed You, suggest a rather complicated connection between two situations related to two sets of actors. Each of the two situations is of a character to constitute the literary interest and given both it is difficult to decide what the psalm is all about. In the prayer psalms, the literary situation must be dominated by the address to Yahweh. But the You-forms stress the importance of a situation of exhortation, which could imply that the prayer situation has a subordinate function compared to the real interest.

This relationship is even further complicated when we take into account the application of the paradigm. In the composition of the psalms analysed

30. The I of these texts as a paradigmatic figure cf. especially Kraus, *Psalmen*, pp. 873, 875, on Ps. 130; Taylor, *Psalms*, p. 679; K. Seybold, *Das Gebet des Kranken im Alten Testament. Untersuchungen zur Bestimmung und Zuordnung der Krankheits- und Heiligungspsalmen* (BWANT 5.19; Stuttgart: Kohlhammer, 1973), p. 76.

earlier, we noted two main types of application, with the compilation of objective statements—usually in the third person—and I-forms, the latter describing the representation of the ideal. But in Psalm 27, we may have to separate between three types of application of the paradigm: the I directly reflecting the ideal figure in general confessions; secondly, representing the ideal in a particular crisis; and thirdly, his fate applied as paradigm for the addressed You.

However complicated, the idea of such a relationship is supported by the formal construction of Ps. 31.20ff. Here we find a composition of third-person statements, vv. 20-21, in hymnic form corresponding especially to 36.6-10. This is followed by first-person forms, which both formally and in motifs correspond to the third-person statements, the I as giving an example of the divine sheltering. Finally, this is followed by a concluding exhortation, vv. 24-25.[31]

Thus, it seems that we have to conclude that these texts could be centred round two interests. One is connected with the I as actualization of the religious paradigm, the other connected with the application of this I as paradigm for others. At the very least, these explicit references to a second layer of actors in some texts must suggest an old tradition of interpretation and application for the other I-texts.

The relationship of the addressed to the literary I must be that of imitation/identification. This is given by the composition of these texts, presenting the I as embodiment of the paradigm. The addressed are related to the religious ideal in the form of some actual figure.[32] Such a relationship is directly expressed by the You-forms in Psalms 130, 131, 31, 62, and possibly also 27 and 55. The addresses are centred round some central terms as *qiwwâ 'ēl*, *hôḥîl le* or *bāṭaḥ be* Yahweh in addition to forms of admonishment connected with the *'al tîrâ*-oracle. Related to the context, the exhortations express a strangely symmetrical relationship. The addressed You seem to face a situation having the same character as, or at least one parallel to, that of the I, and are admonished for a response identical with the paradigm. For the relevant texts without You-forms, this type of application would invite the user to identify with the textual hero, presented as I.

31. Cf. also a similar formal pattern Ps. 55.23-24, with exhortation motivated by a third-person statement followed by a confession in I-form.

32. For parallel expressions of a hierarchical relationship between different sets of actors, the divine 'message' mediated in a link of parallel relationships to the revelation, see Hauge, 'On the Sacred Spot', pp. 30-60.

Such applications must reflect some kind of religious practice, corresponding to the descriptions of the I-figure as expression of the relationship between religious paradigm and actual life experience. Presupposing an immediate connection between the paradigmatic fate, the fate of the I and even of those addressed, these applications also stress the objective character of the motif structure. Either as ideological pattern or biography, the story of the I represents the lawful fate of the human figure in relation to religious reality.

The background to such a combination of two sets of biography, with the experience of the I seen as relevant for others, could be sought in different models of understanding. Thus, the texts could be related to a situation of institutional character, where the I-figure was directly represented as a person among other persons. Such a situation could be presented by for example Psalm 118, as an expression of some kind of initiation. A parallel type of situation could be represented by that of the Wisdom teacher admonishing his 'sons' in I-form, the admonishment connected to biographical experience. The significant number of literary expressions of this situation in the Wisdom tradition attests to its importance. Especially, the traditionally accepted combination of the I of the Wisdom teacher and the I of thanksgiving in some psalms illustrates the relevance of this model.[33] While such a model is relevant only for a limited number of texts, labelled as Wisdom psalms, it can at least illustrate an important layer of interpretation and application of the older texts. Even if the Wisdom psalms should reflect a rather late literary development, the role of the Wisdom teacher—with its emphasis on personal experience coupled with admonishment—represents an influential literary and religious stereotype older then the textual expression in the Wisdom psalms.

For the normal I-psalms, another model could be sought in ideas of mediation and intercession connected with the prophetic function.[34] In

---

33. On the characteristics of the 'Wisdom Psalm', cf. generally R.E. Murphy, 'A Consideration of the Classification "Wisdom Psalms"', *VTS* 9 (1963), pp. 156-67; and especially Beyerlin, *Wider die Hybris*, pp. 81ff. on the author of Ps. 131 as a professional teacher of Wisdom at the temple school of Zion. Such a function would then explain the blending of personal spirituality, personal experience of suffering, the didactic interest, and the authority to address Israel in admonishment (p. 86).

34. E.g. H. Graf Reventlow, *Liturgie und prophetisches Ich bei Jeremia* (Gütersloh: Mohn, 1963) on the 'Jeremiah-confessions' as expressions for the cult prophetic function of intercession.

such a case, the I would have a representative function, his auto-biography relevant for the collective fate.

Because of the connection between different phenomena within disparate texts—some of them touched upon in this study—such a model would have to include a wider background of representative functions. Thus, to Eichhorn, a number of I-psalms which apply the concepts of Yahweh as 'Fels, Burg und Zuflucht', reflect the professional problems of an oracle receiver in connection with some national crisis. The I of the psalm represents a personal crisis immediately connected with the collective one. The personal confession of Yahweh as 'Fels, Burg und Zuflucht' or the prayer that Yahweh should manifest as such in the personal crisis, reflects the function of mediating the revelation of Yahweh as the 'Fels, Burg und Zuflucht' of the people. The close relationship between the fates of the mediator and the collective which this understanding entails is seen as dependent on the ancient Near Eastern concepts of sacral kingship. This entails the idea of democratization, with the individual psalms reflecting the roles of the king, the cultic prophet, the levitical temple-singer, the levitical *Prediger*, and the torah-observing teacher of Wisdom. Common to these roles is the function of mediating the revelation of Yahweh of Zion.[35] The common function can also be related to the Moses tradition, with the cult professionals defining themselves as holding a 'Mittleramt in der Tradition des Mose'.[36]

Against such a background, the highly individual autobiography—by necessity not confined to texts with the concepts of 'Fels, Burg und Zuflucht'—would be relevant for the collective fate, even if the collective is not textually present as, for example, an addressed 'You'.

Both Beyerlin's ideas on the 'wise Psalmist' and Eichhorn's on the 'cultic mediator' are significant in pointing to two socio-religious settings which could illustrate the possible implications of the I-texts as reflecting some type of religious practice. The composition of the I-psalms suggests that the I does not represent a literary device of identification, but reflects a biography presented in ideological terms as an expression of the paradigmatic fate. Thus, when applied to an explicit or implicit You in admonishment, the addressee is implicitly related to a biography for imitation and identification. This raises the question of some religious environment in which such emphasis on personal categories could be central.

Both in the case of the Hebrew Wisdom school and Prophetic

---

35. *Gott als Fels*, pp. 123ff.
36. *Gott als Fels*, p. 87.

institutions we are concerned with institutionalized milieus centred round
personal experience of religious phenomena. Also, for both types of
institution, the personal experience was connected to function and thus
relevant to the recipients of instruction or the divine word. While the I
could not be qualified as 'wise' nor as 'prophet', these two types of
institution demonstrate that phenomena comparable to the characteristics of the I-psalms were found important enough to be given institutionalized expressions in the contemporary environment.[37]

Moreover, the I-figure could have been relevant for both types of
religious practice. As expression of a general religious paradigm applicable
to any type of biographical background and function, the I is relevant to
descriptions of Moses and Elijah, the Old Testament version of the
Wisdom teacher, as well as to more modest fates.

The emphasis on the individual biography as actualization of the
paradigm could be connected with the genre of biography as a whole in
Old Testament literature. Obviously, the presentation of the individual
fate must have been of tremendous importance to generate such a vast
body of literature.

This interest is perhaps best illustrated by the final composition of the
Pentateuch. Whereas the redactional interest may remain rather elusive
for a precise description of some definite theology,[38] the extensive biographical content is plain to see. And while the biography of Moses,
aside from the introductory chapters, is given to ideological materials,
the very concrete and seemingly mundane character of the stories of
Genesis 12–50 is remarkable. For an earlier stage of Pentateuchal criticism, this character could automatically be related to the stories as
historical traditions, reflecting the ancient nomadic past. But when
understood as rather late hagiographical writings—possibly even with
fictitious heroes[39]—the emphasis on normal human events related to
expressions of divine activity is strange indeed. Whatever their meaning,[40]

---

37. Due to the spatial and temporal confinements it is even possible to suppose
that this environment was more uniform than usually thought. Thus the convergence
of traditions illustrated by Beyerlin's author of Ps. 131 as an amalgamation of
Wisdom teacher and Psalm specialist is parallel to the supposed connection of
prophetic associations and temple singers, usual since S. Mowinckel, *Psalmenstudien.
III. Kultprophetie und prophetische Psalmen* (Videnskapsselskapets skrifter. II,
Hist.-filos. klasse; Kristiania: Jacob Dybwad, 1923).

38. E.g. Whybray, *The Making of the Pentateuch*, pp. 221ff.

39. *The Making of the Pentateuch*, p. 240.

the application of the central biographical motifs of the stories must reflect a special theological understanding of the biography as a basic vehicle for religious communication. The biography is the literary mode for a general theological description of divine manifestations.

It is natural to relate this understanding to the parallel interest of the Wisdom tradition, especially as crowned by the books of Job and Qoheleth.[41] The Joseph stories give a sure illustration of the significance of Wisdom to the Genesis stories.[42] The applications of the motif structure of the I-psalms in Psalm 73 and Job both demonstrate the significance of the ideological language of the I-psalms and provide a background for the connection of this language with biographical experience. It is generally acknowledged that both texts express some kind of theological conflict between ideological language and life experience, the relationship of Psalm 73 to Job understood to indicate a gradual development of critical distance—with Qoheleth as the ultimate work.[43] Given the requirement to relate the personal biography to the religious paradigm as characteristic for the religious tradition of the I-psalms, these sapiential texts could be understood as special applications of the traditional piety—representing enlargements of special aspects of the religious tradition.

2. *Psalm 26*

a. *The Psalm as a Whole*
Depending on which parts are emphasized,[44] this psalm has been associated with different situations. The concluding prayers of vv. 9ff. must

40. E.g. Clines, *The Theme of the Pentateuch*; Hauge, 'The Struggles of the Blessed'.

41. Cf. Whybray, *The Making of the Pentateuch*, pp. 238ff. on Job and the Genesis stories as parallel expressions of a learned interest in folktale figures as archetypal persons, 'begun with the Exile' (p. 239).

42. Not only as an isolated 'novella', but with a biographical structure which closely corresponds to the compositional development of the other biographies, Hauge, 'The Struggles of the Blessed'.

43. To the theological significance attached to such a split related also to I-psalms W Brueggemann, 'From Hurt to Joy, From Death to Life', *Int* 28 (1974), pp. 3-19, further developed in 'Shape for Old Testament Theology I' and 'II'; and more concretely Broyles, *The Conflict of Faith*.

44. The rendering of the tenses of the verbs in the first person is in this psalm especially problematical. Craigie, *Psalms 1–50*, pp. 222-23, consistently regards the

obviously be important to the psalm as a whole, pointing to the I in a situation of crisis, his life at peril:

> Do not take away my soul together with the sinners,
> my life with men of blood
> who have wickedness in their hands, whose right hand is full of bribes.
> But I, in sincerity do I walk.
> Ransom me! Have mercy on me!
> My foot stands on level ground. In the assemblies I bless Yahweh.

With the emphasis on vv. 9ff., given the absence of enemy motifs, the I could very well be seen to be in mortal danger due to sickness, which has been the usual interpretation since Gunkel.

But if vv. 9ff. are held together with the introductory prayers in vv. 1-2, judicial categories might serve as a framework for understanding:

> Judge me, Yahweh! for in sincerity do I walk.
> In Yahweh I trust, I do not totter.
> Prove me, Yahweh! Test me! Try my kidneys and my heart!

Moreover, vv. 3ff. could be related to the preceding prayer as protestations of innocence:

> For your grace is before my eyes. I walk in your truth.
> I do not stay with empty men, with dissemblers I do not meet.
> I hate the assembly of the evil. With the guilty I do not stay.
> I wash my hands in innocence so I can walk round your altar, Yahweh,
> to proclaim with sound of praise, to tell all your wondrous deeds.
> Yahweh! I love the dwelling of your house,
> the place which is the place of dwelling for your glory.

Thus, the psalm could reflect a situation of ordeal, vv. 4ff. refuting false accusations by an oath of innocence, perhaps with references to some ritual background illustrated by Deut. 21.6, the whole psalm a *Gebet des Angeklagten*.[45]

---

perfect forms as referring to the past, the imperfect forms rendered as 'I will'. Another solution has been sought in the supposed underlying ritual agenda, e.g., Schmidt, *Psalmen*, p. 47, and Kraus, *Psalmen*, p. 214, who translate vv. 1-5 (Schmidt also v. 11) as referring to the past, vv. 6ff. to the present; and further Vogt 'Psalm 26, ein Pilgergebet'.

45. Schmidt, *Psalmen*, pp. 47-48, with vv. 4-5 as 'Reinigungseid' parallel to Pss. 7.4-6, 17.3-5 and connected to 1 Kgs 8.31, the I in this psalm accused of sorcery. Verse 12 together with 6b-8 reflect the thanksgiving rites taking place after the divine judgement. Cf. also Taylor, *Psalms*, pp. 140-41 (finding the motifs of the oath intended for use for several types of crime); Kraus, *Psalmen*, p. 216; Beyerlin, *Die Rettung*, p. 119 (with apostasy for crime); Dahood, *Psalms I*, p. 161 (with

The judicial motifs could be related differently to other parts of the psalm. Even given a context of accusations, the psalm could be referred to other laments and thus to a normal situation of prayer. Thus, the psalm could reflect a preparatory situation as an ordeal for purification.[46] Or the judicial frame could be connected to the negative attitude of the I towards the evil, and together with the emphasis on motifs of bribery, suggest the I as the royal judge. With this function, he could be in a situation of general national danger.[47] Alternatively the protestations of innocence related to the divine testing and some frame of crisis could refer to rites of renewal of the royal function.[48]

However, these models tend to disregard the 'expressions of delight in worship and the presence of God'.[49] Such motifs could even be emphasized as the main expressions of the situation of the I in this psalm. Thus, it is natural to connect vv. 4-5 to Psalms 15 and 24. Together with the categories of ordeal, these verses could point to the cultic background of entrance liturgy, linked with one of the great pilgrim festivals. The opening statement in v. 1 could presuppose priestly questions connected with admission to the temple, prior to participation in worship. To such an understanding, the declaration of innocence has the function of qualification for admission.[50]

The formal composition of the psalm is characterized by a four times

idol-worship for crime); Ruppert, *Der leidende Gerechte*, pp. 7, 26.

46. 'Reinigungsordal vor der eigenen Bitthandlung'; Gerstenberger, *Der bittende Mensch*, pp. 130ff., with vv. 7 and 11-12 as 'Lobgelübde'.

47. In a 'psalm of protection', Birkeland, *Die Feinde*, p. 298; Mowinckel, *Psalms I*, p. 220.

48. While Eaton, *Kingship*, p. 86, concludes that the psalm not should be used as basis for the description of the royal function during the autumn festival, Croft, *The Identity of the Individual*, pp. 90-91, relates it to Pss. 17, 7, 5, and 139 as an expression for the king being prepared for a cultic role similar to the royal rites of the Akitu-festival.

49. Rogerson and McKay, *Psalms 1–50*, pp. 117-18, with Pss. 5 and 27 for parallels. The hand-washing of v. 6 is seen as a metaphor for 'spiritual preparation' corresponding to 73.13; cf. more concretely Ridderbos, *Psalmen*, p. 207.

50. Especially Vogt, 'Psalm 26'; also Craigie, *Psalms 1–50*, p. 224, and generally to such categories Bentzen, *Jahves Gæst*. To Vogt, 'Psalm 26', p. 336, referring to the ideas of von Rad and Zimmerli, the crisis of vv. 9ff. is related to the ritual of admission. Non-admission into the temple, in the form of a negative verdict by the priests, would mean separation from the source of life. Similarly also Dahood, *Psalms I*, p. 162, with the accused in an ordeal of acceptance or banishment related to the temple.

Between Sheol and Temple

repeated pattern of prayers (vv. 1a first sentence, 2, 9-10, and the conclusion of 11) immediately followed by I-forms of a descriptive nature
(in vv. 1, 3-7, 11, 12).[51] In vv. 1 and 3, the I-forms are connected to the
prayers by the *kî*-element.

The relationship of prayer and the two first I-forms is obvious due to
the motif connection: the I prays for the divine judgment, while the following motivation gives a qualification of the I as prepared for the divine
examination (cf. above to the suggestions of some type of ritual ordeal
or examination). The other I-forms could also be related to such a function. Verses 9ff., in a formal pattern of prayers and I-forms, are naturally
seen to be a continuation of the earlier parts. The I-sentence of v. 11
repeats that of 1a, save for the imperfect form of the verb, and must
have a corresponding function. Moreover, the introductory sentence of
v. 11 contrasts with the description of the evil in v. 10 which expands
the negative nominal qualifications of the evil in the prayer of v. 9.[52]
Against this background v. 12, following the preceding prayer, can be
expected to function as a self-qualification in a parallel relationship to the
preceding prayer. This is also supported by the motif connection
between the I as not tottering (v. 1) and his 'foot standing on level
ground' (v. 12a),[53] while the motifs of 12b correspond to the temple
motifs of, especially, vv. 7-8.

In this way, the psalm is a simple composition with a repeated pattern
of prayers for divine intervention connected with self-qualifications.
Divine intervention—and correspondingly the situation of the I as supplicant—is expressed by parallel motifs of Yahweh as judge, 'examiner',
'not-killer', redeemer and favourable. These motifs might reflect some

51. Cf. especially Ridderbos, *Psalmen*, pp. 206ff., on the psalm consisting of
'Bitten, Beteuerungen der Aufrichtigkeit' and 'Aüsserungen der Erhörungsgewissheit'
(vv. 1d, 12).

52. For the construction of vv. 9-10 with negative nominal qualifications of the
evil in the prayer, expanded by a qualifying *'ašær*-sentence, cf. Ps. 140.2-3, 5-6 and
further also the link of prayer and negative qualification 140.9, 36.12-13, 43.1, 27.12.

53. Cf. Vogt, 'Psalm 26', p. 337, on the possible connotations of the motif 'stand
on level ground' in the context, with the emphasis on its metaphorical function as a
qualification of the I as 'righteous'. The motif surely must be rich in connotations. In
the present context it is natural to relate the concluding v. 12 to the introductory v. 1
(cf. also Ridderbos, *Psalmen*, p. 206; and Dahood, *Psalms I*, p. 163). Together with
non-*mā'ad* related to *bāṭah* (cf. especially Ps. 62), the two motifs refer to the same
basic imagery of 'Firmly going/standing', with an implicit motif of falling for
contrast (cf. below).

line of events, with, for example, an act of divine examination related to more direct acts of intervention into some kind of crisis. The different models of understanding mentioned above—all in different ways related to textual observation—illustrate the possible connotations of the motifs connected with some hypothetical biographical/ritual events. But given the parallel relationship of the prayers in this text, it is natural to understand the motifs to reflect aspects of one act of divine intervention.[54] And the situation of the I, in the text, must correspond to the requested intervention. The category of judgment or ordeal implies both examination and crisis.[55] The I threatened with death at the hands of Yahweh (v. 9) is the most obvious reference to what it is all about.

Similarly, the self-descriptions must basically have a parallel function.[56] Connected with categories of ordeal, they can only have sense as expressions of some ideal. Be it with regard to a particular accusation of some crime or to some life crisis which is translated into judicial categories, to admission into the sanctuary, or to some more ideological application of the motifs, the I is defined according to some notion of how man should be in such a situation.[57] Aside from the references to the evil, this notion is expressed consistently in first-person forms. The self-descriptions clearly define the I as the embodiment of some paradigm.

b. *The Self-Qualifications*
The I as ready for divine examination is expressed by four parallel self-descriptions. Their close relationship is demonstrated by the motif devel-

54. Ridderbos, *Psalmen*, p. 207, understands vv. 9-11 as the concrete prayer to which the poet 'bahnt...sich den Weg'. On the other hand, the Judgment prayer is the comprehensive one, while the other prayers express the different 'Elemente des "Richtens"'.

55. The notes above illustrate how the different models of understanding reflect these aspects, usually with a tendency to give preference to the one above the other.

56. Cf. especially Ridderbos, *Psalmen*, pp. 206ff., simplifying the function of these forms as 'Bitten, Beteuerungen der Aufrichtigkeit' (vv. 1b, c, 3-8, 11a) and 'Aüsserungen der Erhörungsgewissheit' (vv. 1d, 12, the latter in b as 'das Gelübde eines Dankliedes'). On the other hand, the separation of the I-forms into these types of function could reflect that such categories imply unsatisfactory analytical tools. This is demonstrated by the peculiar separation of v. 1, with d isolated from b and c as expressions for different kinds of function.

57. Cf. especially Vogt, 'Psalm 26', p. 331, on Ps. 26 as a 'Gegenstück zur priesterlichen Weisung, die wir aus Ps. 15 und 24 kennen'.

opment based on the imagery of the I as walker (vv. 1, 3, 11).

In vv. 3-8, the introductory v. 3 describes the I as walker, while the main part relates the I to the temple as the dwelling of Yahweh. But the temple motifs are introduced by negative statements in vv. 4-5 of the I as 'not-staying'. Given the relationship between vv. 3 and 4, it is natural to see the repeated *yāšaḇ* (4a, 5b) in negative continuation of v. 3: the walker does not settle. With a verb of movement describing even the temple relationship, the I depicted in circumambulation (6b), also vv. 6-7 could continue the basic imagery of walking / not-staying.

The sentence of motivation in v. 11 repeats the walking motif, while the final motivation of v. 12 combines the motif of 'firmly standing' with a motif on the I as related to Yahweh (*ḇēreḵ*). In this way, the two final self-descriptions in vv. 11 and 12 correspond to the motif combination of the introductory motivation, with the I as walking, as 'not-tottering', and as related to Yahweh.

The subtle variations of the basic imagery must be important for the psalm as a whole, and stress the parallel function of the I-forms in the composition. The relationship between these statements clearly points to vv. 4-8, related to the rest by the introductory v. 3, as central for the composition. This part is dominated by temple motifs. Verses 6-7 must have a background in rites. But the different models of understanding demonstrate that the relationship between textual expression and ritual background is uncertain. In any case, the function of these verses must be found in connection with the context.[58]

Verses 6-8 form the positive contrast to vv. 4-5. This juxtaposition is also stressed by the motifs of hate (v. 5) and love (v. 8). 'I do not stay etc.—I hate' is the negative part of the self-description 'I wash my hands etc.—I love'. These statements involve the I as related to two contrasted types of locality. Temple orientation is juxtaposed to staying *'im* the evil. Together the two statements must explain what is contained in the introductory v. 3, with vv. 6ff. a concrete description of the I as a sincere 'walker'.

---

58. Cf. e.g. Vogt, 'Psalm 26', translating the I-forms of vv. 1, 3-5 in the past tense as expressions for a series of 'gute Eigenschaften' (p. 330), while vv. 6-8 are understood to express what the admittance-seeking pilgrim wishes to do in the actual situation before the temple gates (p. 331). Similarly also Craigie, *Psalms 1–50*, pp. 225-26: vv. 2-5 represents 'prayer' and 'affirmation', while vv. 6-7 ' declare the intention of worship'. Verses 6-7 as 'anticipation of entrance makes the psalmist recall past occasions of entrance, expressed in v. 8' (p. 226).

The use of vv. 4-8 in the context is comparable to the use of the temple motifs in the texts analysed above. The contrasted love and hate motifs can be compared to the expressions of deep longing of Psalms 84 and 42 (cf. Ps. 27.3-4). In addition, the contrast of vv. 4-5 and 6ff. corresponds to the contrast of Ps. 84.11 with 'standing at the threshold of my God' juxtaposed to 'dwelling in the tents of evil' (cf. above to Ps. 42.7). The I is related to two alternative localities of orientation, choosing between them. Thus, the self-descriptions refer to categories of confession. With such a function the temple motifs obviously do not refer to rites connected with some biographical crisis or any other definite ritual situation, but are used in a general sense for life orientation and denote the locality of orientation. Even as connected with some serious crisis—as is the case in both these texts—the choice of temple relationship is presented as an act of confession, and used for self-qualification (cf. above on the relationship of 27.1-3 to vv. 4ff.). Obviously, the confession to the temple represents the religiously right choice—taken by the I of Psalm 84 as related to the blessed paradigms of vv. 5ff. and by the I of Psalm 26, presenting himself for divine examination.

This means that the function of the I-forms in vv. 4-8 corresponds not only to the first-person forms in Ps. 27.1-6 and also Pss. 42.2ff., 43.3-4, but also to the third-person statements of Pss. 84.5-8, 36.6-10, 140.14 as applied to the I-forms of the contexts. The relationship extends not only to comparable function and basic motifs, but seems also to be reflected in the elaboration of the material. Thus, aside from the material common to Psalms 84 and 26, we find a peculiar connection between 26.3ff., the hymnic 36.6ff. and the prayer 43.3-4.

The introductory Pss. 26.3 and 36.6-8a contain central terms which comprehensively describe the divine reality as related to humankind: 'your grace' and 'your truth' in 26.3, corresponding to the repeated 'your grace' in 36.6, 8 in addition to 'your faithfulness', 'righteousness' and 'judgments'. And in the first prayer of 43.3 we find 'your light' (cf. 36.10) and 'your truth' (cf. also 27.11 with 'your way' and 'the even path').

The parallel applications of these terms, related to the following temple motifs, in texts representing such different formal genres can hardly be coincidental. In addition, the applications overlap. Thus, the hymnic declaration centred round divine grace in 36.6-8 could be characterized as an expression asserting 26.3a 'Your grace is before my eyes'. And the application of the terms in 26.3 and 43.3 refers to the same type of imagery: the I walking with 'your grace before my eyes' and '*be* your truth' corresponds to the divine 'light' and 'truth' being sent to lead the I towards the temple (cf. also 27.11 with the I taught 'your way' and led 'upon the even path' and, also, vv. 4ff. on the I brought into the temple by the divine subject).

In the three texts, these applications are followed by motifs on movement towards and relationship to the temple. Save for the different types of motif exposition, due to the individual compositional needs, the first-person description 26.6-8 corresponds to the statements of 36.8ff., while 43.3-4 is dominated by the imperative forms of prayer. On the other hand, the compilation of terms for the temple, as well as the formal order of two and two terms in 43.3-4, corresponds to the arrangement in 26.8. This compilation must have a climactic effect of conclusion. In all the three cases, the temple forms are ended by sentences formally differing from the preceding verses (26.8, 36.10, 43.4 second line). These conclusions are all in first-person forms, in different ways representing a style of elation for describing the personal relationship to the divine presence in the temple.

This correspondence[59] can hardly be coincidental. It demonstrates a common dependence on given sets of concepts and motifs linked to specific central terms and must also reflect a common background of formal tradition. On the other hand, the applications in hymnic form, prayer and protestation of right confession illustrate the freedom of allusive application.

This combination of stereotypes and freedom is also illustrated by the other self-qualifications parallel to vv. 3-8. The formally independent motivations in vv. 1, 11, and 12 together with v. 3 demonstrate statements of parallel significance as short forms of religious self-description. The introductory location of v. 3 together with the negative and positive form of vv. 4-8 even suggests v. 3 as the central statement explicated by vv. 4ff.

The significance of these short forms as self-contained expressions[60] is illustrated by Psalm 84. The relationship between the three parallel beatitudes vv. 5, 6-8, 13 is comparable to that of the motivations in Psalm 26. Psalm 84.5 as the comprehensive form is elaborated by the motifs in vv. 6-8. This corresponds to 26.3 introducing vv. 4ff. And 84.13 has a

59. Cf. also the formally parallel constructions 26.7 and 27.4b on the temple relationship.
60. Cf. also Pss. 140.13 and 84.12 related to their contexts.

concluding function, its form referring to vv. 5ff., on the other hand isolated as a self-contained statement.[61]

The motifs of the self-qualifications correspond to the basic motif structure. Verses 3-8 illustrate the significance of temple motifs as the central expression of personal confession. Relationship to Yahweh is defined as longing for, and on the way to, and in the temple as the place of a special relationship to the divine presence. While the motifs of way in separate statements could have general connotations of mode of life or fate or of Torah-piety, 26.3 related to 43.3 demonstrates the dependence on given motif sets. I as 'walker' describes the I in movement towards the temple. On the other hand, the application of the motif in this psalm suggests its significance as a relatively independent motif. In the other psalms, motifs of movement related to the temple are usually presented within a set of motifs which emphasize the significance of dwelling in the temple (cf. Pss. 42.3, 43.3-4, 36.8, 27.5). Of these texts, primarily 84.6ff. with references to a miraculous pilgrimage and also the qualifications of 27.11 with a divine guide (cf. also 140.5-6), illustrate that motifs of way could refer to a cluster of relatively independent connotations.

The composition of the psalm suggests that also the other motifs of qualification refer to the basic motif structure. The significance of non-*mā'ad* together with *bāṭaḥ*[62] in v. 1 is illustrated by the motif development in Ps. 62.2-8, 9, 11 connected with non-*môṭ* and *bāṭaḥ*. The imagery refers to the contrast between standing/falling. But in Psalm 26, the context of 1a, 3 connects the 'not-tottering' to the way motifs (cf. Pss. 18.37, 37.31). This is comparable to the motif application Ps. 140.5-6 (connected with a motif of firmly standing v. 12; cf. also 118.13 and 36.13). Here the falling is connected with the activities of the enemies as 'pushing', while in Psalm 26 the not-tottering illustrates the I as the 'sincere walker'. On the other hand, the connection of falling/enemy attack in Ps. 140.5-6 is interesting as an illustration of the connotative significance of the two negative statements in 26.1b and 4-5. Formally the two statements correspond, as parallel negative self-qualifications related to positive forms. Ps. 140.5-6 together with 118.13 and 36.13 demonstrate that the formal relationship of the I as 'not-tottering' and as 'not-settling' among the evil also has a connotative background connected

61. 84.13 together with 26.1b suggest that *bāṭaḥ* is important as a central term for such short forms (cf. also 27.3b with this verb concluding the introductory vv. 1-3, preparing the temple motifs vv. 4-7).
62. To the combination of the two words cf. Prov. 25.19.

with the basic concept of evil enemies. This background stresses the consistent rendering of these motifs in Psalm 26 with the I for subject in self-qualifications.

A corresponding contrast of falling is also implied in the concluding v. 12a. The qualification of *mîšôr* is usually connected to way motifs.[63] But related to 'standing' and to the motifs of v. 12b, the imagery is framed by the situation of dwelling in the temple. This can be related to the self-descriptions of 62.2ff., depicting the I as not-tottering on the rock.

As to function, these motifs as well as those of vv. 4-8 are parallel expressions of the I as fit for divine examination. Thus, motifs of the evil, temple, walking, firmly standing etc. are used in self-qualification. The thrice repeated motif of I as 'wholly walking' obviously is central for the composition, dominating the application of the other motifs. This corresponds to the formal character of Psalm 26 as a consistent expression of the volitional aspects of the motif structure. At the same time, the composition also reflects a second type of motif application, round a meticulous development of the I as walking/non-falling, walking as not-settling among the evil/but entering the temple, walking and finally standing (/not-falling).

The significance of this subtle motif development can be illustrated by Psalm 23. For the composition of this psalm, the obvious formal characteristics of the two parts are connected with a basic motif exposition centred round introductory motifs of way and concluding motifs of dwelling in the temple (cf. above). Psalm 15 could be an even more interesting parallel, due to the relationship of third-person qualifications and temple motifs corresponding to the I-forms of Psalm 26.[64] In 15.1 (cf. also Isa. 33.14b)[65] dwelling in the temple is the central motif. The following list of characteristics is introduced by *hālak* (Isa. 33.15). The conclusion, on the fate of the paradigmatic figure, returns to the situation of dwelling in the temple. But while Isa. 33.16 refers to the comprehensive motif of dwelling, Psalm 15 applies the motif of eternal not-tottering. This corresponds to the conclusion of Psalm 26. The application of this motif in such contexts must reflect the connotative background of the motif as connected with dwelling in the temple.[66]

63. Pss. 27.11; 143.10; Isa. 40.4; 42.16; Mal. 2.6.

64. To this connection Vogt, 'Psalm 26'.

65. The use of verbs of entrance in the parallel Ps. 24.3 must reflect the compositional interest with a concluding presentation of a parallel divine enterer, vv. 8ff.

66. On the other hand, Isa. 33.16 with dwelling and motifs of meal related to a

Given this background, Psalm 26 can be characterized as a literary elaboration of the basic motif structure. The individual expressions refer to the connotations of the sacred topography, centred round the concepts of temple with a contrast locality, and of the way. While Psalm 42 seems to define the way as leading from the contrast locality of Sheol to the temple (cf. the applications in 1 Kings 19 and Exodus 15), the imagery of Psalm 26 corresponding to 84.11 could relate the way differently to the two localities, the sincere walking possibly interrupted by the attraction of the negative locality.[67]

On the other hand, the application of Psalm 26 differs considerably from those analysed above. Except in what we termed the 'volitional' aspects of Psalm 84, we have repeatedly noted the character of the I as consistently passive in these texts, with a corresponding emphasis on miraculous categories. Not only with regard to God, but also to the enemies, the I is object for the acts of others. In this mode, the I is depicted as the sufferer, with the prayer for divine intervention as the only effort. While the prayer is an expression of the I as confessor, with, for example, *bāṭaḥ* for a comprehensive term, the ideal confession as described in Psalm 27 is that of the ultimate quietist, with the I surrounded by enemies praying for the one thing of temple admission!

Against this background, the activist mode of the I in Psalm 26 is remarkable. Here, the main motifs are not related to the divine subject, but to the perfect actualization of the I. The application of the way and temple motifs demonstrate the significance of the I as active. In 43.3-4 and 27.11, the way is the result of the miraculous intervention, signifying the way of salvation. In Psalm 26, the relationship to the way is proof of total commitment. And the temple motifs, which usually express the

locality of a mountain fortress under siege demonstrates the combination of stereotyped language (cf. also the reference to the beatific vision in the You-application v. 17) and individual expression which seems to be characteristic for the application of the motif structure.

67. Cf. also Ps. 1 as a further elaboration, contrasting not only the negative and positive localities (vv. 1b, 5), but also the two ways (1a, 6). While the imagery of the tree and wind-blown chaff could express connotations of dwelling/not-dwelling in the temple (cf. v. 5 and, e.g., Pss. 52.7, 10-11; 92.8, 13ff.; and especially Jer. 17.5ff. with a motif contrast of tree and dwelling in the wilderness), the verbs of v. 1 express a subtle development of some basic motifs. Here walking-standing-staying is used for the fatal attraction of the negative locality. This application, together with the use of these motifs in Ps. 26, serve for good examples to illustrate the refined literary character of the tradition in question.

ultimate goal, are in this psalm used in a contrasting mode (cf. Psalm 5, Chapter 5 below). The application of the evil motif corresponds to this type of exposition. The I is not the object of their attack, but the not-attracted walker passes by their evil dens. The basic motifs of way, temple, and evil are used for the description of the I as the religious hero, the perfect embodiment of the paradigm.

This change can hardly reflect a critical valuation of the traditional application of the other texts. If that were the case, Exod. 33.18ff. would illustrate that we could expect identifiable expressions of a new under-standing. Psalm 26 must reflect the motif structure as applied in a voli-tional mode.

The application of the motif structure as a whole and as stated corre-sponds to Ps. 27.1-6. There, temple entrance and stay are expressed in stating forms. And the functions of the I-forms are comparable, the I describing himself as the perfect *bôṭēaḥ*. The main difference between the two expressions of the motif structure is the consistent motif applica-tion in Psalm 26 by sentences with the I for subject. Also, the composi-tion of Psalm 27 is centred in the enemy situation, while Psalm 26 is dominated by a situation based on the way motif.

The significance of a composition centred around way motifs could be illustrated by Psalm 84. The relationship of the beatitudes vv. 5-8 to the I-forms of v. 11 demonstrates the I as an actualization of the given paradigm, choosing the alternatives of orientation. Thus, Psalm 26 as a whole could be seen as a composition in I-form parallel to the combina-tion of third-person and first-person forms of 84.5-8, 11. In both cases, the application of way motifs in the volitional mode is connected with the absence of enemy motifs.[68]

In the relationship of Psalm 26 to Psalm 84, the former stands apart with its consistent application of the main motifs in sentences with the I

---

68. As illustrated by the discussion Vogt, 'Psalm 26', pp. 328ff., absence or presence of concrete enemy motifs have traditionally been important for the under-standing of the concrete life/ritual setting of the text, the former, for example, to a situation of sickness, the latter to ordeal or to national distress, e.g., Schmidt, *Psalmen*, pp. vi-vii; Birkeland, *Die Feinde*, pp. 20ff. Correspondingly, the different juxtaposition of the I / enemies or I / the evil as seducers has been seen as significant, suggesting development from a ritual and conceptual reality concerned with social categories to a later, 'spiritualized' type of pious application, e.g., Beyerlin, *Die Rettung*, pp. 158-59; Kraus, *Psalmen*, pp. 3-4. Aside from the applications of Pss. 36 and 5, Ps. 17.3-5 related to vv. 7ff. is a good example of an immediate connection between the evil as the negative paradigm, corresponding to Ps. 26.3ff., and the evil as enemies.

for subject. This must be linked to the formal character of the psalm as a whole. The I is surely the confessor, but not addressing the confession to Yahweh with a function of immediate adoration and worship (cf. v. 8 contrasting v. 5). Instead, the self-descriptions seem to have a function as argumentative self-qualifications. The relationship to the temple as 'beloved' certainly corresponds to the longing I of Psalm 84. But in this psalm, the temple motifs of vv. 4-8 are used to qualify the I as not-evil (vv. 5-6).

A corresponding interest in self-qualification seems to be relevant also to the other texts. This could be related to the common situation of prayer, with a basic orientation towards divine intervention on behalf of the supplicant, with implications of categories of ordeal. Thus, the basic elements of the paradigm correspond to the other psalms. Aside from the fundamental *bāṭaḥ*-relationship to Yahweh, temple orientation is the expression of the confession, with dwelling in the temple, here as a situation of praise and thanksgiving, as the ultimate aspiration (v. 7).

What makes the composition of Psalm 26 so special is the absence of enemy motifs. In the other texts—aside from Psalm 84—the I as confessor is linked to his situation of suffering in the hands of enemies, the enemies consistently qualified as evil. Thus, the description of enmity and suffering represents in itself a self-qualification of the I presenting himself for divine judgement. This text represents only the aspect of evilness of the enemy motif, corresponding to the presentation of the I as not-evil. This must be linked to the prayer of v. 9, which depicts Yahweh as the threat to the I.

The function of the self-qualifications, presenting the I as an embodiment of the paradigm, fit for divine examination, is given a significant expression by the central qualification of 'wholeness'. The I is 'wholly walking' (1a, 11), the total commitment illustrated by the motifs of trust and not-tottering (1b) and firmly standing (12a) and by the temple orientation of vv. 4-8 as the expression of the way-motifs in v. 3. Moreover, the total commitment is internalized, related to 'heart' and 'kidneys', in addition to the verbs of 'hate' and 'love'. In this way the I is related both to outer and inner manifestations of the paradigmatic walking. Implicitly contrasted to forms of 'insincere walking' (cf. especially Ps. 84.6b on the blessed with 'highways in their hearts'), the paradigm must also be connected with categories of inner integrity.

On the other hand, this could be related to aspects of the other texts. Especially for Psalms 84 and 42–43 (cf. also 36) we have noted different expressions for a similar interest, while the I of Ps. 27.1-6 could also serve as an example of perfect confession in connection with the enemy situation. The expressions of longing for the temple in Psalms 84 and 42–43 witness that the application of the motif structure was also connected with emotional and psychological categories.

Thus, Psalm 26 seems to reflect an elaborated version of the motif structure, with the composition centred round aspects of aspiration and striving. This makes this psalm an important example of how the motifs can be related to religious practice. Psalm 26 clearly demonstrates a practice of religious commitment including inner emotional and mental attitudes in addition to outer manifestations. The description of human inner and outer reality, presented for inspection by the divine examiner, is totally given to the ideological categories of the motif structure. Thus, while it is possible to envisage types of usage which could make the recitation of such a text into, for example, a magical incantation of appeasement, the very fact of such a composition demonstrates a religious paradigm—which must presuppose some type of practice—centred round the main motifs, connected with human striving and experience. The I of this psalm represents an embodiment of the religious ideal, the ideological motifs translated into personal being.

c. *The Prayers*
In the four times repeated pattern of prayers and motivations, the motif connection stresses the parallel function of the motivations. It is natural to assume a similar relationship between the prayers. Among the motivations, vv. 4-8 stand out as the elaboration of the I as 'wholly walking'. A similar function with regard to the prayers could also be ascribed to vv. 9-10:

> Do not take away my soul together with the sinners,
> my life with men of blood!
> who have wickedness in their hands, whose right hand is full of bribes.

This prayer clearly represents an application of the preceding self-description. The repeated *'im*-elements of vv. 4a, b, 5b and 9a, b stress the connection between two situations with the I as not 'together with' the evil: in the one the I is the subject of separation, in the other Yahweh. Having separated himself from the evil, Yahweh should not cause 'togetherness'. In vv. 4-5 the motifs refer to local categories, the locality of the evil juxtaposed to the temple. The use of *'āsaf* with divine subject suggests that also in the prayer, the 'togetherness' alludes to a locality to which one is brought. With 'soul' and 'life' for objects of the divine collecting,[69] Sheol is naturally the place of 'togetherness'.[70] Thus the prayer presupposes Sheol as the given locality for the evil. This refers to categories we have found earlier for, especially, Pss. 36.13 and 42.7-8 and for 140.11b, 12. Contrasted to the temple as the wished-for locality, the negative fate is described by motifs of Sheol/death. The relationship of the I to the negative place in Psalm 26 is comparable to that of 36.12-13 (cf. also in 140): the I is evidently not localized to the place of death, but could be 'brought' there, in Psalm 36 (and 140) due to the onslaught of the evil enemies. Psalms 42–43 show a different type of motif application, with the I localized to Sheol. But connected with motifs of way and temple in addition to motifs of the evil, the differences reflect individual applications of the basic motif structure.

In this way, the motif execution demonstrates a close relationship between the self-description of vv. 3ff. and the prayer, the former as a motivation preparing the prayer. This close relationship is also expressed by the extension of the prayer in v. 10. The hand motifs in the qualification of the evil contrasts with the purification motifs in v. 6a.[71] As not only a non-dweller among the evil, but entering the contrast locality with pure hands, the I is obviously not-evil and should not be brought to the locality of the evil by Yahweh!

This connection between motivation and prayer stresses the impression of vv. 4-8 as an 'active' or volitional application of the motif structure, with vv. 6-8 forming the positive counterpart to the negative vv. 4-5. On the other hand, in v. 9 the motifs are applied with the I in the usual passive mode, his fate dependent on divine intervention. In this way, the function of the volitional self-qualifications related to a situation of prayer must be comparable to, for example, the pattern of self-descriptions and prayers in Psalm 27. In both cases, the basic motifs of the motif structure are stated and then related to prayers which apply the motifs in the subjunctive mode, connected with the miraculous categories of divine intervention.

As to contents, the prayer of v. 9 corresponds closely to that of Ps. 36.12-13. The two texts differ as to the subject of the I's movement towards the negative locality: 26.9 with Yahweh as potentially bringing

69. With Yahweh for subject and life/soul for object cf. especially Ps. 104.29 and Job 34.14; further also 2 Kgs 22.20 with 'you' for object.

70. Cf. especially Ps. 88 with a combination of Sheol and 'togetherness' motifs.

71. E.g. Isa. 1.15ff. with corresponding motif contrasts.

him into Sheol, 36.12-13 with the enemies doing that. But common to the two prayers is the imagery of the I brought into Sheol as the locality of the evil.[72] And in both cases, the movement towards Sheol is qualified as the fate of the evil: in 26 by the motif of togetherness, in 36 by the general description of the locality as the place of the evils' falling.

The application of the motif structure in an active and passive mode also suggests that the negative locality—correspondingly also the positive locality—can have two functions in these texts. The prayers of Psalms 36 and 26 qualify the negative place as an expression for the fate of the evil, with connotations of retribution and punishment. As the place of death, the negative place stands for defeat and failure and terror. This corresponds to the use of the way and temple motifs in most of the texts, with the temple as the place of longing and aspiration, and dwelling in the temple as the fate of the paradigmatic righteous, connected with divine intervention and *hæsæd*.

But the applications of Ps. 84.11 and, especially, Ps. 26.4-5 define the negative locality as a place of attraction and temptation, marking the alternative to longing for the temple. Also in this case, the motif applications presuppose that the negative place of attraction and staying is inhabited by the evil.

The relationship of vv. 4-8 and 9 in Psalm 26 demonstrates that the two types of application are closely connected as two aspects of one concept. Also the relationship between Ps. 42.7 and 8 could reflect this connection. On the one hand, the verses are parallel descriptions of the I's localization, on the other hand the motifs of v. 7 refer to connotations of revolt, of v. 8 to categories of suffering and divine punishment.

d. *Conclusions*
Psalms 26 and 27 represent interesting applications of the motif structure. In both cases the central motifs of I contrasted with the evil and connected to local categories of temple/Sheol and way, form the thematic basis of the individual composition, both with regard to material and to structure. And at the same time, the exposition reflects the

---

72. Cf. above to Pss. 42–43 which refer the suffering of the I both to the categories of divine punishment (v. 8) and to the enemies. The connection between the two modes of description is illustrated by the narrative forms of Ps. 118.5, 13-14, 18. In the parallel descriptions of the crisis and the salvation, the crisis is related to different types of situation. I in confinement, Yahweh as 'punishing not completely unto death', and You as 'pushing unto falling' express different aspects of the crisis.

literary freedom of application, Psalm 26 elaborating way motifs, 27 motifs of dwelling in the temple.

The compositional development of both Psalms 26 and 27 repeats the basic motif structure, partly in a series of statements, partly in references in the prayers. This corresponds to the other texts, with the prime difference being that the statements in Psalms 26 and 27 are expressed in the I-form. In all the texts, the prayer situation is presented as an actualization of the paradigm. The motif structure stated in first-person forms has a function parallel to the third-person statements as expressions of the paradigm. Such a background, with the third person statements as the basic type of expression, could be reflected in the relatively independent character of the self-descriptive statements in the context. With Ps. 27.1-6 often isolated as an independent psalm, and the four times repeated self-qualifications of Psalm 26, the special formal character of the motif structure as stated is underlined. Also, the special motif application, with dwelling in the temple stated and even used for self-qualification, while the prayers refer to a crisis and thus to a situation of 'not yet' prior to the climax events of the motif structure, must reflect that statements and prayers employ different types of application.

The special character of the paradigm connected to I-forms is demonstrated by the mode of application. The normal application of the motif structure in connection with the prayer situation stresses the significance of miraculous categories, with the I presented as the passive sufferer and supplicant. But as the perfect confessor in Ps. 27.1-6 and the total walker in Psalm 26, the motifs serve for the self-qualification of the I (cf. also 92.13ff. on the fate of the righteous compared to the self-qualification of 52.10-11). This type of application dominates Psalm 26, with the basic motifs presented not with a divine, but with a human, subject. Compared to the usual type of application, the self-qualifications of this psalm present the motifs in what we could term a volitional or active mode. But the prayer situation of this psalm reverts to the basic mode of divine intervention.

In this way, the I of these two psalms is presented as an embodiment of the paradigm. This character can also be illustrated by the texts' relationship to other texts. As we have seen, Psalm 26 can be related both to the beatitudes of Psalm 84 and to the proclamation of admittance rules in Psalm 15. And the fearless confessors of Pss. 27.1-6 and 23 can be seen as the perfect realization of the holy war admonishments of, for example, Exod. 14.13-14 or Deut. 20.1ff. aside from the bourgeois ideal of Ps. 112.5ff. The connection between the motif structure as stated in first- and third-person forms can be compared to the relationship of Ps. 52.10-11 and Ps. 92.13ff. In both cases, the positive ideal is contrasted to a negative paradigm, 52.8-9 concluding the You-description of vv. 3-7, and 92.8. Either as a *ṣaddîq*-saying related to I-forms in Psalm 92, or as a contrasting self-description in I-form stated by the *ṣaddîqîm* in Psalm 52, the motifs clearly represent the paradigmatic figure.

In this way, Psalms 26 and 27 add to our understanding of the I-figure of the other texts. Psalm 26, related to Psalms 84 and further 52 and 92, also demonstrates that the positive paradigm of the 'righteous' is balanced by the evil—with *rāšā'* for the obvious contrast term—as the negative one. The category of 'evilness' is characteristic for the negative figures, applied either as mortal enemies or as figures of attraction. In both cases, their function is identical within the motif structure, negating temple relationship, relating the I to Sheol.

Fundamentally, the I of these texts is presented as a being in between the paradigmatic figures. Even as orientated towards the positive ideal, the I in the prayer situation is evidently given to the negative fate save for divine intervention. This must be basic to the function of the motif structure, as even the perfected heroes of Psalms 27 and 26 share the same type of crisis with those of the other texts. Even as the 'total walker' led by the divine light, the hero of Psalm 26 can be brought to the 'togetherness' of Sheol, with prayer as the means of avoiding the negative fate. In this way, the two psalms with their special character stress the importance of miraculous categories for the motif structure. Whatever the exposition, these texts are dominated by a basic structure of ultimate goal/non-goal which is unattainable/given depending on the divine intervention. The divine manifestation is an integral part of the paradigmatic fate.

Psalms 26 and 27 also support the impression of these texts as expressions of ideological language. The basic motifs are determined by a function of general religious interpretation, providing terms and ideological coherence for the religious description of human reality.[73] The textual shape and the motif execution of Psalms 27 and 26 stress the significance of the basic motifs as parts of an ideological language. In the

---

73. For a traditional conceptual frame for such categories cf. especially Mowinckel, *Psalms*, II, pp. 18ff., 126-145, with a contrast of 'traditional' and 'personal' language, the former dependent on cultic function, the latter connected with categories of individual experience, emotion and poetical inspiration.

present textual frame, their function is not dependent on an accompaniment of parallel ritual experience in the traditional sense. As expressions of life orientation, they describe the reality of humankind interpreted in a set of religious concepts. The applications of the temple motifs in Psalms 52 and 92 related to 26.4ff. (cf. also above to 27.1, 13) even suggest that a relationship to a physical temple could be completely irrelevant for the realization of the ideological language, with dwelling in the temple as an expression for a special state of being.

On the other hand, such applications do not, of course, exclude levels of interpretation and application connected with real-life temple institutions. Given the ancient connotations of Near Eastern concepts of the temple,[74] the 'temple' being part of a 'symbol system' in the sociological sense,[75] it is possible to surmise a type of ideological language dependent on and presupposing actual contact with physical temples both as buildings and as institutions. In our context, the emphasis on the ideological character of the language refers mainly to the traditional models of understanding for texts like Psalms 27 and 26, and thus to the need to ponder alternative settings for the production and original function of these texts.

Thus, while the texts could have some relationship both to historical-biographical and ritual reality, as envisaged in the usual models of understanding, the motif application suggests a basic character of ideological language. However, it must be important that these texts relate the ideological language to biographical experience. The very fact of I-forms in connection with the paradigmatic language, in addition to the situation of prayer connected to a crisis defined by the ideological categories, points to such a connection as basic for these Psalms.

In this respect, Psalms 26 and 27 are of special importance. In both texts, the self-qualifications link ideology and biography through the person of the I as the embodiment of the ideal figure. In addition, the relationship between statements and prayers in Psalm 27 could directly reflect a relationship of paradigmatic crisis and some life crisis as interpreted within the categories of ideological language. But it is especially in Psalm 26 that ideology and biography seem to be closely linked. Here, the idea of a totally integrated paradigm related to the divine examination of heart and kidneys indicates a close connection between ideology

74. E.g. Tromp, *Conceptions of Death*, pp. 205ff.; Clifford, *The Cosmic Mountain*.

75. Geertz, *The Interpretation of Cultures*; Ollenburger, *Zion the City*, pp. 19ff.

and biographical reality. For the argument of the psalm to be effective, the I must *be* the ideal figure, bearing in his own flesh and blood the characteristics of the *ṣaddîq*, both 'heart' and 'hands' expressing his total devotion.

Such a qualification must refer to a practice of religious observance, connected both with mental and emotional categories. Similarly, the I of 27.1-6 must at the very least be intended to describe a state of religious enthusiasm and emotional fervour. In these texts, biographical and ideological language seems to be identical. And a concept of an 'ideological biography' would indicate a setting of religious observance committed to the internalization and integration of the paradigm. When related to similar findings in the other texts, both Psalms 26 and 27 could mirror the experiences of a religious *milieu* in which the motif structure represented a conceptual vehicle of religious practice and inner development. Thus, the heroes of, for example, Psalms 27 and especially 26 suggest rather perfected actualizations compared to the I of, for example, Psalms 42/43 and especially 36.

This would imply that the qualification of the language of these texts as 'ideological' only covers certain aspects. The application of the motif structure in Psalms 26 and 27 above all points to an interest in religious practice, concerned with the internalization of the religious paradigm in biographical experience expressed by the I as mental-emotional-physical integrity.

Such an interest could also be related to indications of these texts as expressions for an interest in admonishment. Thus, the relationship between Ps. 26.3-8 and 9-10 provides an elegant, rather subtle argument for a situation of prayer totally given to the experience of crisis and supplication before God. But the I presented to others as a paradigmatic figure for identification, with a corresponding emphasis on the self-qualifications for imitation and identification, would make such expressions natural. Both the rather assured self-description and the rhetorical subtlety of the prayer would correspond to a function of indirect admonishment, comparable to, for example, the third-person beatitudes of Psalm 84.

Chapter 5

PSALM 5: THE STRUGGLE TO DWELL IN THE TEMPLE

1. *The Psalm as a Whole*

With the introductory invocation in vv. 2-3a and the prayers in vv. 9 and 11, Psalm 5 is traditionally recognized as an individual lament. Verse 4 is usually understood as a reference to a morning sacrifice.[1] Thus, the psalm could generally be connected to a cultic situation in the night before or during the morning sacrifice.[2]

On the other hand, the absence of complaints seen together with forms which could be understood as protestations of innocence (vv. 5ff.) related to enemy motifs, could suggest that this psalm reflects a more special setting. *'ārak*, v. 4b, understood as a sacrificial term, together with *ṣippâ*[3] could refer to divinatory rites of omen or *Schauopfer*.[4]

---

1. With *'ārak* as a technical term for sacrificial preparations. On the other hand, Dahood, *Psalms I*, p. 30, understands the verb as a technical reference to forensic categories, 'draw up my case'. Correspondingly, also v. 6a is understood to refer to a situation in law court comparably to Job 33.5 (p. 31). The parallel verbs and nouns connected with the I in the context vv. 2-4, stressed by the motifs of the contrast description v. 10 (cf. below), suggests that the verb refers to a situation of prayer.

2. Weiser, *Psalmen*, pp. 76-77; Taylor, *Psalms*, p. 37; Rogerson and McKay, *Psalms 1–50*, p. 30, the latter referring to Ps. 17 for a close parallel.

3. This is understood by Delekat also, *Asylie*, p. 57, as a technical sacrificial term 'auftischen'. But as argued by Kraus, *Psalmen*, p. 39, the usage should be related to Mic. 7.7 in the context of vv. 7-10 and Hab. 2.1 with closely parallel usages: watch, observe. Parallel to *hôhîl*, Mic. 7.7, the I as 'watching' in connection with a situation of prayer corresponds to the use of *qiwwâ*, Ps. 27.14 and *hôhîl*, Pss. 42.6, 12, 43.5.

4. Cf. especially Mowinckel, *Psalms II*, p. 54, emending the second *bōqær*, v. 4b, to *biqqer* corresponding to Ps. 27.4b, understood as a technical term for divination; Delekat, *Asylie*, p. 57; Gerstenberger, *Der bittende Mensch*, pp. 149-50. While this understanding seems rather uncertain in view of the context of vv. 2-4 with parallel terms pointing to a general situation of prayer, such a situation implies *eo ipso* some type of divine manifestation. Either as intimately connected with sacrificial rites

Connected to such a setting, the psalm could reflect introductory rites preparing the real prayer ritual.[5] Or the divination could point to a judicial situation, the I accused by slandering enemies (cf. v. 10 immediately connected with the enemy prayer, v. 9), bringing his case before the divine judge in some kind of ordeal situation.[6] Or, given the absence of complaints and what is understood as a lack of motifs for an actual conflict, the psalm could refer to protective rites of a more general nature, with a setting prior to any conflict or battle.[7] With emphasis on vv. 5ff. as protestation of innocence and connected to a royal I, the psalm could be related to similar royal protestations of the Babylonian Akitu-festival, reflecting a ritual of renewal of the royal function.[8]

With a basis in textual phenomena, these proposals as to setting and application are equally plausible as to what might have taken place in the original situation of application and reflect equally aspects of the textual situation. In our connection, in a context of Psalm 26 related to the other I-psalms, the combination of self-qualification and enemy motifs is interesting. Psalm 26 lacks enemy motifs and is characterized by special self-qualifications. Related to, for example, Psalms 15 and 24 traditionally regarded as expressions for a situation of examination referring to specific religious virtues connected with temple entrance, one could isolate Psalm 26 from the normal enemy psalm.

In this respect, Psalm 5 is important. It is decisively linked to Psalm 26 and texts like Psalms 15 and 24, being dominated by the interest of admission to the temple, and also to the enemy motifs of the other texts. Further, the execution of the temple motifs in this psalm, with the evil related to dwelling in the temple, provides a significant link between Psalm 5 and Isa. 1.10-20[9] and Jer. 7.1-15, thus supporting the generally

(e.g. Num. 23!) or not, the I is praying for a miraculous intervention of guidance (v. 9).

5.   Gerstenberger, *Der bittende Mensch*, pp. 149-50, the relevant rites characterized as 'Befragung des Propheten oder Priesters' or as purificatory rites (pp. 148-49).

6.   Schmidt, *Psalmen*, pp. 9-10; Kraus, *Psalmen*, p. 37; Delekat, *Asylie*, p. 57; Beyerlin, *Die Rettung*, p. 90; cf. also Ruppert, *Der Leidende Gerechte*, p. 37, and Dahood, *Psalms I*, pp. 29-30.

7.   As a 'protective psalm', Birkeland, *Feinde*, pp. 104ff.; Mowinckel, *Psalms I*, p. 220, both with the I as a representative figure; and Craigie, *Psalms 1-50*, p. 85.

8.   Croft, *The Identity of the Individual*, p. 90, relating the psalm to Pss. 26, 17, 7 and 139, further Eaton, *Kingship*, pp. 64-65.

9.   From the traditional form-historical viewpoint vv. 10-17 and 18-20 are independent units in a secondary composition, e.g., H. Wildberger, *Jesaja*. I. *Jesaja*

accepted[1] linkage between these prophetic texts and Psalms 15 and 24. In this way, Psalm 5 demonstrates the connection between important motif groups.

1–12 (BKAT 10.1; Neukirchen-Vluyn: Neukirchener Verlag, 1972), pp. 34ff., 50; O. Kaiser, *Isaiah 1–12* (OTL; London: SCM Press, 1972), p. 24; H.W. Hoffmann, *Die Intention der Verkündigung Jesajas* (BZAW 136; Berlin: de Gruyter, 1974), pp. 92-93. But in connection with the 'covenant lawsuit' genre, the verses are found to represent parts of a composition, e.g. on vv. 2-31, S. Niditch, 'The Composition of Isaiah 1', *Bib* 61 (1980), pp. 509-29; on vv. 2-26, E.W. Davies, *Prophecy and Ethics. Isaiah and the Ethical Tradition of Israel* (JSOTSup 16; Sheffield: JSOT Press, 1981), p. 4; on vv. 2-20, Y. Gitay, 'The Study of the Prophetic Discourse', *VT* 33 (1983), pp. 207-21; on vv. 2-20, J.T. Willis, 'The First Pericope in the Book of Isaiah', *VT* 34 (1984), pp. 63-77; on vv. 2-23, J.D.W. Watts, *Isaiah 1–33* (Word Biblical Commentary 24; Waco: Word Books, 1985), pp. 15-16. While the present composition of ch. 1 must be significant, the isolation of vv. 10-20 in this context reflects the significance of the elaborate introduction, v. 10, and the address to a plural You in addition to the application of the motif structure ending in the conditioned statement on the fate of the addressees in vv. 19-20.

10. Traditionally linked to formal categories, cf. J. Begrich, 'Die priesterliche Tora', *BZAW* 66 (1936), pp. 63-88, reprinted *Gesammelte Studien zum Alten Testament* (TB 21; Munich: C. Kaiser, 1964), pp. 243, 249 on Isa. 1.10ff. and Pss. 15, 24 as 'Nachahmungen' of a priestly or cultic torah. More directly related to cultic categories, S. Mowinckel, *Le décalogue* (Études d'histoire et de philosophie religieuse 16; Paris: Alcan, 1927); cf. K. Koch, 'Tempeleinlassliturgien und Dekaloge', in R. Rendtorff and K. Koch (eds.), *Studien zur Theologie der alttestamentlichen Überlieferungen. Gerhard von Rad zum 60. Geburtstag* (Neukirchen: Neukirchener Verlag, 1961), pp. 45-60; and especially comprehensively H. Graf Reventlow, 'Gattung und Überlieferung in der "Tempelrede Jeremias", Jer 7 und 26', *ZAW* 81 (1969), pp. 315-52. With the cultic aspect recently more downplayed, the texts have been connected to the categories of the 'covenant lawsuit' (cf. also the references of the preceding note) in addition to the discussion on the Deuteronomic influence on Jer. 7, e.g. Wildberger, *Jesaja 1–12*, p. 49; Kaiser, *Isaiah 1–12*, pp. 24ff.; R.P. Carroll, *The Book of Jeremiah* (OTL; London: SCM Press, 1986), p. 209; W.L. Holladay, *Jeremiah 1. A Commentary on the Book of the Prophet Jeremiah Chapters 1–25* (Hermeneia; Philadelphia: Fortress Press, 1986), pp. 236ff. On the Deuteronomic influence cf. especially W. Thiel, *Die deuteronomistische Redaktion von Jeremia 1–25* (WMANT 41; Neukirchen-Vluyn: Neukirchener Verlag, 1973), pp. 105ff; A. Graupner, *Auftrag und Geschichte des Propheten Jeremia. Literarische Eigenart, Herkunft und Intention vordeuteronomistischer Prosa im Jeremiabuch* (Biblisch-Theologische Studien 15; Neukirchen-Vluyn: Neukirchener Verlag, 1991); H. Weippert, *Die Prosareden des Jeremiabuches* (BZAW 132; Berlin: de Gruyter, 1973). A confluence of traditions has been suggested by Kaiser, *Isaiah 1–12*, pp. 27-28 for Isa. 1.10-17 (cf. also J. Jensen, *The Use of Tora by Isaiah. His Debate with*

Formally, the psalm is characterized by a structure of prayers followed by stating sentences introduced by *kî*. This corresponds to the structure of Psalm 26. The prayers are found in vv. 2-3a, 9, 11a and probably also v. 12.[11]

2-3a:
To my words—give ear, Yahweh!
consider what I whisper.
Give attention to the sound of my cry,
my King and my God.

9:
Yahweh, lead me in your righteousness! because of my enemies.
Make your way even/straight before me!

11a:
Make them bear their guilt, God!
so they fall from their schemes.
For their abundant crimes—cast them out!

12:
So they may rejoice, all those seeking refuge with you!
for ever they be jubilant!
Screen them! so they can exult in you, those who love your name.

With the first prayer an invocation, and the concluding one expressed in third-person forms related to general motifs of praise, vv. 9 and 11a clearly represent the prayers reflecting the present crisis of the I.[12]

the Wisdom Tradition [CBQMS 3; Washington DC: Catholic Biblical Association of America, 1973]). Reflecting both Sapiential influence and Deuteronomistic theology, the composition as a whole is related to the group of temple singers in the post-exilic period with the function of handing on and increasing the spiritual possession of their people. Such ideas of confluence can also be related to the assertion of Weippert, *Die Prosareden*, pp. 32, 44-45, that a number of the central terms in Jer. 7.1-15 reflects cultic language and especially to W. Beyerlin, *Weisheitlich-kultische Heilsordnung. Studien zum 15.Psalm* (Biblisch-Theologische Studien 9; Neukirchen-Vluyn: Neukirchener Verlag, 1985).

11. The imperfect forms of the stereotyped form v. 12 could have different functions. Because of the context (cf. e.g. Pss. 40.17 and 70.5 with a similar location), it is natural to understand v. 12 in the present position in the subjunctive mode, dependent on the verbs addressed to Yahweh in vv. 11a and 12a; Ridderbos, *Psalmen*, p. 128; Taylor, *Psalms*, p. 39; Rogerson and McKay, *Psalms 1–50*, p. 29; Craigie, *Psalms 1–50*, p. 88. Both as to formal type and to location, the relationship of v. 12 to the context can be compared to Ps. 140.13-14 related to vv. 11-12 (cf. below).

12. Cf. especially Ridderbos, *Psalmen*, p. 128, on vv. 9-12 as 'das eigentliche, das zentrale Gebet'.

The motivating sentences introduced by *kî* are found in vv. 3b-4 in I-forms immediately followed by 5-8, then in the pattern of prayer/ statement in 10, 11b, 13.

3b-4:
For to you do I pray.
Yahweh, in the morning you hear my voice.
In the morning I 'set forth my case' for you
and I keep watch.

5-8:
For you are not a god who delights in guilt.
Not shall the evil sojourn with you.
Not shall the boasters stand in front of your eyes.
You hate all those who do evil.
You shall annihilate those who speak lies.
The man of blood and deceit is abhorred by Yahweh.
But I, due to your abundant grace, can come to your house.
I prostrate myself before your holy temple in fear of you.

10:
For there is nothing firm in his mouth.
Their inner is a void.
An opened grave is their throat, their tongue they make smooth.

11b:
For they have rebelled against you.

13:
For you bless the righteous, Yahweh.
As with a shield you encompass him with favour.[13]

The types of this series of statements are familiar from the texts analysed earlier. Contrasted sentences describe the I (3b-4, 8), the evil (5-7), the enemies of the I as evil (10, 11b) and the righteous (13), all as related to Yahweh. Moreover, as to formal character, the sentences can be related to each other as representing two types: vv. 12-13 as third-person state- ments on the fate of righteous correspond to the sentences of vv. 5-7 on the fate of the evil, the two types of being characterized by qualifying

13.   Verse 13, isolated or together with v. 12, is usually seen as an expression of confidence directly or stylistically reflecting ritual expressions for the divine response to the prayers, e.g. Ridderbos, *Psalmen*, pp. 128, 71-72 cautiously on a 'Nachwirkung des kultischen Rituals'. While the concluding location of vv. 12-13 gives these forms a special function, it is natural for our purposes to stress the relationship of v. 13 to the preceding parallel statements.

nouns. Connected with these statements are the self-descriptions of
vv. 3b-4 and descriptions of the evilness of the I's enemies in vv. 10,
11b, both related to the prayers. The composition of these sentence
types corresponds especially to Psalm 26. Of special significance is the
similar juxtaposition of central prayers (vv. 9ff.) following an elaborated
series of self-qualifications (3b-8). This connection would suggest that
v. 9 is of special significance in Psalm 5.

For the other texts, we have found that such a composition of third-
person statements on the righteous and the evil related to I-forms and
descriptions of 'my enemies' reflects a connection between paradigm
and actualization. Thus, while Psalm 26 lacks the objective statements in
the third person, the ending of Ps. 5.12-13 is especially close to 140.13-
14 (cf. also the negative 36.13 and the positive conclusion of 84.12-13).

The special conclusions of Psalms 5 and 140 could be related to the
indications we have noted earlier of an admonishing function as significant for these texts. The third-person statements as objective confessions
could reflect a similar interest (cf. especially Pss. 31.24-25; 32.10-11;
55.23-24 with corresponding forms and locations connected to explicit
expressions of admonishment). The formal structure of the two psalms
ending with *ṣaddîq*-sayings, connected with the composition of Psalm 84
centred round the beatitudes and ended by v. 13, could even indicate
that such interests have been decisive in the composition of these texts.

In addition, we note a more subtle motif development underlying the
compositional development of the different sentence types, which corresponds to Psalm 26. Connected with the basic temple motifs, the evil are
negatively depicted as 'staying' (5b, 6a), to be 'cast out' (11a), in contrast to the I as 'coming' and as 'guided on the way' (9), while the concluding vv. 12-13 refer to the happy outcome of permanent dwelling in
the temple for the righteous.

2. *The Paradigm (Verses 5-7, 12-13)*

In contrast to the I-forms of Psalms 26 and 27, the paradigm is
expressed in third-person statements in Psalm 5. Verses 12-13 are easily
recognizable as singular expressions of stereotypical sentence structures
which correspond to Ps. 140.13-14 (cf. 84.12 and as a prayer 36.11).
Two basic types are represented, both consisting of three elements. One
nominal element refers to God, the other represented by nouns or participle constructions implies a religious qualification of the human actors
('those who seek refuge', 'those who love your name', with *ṣaddîq* for

a central term). A third element, usually a verb, expresses some act or situation or relationship between the divine and human actors. The sentences in v. 12—rendered as statements—represent one type:

> They rejoice, all those seeking refuge with you.
> For ever they are jubilant.
> They exult in you, those who love your name.

This corresponds to the similar sentences of Ps. 140.14:

> The righteous praise your name.
> The upright dwell in your presence.

These sentences reflect a structure with a given relationship between the three elements:

A. Terms of qualification in singular or plural forms function as subject in the sentence.

B. Verbs refer to a situation of dwelling in the temple (directly as in Ps. 140.14b, usually connected to a situation of praise and thanksgiving, with *śāmaḥ* as a typical word).

C. The verbs are usually connected to expressions for the divine presence ('in Yahweh', 'in your presence' etc.).

This type is represented by a number of constructions in the Psalms.[14]
A second important sentence type is expressed in v. 13 and v. 12a:

> You bless the righteous, Yahweh.
> You encompass him with favour.
> You screen them.

Corresponding sentences are used in Pss. 140.13 and 84.12:

> Yahweh judges the afflicted.
> He (Yahweh) executes justice for the poor.
> Yahweh gives grace and glory,
> no good is withheld for those who walk in sincerity.

And the prayer of Ps. 36.11 shows a corresponding structure:

> Prolong your grace for those who know you!
> your righteousness for the upright of heart.

---

14.   Confined to the Psalms and with *ṣaddîq* for word of reference: 58.11; 64.11; 68.4; 140.14; in addition to singular expressions elaborating aspects of the praise motif 92.13ff. (cf. the corresponding 52.10-11 in I-form), 118.15-16; 52.8-9; 118.19-20 and possibly also 142.8b; in imperative form 32.11; 33.1; 97.12.

In this sentence type the relationship between the three elements consists of:

A. Divine subject.
B. Verbal or nominal form relating the divine subject to
C. Nouns or participle constructions which imply a religious qualification, expressing the human objects of the divine action or attitude.

This type also reflects a traditional structure.[15]

The stereotypical character of these sentences both as to form and to motifs must reflect a traditional background. Their formal characteristics and application indicate that they basically have a function as statements of religious truths. With expressions for the divine grace and religious qualification as fixed elements, their subject matter is the good fate of certain types of people as related to God's special favour.

In Psalm 5 these sentence types are negatively mirrored by contrast statements in vv. 5-7. This corresponds to the relationship between 140.13-14 and v. 12. Both types described above are represented. With human subjects religiously qualified in 5b, 6 and 140.12:

> The evil shall not sojourn with you.
> The boasters shall not stand in front of your eyes.
> The man of tongue shall not stand firm in the land.

Also the basic structure of 36.9 can be related to this type:

> They fall, those who do evil.

With divine subject in 5a, 6b, 7:

> You are not a god who delights in unrighteousness.
> You hate all those who do evil.
> You annihilate those who speak lies.
> Yahweh abhors the man of blood and deceit.

A related construction with evil fate for subject is found in 140.12:

> The man of violence—evil 'shall hunt' him speedily down.

These statements correspond to the positive statements not only with regard to structure, but also to motifs. The sentences with divine subject

15. Also here confined to Psalms and *ṣaddîq*, cf. the nominal constructions 14.5b; 34.16; 37.39; participle constructions 1.6a; 34.21; 37.17b; 146.8b; with finite verbs 5.13; 7.10; 11.5a; 34.20b; 37.33, 40; 55.23 second line.

describe Yahweh in negative and positive relationship to two types of human being. For words like *rāṣôn* and *tā'ab*[16] the cultic connotations of divine acceptance and non-acceptance are obvious, while especially *ḥāpeṣ*[17] and also *śānâ* with Yahweh for subject link to the connotations of *rāṣôn*.[18] Thus, the introductory negative statement in v. 5 on Yahweh as *lô ḥāpeṣ* related to the object of *ræša'* corresponds to the concluding statement, v. 12, relating the divine *rāṣôn* to the *ṣaddîq*. These statements complement each other as descriptions of Yahweh in positive and negative relationship to good and bad humans. Their relationship could even suggest that the application of the contrast statements could be significant for the composition of the psalm as a whole.

The sentences with human subject of vv. 5a, 6a and in 12 refer to motifs of dwelling in the temple, the eternal rejoicing corresponding to 'sojourning' and 'standing' related to Yahweh. Moreover, the motifs of the two sentence types in Psalm 5 correspond, with the idea of admission into and stay in the holy precinct connected with divine examination and acceptance.

Such negative statements, contrasting positive statements, are found in a number of applications.[19] In Wisdom literature contrast of this type is a typical fixture. In the psalms, Psalms 34 and 37 could be regarded as collections of contrast statements representing the two sentence types described above. Psalms 1 and 52 are of special importance in this connection. In Psalm 1, v. 6 represents a typical contrast statement. But in addition, the psalm as a whole is traditionally seen as a composition of contrasting descriptions of the positive and negative type, with regard to qualification and to fate. Psalm 52 can be regarded as another example of a composition of contrast, here with the negative figure addressed as You (vv. 3-7), contrasted by the positive figures of the *ṣaddîqîm* connected with a self-description in I-form (vv. 10ff.). These two psalms

16. Cf. the application of the noun Isa. 1.13 and Jer. 7.10, Weippert, *Die Prosareden*, pp. 42-43.

17. Isa. 1.11.

18. E.g. Gerlemann, *ḥpṣ*, THAT, I, pp. 623ff.; *rṣh*, THAT, II, pp. 810ff., cf. also Gerstenberger, *t'b*, THAT, II, pp. 1051ff.

19. Aside from the repeated contrast sayings of Pss 34 and 37 cf. especially 1.6, 7.10, 11.5 and further 92.13-15 with the antithetical v. 8, and further 32.11 as related to v. 10, 68.4 as related to vv. 2-3, and also 55.23 followed by v. 24, 14.5a and b, 75.11, in addition to the elaborate constructions 112.5-9 related to v. 10, and 146.7-9a related to 9b. In this context 58.11 reflects the contents of an antithetical saying, contracting the plus and minus-fate into one scene.

demonstrate that the literary significance of contrasted paradigms is not limited to the application of certain statements, but can be applied as a conceptual frame for a whole composition. This is also relevant for the more complex compositions of Psalm 5 and also 140.

Psalms 34 and 37 also illustrate the proverbial character of these statements as short and general descriptions of religious laws. In a number of cases, the saying might even represent a traditional statement being cited (cf. especially the introductions in Ps. 140.13-14). The transition from singular to plural forms in Pss. 5.5-7, 12-13 and from Yahweh's being addressed to being mentioned in the third person in v. 7 might reflect such a background, with the present composition representing a compilation of traditional sayings. Alternatively, the individual statement could represent an individual *ad hoc* construction. Even as such, its shape must define it as a statement of a certain character and function as dogmatic expression of a religious truth.[20]

The stereotypical formal character of these statements goes with a marked freedom of individual application. Thus, Ps. 36.11, which reflects the stereotypical structure of the three sentence elements, is presented as a prayer (cf. also the *śmḥ*-sentences in indicative and imperative forms). In the same way, the imperfect forms of Pss. 140.12 and 5.12 as immediately related to preceding prayers, probably should be rendered as subjunctives. On the other hand, the following stating sentences (140.13-14, 5.13) must have repercussions for the function of the preceding sentences, serving both as prayers and as preparing the concluding statements.

Moreover, the application of such truths is not limited to the stereotypical sentence constructions, but can also be used as a conceptual frame for the composition of whole psalms like Psalms 1 and 52 and possibly also prayer psalms like 5 and 140. In addition, the significance and applicability of these concepts are demonstrated by the other expressions of the paradigmatic figure in the texts analysed above. The linkage of this paradigm with concepts of dwelling in the temple connected with categories of admission and divine acceptance relates the

20.   Often applied as conclusion in prayer psalms, such statements are traditionally given a function as statements of 'confidence', connected with the psychological categories of Gunkel's 'Sich-Aufschwingen zu einer festen Gewissheit' or with more objective phenomena of an intermittent oracle response, e.g. Ridderbos, *Psalmen*, pp. 71-72.

statements in Psalm 5 to the literary and religious tradition expressed by Psalms 15 and 24.

These connections are stressed by the simplified motif usage in the paradigmatic statements in Psalm 5. In vv. 5-7, the evil are related to the sanctuary as dwellers also. Centred round motifs of divine favour/disfavour and dwelling in the temple, the righteous and the evil are related to the same goal of 'dwelling before Yahweh'. The confluence of the contrasts into this basic imagery, with the two groups of humanity depicted as competitors for the same goal, could be explained as a rhetorical simplification reflecting the interest of this singular composition. On the other hand, the very fact of contrast statements which describe the contrasted fate of two contrasted types of human being must presuppose a basic connection between the positive and negative fate. Such a constellation would correspond to the contrast of basic terms like *ṣaddîq* and *rāšā'*. With Deut. 25.1ff. as an illustration of the connotations of the terms, their application could imply a constellation of struggle for the same coveted object in front of the judge.[21] In addition, such a confluence of motifs could be implicit in the other texts. It corresponds to the basic contrasts of temple and Sheol/death, death signifying the fate of the evil.

That such a connection is basic is also demonstrated by the relationship of these texts to Psalms 15 and 24 together with Isa. 1.10ff. and Jer. 7.2ff. While Psalm 5 contrasts the negative and positive paradigmatic figures, both as related to dwelling in the temple, Psalms 15 and 24 are given to the description of the positive figures which qualify for the coveted goal of dwelling in the temple. The prophetic texts express a special application of the paradigm, with a special allocation of the main roles: the evil are entering the temple for worship (Isa. 1.12; Jer. 7.2). As entering to see/be seen by the divine face (Isa. 1.12, heightened to a prayer situation, v. 15; cf. the motif correspondence with v. 16), standing themselves before the divine presence in acts of confession and trust (Jer. 7.10)[22], their temple orientation[23] and behaviour correspond to the

21. Cf. also the traditional model of ordeal as basic for the enemy psalms.
22. Cf. also the threefold repetition of *bāṭaḥ*, vv. 4. 8. 14, which we have found to be significant for this type of piety; 'the Temple of Yahweh', v. 4; and *šæqær* vv. 4, 8, 9; Weippert, *Die Prosareden*, pp. 32ff. A negative confession related to 'falsehood' and contrasted by positive exhortations can be compared to the use of *bāṭaḥ* Ps. 62.9ff. (cf. below).
23. This aspect is pronounced in Jer. 7, cf. the preceding note and stressed by

those of the I in Psalm 5 and the other psalms. But as 'evil' (cf. especially Isa. 1.15 and Jer. 7.9 with a strong connection between motifs of evilness and cult acts) their praying with bloody hands and their confession before the divine presence corresponds to the visualization of the evil in Ps. 5.5-7.

While the usual application contrasts two types of religious being as represented by two contrasted groups, the addressed You as evil are the sole actors in the two prophetic texts. On the other hand, the exhortations (Isa. 1.16-17; Jer. 7.3-6)—at least rhetorically—presuppose that the addressed You can change their roles in the drama.[24]

Correspondingly, the addressees are related to two contrasted types of fate. *hišlîk* from the divine face v. 15, juxtaposed to *šākan* in pi'el form vv. 3, 7[25] corresponds to the motif application of Psalm 5. Also the contrast eat/being eaten in Isa. 1.19-20 can be referred to the fundamental contrast of life/death inherent to the motifs of dwelling in the temple and could represent a singular application of the stereotypical meal motif. In this way, these texts could be seen as expressions of important aspects of the complex situation depicted in Psalm 5.

3. *The Actualization of the Paradigm (Verses 3b-8, 10 and 11)*

The negative statements in vv. 5-7 are framed by contrasting I-forms (vv. 3b-4 and 8). This connection corresponds to the immediate

---

Carroll, *Jeremiah*, p. 209, who finds the sermon not to reflect entry requirements for worshippers, but a 'thoroughgoing critique of Jerusalem's cultic ideology'.

24.   That this not is an isolated case of application is demonstrated by Isa. 33.14 relating dwelling in the temple to 'sinners' and 'polluted'. This type of introduction in so stereotyped forms is significant when added to the two independent applications in Isa. 1 and Jer. 7.

25.   The peculiarly tenacious emendations based on the Vulgata (Holladay, *Jeremiah 1*, pp. 236-37) disturbs this contrast. With the Masoretic vocalization, the application of *māqôm* (vv. 3, 7, 14) makes an ambiguous effect (Carroll, *Jeremiah*, p. 209), with a subtle shift from temple to land as the blessed locality of divine relationship. That the categories of dwelling in the temple are open to flexible use is demonstrated by Jer. 22.1ff. Reflecting an application of the motif structure which correspond to 7.1-15 (Reventlow, 'Gattung und Überlieferung in der "Tempelrede Jeremias", Jer 7 und 26', p. 332), the immediate meaning of the locality motifs vv. 2-4 must be connected to associations of the royal palace, extended to land vv. 6-7 and city v. 8. At the same time, the connection of vv. 2-3 would make the message viable by its subtle undertones of temple ideology.

transition from enemy motifs in the prayers of vv. 9-11 to the positive statements in vv. 12-13. With this arrangement of the materials, the I is related to the negative, the enemies to the positive paradigm.[26]

As concluding the introductory prayer in vv. 2-3a and preparing the main prayers of vv. 9ff., the location as well as the main motifs of 3b-8 correspond especially to Ps. 26.3-8 located between vv. 1-2 and 9ff.[27] The formal structure of these statements corresponds as well: vv. 3b-4 qualify the I positively (cf. Ps. 26.3), 5-7 give a contrasting description of the evil (cf. Ps. 26.4-5 in I-form),[28] contrasted by a description of the I in the temple (cf. Ps. 26.6-7). In both cases, the negative statements are introduced by relatively independent I-forms. Ps. 26.3 refers to the repeated statement of the I as walking (vv. 1 and 11), while 5.3b-4 and 5ff. are both introduced by *kî*. The connections of structure and motifs are too obvious to be coincidental, while the individual character of each composition makes a direct relationship of literary dependency improbable. The I-forms in both cases must reflect a traditional background of some given pattern. Ps. 26.3ff. in I-form and the pattern of I-forms and third-person statements in 5.3b, 4ff. must have a similar function in the context.[29]

As composed by I-sentences, the expression of this tradition in Ps. 26.3ff. represents the simpler form. Ps. 5.3b, 4ff. is more complex, with I-sentences related to independent third-person statements on the evil. Thus, while the I of Psalm 26, both in self-qualifications and prayers, is related to the evil in plural form, the composition of Psalm 5 relates the I to the evil mentioned both in singular and plural: aside from 5a with evilness for the central noun of negative qualification, 5b introduces the third-person statements with the evil in singular, followed by plural forms until the singular form of the last third-person statement, v. 7 second line. Contrasted by the I-form of v. 8, the concluding singular form as well as the introductory must have a function of linking the I-forms and the third-person statements. Thus, while the enemies in the

26. For an alternative arrangement cf. Ps. 140, with the I related to the enemies qualified as evil, followed by a gradual transition (vv. 11-12) from prayers into negative (v. 12) and positive (vv. 13-14) statements.

27. Dahood, *Psalms I*, p. 32.

28. Cf. concretely the series of *lô*-sentences followed by a sentence introduced by *šānā* 26.4-5 and 5.5-6.

29. Cf. especially Dahood, *Psalms I*, p. 29 and Croft, *The Identity of the Individual*, p. 90, on these verses as protestations of innocence.

prayer are mentioned in plural (v. 9a), the enemy-qualifications in the prayers have an arrangement of singular and plural forms which correspond to vv. 5ff. Here an introductory—often emended—singular in v. 10 is followed by plural forms in vv. 10 and 11. The absence of a concluding singular form in v. 11 corresponds to the plural forms of the positive statement, v. 12, which contrasts the evil enemies with the blessed rejoicers. The singular form *ṣaddîq* of the concluding statement v. 13 reverts to the frame of singular forms, and must reflect a similar compositional interest. Thus, it both balances the introductory third-person statement (v. 5) and must in this context link to the I-figure.

This meticulous composition underlines the connection of the positive and negative third-person statements with the positive and negative descriptions of the I and the enemies. On the other hand, the different formal background must have repercussions for the function of the different types of statement. In the present composition, the common temple motifs of vv. 5b, 6a and 8 link the I and the evil in a contrasting relationship to the temple. Usually, the two statements are seen as materially identical: the evil are not allowed to enter the sanctuary, the I is allowed to enter. Correspondingly, the I is found to designate himself—at least indirectly—as 'righteous'.[30]

But as an expression of a stereotypical saying, vv. 5-7 has a special connotative function, parallel to vv. 12-13 as a contrast statement. The statements describe the fates of two types of human being under divine favour and disfavour, as rejoicing and not-dwelling in the temple (to the latter contrast cf. Ps. 140.14 related to v. 12). While the I-forms are connected to the negative paradigm, the enemy prayers are connected with the positive vv. 12-13.

Thus, the present relationship between vv. 5-7 and v. 8 must be more subtle.[31] Together with vv. 3b-4, v. 8 is not an expression for the ultimate fate of the I, but must be related to the following prayers. The solution of the crisis depends upon divine intervention.[32] Similarly to the

---

30. E.g. Kraus, *Psalmen*, pp. 39-40; Ruppert, *Der leidende Gerechte*, p. 37.

31. That the motifs of v. 8 cannot be automatically identified with the situation of vv. 12-13 is also illustrated by Ps. 118.19-20, referring to a special entrance for the righteous. Cf. also Jer. 7.2, 3, 5-7, 10 with the normal ritual 'come to prostrate oneself' and 'come and stand oneself' contrasted with a special 'dwelling' reserved for the non-evil, and Isa. 1.12, 19-20 separating between the ritual 'come to see/be seen' and an ultimate goal of 'eating' contrasted with 'being eaten'.

32. This is also illustrated by the tendency to reconcile the tension between v. 8,

parallel 26.3ff., the I-forms contrasted by the negative statements must have a function of self-qualification in preparation of the following prayers. This corresponds to the motifs use.

hištahawâ connected with *bô* refers to temple categories and could simply mean 'go to the temple to take part in the proper rites'.[33] But more pregnant usages suggest that with this meaning the motif has retained its original meaning of 'bowing down', referring both to confession and submission.[34] The prostration as orientated *'æl hêkāl* (Pss. 138.2 and also 28.2) could be significant. In Ezek. 8.16 the apostates demonstrate the utter perversion by their prostration towards the east, their backs *'æl hêkāl*.[35] This scene could represent an elaboration of the connotations of the motif as expression for the right form of worship.[36]

In this context, it is natural to stress the connotations of submission in connection with the act of prayer, due to the connection of vv. 8 and 3b-4. As illustrated by Ps. 28.2, the motifs of vv. 8 and 3b-4 could reflect the one scene of the I as praying. The significance of this situation is underlined by vv. 3b-4 where four parallel sentences describe the act of

presupposed to demonstrate an attained status, and vv. 9ff., orientated towards the decisive future acts, by Ps. 5 understood to refer to preparatory rites.

33.   Jer 7.2; 26.2; Ezek. 46.2, 9; and further Ps. 132.7; Isa. 27.13; 66.23.

34.   On the latter aspect cf. especially Ps. 99.9.

35.   Zimmerli, *Ezechiel 1–24*, p. 221 stresses 'die Verletzung der geordneten Gebetsrichtung' as their real sin.

36.   Cf. the constructions with *lifnê* the right altar in 2 Kgs 18.22, Isa. 36.7, 2 Chron. 32.12 in addition to 2 Chron. 29.6 connected with temple motifs and further also Jer. 2.27, 32.33 on turning the back and not the face towards Yahweh. These applications could allude to a special conceptual background of proper ritual localization. Thus Ps. 5.8 together with 28.2, 138.2 and also 26.6 could be related to Ezek. 8.16, Joel 2.17, and 2 Kgs 18.22 as references to a certain location connected with the altar. Cf. also Beyerlin, *Weisheitlich-kultische Heilsordnung*, pp. 94ff., who links Ps. 15, Ezek. 46.3 and Ps. 118.19-20 to the parallel localizations of 'gate' and 'forecourt' in Jer. 7.2 and 26.2 and relates the pilgrims to the outer temple forecourt and orientated to the gate leading into the inner forecourt with the altar (cf. also Reventlow, 'Gattung und Überlieferung in der "Tempelrede Jeremias", Jer 7 und 26' pp. 326ff., 333). On the other hand, Ezek. 46.2, 3, 9 warns against too simplified models of cultic reality by illustrating that the general expression 'coming to prostrate oneself' could refer to different locations within the temple compound for different classes of people; cf. Hauge, 'On the Sacred Spot. The Concept of the Proper Localization before God', pp. 30-60 and also the suggestions Beyerlin, *Weisheitlich-kultische Heilsordnung*, p. 95 on 'Wenigstens zwei' 'Grenzlinien'.

prayer. Moreover, the description continues the invocation vv. 2-3a with the divine attention related to the parallel 'my words', 'my whispering' and 'the sound of my crying'. And with 'my words' introducing the whole composition, the first part of the psalm puts a marked emphasis on the situation of prayer. The I—in contrast to the paradigmatic evil—of vv. 2-8 describes himself as supplicant.

With v. 8 as part of this imagery, the final motif of I coming 'due to your abundant grace' (cf. especially in the similar context Ps. 26.3) and prostrating himself 'before your holy temple' 'in fear of you' contrasts with the motifs of the evil in vv. 5b, 6a as 'sojourning' and 'standing' as 'boasters' 'in front of your eyes'. The image of the I as humbly prostrated corresponds to the boastful[37] standing,[38] comparably to the execution of the motifs of walking and staying in Psalm 26.

In this way, vv. 3b-8 have a function corresponding to the self-descriptions of Pss. 26.3-8 (and its parallel forms), 27.1-6, 42.2ff., 84.2-4. The application of the negative statements of vv. 5-7 within the self-description can be compared to the motifs of the evil in Ps. 26.3ff., and also to the self-description of Ps. 84.2ff., which is immediately followed by beatitudes in vv. 5ff., and to the special composition of third-person forms in Ps. 36.2-10. Whatever the particular motifs, the I is describing himself as related to Yahweh as confessor, the confession preparing for the prayers. In all cases the relationship to Yahweh is expressed by the I's temple orientation. With this temple orientation also connected to third-person statements (cf. especially Psalms 140, 36, 84 and 5), the confession of the I expresses aspects of the positive paradigm, contrasting with the negative. The renunciation of the example of the evil is especially significant in this psalm which depicts also the evil as related to the temple and 'cast out'.

The application of the enemy descriptions in vv. 10 and 11b is parallel to the I-descriptions, introduced by *kî* and related to the prayers. The

37. *hālal* with its connotations of 'praise' could be related as a contrast to especially the *hitpallel* of the I; cf. also Dahood, *Psalms I*, p. 31 and Craigie, *Psalms 1–50*, p. 84 on the 'pagan overtones' of this motif. The scene of Jer. 7.10 with the complacent self-qualification 'we are delivered!' from the evil standers represents a parallel visualization (cf. also Isa. 1.12 on the entrants as 'trampling'). That the texts reflect traditional expressions can also be seen from the elaboration Isa. 1, with motifs of uncleanliness (vv. 15-17, 18) comparable to the self-qualification Ps. 26.6.

38. Cf. also a similar word-play Ps. 99.9 with the challenge to prostrate for the holy mountain parallel to 'make high' their God.

parallel relationship is stressed by the arrangement in the context, with the I-forms connected with the negative third-person statements, the enemy descriptions with the contrasting vv. 12-13. The motifs of vv. 10, 11b clearly describe the enemies as evil. Especially the motifs of 'deadly' talking in v. 10 correspond to v. 7. Related to such 'smooth-talking[39] graves',[40] the I is evidently exposed to certain death save for the divine intervention. In addition, the pattern of singular and plural forms in the enemy descriptions corresponds to vv. 5-7 (cf. above). Similarly to the I actualizing aspects of the positive paradigm, the enemies are representatives of the evil.

This could also be related to the qualifications used. The I entering the temple 'due to your abundant grace' and the enemies cast out 'due to their abundant crimes' reflect the contrast relationship.[41] Especially, vv. 2-4 puts a peculiar emphasis on the I as 'talking', connected with the prayer situation. Aside from the connection with vv. 5ff., this can be related to the parallel emphasis—expressed by four sentences—in v. 10 on the enemies as deadly talkers.[42] Conversely, this would add to the significance of the I as supplicant as the expression for the positive paradigm.

By these arrangements, the enemy relationship is described within the categories of the paradigm. The text may reflect a relationship in some hypothetical life situation isolated from these categories. But within the textual frame, the significance of the relationship consists in the I and the enemies depicted as contrasted types of religious being in conflict. And with the conflict as an expression of the evilness of the enemies, this is

---

39.   Cf. the similar use of *ḥālaq*, Ps. 55.22 and Prov. 2.16ff. (cf. also Prov. 5.3, 6.24, 7.5, 21) with a parallel contrast between spoken smoothness and inner reality of death. In both cases the description of the evil enemy is connected to general third-person contrast statements (Prov. 2.21-22 and Ps. 55.23 second line, 24a), Prov. 2.20-21 also to positive way motifs with wisdom providing the special guidance. Either as related to the sexual seduction of Prov. 2 or the intimate friend of Ps. 55 or to the devourers of Ps. 5, the imagery obviously draws on stereotyped motifs, motif patterns, and forms.

40.   Connected with 'grave', *hawwôt* could be expected to refer to an imagery of 'gape', 'chasm', 'void', with the enemies as 'devouring' corresponding to Ps. 27.2a, Prov. 1.11-12; cf. Dahood, *Psalms I*, p. 34-35; also A.R. Johnson, *The Cultic Prophet and Israel's Psalmody* (Cardiff: University of Wales Press, 1979), pp. 258-59.

41.   Ridderbos, *Psalmen*, p. 129.

42.   Craigie, *Psalms 1–50*, p. 88, stresses the significance of talk motifs for the characterization of the enemies in this psalm.

part of the paradigmatic description of reality. This is stressed by the
special motifs of the prayers.

4. *The Prayers (Verses 9-11)*

Verses 9-11 correspond to Pss. 27.11-12 and 43.1-4. In the parallel
prayers we find the pattern of address to Yahweh and motivating sentences (cf. 27.12b like 5.10, 11b describing the evilness of the enemies,
while the enemy qualification in 43.1 is directly connected to the
address). In all cases, the prayer consists of two parts (Ps. 27.12-13
without any formal separation). One part is given to the prayer for divine
guidance connected with way motifs, the other for the divine intervention related to the enemies. The two parts are closely linked. This is
expressed by the element 'because of my enemies', v. 9a and 27.11b
attached to the guidance prayer. Even with 'your righteousness' for the
way unto which the I shall be led (cf. Pss. 26.3 and 43.3 connecting the
way with similar divine attributes), the two parts must basically refer to
the same situation.[43] In Psalm 5 this linkage is especially close, with the
main enemy qualification in v. 10 closely connected to the way-prayer.

While the elements of v. 9 and 27.11 obviously represent stereotypical
language with allusive effect, Ps. 43.1ff. provides a frame for the visualization of the connection between the various motifs: under divine guidance the I can be brought from a place where he is delivered into the
hands of his enemies to the temple. But both in Psalms 27 and 5 such a
connection between way and temple motifs is rhetorically 'impossible'.
Due to the prior application of the temple motifs in the self-qualification,
the visualization of the I in the temple has been pre-empted. Instead the
temple relationship as the ultimate goal of the I's prayer is, in Psalm 5,
expressed by the stating third-person forms of vv. 12-13; in Psalm 27 by
the substitute motifs of seeing in the land of life v. 13 (cf. also the similar

---

43. This connection poses no problem when the 'real' crisis is connected to
social-biographical categories of, e.g., judicial or national problems, the results of
divination immediately to be interpreted as expression for the divine will to annihilate
the 'real' problem out in life. But when, e.g. Ridderbos, *Psalmen*, p. 128, on the one
hand recognizes the 'spiritual' contents of the way motifs ('- ist der Weg von Gottes
Satzungen'), on the other hand seems to retain the traditional understanding of the
Enemies, he has difficulties in combining a pious and an obviously 'selfish' prayer:
first the I prays for 'Unterweisung in den Geboten' and only then 'wagt er von
seinen Feinden zu sprechen'!

motif relationship in the self-qualification Ps 26.6 compared to the negative motifs of the prayer, v. 9).

The enemy prayer Ps. 5.11, immediately preceding vv. 12-13, connects to these categories. In parallel imperatives Yahweh is asked to *'āšam* in hiph. form so the enemies *nāpal*, and to *nādah* in hiph. form.

The negative fate described as falling corresponds to the motifs of Pss. 140.5b, 11, 12a; 36.13; 27.2b. It can be related to a contrast motif of standing as with *hityaṣṣeb* (v. 6a), further *qûm* (Pss. 140.11b, 36.13), *kûn* (140.12a), *'āmad* (26.12) and non-*mā'ad* (26.2b). Probably also *rûm* of Ps. 27.5b, 6 reflects the same imagery, in addition to the motif of 'even ground' (Ps. 26.12) and also as one set of connotation of *yšr* linked to way (Pss. 27.11a and 5.9b).

nādah in hiph. form is usually understood as a general term for destruction and annihilation. But the word could have more specific connotations.[44] The other usages indicate that the word is of a referential nature related to local categories and means 'remove from a place'. With Yahweh for subject, the word is used as a technical term for Israel as exiled.[45] So even in this stereotypical application, the verb has retained its meaning of forcible removal from one (preferred) place to another.

With this meaning, the enemy prayers correspond to the special third-person statements in vv. 5b, 6a, with the enemies, 'falling' parallel to the not-standing of the evil, 'being cast out' parallel to the not-sojourning. Such a relationship between stated and requested fate would correspond to the relationship between vv. 5-7 as expression of the negative paradigm and the enemies of the I as actualization of the negative paradigm. Moreover, this correspondence of motif usage would imply that in v. 11 also the enemies are cast out from the divine presence. Such a relationship between *nādah* in hiph. form and a negated *gûr* connected with motifs of divine rejection is given a dramatic illustration in the scene from Lam. 4.15:

44. A more direct relationship to the context is suggested by Delekat, *Asylie*, p. 59 ('In der Fülle ihrer Frevel verstosse sie!') and especially Dahood, *Psalms I*, p. 36, who argues that the word, with *dāhâ* as 'congeners', sometimes signifies to 'thrust into Sheol'. Correspondingly, *nāhâ* of v. 9 is supposed to mean 'lead into Paradise', with references to 23.3, 73.24, 139.24 (pp. 33-34).

45. Deut. 30.1; Jer. 8.3; 16.15; 23.3, 8; 24.9; 27.10, 15; 29.14, 18; 32.37; 46.28; Ezek. 4.13; Dan. 9.7. The exception is Joel 2.20 on Yahweh removing the enemy 'from you' and 'thrusting' them into a 'dry land'.

Go away! Unclean! they shout to them.
Go away! Go away! Don't touch!
For they flee, yes, they stagger.
They say among the peoples:
They shall not sojourn any longer.

Comparably to the evil as 'men of blood' and the contrast of evil and
righteous in Psalm 5, the beings of Lamentations 4 are described as
staggering[46] around, defiled and unclean from the 'blood of the righteous'. In v. 16a they are negatively related to the divine face which
'have scattered (*ḥilleq*) them' and 'shall not look upon them any
longer'. The sentence construction of v. 15bß corresponds to v. 16bß,
connecting the 'not-sojourning' and the divine 'not-looking' similarly to
the 'not-sojourning' and 'not-standing' before the divine eyes (Ps. 5.5b,
6a).

This motif compilation corresponds with that of Ps. 5.5-7, 11, and
depicts in a vivid scene the implications of the motif connection: the 'evil'
shall not sojourn and not stand themselves in front of Yahweh, but shall
fall and be cast out—the casting out connected with relationship to the
divine presence.[47] Such a connection corresponds also to the immediately following contrast forms in vv. 12-13, which depict the contrast
fate of dwelling in the temple and divine favour for the *ṣaddîq*-group.

In v. 11 the 'casting out' is parallel to the divine *'āšam* in hiph. form.
This can be compared to the compilation of statements in Ps. 140.13-14,
where the motifs of dwelling in the temple (v. 14) are parallel to the
divine making of *dîn* and *mišpāṭ* for the favoured group. The motif
composition of the positive judgement related to dwelling in the temple
and contrasted with negative statements on the disfavoured group
(Ps. 140.12-14) corresponds to that of Ps. 5.11-13, with the negative
judgement related to banishment and contrasted with positive sentences
on the fate of the favoured group. The significance of some divine

---

46. *nû'a* can be related to the motif firmly standing, cf. words as *kûn, môṭ, mā'ad,*
dāḥâ, kāšal in these texts in addition to the motif of *mîšôr*. On the other hand, to
Beyerlin, *Weisheitlich-kultische Heilsordnung*, p. 55, the application of *môṭ* Ps. 15.5
is important for the argument for Sapiential background for Ps. 15.

47. That these texts represent individual expressions for a given motif group is
also illustrated by the parallel elaborations of these motifs in Isa. 1.10ff. and Jer. 7.1-
15 (cf. above). For the negative fate as described in Ps. 5, cf. especially the 'hiding of
the divine eyes' (Isa. 1.15 corresponding to Ps. 5.6a, Lam. 4.16), and Yahweh's
'hišlîk from his face' contrasted with *'šākan* for the good fate (Jer. 7.15, 3, 7).

examination in connection with the situation of admission/non-admission to the temple is stressed by Psalm 26, here in connection with the I being brought to Sheol by Yahweh.

In Psalm 5 connotations of death as the contrast fate are alluded to by the motif of falling in v. 11. The function of this motif in the context is seen in the relationship to the motif of standing in v. 6a and the even way of v. 9b. But when we pay attention to the applications of the motif in Pss. 140.11ff., 36.12-13 and also 26.9-10, 'falling' in connection with forced movement and in contrast to dwelling in the temple implies connotations of death and Sheol as the negative locality. Similarly, the I led on the way (v. 9) refers in this context to the opposite movement towards dwelling in the temple. For the I, related to the enemies as described v. 10, death is the negative alternative.

Given this background, we find a relationship between the prayer in v. 11 and the description of the fate of the evil in vv. 5-7. What is stated as lawful fact in vv. 5-7, is asked for in v. 11. The connection between statements and prayer is given by the qualifications of the enemies in vv. 10 and 11: the enemies of the I are truly evil and should have the corresponding fate. In this way, the enemies are representatives of the negative paradigm.

The expression for the I as representative of the positive paradigm is more subtle and indirect. The self-qualifications in vv. 3bff. contrast the I as the humble supplicant with primarily the negative example of the evil. In addition, the way motifs of v. 9 with the I under divine guidance and set on the 'even way' contrast with the negative movement of the enemies as 'cast out' and 'falling'. But motifs of ultimate dwelling in the temple are reserved for the concluding third-person statements in vv. 12-13. This reticence corresponds to the concrete situation of crisis and supplication directed towards the divine judgement. Here as in the other texts, the application of the motif structure presupposes the I as a being outside the sacred state described in v. 12.

5. *Conclusions on the Motif Structure*

a. *The Basic Structure*
Given this background, Psalm 5 represents a meticulous composition: on the one hand remarkably simple due to its internal balance of juxtaposed elements, on the other hand presenting a compilation of complex and richly allusive materials. It is closely connected with the texts analysed above, and is important in linking different phenomena which characterize

single texts or single groups of texts.

This text elaborates motifs which reflect a basic structure of sacred topography. The temple is juxtaposed to an outside. While most of the other texts refer more to outside situations, Psalm 5 is centred round the concept of dwelling in the temple. Thus, in this psalm the evil and the enemies are negatively related to dwelling in the temple. The motifs which implicitly refer to localities outside are related to the temple as the sole relevant locality; the I related to the sacred way, the enemies 'cast out'. While the motif of falling implies connotations of death, the main function of this motif is here linked to the idea of dwelling in the temple and contrasts with standing before the divine eyes.

Secondly, the two localities—here dwelling in the temple and not dwelling in the temple—are linked to two types of human being. This linkage is especially clear in this text due to the use of contrasted third-person statements. The 'righteous', 'those who seek refuge with you', 'those who love your name' (vv. 12-13) are linked with the temple, while those of 'guilt', the 'evil', 'those who boast', 'those who do evil', 'those who speak lies', 'the man of blood and deceit' (vv. 5-7, cf. also vv. 10 and 11b) are linked to an implicit outside of not dwelling.

Thirdly, the linkage of locality and type of human being is connected with categories of fate. Dwelling in the temple represents the ultimate goal within the motif structure; being 'cast out' represents a negative fate. The connotations of death, with Sheol for the contrast locality, stress this aspect.

In addition, this text applies the temple motifs not only as the ultimate fate, but also as the qualification of the I as separate from the evil/the enemies. The application of temple motifs in this volitional mode, corresponds especially to Psalm 26 (cf. also Pss. 84 and 27.1-6). At the same time, the applications of these motifs in these texts clearly distinguish between the I as related to the temple and the special dwelling in the temple as the possible outcome of the divine intervention, reserved for a special group.

Fourthly, the connection of categories of locality, types of human being and their contrasted fates, is linked to the fundamental concept of relationship to Yahweh. The significance of the temple as well as the negative outside is given by the temple being the place of divine dwelling. Admittance into the temple means a special relationship to the divine dweller. In this text, this is expressed by vv. 5-7 (cf. also vv. 12-13) which define the special dwelling in the temple as spatial closeness to

Yahweh, 'sojourning with' and 'standing before the eyes of' Yahweh, over and above the use of verbs which describe an emotional relationship of divine disgust and favour.

Finally, these concepts are linked to the idea of divine decision and intervention. The *'āšam* in hiph. form related to the enemies of v. 11 corresponds negatively to the divine *dîn* and *mišpāṭ* related to the 'afflicted' and the 'poor', Ps. 140.13, and to the more comprehensive *šāpaṭ* as divine examination and testing, Ps. 26.1-2.

Ultimate admission to the temple—in this psalm also the exclusion—depends on divine judgment. And the central terms of *rāšā'* and *šaddîq*, together with the positive and negative qualification of the I and the enemies, must reflect the significance of the divine intervention connected with categories of examination.

In this respect, Psalm 5 is of special importance. This text explicitly links a normal enemy situation to concepts of divine examination in connection with admission into the temple. The latter obviously corresponds to the situation of the I in Psalm 26. The prayers on the enemies of Ps. 5.11 and on the fate of the I in 26.9 (cf. also 36.12-13) reflect a common set of basic concepts: the evil are removed from the temple and/or brought to a negative locality by Yahweh. Psalm 26 links, also, to Psalms 15 and 24. As suggested by Vogt, Psalm 26 must somehow be connected to the situation[48] of these psalms (cf. above). And while Psalm 26 does not contain any explicit references to enemies,[49] Psalm 5 clearly links the enemy situation to the situation of divine examination connected with dwelling in the temple.[50] Immediately following vv. 9-10, the

48.   In our connection, the term 'situation' does not refer to speculations on cultic setting, but to literary categories, with a combination of motifs related to dwelling in the temple and the description of the 'stayer's' qualifications and fate, connected to a religious paradigm. For a carefully considered presentation of the cultic setting of Ps. 15, cf. especially Beyerlin, *Weisheitliche-kultische Heilsordnung*, pp. 90-97. To Beyerlin the textual evidence of Ps. 15 does not point to a 'Kontrol- und auf kein Selektionsverfahren', but to the Sapiential confidence of the addressed as willing and able to accept the teaching (p. 92). Thus, the 'Festkultteilnehmer' are inside the sanctuary, in the outer forecourt, related to the gates leading into the inner forecourt. On the other side, the application of the genre Isa. 33.14 with 'sinners' and 'polluted' related to dwelling in the temple—i.e. a connection parallel to Ps. 5.5ff., 11—makes such a translation of the text into cultic reality rather problematical.

49.   Which results in Vogt's separating the psalm from 'Gebeten Angeklagter', 'Psalm 26', p. 329.

50.   Cf. also the parallel linkage of situations in Isa. 33.14-16 compared to Pss. 15

prayer of v. 11 must have a function similar to, for example that of Pss. 27.12, 36.12, 43.1, 140.2, 5, 9ff. and also mean 'Save me from my enemies!'. Correspondingly, the prayer for guidance in v. 9 is linked to the enemy situation.

In this way, Psalm 5 must reflect a complex situation. The blurring of the imagery by the connections between the different motif groups must reflect the stereotypical and allusive character of the literary expressions of the basic situation.

The connection with Psalm 26 and further Psalms 15, 24 and Isa. 33.14ff. in addition to Isa. 1.10ff. and Jeremiah 7 stresses the serious character of the divine examination for the I. This corresponds to the self-qualifications of Ps. 5.3b-4 and 8 connected to the negative statements vv. 5-7. As in 26.3ff., the I is primarily designated as not-evil, with temple relationship for positive qualification. The relationship to the temple is, in Psalm 5, expressed by the I as humble supplicant, in Psalm 26 by his pure hands. But in both cases, the positive qualifications contrast with the negative qualities of the evil and thus stress the character of the I as not-evil. The traditional character of these two negations is stressed by the applications of Isa. 1.10ff. and Jeremiah 7. The imagery of the evil complacently standing in the temple (Jer. 7.8-10; cf. also Isa. 1.12, and further Ezek. 8.16 on perverted orientation) corresponds to the contrasts of Ps. 5.5-8. And the 'unpure, bloody hands' related to supplication in the temple in Isa. 1.15-16 correspond to the imagery of Ps. 26.6-7.

The I as a contrast to the evil—together with the situation of supplication—demonstrates that the I is an object for divine examination. Compared to the paradigms of the righteous and the evil, the I and his enemies are beings 'in between', their fate dependent on the divine judgment. For the I, this state of 'in between' is expressed by the way and guidance motifs of the prayer. As aspirants to dwelling in the temple, the contenders, one praying for guidance on the way and the others 'cast out', represent opposite movements in relation to the two fundamental localities in the human universe.

This means that these applications of the motif structure could reflect a theological understanding of humanity as representatives of different types or states of being. The righteous and the evil represent the zenith

and 24. While the two psalms have no reference to the evil/enemies, Isa. 33.14 relates the evil to dwelling in the temple while v. 16 describes dwelling in the temple by meal motifs applied in the imagery of the accepted staying in a secure fortress.

and nadir of human being, related to the divine presence in the temple and as 'cast out', with Sheol for the implicit locality. The fate of the I and his enemies is dependent on the divine judgment. But they illustrate the different character of beings 'in between', the I defining himself as not-evil, while the actions of the enemies define them with the qualities of evilness. The applications of the motif structure in Isa. 1.10ff. and Jeremiah 7 (cf. also Isa. 33.14) demonstrate the versatility of the motif structure and the shades of meaning inherent in the motifs. Here, the worshippers coming to the temple are qualified as evil and threatened with the negative fate. And to this transfer of roles is added a possible second transfer, with the admonitions making the transition from evil to 'dweller' possible. Thus, as expressions for stereotypical forms of evilness, the addressees are at least rhetorically supposed to be in a position of possible change. Compared to them, the humble supplicant of Psalm 5 and the purified pilgrim of Psalm 26 represent advanced states of religious being.

b. *The Relationship of Text to Ritual Practice*
These applications of the motif structure permit us to draw some conclusions about the type of language being used. It is natural to relate the motifs in Psalm 5 to a background of ritual practice. Diverse ritual acts could form the basis for the single motifs and motif groups, as, for example, rites of prayer, of purification, of denunciation (also of self-denunciation) by oath or incantation. Also more complex ritual situations might be involved, as in the case of Psalms 15 and 24 traditionally connected to some special entrance ritual of examination or to some exhortatory proclamation connected with entrance into the temple.

The applications of the motif structure in Isa. 1.10-20 and Jer. 7.1-15 stress this connection to some ritual background and also provide a firmer basis for suppositions about original settings for the language involved than the traditional speculations based on the form of Psalms 15 and 24. As we have seen, a number of motifs which describe the ritual acts of the addressees correspond to the language of the I-psalms: the 'You' *bô* to *rā'â* the divine face (Isa. 1.12) or to *hištaḥawâ le* Yahweh (Jer. 7.2) or as parallel to *'āmad lipnê* Yahweh (Jer 7.10). They *šākan* (Jer. 7.3.7) contrasted to the divine *hišlîk* from 'my face' (v. 15), while the positive fate in Isa. 1.19 is described by meal motifs. In Isaiah 1, dwelling in the temple is connected to the 'spreading out of hands' in front of the divine 'eyes' in a situation of prayer and related to motifs of purification (vv. 15-16). In Jeremiah 7, the element *niṣṣalnû*

v. 10 would refer to some situation of confession.

Such terms refer to the central motifs of temple entrance and dwelling. The acts of the addressed You in these texts correspond to those of the I and the righteous in Psalm 5. And in the prophetic texts, these acts clearly refer to the normal ritual behaviour of any worshipper, both entrance and worship undertaken as uncomplicated and habitual acts of right religious behaviour.

Moreover, the confession of the people in Jer. 7.4 is usually understood to refer to temple ideology, reflecting a confession to the religious significance of the temple. Added to by the introductory *bāṭaḥ*, this confession can be compared to the glowing declarations about the temple which seem to function as the main qualification of the I as confessor. Further, the self-description 'we are saved!', v. 10, must refer to categories of crisis, corresponding to the I-psalms.

This suggests a strong connection between the ritual behaviour of the You in the prophetic texts and the I of the Psalms. As in the case of Hezekiah's sickness in 2 Kings 20, the actors of Isa. 1.10ff. and Jer. 7.1ff.—at least prior to the prophetic invectives—must have been in a position to identify with the I-figure, with, for example, Psalm 5 as a fitting text for the prayer ritual suggested by Isa. 1.15.

On the other hand, the application of the motifs of entrance and dwelling are completely different in the two sets of descriptions. To be meaningful, Isa. 1.10ff. and Jer. 7.1ff. obviously envisage some type of unproblematical ritual entrance and dwelling in the temple connected with normal religious behaviour, completely acceptable according to tradition, now suddenly refused by the prophet. And correspondingly, in none of these texts is the ritual character of these acts criticized, nor the ritual qualifications of the addressees to enter the sanctuary questioned. Obviously, the participants have neither undergone nor evaded any kind of entrance examination as proposed in connection with Psalms 15 and 24, nor is the prophet making a personal twist to the ritual. The blessed state in the form of 'dwelling in the land' or 'eating the goodness of the land' is removed from the categories of ritual temple entrance and dwelling and related to the divine intervention. This corresponds to the I-psalms, where the corresponding motif groups refer to miraculous categories, with Yahweh related to those accepted as righteous.

Moreover, it is clearly impossible to translate the motif structure or the specific applications of the motif structure directly into some ritual pattern of the traditional *Sitz im Leben* mode. The versatility and subtlety of the motif structure demonstrated by the application of Psalm 5 compared to especially Psalms 26, 15, 24, and Isa. 33.14ff. together with Isa. 1.10ff. and Jeremiah 7, suggest that the motif pattern primarily is of conceptual and ideological nature, applicable as a religious and interpretative description of human reality.

In this way, the motif structure must presuppose a *background* in normal ritual practice. Similarly, as demonstrated by Isa. 1.10ff. and Jeremiah 7 and also 2 Kings 20 and Isaiah 38, it is *applicable* to such a practice. This suggests some kind of parallelism between religious language and ritual practice. Whatever manifestation represents the original expression, some of the aspects of the relationship between ritual practice and religious language could be expressed by the sociological term of 'symbol' and 'symbol system'. As meaningful, the language refers to the temple institution and the religious-social experiences connected with the normal temple cult, but with the emphasis on the connotations of this experience as relatively independeñt and further developed concepts.

The relative independence of the religious language as related to normal temple cult is stressed by its possible background in some type of special religious practice. Connected with such *milieus* and expressed in stereotypical literary expressions, this type of practice automatically entails categories of rite and cult as relevant.[51] But our fundamental ignorance of ritual development in Israel, seen together with the traditional massive cultic interpretation of the Psalms in connection with speculations as to *Sitz im Leben*, suggest that the terms of rite and cult should be rather cautiously applied at the present stage of research.[52]

51. Cf. the staid opposites 'private' versus 'cultic' phenomena of the Gunkel-Mowinckel controversy, e.g. Mowinckel, *The Psalms II*, pp. 18ff. The tenacity of these categories is demonstrated by the discussion on the setting of Ps. 34 in L.O. Eriksson, *'Come, children, listen to me!' Ps 34 in the Hebrew Bible and in Early Christian Writings* (ConBOT 32; Stockholm: Almqvist & Wiksell, 1991), pp. 82ff. A 'cultic situation' is contrasted to a 'situation of fellowship and community', including 'instruction, even preaching' (p. 88), the latter obviously found to be non-cultic.

52. Possible models could be connected to von Rad's suggestion about different types of temple rituals for different types of person, '"Gerechtigkeit" und "Leben"', p. 239, or to Gerstenberger's ideas about more private rituals taking place outside the temple proper in individual crises of, for example, sickness, with a special ritual personnel and participants proper for the rites in question, *Der bittende Mensch*, p. 142, in addition to the types of setting connected with Wisdom texts, Eriksson, *'Come children'*, pp. 83ff. But also other models must be possible. Thus, the texts

For the character of the religious practice reflected in the I-psalms, the connection between paradigm and biographical experience seems to be significant. This connection is linked to individual acceptance of the paradigm in the form of identification, related to categories of integration and internalization of the paradigm. Centred round ideas of intimate relationship to Yahweh and experience of the divine presence, the character of this practice must have been profoundly 'religious'.

The basic linkage between this practice and the normal ritual behaviour is demonstrated by Isa. 1.10ff. and Jeremiah 7. As applications in You-form, the prophetic texts are parallel to the applications of the I-psalms, immediately presenting the ideals of a religious élite as relevant for all worshippers. On the other hand, they are significant for our understanding of the underlying religious practice. With the addressees identified both with the negative and positive paradigms, the importance of processes of identification and internalization in connection with the paradigm is stressed.

Related to the large number of I-psalms, it is natural to understand the prophetic texts as dependent on the applications of the I-psalms. This secondary character could also be demonstrated by the new criteria of qualification (Isa. 1.16-17; Jer. 7.3-7).[53] The list of virtues makes

relating to the social and religious association of the *mrzh*-institution considerably widen the scope of possible ritual behaviour, H.M. Barstad, *The Religious Polemics of Amos. Studies in the Preaching of Amos 2,7B-8; 4,1-13; 5,1-27; 6,4-7; 8,14* (VTSup 34; Leiden: Brill, 1984), pp. 127-42. To the present author, the ritual life of Beth-Shan during the reign of Sethi I and Ramses II offers an especially intriguing model for the visualization of interconnected types of ritual. According to Patrick McGovern, Department of Oriental Studies, University of Pennsylvania, the archaeological evidence points to three levels of religious activity within one contained community: the official state religion, the cult in the 'Workers' Temple', and finally private cult in the homes (in private communication during the annual meeting of the Norwegian Old Testament Society, Oslo 1991). Nor need these models be mutually exclusive, but could be added to each other: the cult in the temple 'proper' related to interests of state and sub-groupings of official importance could co-exist with other religious strata centred round specific interests of social sub-groupings connected with blood or profession etc. and specific places of meeting in addition to religious activity connected with the interests of the singular 'house'. Moreover, the present composition of Exod. 12 demonstrates the Paschal ritual as a combination of collective gathering and private family/'house' rituals, 1 Sam. 1 that regular pilgrimage to the temple could include non-regulated 'ritual' behaviour connected with rather private interests.

53.	Cf. also the addressed related to dwelling in the 'Land of the Fathers'. This

conspicuous the lack of similar *thora* motifs in the self-qualifications in
the I-psalms. With a corresponding interest dominating Psalms 15, 24,
Isa. 33.14ff. and the definition of the *ṣaddîq* Ezekiel 18 [54] together with
33.1-20 and 3.17-21, the two prophetic texts could reflect a later stage
of application. Related to the I-psalms, these texts point to some need at
some time to combine the religious paradigm with positive requirements,
connected to the religious behaviour of the general population. In our
connection, the text group represented by Psalm 15 is of special interest.
Its stereotypical form together with its emphasis on the significance of
dwelling in the temple must reflect a new and codified understanding of
the qualifications for dwelling in the temple.

In their relationship to Psalm 5, Isa. 1.10ff. and Jeremiah 7 could provide illustrations of this understanding introduced as something new, as
well as of situations which necessitated a new understanding of dwelling
in the temple. These texts would lose their rhetorical effect if they simply
represented watered down expressions of any entrance *thora* genre.[55]
The negative qualifications of the addressed worshippers, together with
the necessity of giving a determinate list of the required qualities, suggests that the addressees are as ignorant of the *Gattung* as of its supposed *Sitz*. But related to the I-psalms, the negative qualifications can
be seen as applications in You-form of the negative qualifications
of the evil. And with the required qualities presented as a series of
exhortations, the prophetic texts could represent a democratized application of the élite religious paradigm. Such a change to popular address
could also be reflected in the shift from dwelling in the temple to relationship to the land as the *summum bonum*.

Against this background, some tentative suggestions on the relationship of the I-psalms to normal cultic practice could be possible. The
religious language of these psalms is based on concepts derived from

reinterpretation of the temple motif corresponds to Exod. 15.13, 17 with the guidance
of the people from Egypt ending in permanent dwelling in the temple.

54. Cf. especially Beyerlin, *Weisheitlich-kultische Heilsordnung*, pp. 47ff.
pointing to some connection between Ps. 15 and Ezek. 18, 22.1-16.

55. Cf. also that Reventlow, 'Gattung und Überlieferung in der "Tempelrede
Jeremias", Jer 7 und 26', pp. 337-38, finds the form of 'Einzugstora' disturbed by
the negative reference to 'words of falsehood' in Jer. 7.4, 8, understood to reflect the
intermixed genre of 'prophetische Scheltrede'. In the context of Ps. 5 and the related
texts, such forms can be seen as immediate applications in You-form of the negative
qualifications of the evil in the motif structure.

normal temple practice and ideology. On the other hand, the development of the concepts reflects a parallel practice connected with an élite
milieu of spiritual experience. Because of the connection between the
basic concepts of the religious language and the ongoing normal cult, it is
possible to suppose constant interaction between the two sets of
practice.[56] Thus, the I-psalms could have been applicable also to prayer
situations connected with ordinary life crises (2 Kings 20 and also 1
Sam. 2.1ff., stressed by the connection between Psalm 5 and the
description of the worshippers in Isa. 1.10ff. and Jeremiah 7). Finally,
Isa. 1.10ff. and Jeremiah 7 could witness a secondary type of application,
with the élite ideals applied critically to the normal cultic behaviour. In
these texts, the application of the religious language is connected with a
reinterpretation of the paradigm, expressed by *thora* motifs in exhortatory form. The lasting influence of this reapplication and reinterpretation
could be illustrated by Psalms 15, 24, Isa. 33.14ff. and by Ezekiel 18
together with 33.1-20, 3.17-21. Such an interest could also be related to
the indications of an exhortatory interest found in some I-psalms.

c. *The I and the Enemies: Internalization of the Conflict*
Psalm 5 adds to our understanding of the use of the enemies motifs in
these psalms. In this text, the enemies are described by two types of
motif in the parallel prayers, vv. 9-10 and 11.

Verses 9-10 link the enemies to the usual type of crisis. The prayer for
guidance is related to the enemy situation. And the following qualification in v. 10 describes the enemies as 'deadly talkers'. This corresponds
to most of the other texts, where some kind of linkage with way motifs
is the most common type of application.[57] Within the categories of
locality, the enemy situation of crisis and divine intervention takes place
on the outside. Consistent with this type of imagery, with the enemies

56. Ps 118.19-21 makes it also possible to link the parallel 'esoteric' practice to
the temple institution, especially seen in connection with the language of the regulations of temple admittance Ezek. 44.1-3; Hauge, 'The City facing Death', pp. 8-9. On
the other hand, the reference to the 'Tents of the Righteous', v. 15, comparable to the
motif 'localities of the Evil', Pss. 26.4-5 and 84.11, shows that also the 'Gates of the
Righteous' could reflect conceptual applications of the gate motif.
57. 27.11-12; 26.4-5 (cf. also 84.11); 140.5-6; and 36.12-13 with a negative way
motif. Also the relationship between Pss. 27.1-3 and 4ff. and between 43.1-2 and 3-4
links the enemy motifs connected with the 'outside' to the motifs of 'coming to the
temple'.

killing or somehow impeding the movement towards the temple, the evil can be depicted as representatives of an alternative locality, contrasting with the relationship to the temple (Pss. 26.4-5, cf. also 84.11).

Compared to this, probably central, type of imagery, Ps. 5.11 introduces a different type of situation. Seen in isolation, v. 11 could be understood simply as a prayer for the death of the enemies, to be 'cast out to the place of falling' (cf. Ps. 140.11-12). But related to the positive contrast statements in vv. 12-13 and to the negative statements of vv. 5-7, v. 11 obviously refers to a more consistent imagery of the enemies cast out from the temple.

This imagery corresponds to the parallel prayer in v. 9. Together, the two prayers contrast two movements relative to the temple: the I led on the way, the enemies cast out of the temple. This consistent imagery implies that the I and the enemies are both contenders for dwelling in the temple. The significance of such imagery is attested to by the elaborations of Isa. 1.10-20 and Jer. 7.1-15 and by the special introduction to the questions in Isa. 33.14. Also the elaborations of the triumph scenes of Pss. 23.5 and 27.5-6 illustrate the literary possibility of placing the enemies in the sanctuary.

From these texts we can at the very least conclude that 'the enemies/ evil in the temple' reflects an established literary theme. The different expressions of this theme make it natural to stress its literary and ideological character. They can hardly reflect historical or cultic reality.

This corresponds to other elaborations of the enemy threat. In Psalms 26 and 84, the evil are depicted as representatives of the alternative locality, while the enemies in 36.12 simply frighten the I away to a place of falling. This is stressed by combinations of motif types similar to that of Ps. 5.9, 11. Thus, in Psalm 42, the enemies as 'taunting' suggest that they people Sheol together with the I, while the prayers of Ps. 43.2 refer to a situation of struggle. In Psalm 26, the evil represent both localities of temptation and are inhabitants of Sheol—the I who has resisted 'togetherness' on his way to the temple risks 'togetherness' in Sheol. And while Ps. 27.1-3 refers to a scene of war from which the I is taken to the temple, v. 11 links the enemy situation to the I related to way and divine guidance. But in vv. 5-6, the scene of triumph is extended to include also the enemies as present in the temple.[58]

These examples demonstrate the free and creative character of motif

---

58. Cf. also 23.5 with the enemies witnessing the sacred meal, while Isa. 33.16 describes a meal in a beleaguered fortress!

elaboration. A stereotypical set of basic motifs is clearly given. But these motifs seem to be of allusive and plastic character, the shape of the motif application moulded according to the needs of the individual composition. This must illustrate that the elaborations of the enemy situation do not have a direct and literal relationship to historical or cultic reality, but are of ideological character.

Thus, for the absurd scene of Ps. 5.11, the prayer should be connected to the basic connotations of the motifs. With temple as contrast to Sheol, the prayer must have a function which corresponds to, for example, Ps. 140.11-12. Parallel to the I's being brought from relationship to temple to Sheol in Ps. 42.5-8 or frightened to Sheol by the enemies in 36.12, the negative movement of death is implored for the enemies. In this way, the imagery represents a natural extension of the conflict into local categories. Especially with stay 'in the land' (Ps. 140.12) or 'in the land of life' (Ps. 27.13; Isa. 38.11) as parallel expressions for the concept of dwelling in the temple, it is natural that the actors are juxtaposed as contenders for dwelling in the temple.

This could also suggest that the imagery of Ps. 5.11 together with vv. 5-7 could be more significant than merely to represent an elaboration comparable to, for example, Pss. 23.5 and 27.5-6. The idea of the I and the enemies locked in struggle for one disputed object corresponds to the relationship suggested by the *ṣaddîq/rāšā'* concepts. Connected to the categories of divine judgment, these concepts could make the imagery of Ps. 5.11 an expression of the character of the conflict.

When we pay attention to the consistent negative qualifications of the enemies as evil in these texts, the conflict as a contest for a common aim seems probable. The general character of these qualifications transcends the confinements of a straightforward enemy situation of mortal threat and links in to a wider frame of meaning. They describe the enemies not only as simply terrible (Ps. 27.2a) or as hostile and mighty (Ps. 27.3a), but as generally 'evil'. This suggests that the conflict not is fully described by the enemies seeking the life of the I, but has wider implications. In Psalm 5 the general character of vv. 5-7 is unnecessary as an isolated motivation for the prayer of v. 11. But in contrast to vv. 12-13 and connected to the self-qualifications in vv. 3-8 and vv. 5-7 as a preparation for the prayers, vv. 9-10, 11 could provide a frame of understanding for the negative qualifications of the other texts.

The possibility of some wider implications is stressed by the parallel self-qualifications of the I. They are linked to the idea of divine

examination and judgment, and imply the same function for the qualifications of the enemies. Conversely, the category of *rāšā'*-hood is
relevant not only for the enemies, but also for the I. This is illustrated by
the prayers of Psalms 26 and 36 (cf. also 42.5-8), where the I is related
to the negative fate of Sheol in contrast to motifs of temple relationship.
Also, the I facing not only the enemies but Yahweh as the ultimate
threat (cf. *in nuce* the parallel descriptions of the past crisis and salvation
in Pss. 118.5, 13, 18 in addition to 26.9 in which Yahweh is the sole
subject of the crisis), the enemy conflict clearly is of a complicated
character. With the I as the central figure in these texts, the evil enemies
represent actualizations of the motifs which are relevant also, possibly
even mainly, for the I.

In this way, the imagery of Ps. 5.11 could reflect significant aspects
of the motif structure, with a type of conflict and role allocation
more subtle than a simple contrast of enemies in external conflict. This
can be related to the motif application of Isa. 1.10-20 and Jer. 7.1-15. In
these texts, the contrast of the central figure and the evil is internalized.
The contrasted roles of the motif structure are both allocated to the
addressed You. This is elaborated by a threefold exposition.

The addressees are related to the temple as enthusiastic worshippers.
In their ritual acts connected to supplication (Isaiah) and confession
(Jeremiah), they perform acts which correspond to those of the self-
descriptions in the psalms—there clearly described as meritorious.

With the divine examiner differentiating between outer ritual behaviour
and real religious contents, the pious worshippers are identified as evil,
deserving the negative fate of death (Isaiah) or 'being cast away'
(Jeremiah). But the ritual actors, denounced as really embodiments of
the role of the evil, are not bound to enact the negative role. The exhortations presuppose that the condemned evil can change their roles and
qualify for the positive fate. In this way, the seemingly fixed roles of the
I-psalms are dissolved by being related to one set of actors who embody
a series of roles. The conflict between different sets of actors is internalized as expressions of inner attitudes and real acts. For the decisive
transition from one role to the other, categories of identification or role
assignment are central. These include both the divine intervention and
human choice/acts. The divine intervention—both as examination and
judgment/execution—clearly is important. This is illustrated by the worshippers qualified as evil and threatened with the negative fate. But the
contrast fate presented in connection with a series of exhortations

demonstrates that mental and psychological categories of a different mind-set and a different way of acting are equally important. The human actualization of the exhortations makes possible the role transition from evil to dweller.

As we have seen, both aspects can be related to the I-story of the psalms. The categories of divine examination and judgment are as decisive for the I, in addition to the character of these texts as prayers and thus totally orientated towards the divine intervention as the central act of the I-story. In the psalms, the I's supplication must effect a series of events similarly open-ended. Related to the divine verdict, the self-qualifications must be of as little real significance as the complacency of the worshippers in Isaiah 1 and Jeremiah 7. Thus, different versions of the I-story imply change of role identification.

In addition, the volitional aspect and categories of religious practice correspond to the I-psalms. With the I as the actualization of the paradigmatic figure, both the positive ideal figure of the righteous and the negative evil refer to categories of identification and internalization. As a figure in between paradigmatic righteousness and paradigmatic evil, the I can actualize the qualities and fate of both paradigms. Related to religious practice, this means inner activities of a mental and emotional nature comparable to the three situations of the addressed You in the two prophetic texts.

This must have consequences for the function and application of the I-psalms. Earlier we found two types of application possible. As a genre, the I-psalm reflects individual experience, with the I-figure as an embodiment of the paradigmatic figure. But there are signs of a secondary application, with a wider group related to the experiences of the I. The relationship seems to have consisted in forms of imitation and identification, with addressees or users related to the religious ideal in the form of a person. This means that the role of 'I' is open for new actualizations (cf. above Chapter 4 and also below to Psalm 62). What can be ascertained within some texts is that the literary situation with the I-figure described in a situation of prayer is extended to comprise a second group of actors who are related to the experience of the I. But given the fact of the textual fixation and transmission of the singular I-experience, it must be possible to suppose further types of application, with the I as a literary device for imitation and identification by some reader or listener.

Applied by the You of Isaiah 1 and Jeremiah 7, Psalm 5 would have at least a threefold function. The enthusiastic and complacent entrants could have identified with the I-figure of Psalm 5. For the denounced You, the psalm would have the function of a threat and an indirect exhortation. For those influenced by the prophetic exhortations, the psalm would have the function of promise and prayer, strengthening the identification with the positive paradigm.

Moreover, with a type of application including both the I-figure and a wider group of applicants, these three forms of application would not be mutually exclusive, but could have been actualized for one situation of usage. Depending on the religious status of the different members of the group and even on the state of the individual member, a series of different types of applications would be actual for the one situation of usage.

This must have consequences for the understanding of the evil enemies in these texts. We have earlier found that the I and the enemies of these texts represent actualizations of the positive and negative paradigms of the righteous and the evil. For the I as confessor, embodying the positive paradigm, this implies processes not only of imitation and identification, but also of repudiation and renunciation. Psalm 5, especially when related to the applications of the motif structure in Isaiah 1 and Jeremiah 7, stresses the significance of the latter, negative aspects. The conflict between the confessor and the evil enemies can be internalized, with the religious subject as a real or imagined actualization of one type and potential actualization of the other type. All three states are a psychological possibility in the inner reality of one group or one individual at the same time.

d. *The Evil in the Temple: Numbers 16, 12, 2 Chronicles 26.16-21*
i. *Numbers 16.* Numbers 16 is a good illustration of the motif structure applied as a series of events and with a relationship of conflict between two groups of actors contending for the same coveted goal of dwelling in the temple. The description of the enemies represents a peculiar collocation of diverse materials. The composition of the disfavoured group is uncertain,[59] while the divine intervention is described as two acts directed against two sets of evil (Num. 16.28-33, 35). The collocation of materials—

59. According to H. Schmid, *Die Gestalt des Mose. Probleme alttestamentlicher Forschung unter Berücksichtigung der Pentateuchkrise* (EdF 237; Darmstadt: Wissenschaftliche Buchgesellschaft, 1986), pp. 97-98, Num. 16 combines a series of traditions on revolts against Moses (Dathan and Abiram) and against Aaron (Korah, the 250 men, the Levites), united first orally and later as written text 'unter dem Gesichtspunkt der Ahndung der Rebellion durch Gott'.

Between Sheol and Temple

so striking that it surely must have been felt also by ancient readers—is usually[60] understood to result from separate traditions of different origin[61] and historical significance for the understanding of the development of Hebrew priesthood[62] and of traditio-historical development.[63]

It is generally accepted that the Korah materials and the juxtaposition of Korah and Aaron is central for the present composition.[64] Within this story, the contention is connected with relationship to Yahweh expressed in local categories as 'nearness'—expressed as *hiqrîb* (Num. 16.5ab, 8, 10 with divine subject, 17, 35 with human subject, as qal 17.5) and localization *lipnê* Yahweh (vv. 7, 16, 17, 35, 17.5) in addition to other terms for priestly function (vv. 9-10). Within the development of the story, a special pregnancy is attached to the contenders' *'āmad lipnê*

60.   Without refusing a composition of materials of different origin, the significance of Num. 16 as a literary creation by an author can be stressed. G. Richter 'Die Einheitlichkeit der Geschichte von der Rotte Korach (Num. 16)' *ZAW* 39 (1921), pp. 128-37, puts the blame for the present confusion in an originally masterful composition on the mistakes of a later 'Abschreiber'; Pedersen, *Israel III–IV*, pp. 283ff., 694-95, qualifies Num. 16–17 as a 'typical ecclesiastical legend' (p. 286), entirely from the post-exilic period, 'longwinded and badly told' (p. 695), but not the result of independent stories mechanically combined by a redactor. When the literary coherence of the present composition is sought, the assertions by Brichto, 'The Worship of the Golden Calf', pp. 1-44 on Exod. 32–34 as a 'Fable' composed by succeeding 'episodes' in a narrative structure are especially relevant.

61.   Cf. especially S. Lehming, 'Versuch zu Num 16', *ZAW* 74 (1962), pp. 291-321, while Aurelius, *Der Fürbitter*, pp. 191-92, rejects a 'pure' traditio-historical approach, understood to imply ch. 16 as the result of one author's compilation of given traditions. Only a literary-critical analysis will suffice, the text a result of 'der Zusammenfügung verschiedener, bereits literarisch fixierter und treu wiedergegebener Quellen'.

62.   E.g. Wanke, *Die Zionstheologie*, pp. 24-25, 27-28; A.H.J. Gunneweg, *Leviten und Priester. Hauptlinien der Traditionsbildung und Geschichte des israelitisch-jüdischen Kultpersonals* (FRLANT 89; Göttingen: Vandenhoeck & Ruprecht, 1965), pp. 171ff.; A. Cody, *A History of Old Testament Priesthood* (AnBib 35; Rome: Pontifical Biblical Institute, 1969), pp. 172-73; Schmid, *Die Gestalt des Mose*, pp. 88ff.

63.   E.g. G.W. Coats, *Rebellion in the Wilderness. The Murmuring Motif in the Wilderness Tradition of the Old Testament* (Nashville: Abingdon Press, 1968), p. 184, on Num. 16 as the traditio-historical 'point of departure of the development of the murmuring tradition'; cf. also Lehming, 'Versuch zu Num 16', p. 302.

64.   E.g. P.J. Budd, *Numbers* (Word Biblical Commentary 5; Waco: Word Books, 1984), p. 184, on Num. 16.1a, 3, 8-11, 16-17, 19-24, 26-27a, 32b, 33b as the contribution of the 'author of Numbers'.

Yahweh (v. 16) or as related to the door of the sanctuary (v. 18; cf. the contrast v. 27b). Connected to the hostile gathering of the people (v. 19), this special place refers both to the contended function as well as to a place of judgment.[65]

Those admitted to 'nearness' represent certain qualities. Here their special character is expressed by the terms of *qādôš* and the divine *bāhar* (v. 3 connected with Yahweh in 'their midst', vv. 5, 7) and the divine *hibdîl* (v. 9). The usurpers are negatively qualified, they 'gather against' Yahweh (v. 11) and 'contemn' him (v. 30) in addition to the qualification of *rešā'îm* (v. 25), *zār* (Num. 17.5), and the term *ht'* (v. 25, 17.3).

It is interesting to note that the relationship of the two groups is not determined by a balanced description of human good[66] and bad qualities. Nearness is dependent on divine intervention. But the usurpers are obviously 'bad' through their own acts of usurped nearness, their negative character revealed and punished through divine intervention.

Aside from this emphasis on the divine action, the story includes what we might term a volitional form of qualification, in the negative form of separation from the evil. Moses and Aaron are told to *bdl* in niph. form (v. 21) and the people are told to *'ālâ* in niph. form (24, 27) and to *sûr* (v. 26) from the condemned. In the context of the I-psalms it is interesting that connected with this type of volitional language, the threat of the evil is described as a relationship to dwelling places (cf. above to Pss. 26 and 84.11). Staying with the evil means death.

The execution of this motif (vv. 19-27) stresses its significance for the story as a whole. The description of the evil, v. 27b—peculiarly graphic within a story told with so few embellishments outside the vital points—leaves a moving impression of doom not only for the active revolters but for 'their wives and their children and their small-trippers'. Prepared by the repeated exhortations (vv. 21, 24, 26) and the statement of v. 27, this scene must be important for the composition. This corresponds to the dramatic description of the terrible punishment, vv. 28-34, and is

---

65. Cf. Delekat, *Asylie*, pp. 207ff., on the significance of the holy rock in the Zion temple as a place of concrete ritual localization, connected with the plea for acceptance of the asylum-seeker and the divine verdict; also Eichhorn, *Gott als Fels*, pp. 83ff.

66. Verse 4 might represent an exception by the much-discussed prostration of Moses (e.g. Budd, *Numbers*, p. 181). Within the present context, his 'falling on his face' can be connected with the immediately preceding accusation of 'self-uplifting', and thus with a function corresponding to Num. 12.3 after the accusation v. 2. Such a contrast can be compared with Ps. 5.6, 8.

emphasized by repetition. It is expressed both as predicted and as stated fact, in addition to a third indirect description by the reaction of terror, v. 34.

Moreover, as mainly connected to Dathan and Abiram (cf. the parallel introductions in vv. 24-25 and 27), this scene should be connected to vv. 12-15. These verses are usually thought to refer to an original protest of 'going up' to the conquest of the land. But the repeated refusal to *'ālâ* (vv. 12, 14) is related to the challenge of v. 12a, which within the present composition refers to the preceding arrangements for ordeal. The scene of vv. 12-15 prepares for the scene of separation, vv. 19-27, where *'ālâ* in niphal is the central term for the people removing themselves from the place of death (vv. 24, 27), contrasting the terrible *yārad* to Sheol (vv. 30, 33).[67] Such a connection is also stressed by the parallel linking of the motif 'going up' and the position of Moses as leader in vv. 12-15 and v. 28 in the context. Thus, vv. 12-15 should be connected to vv. 21ff. as an intimation of the importance of the theme of separation from the evil, preparing the description of revolt and tragedy in v. 27b followed by the terrible climax of retribution.

Compared with the detail of vv. 28-34, the parallel and concluding description of the punishment in v. 35—which after all refers to the central issue for the story as a whole—comes almost as an anti-climax. On the other hand, it is continued in the following stories on the covering of the altar, Aaron as atoning offerer of incense, and the theme of Aaron's rod in ch. 17.

But in our connection, it is important that in both descriptions of retribution, death is the outcome for the disfavoured group. For the positive group, the sign of victory is obviously that their lives are spared as they stand on the sacred place of nearness. But the story of Aaron's rod in ch. 17 demonstrates that also positive aspects might form the literary basis of a parallel story,[68] with the emphasis on the hero of the judgment.

---

67.   This context—within the present composition—provides the basic frame of reference for the understanding of the verb, while the application in hiph. form v. 13a must have an argumentative function dependent on the connotations of the verb: 'We left a good place to "go up" to a bad place!' corresponding with the refusal to 'go up' from their tents.

68.   To G.J. Wenham, 'Aaron's Rod (Numbers 17:16-28)', *ZAW* 93 (1981), pp. 280-81, Num. 17.16-28 is a 'symbolic reenactment of the rebellions—described in Num 16', the first set of traditions showing the status of Aaron in a negative

The contrasts of nearness and death due to divine intervention which dominate the present composition correspond to the I-psalms, with the fate of death juxtaposed to relationship to Yahweh/dwelling in the temple as the outcome of the story. For our purposes, the description in vv. 30-34 is of special interest. Here, the fate of death is graphically described in local categories with the usurpers in a movement of *yārad* from their dwelling-places to Sheol. The contrasting movement of *'ālâ* (vv. 12, 14, 24, 27) is not qualified in the immediate context and could, similar to *bdl* in niph. form (v. 21) and *sûr* (v. 26), simply have the connotations of removing oneself from uncleanness. Thus, the imagery of v. 34 simply implies the 'going up' to have ended 'round' the doomed locality. But within the received composition, the fate of the usurpers is framed by the central issue of ritual 'nearness'. Within this context and subordi- nated to the revolt and test described in vv. 1-7, 16-19, the contrast of 'going down' to Sheol must be related to the dominating scene of proper localization before Yahweh in the sanctuary (cf. the scene of vv. 18-19 continued in v. 35). The proper place must be connected to the challenges of vv. 12, 14b, 24-27 with implications of a special rela- tionship to Moses as the representative of the divine presence (vv. 28-30 and also v. 15).[69] For the usurpers, the fate of being 'swallowed' by the earth or 'eaten' by the sacred fire contrasts with the fate of temple rela- tionship, here by the movement of *'ālâ* related to Moses as 'sent'.[70]

In this way, the story of Numbers 16 can be related to the motif struc- ture of the I-psalms, especially as expressed in the application Psalm 5 with the evil and the righteous contending to dwell in the temple. As to basic motifs, the relationship of the two text types is so close that Numbers 16 could be regarded as an application of the motif structure as a story. For this application, the central motif of dwelling in the temple is expressed in priestly categories of nearness connected to ritual

way, the second a positive demonstration.

69. Cf. also the imagery of the two scenes of the evil standing at the 'opening of their tents' (v. 27b) and the contenders standing at the 'opening of the Tent of Meeting' (vv. 18-19). Within the present context, and given the narrative economy of detail, the two scenes must be connected, as an allusion to connotations of contrasted localities (cf. below).

70. Ps. 52 provides a corresponding imagery, with the evil pulled out from 'his tent' and 'the Land of Life' (v. 7), contrasting the I as tree in the temple (v. 10). A similar motif elaboration can also be found Prov. 2.16-22, with Sheol and land for basic contrasts, both localities related to corresponding ways. To this basic imagery is added the motif of the evil 'house', here as sinking down into Sheol (v. 18).

function. Given the diverse materials of Numbers 16, it is possible to conclude that for the author, the motif structure presented a literary frame of formative and interpretative nature for the theological elaboration of existing traditions.

The special form of Numbers 16 could also be relevant for our understanding of the I-psalms. The categories of priestly nearness are central, as is demonstrated by vv. 1-11, 16ff. This corresponds to the continuation in ch. 17 given to the covering of the altar from the ritual implements of the usurpers; Aaron offering incense in atonement for the sins of the people, and finally the miracle of Aaron's flowering rod. Within such a composition, the application of Num. 16.12-15, 20-34 is peculiar. This is especially the case for vv. 28-34 which disturb the significance of v. 35 as the decisive event in relation to the ordeal of vv. 19-20 and also to ch. 17. In the same way, vv. 20ff. disturb the tension of the confrontation of vv. 19-20, both Aaron and, especially, Moses rushing into other matters.

The inclusion of vv. 12-15 and 20-34 could of course reflect respectful but clumsy intercourse with ancient traditions impossible to disregard, with some well-meant scattering of proper names to give the appearance of literary coherence. On the other hand, both the very fact of inclusion as well as the elaborate, repetitive style of vv. 20-34 could suggest that the verses express an important concern of the author.

This is stressed by the development of similar themes in Num. 17.1-5, 6-15, 16ff. As to motifs and literary coherence, these stories are strongly connected with the fundamental motifs of ch. 16, centred round Aaron in his priestly function as offering incense and as the one chosen for ritual 'nearness'. Given the immediate connection between the Aaron-Korah themes of ch. 16 and the stories of ch. 17, the inclusion of other elements, especially vv. 12-15, 25-34, cannot reflect respectful treatment of original traditions impossible to disregard, but must on the contrary represent a certain interest which formally disturbs this connection.

The two sets of repetitions, vv. 20-27 and 28-34, stress on the one hand the theme of 'separating oneself from the evil', on the other hand the impression of the terror of the doom. The exhortation is related to the doom (v. 21): the addressees shall separate themselves from those doomed. According to vv. 20-21, everyone in the 'congregation' (cf. also *'ēdâ* as the addressee, vv. 24 and 26, *qāhāl*, v. 33, the 'whole of Israel', v. 34) except Moses and Aaron are to be destroyed. Within the context, the destruction announced refers to the ordeal scene of

vv. 18-19 and is described in v. 35. In this way, vv. 20-34 represent an intermission scene, with a description of the frantic efforts of Moses to save as many as possible from destruction (cf. 17.9-10 in relation to vv. 11ff.).

In the intermission scene, the emphasis is changed from the real contenders to the people in between. The repeated exhortations together with the description in v. 27 of what resulted, stress the volitional aspects of this situation, those heeding the instruction moving away, the hard core remaining, standing defiantly in the door. The defiance of the real evil is stressed by the introductory vv. 12-15.

The significance of vv. 20-27 together with vv. 12-15 as expressions of a relatively independent theme of self-separation is also demonstrated by the local categories. While the whole congregation really is present in the situation of ordeal in vv. 18-19 at the sanctuary, the local categories in the intermission scene give the author's concern illustration in the imagery of the bodily movement away from or remaining at the doomed locality of the tents of the evil. This motif elaboration can be seen as a narrative parallel to the motifs of Pss. 26 or 52.3-7.

In this way, the addressees with their subjective reactions to the warning represent the main actors in vv. 12-15, 20-27. As people in between in relation to the aligned contenders of vv. 18-19, their role corresponds to the addressed You of Isa. 1.10ff. and Jeremiah 7. But also the role of Moses is changed accordingly. In the intermission scene he is acting not as contender, but as the caring exhorter. His position as leader is certainly stressed both in vv. 13-15 and 28-30. In both cases his leadership is connected with his challenge to 'go up'. This means that the terrible doom of vv. 31-33 is connected to Moses' function as exhorter, the divine intervention demonstrating that he is truly sent. And the evil here are engulfed not as contenders, but as people in contempt of Yahweh by their refusal with regard to the exhortation.

After this intermission on Moses as exhorter and the people's reaction on his exhortation, v. 35 returns to the fundamental situation of impending doom held in suspension (vv. 18-21), immediately followed by the closely related stories of ch. 17. While the inclusion of 16.12-15, (20-24) 25-34 formally disturbs the compositional frame, the parallel story in 17.6-15 corresponds to the frame.

What characterizes 16.12-15, 20-34 compared to 17.6-15, is its presenting of Moses as the main actor, while the parallel story is centred round Aaron. Secondly, the volitional aspects of acceptance/refusal are stressed in ch. 16, in addition to the emphasis on Moses as the truly sent exhorter. This is connected with a different understanding on how the people are saved or doomed in the two stories. In the priestly narrative, the atonement takes place by the magic application of incense. As soon as the official is in function, the divine striking stops, so that the fate of death or life depends exclusively on priestly efficacy. But in the Moses story, the corresponding fate depends on willingness to heed the warning and the appropriate acts of moving away from the place of the evil. With the emphasis on the refusal and the resulting doom, Numbers 16 as a whole must have a function of admonishment and warning. Dathan and Abiram are illustrations of stiff-necked stupidity causing the destruction of themselves, their wives, their children and even their 'small-steppers'. In such a context and framed by the Moses references, Num. 17.9-10 and 15, the parallel Aaron story of atonement would be connected to this frame of meaning.

This can be connected with what we have found as typical for the religiosity of the I-psalms, centred round volitional categories of identification with the positive/negative paradigm. Together with the applications in Isa. 1.10ff. and Jeremiah 7, Numbers 16 stresses that the process of identification also takes the form of transition from the role of evil to the positive role. The way in which this theological interest is expressed in Numbers 16 even suggests that at some definite time this interest dominated the application of the motif structure. Here, this transition from the negative to the positive state is linked to relationship to Moses as the truly sent.

Moses as the authoritative expression of the religious ideal probably represents a special and late stage of application, seen in relationship to the other texts. But also, this type of application can be related to what we have found as relevant for the genre of I-psalms. The importance of ideological autobiography witnessed by this genre demonstrates the interest in the religious paradigm as represented by human embodiments. The very genre of I-psalm, with the I depicted in a situation of prayer or confession, could reflect the paradigmatic significance of such a figure for the religious address to a wider group. Thus, we have found indications that a function of admonishment could be central for this genre. Together with Jeremiah 7 and Isa. 1.10ff., Numbers 16 represents an interesting application of the motif structure outside the conventional frame of the I-psalm, illustrating aspects of the religiosity and practice behind the stereotypical literary expressions.

Numbers 16 together with the parallel stories Num. 17.6ff. and especially vv. 16ff. has repercussions for our understanding of the different versions of the I-story in the psalms. While ch. 16 is dominated by negative aspects of revolt and usurpation, centred round embodiments of the evil given to doom, Num. 17.16ff. unfolds the positive aspects of the contention with the victorious hero as the central figure. This can be related to the different versions of the motif structure in other texts. The I-psalms represent versions with different emphasis on positive and negative aspects of the motif structure (e.g. Ps. 52 compared to Pss. 23, 26 and 84, and further the different elaborations Isa. 1.10ff., Jer. 7, 1 Kgs 19.3ff., Exod. 33.18ff.). The connection of the fate of the I-figure as primarily related to the evil fate of death (e.g. Pss. 26 and 36) or to the positive categories of dwelling in the temple (e.g. 42-43, 84), can also be illustrated by the relationship between Numbers 16 and 17.

Within Numbers 16, the shifts of emphasis from the heroes of contention to the congregation as related to Moses or to the dwelling-places of the evil, express how different aspects of meaning can be both differently elaborated and also combined as expressions of one story. The unworried adding and subtle changes of different groups and persons as representatives of the negative group in Numbers 16 is especially relevant for the execution of the enemy motifs in the psalms.

The resulting story is so peculiar in its form that it even tempts speculations on the character of the literary language applied. For the coherence of the story, the fundamental juxtaposition of Aaron and Korah is obviously important. But in the development of the story, the evil are on the one hand headlined as one group of rival usurpers, on the other subdivided as localized to a place of contention in front of the sacred tent door, and to a place of refusal in front of the tent door, the latter subdivided into a hard-core group remaining on the place of refusal, and those 'going up' to a place 'around' (16.34).[71] Correspondingly, Moses is partly a ritual rival located to the sacred locality, and is partly (with his function contended) leading the exodus from the locality of the evil. The I-psalms abound in corresponding literary operations connected to the interplay of *parallellismus membrorum*. The results must presuppose some mental fluidity most illogical for modern readers, but obviously conventional for the ancient authors and readers. The elaboration of parallels in Numbers 16–17, with parallel and repeated scenes of conflict

---

71.   Cf. the similar elaboration Ps. 118.15 on the righteous jubilant 'in their tents', while they 'really' should be locally related to the divine presence (vv. 19-20).

and divine intervention, can be compared to the psalm language.[72] Fundamentally, this must be due to a common background of basic motifs and concepts. But the result in Numbers 16–17 is so peculiar that it is even possible to speculate that this type of narrative technique utilizes effects comparable to the conventions of poetic literature.[73]

ii. *Numbers 12.* The received composition[74] of Numbers 12 presents a story closely related to that of Numbers 16. A conflict for religious authority defined by categories of relationship to God, with a hero contrasted with challengers, is decided by divine intervention. Here the special position is not defined as cultic 'nearness', but with a relationship to Yahweh defined in personal categories of being 'spoken to' as prophets (vv. 2 and further 6-8). In v. 8, the special mouth-to-mouth and vision relationship of Moses—here meaningful as contrasted to 'riddles'[75]— is even extended to contemplation of the divine form. Seemingly unnecessary[76] in a context of prophetic function (cf. the connection between

72. In the context of, e.g., Ps 140.11-12, Num. 16.28-34 and 35 as parallel expressions of one event would refer to conventional attitudes of literary discernment! Also the 'unnecessary' repetition of the confirmation of Aaron's status in Num. 17.16ff. would with such a background be a natural expression for a positive parallel. On the other hand, the embellishment of the descent to Sheol must reflect some special concern (cf. below).

73. Cf. the term 'Narrative Poetics', D.L. Christensen, 'Narrative Poetics and the Interpretation of The Book of Jonah', in E.R. Follis (ed.), *Directions in Biblical Hebrew Poetry* (JSOTSup 40; Sheffield: JSOT Press, 1987), pp. 29-48, applied in connection with a metrical analysis of Jonah as consisting of both 'narrative and lyric poetry' (p. 30), and also Brichto, 'The Worship of the Golden Calf', pp. 1-44.

74. According to G.W. Coats, 'Humility and Honor: A Moses Legend in Numbers 12', in D.J.A. Clines, D.M. Gunn and A.J. Hauser (eds.), *Art and Meaning: Rhetoric in Biblical Literature* (JSOTSup 19; Sheffield: JSOT Press, 1982), p. 97 a 'prime example of literary and traditio-historical disunity' for past interpreters, related to three stages of growth: a Miriam story connected with the Cushite woman tradition, a second stage characterized by Aaron as culprit together with Miriam and a conflict for authority of mediation, a third stage centred round Moses and his unique position. For an illustration of the traditio-historical complexities concerned see, for example, Schmid, *Die Gestalt des Mose*, pp. 89-95.

75. Cf. the discussion J.S. Kselman, 'A Note on Numbers XII 6-8', *VT* 26 (1976), pp. 500-505 on *mar'â*, v. 8a, concluding that vv. 6-8 is 'archaic poetry preserved by J' (p. 504).

76. And a later addition according to M. Noth, *Numbers: A Commentary* (OTL; London: SCM Press, 1966), p. 96.

vv. 2, 6b and 8aα), this description corresponds to the categories of dwelling in the temple (e.g. Pss. 17.15, 27.4).

The enemy situation of vv. 1-2, 8b is comparable to Num. 16.1-3 and the motifs of evil talking in the I-psalms. But here the slandering takes place in secret and is revealed by Yahweh. The contrasted qualification of Moses in v. 3 is a peculiar element in the context, introducing a secondary level of comment in relation to the narrative.[77] Located immediately after the enemy description and qualifying Moses as 'meek', it corresponds to the similarly contested element in Num. 16.4. It can also be compared to the application of self-qualifications in the psalms, as, for example, Ps. 5.8 related to vv. 5-7. And corresponding to the function of the self-qualifications in the psalms which motivate the prayed-for divine intervention (e.g. Ps. 5.8 related to 9ff.), the qualification of Moses is followed by Yahweh's intervention in vv. 4ff.[78]

Within the development of the story, the negative aspects of punishment are stressed (cf. vv. 11ff.). This corresponds to the application of Numbers 16 and also to those I-psalms centred round the destruction of the enemies as the decisive event (e.g. 140), while positive aspects of acceptance and dwelling in the temple are expressed more indirectly. But introduced by vv. 4-5, the divine description of Moses in vv. 6-8 must be seen as an expression of the positive aspects of the intervention related to the victor of the conflict, corresponding to Num. 17.16ff. and especially 16.28ff.[79]

77. A later addition which disrupts the close connection between vv. 2b and 4 according to Noth, *Numbers*, p. 95. But to Coats, 'Humility and Honor', p. 99, v. 3 is now the centre of the unit. The old narrative tradition about a rebellion against Moses has been transformed into a 'legend' which focuses on the virtues of Moses.

78. This would correspond well to Schildenberger's argument on 'Moses als Idealgestalt eines Armen Jahwes', *À la rencontre de Dieu. Memorial Albert Gelin*, pp. 71-72 (cited by Coats, 'Humility and Honor', p. 106 note 10). To Coats (pp. 100ff.) the qualification of Moses as 'meek' conflicts with vv. 6-8, especially the qualification of Moses as the responsible servant in v. 7. The word here has the connotations of honor and integrity and is translated as 'honorable' (cf. also in *Moses*, pp. 127-28), while Schmid, *Die Gestalt des Mose*, p. 73 relates the two descriptions to their different contexts of meaning.

79. Within a traditio-historical context, vv. 6-8 disrupt the thematic development of rebellion. Thus, to Coats, 'Humility and Honor', pp. 99ff., the interest in the special qualities of Moses, vv. 3, 6-8 represents the transformation of the old tradition into legend. It is possible that the special Moses-elements both in Num. 17–18 and 12 represent younger elaborations of given materials (cf. above). But with a

Thus, within this story, the divine glorification of Moses' virtues in vv. 6-8 is addressed to the usurpers (vv. 5b, 8b, cf. also in v. 6aα).[80] Within such a frame, and immediately followed by the punishment (vv. 9-10), the vindication of Moses motivates the punishment. Such a connection corresponds to the intercession scene in Numbers 16, where the punishment of descent into Sheol demonstrates the position of Moses as truly sent (vv. 28-31; cf. also 12-15). The composition of the two stories must reflect a parallel concern for the understanding of Moses as embodiment of the religious hero.[81]

In vv. 11ff. the clear connection with the enemy situation is changed. The juxtaposition of righteous and guilty is dissolved, by the victor interceding on behalf of the defeated. This corresponds to the elaboration of the motifs in Numbers 16. In Numbers 16 the scene of intercession took place as an intermission. Here it represents an additional event, added to the completed intervention scene. Yahweh has left and the cloud moved away. In both cases the immediate structure of events which corresponds to the story in the I-psalms is extended. And also, in both texts, the enemy group is broken up by juxtaposition of really evil and figures in between. Here Aaron is the repentant sinner,[82] interceding on behalf

---

background in a motif structure connected to conflict between enemies and divine intervention, both negative and positive aspects are included and form a connotative background for the literary application centred round one set of aspects. On such a background, a formally disturbing elaboration which, for example, dwells upon the positive qualities of the hero within a context given to the fate of the evil is a natural exposition of the significance of the story.

80.   This also implies that Moses may rest undisturbed in his 'meekness', cf. the dangers of 'public celebration of deeds or character' according to Coats, 'Humility and Honor', p. 102.

81.   Cf. also Coats, 'Humility and Honor', p. 105 on the Moses function as intercessor in Num. 12, traditionally related to the prophetic or the royal function. A third source is proposed, 'a pattern for depicting particular leadership figures that is not limited to one institution', derived from folklore and described as 'heroic', cf. also in *Moses*, pp. 155ff. Aside from the arguments of the present study linking these texts and I-psalms, the model of Eichhorn in *Gott als Fels* on a number of I-psalms as 'Gebet des Mittlers' is of particular interest for the Moses tradition. On the other side, it is obvious that the function of Moses in Num. 12 is defined as related to the categories of the prophetic function, corresponding to the application of Num. 16–17 with the motif structure mainly in priestly categories.

82.   According to Aurelius, *Der Fürbitter Israels*, pp. 148, Exod. 9.27-33, 10.16-19 and Num. 12.13 relate the intercession of Moses to a preceding confession of sins.

of Miriam. Aaron's plea is addressed to Moses, so that the real intercession related to Yahweh depends on Moses. Such a concentration on the
Moses figure corresponds to the intercession scene in Numbers 16.

In Numbers 12 the intercession is effective also with regard to the
really evil. But the normal pattern of retribution is upheld, here by the
application of local categories, with Miriam shut up outside the camp.
Within the motif development, the contended position of close relationship to Yahweh is contrasted by the confinement on the 'outside'.

iii. *2 Chronicles 26.16ff.* 2 Chron. 26.16ff. can be related both to
Numbers 12 and 16. The punishment of leprosy and the concluding
spatial confinement on the outside corresponds to Numbers 12, while
the usurpation of priestly prerogatives of incense offering corresponds to
Numbers 16. On the other hand, in the Chronicles story, the local categories are more immediate with the priestly function connected to the
temple, contrasted with the house of confinement.

The introductory description v. 16a qualifies the king as 'evil'—with
his 'high heart' linked to his usurping entering of the temple to perform
rites reserved for the qualified (vv. 16b, 18). The king is confronted by
the positive group who similarly to Num. 12.3 and 16.4 are given
a positive qualification corresponding to the situation of contention
(v. 17b). Also here, the confrontation of the human actors is decided by
the divine intervention.

In this way, the story can be seen as a rather direct application of the
basic motif structure centred round the negative aspects of the evil for
main figure. With the connection to temple motifs, the story can be seen
as a parallel in narrative form to the events of Psalm 5 with the evil cast
out of the sanctuary.

The qualification of the place of confinement as 'house of freedom'
could allude more directly to the connotations of stay on the outside
relative to dwelling in the temple. *bêṯ haḥŏpšîṯ/haḥŏpšûṯ* in 2 Kgs 15.5
and 2 Chron. 26.21 has been linked to the Ugaritic *bt ḥptṯ* related to the
underworld and translated as 'charnel house'.[83] Isolated to the term in
the Kings version, the connection to a possible Ugaritic parallel term
could refer to different connotations.[84] But in the Chronicles version the

---

83. W. Watson, 'Archaic Elements in the Language of Chronicles', *Bib* 53
(1972), p. 193; further J.A. Soggin, 'Tod und Auferstehung des leidenden
Gottesknechtes', *ZAW* 87 (1975), p. 352.

84. T. Willi, 'Die Freiheit Israels. Philologische Notizen zu den Wurzeln *ḥpš*, *'zb*

significance of the term 'house of freedom' has been added to by its contrast to the 'house of Yahweh' from which the king was 'cut off'. The compilation of the rare words *ḥŏpšût* and *niḡzar* contrasted to temple could correspond to the motif usage of Ps. 88.6 where the I in Sheol is described as 'free among the dead' and like those whom Yahweh does not 'remember, they are cut off from your hand'.[85] The emotive function of these terms is stressed by the frame of references to the king's death (vv. 21aα, 23a), the king living 'cut off' like the dead until his death.

With this literary application related to the older tradition in 2 Kgs 15.5, it is also a good illustration of how the motif structure can be applied to given materials. By subtle additions, biographical references are connected to a conceptual frame of religious implications. The biography is enlarged and retouched into a paradigm of the evil, a warning valid for everyone. The relationship of the Chronicles version to the older tradition is the more interesting as Numbers 12 and 16 must also be the result of similar processes of theological adaptation. Together these stories illustrate the potential range of motifs applicable for the composers, and the corresponding flexibility of the basic motif structure as providing religious depth to diverse materials.

The relationships between the three versions are especially interesting with regard to the I-psalms as usually related to different social or institutional settings. The three stories must reflect a common motif structure. In particular Numbers 16–17 and 12, centred round a parallel situation of conflict related to 'nearness' and religious authority, with Moses and Aaron as actors in both stories, must have a rather close literary or traditio-historical relationship. Given this background, the change from a conflict described in priestly to prophetic categories is remarkable. What is common to these stories evidently transcends the usual criteria of institution and is applicable as a theological frame of interpretation for diverse types of religious behaviour.

und *drr*', in H. Donner, R. Hanhart and R. Smend (eds.), *Beiträge zur alttestament- lichen Theologie. Festschrift für Walther Zimmerli zum 70. Geburtstag* (Göttingen: Vandenhoeck & Ruprecht, 1977), p. 536, stresses positive aspects of a 'Haus des Ruhestandes', while W. Rudolph, 'Ussias "Haus der Freiheit"', *ZAW* 89 (1977), p. 418, understands the expression as an euphemism for 'Isolierhaus'.

85. Cf. also the use of *niḡzar*, Isa. 53.8 and Lam. 3.54; Soggin, 'Tod und Auferstehung', p. 352.

iv. *Conclusions: the evil as religious hero.* These stories are centred round the negative aspects of the motif structure, depicting the evil as usurpers. But the varied inclusion of positive contrast figures—with Moses and Aaron in Numbers 16–17 as the most active contenders in a situation of confrontation, the Moses of Numbers 12 passively slandered and not included in the situation of divine intervention, the priests of 2 Chronicles 26 trying to stop the usurper and divinely helped—illustrates the more comprehensive background of connotations. The interest of the exposition also results in different expressions for the happy end of the story. It obviously can be satisfactorily expressed in purely negative terms as the 'destruction of the evil'. But included in the destruction or elaborated within different types of exposition, the positive aspects of some kind of victory for the hero can be expressed. This corresponds to the different expositions of the motif structure in the I-psalms.

In this connection, it is interesting to note the different expressions for the contended aim. In the I-psalms, it has been convenient to use the label 'dwelling in the temple' for a comprehensive aim. 2 Chron. 26.16ff. is an expression of the significance of local categories. But both Numbers 12 and 16—the latter obviously closely connected to temple categories—link the contention to what we have found as a central aspect of dwelling in the temple, namely personal categories of intimate relationship to Yahweh. The expositions of this relationship into categories of priestly and prophetic function in the two stories underline the significance of the concept of a basic special relationship to Yahweh as it is expressed in the I-psalms. On the other hand, these two stories are interesting illustrations of the connection between the special relationship to Yahweh and local categories of dwelling in the temple and contrast locality.

Finally, these stories illustrate the religious significance of the figure of the evil/enemy. In the I-psalms, we have found many indications that the transference of the religious paradigm into biographical reality implies the dissolution of the seemingly stark contrast between positive and negative figures in, for example, Psalm 140. The applications of Isa. 1.10ff. and Jeremiah 7 are expressions of such an interest. The expositions of the motif of the evil enemy in the compositions of Numbers 16 and 12 stress the admonishing function of this motif.

In this way, Numbers 16–17, 12 and 2 Chron. 26.16ff. can be seen as parallel applications of the motif structure centred round aspects here labelled thematically as 'the evil in the temple'. A number of texts could further be related to these stories. It has been proposed[86] that the Chronicles version has been influenced by the description of Isaiah's temple vision in Isa. 6.1ff. The argument is based on the reference to the book of Isaiah in 2 Chron. 26.22 and on the element *niḏmêtî* in Isa 6.5 understood similarly to Isa. 14.14 and Ezek. 32.2 to refer the usurper's self-comparison with God. The central theme of *hubris* is related both to the royal usurpation of Isaiah 14 and to the Eden myth in Genesis 2–3, Job 15.8 and Jer. 23.18. Other elements of the Chronicles story are traced to Lev. 10.1ff. and 1 Kgs 12.33, 13.1ff., the story itself understood as *eine eklektische Erzählung* compiled of elements from different biblical stories.[87]

In a context of 'the evil in the temple', Zeron's ideas on the relevance of the Eden tradition and the royal usurpation of Isaiah 14 are of special interest. Ezek. 28.12-19 connects the fate of the usurper to local categories based on the contrasts of stay on the holy mountain (vv. 13-15) being 'defiled' from the mountain and 'thrown down on the earth' (vv. 16-17). Similarly to the parallel descriptions of punishment in Numbers 16, the negative fate of being 'on the earth' is extended to a fate of destruction by fire (v. 18).[88] This corresponds to the introductory address in vv. 2-10, with a local contrast of stay in the divine dwelling 'in the heart of the seas' (v. 2) contrasted to being 'made to go down' to the grave to die 'in the heart of the seas' (v. 8). Parallel to the contrast of divine dwelling/grave, here the fate of the usurper is described by more obvious motifs of death (vv. 9-10 in addition to 8b).

In Isa. 14.4-20 the usurper is described by categories of movement between contrasted localities. Different motif groups are used as parallel expressions for the basic structure. Here the usurpation is described as a movement of *'ālâ* up to 'heaven' to *yāšab* on the 'divine mountain' (vv. 13-14), in contrast to the movement of *yāraḏ* to Sheol (v. 15 in addition to v. 11). In addition, v. 12 connects the imagery of 'falling from heaven' to the king as 'hewn down to earth', corresponding to the fall from Eden-mountain to earth in Ezekiel 28. And in v. 8, the king as

---

86. A. Zeron, 'Die Anmassung des Königs Usias im Lichte von Jesajas Berufung. Zu 2.Chr. 26,16-22 und Jes. 6,1ff', *TZ* 33 (1977), pp. 65-68.

87. 'Die Anmassung', p. 68.

88. Often understood as secondary additions, e.g., W. Zimmerli, *Ezekiel 2. A Commentary on the Book of the Prophet Ezekiel, Ch 25–48* (Hermeneia; Philadelphia: Fortress Press, 1983), pp. 94-95, the seemingly different motif groups can be seen as parallel expressions for connotations of the basic concept.

'lying down' contrasts his former *'ālâ* as hewer up to the cedars of Lebanon. Finally, the fate of the king as dead is described by motifs of burial (vv. 18-20).

The connotative wealth of the basic motifs and the possibility for individual literary expression suggested by the motif exposition in Ezek. 28.2-19 and Isa. 14.4-20 is stressed by the application of the Eden theme in Genesis 2–3. The connection to the local structure of Ezekiel 28 is easily recognizable, with the 'usurper' related to Eden and a contrast stay on the outside, qualified as no relationship to the tree of life (Gen. 3.22, 24) and relationship to *'adāmâ* (v. 23 in addition to vv. 17-19)[89] / death (v. 19 in addition to Gen. 2.17, 3.3ff.).

The subtle literary elaboration of this structure in Genesis 2–3 is continued in ch. 4 with the contention of the brothers for divine recognition. The connection to the basic motifs is illustrated by Cain leaving 'from before Yahweh' (cf. also v. 14 on Cain hiding himself from the divine face) to stay (*yāšab*) in the land of 'moving' 'east of Eden' (v. 16).[90] At the same time the description of the negative place in vv. 12, 14 continues the motif exposition of chs. 2–3. While the negative fate for Adam consisted in relationship to *'adāmâ* (Gen. 3.23), such a relationship now represents the positive fate, contrasted to a fate as 'out-cast' into 'tottering and moving', connected to a permanent threat of death.

In this way, a set of basic motifs centred round local categories of sacred topography indicates a fundamental connection between these stories, both as related to each other and to the motif structure of the I-psalms. In these stories, dwelling in the temple and the main figure described in movement relative to dwelling in the temple serve for an ideological interpretation of human reality. The character of the evil is described as usurpation linked to local categories. Even in the Cain story where divine acceptance is the object of contention, the interpretative frame links the story to basic localities. The flexibility of application is striking. The usurper king can be localized to the sacred mountain to be

89. On the significance of the 'ground' motif, cf. especially A.J. Hauser, 'Genesis 2–3: The Theme of Intimacy and Alienation', in Clines, Gunn and Hauser (eds.), *Art and Meaning*, p. 21.

90. Related to a basic concept of 'dwelling in the temple', the parallel relationship of the motifs is natural; cf. on the other side the discussion C. Westermann, *Genesis 1–11* (BKAT 1.1; Neukirchen-Vluyn: Neukirchener Verlag, 1974), pp. 421-22, on the connection between 'Verbannung aus diesem Lebensraum' and the removal from the divine face as removal from the divine wrath.

cast out due to his usurpation, or the usurpation is depicted as a movement of *'ālâ* towards the coveted locality, in addition to the submotifs
which qualify the central motifs within the single text. In both cases, the
story of the main figure mirrors the story of the I in the psalms linked to
motifs of way or aspiration and dwelling in the temple. The basic events
of the motif structure characterize both the evil and the religious hero.

The present composition of Numbers 16–17 is especially important as
an illustration of the connection between the different individual applications. The narrative line of ch. 16 is linked to a scene of conflict centred
round the evil actors. And the story of Aaron's election in Numbers 17
demonstrates that this story is mirrored by a story centred round the
positive hero. In the same way, the added elaborations within ch. 16
suggest other connotations. Parallel to the evil usurpers standing on the
usurped spot of 'nearness', the evil refusing to 'go up' are localized to
their 'tents' as the anti-locality. In this subordinate scene, the group of
evil is dissolved into really evil and a group which heeds the warning of
Moses and separates from the negative locality and from Sheol.

Numbers 16–17 demonstrates the richness of connotations interwoven
within one composition. When one literary composition can bear such a
connotative load within the narrative development, it is easier to recog-
nize the essential connection between the other stories. Thus, for example,
Genesis 2–3 and Ezekiel 28 or Numbers 16 and 2 Chron. 26.16ff. are
on the one hand independent literary expressions, on the other hand
parallel versions of given traditions, and could be related as parallel
expressions for different connotations within one story of usurpation.
While Genesis 2–3 is continued by the conflict story in ch. 4,[91] and the
two versions of royal usurpation Ezekiel 28 and Isaiah 14 are immediately recognized as somehow[92] connected, the pattern of connotative
interrelationship demonstrated by Numbers 16 is transferable to the
other texts.

What may be most important for the understanding of the I-psalms is
the treatment of the evil/enemy motifs. A number of these texts describe
the figure of the evil within the same stark categories of evilness as the
normal I-psalm. But with the evil motifs of, for example, Isa. 1.10ff. and
Jeremiah 7 related to Psalm 5, the elaboration of the evil figure within

---

91. E.g. Westermann, *Genesis 1–11*, pp. 389-90.
92. E.g. Clifford, *The Cosmic Mountain*, p. 162, on Gen. 2–3, Ezek. 28 and
Isa. 14 representing some of the 'fragmentary references in Ugaritic and the Hebrew
Bible to the revolt in the heavens'.

Numbers 16, 12 and especially Genesis 2–4 is of special significance. Thus, Adam evidently represents the evil hero 'cast out', corresponding to the usurper of Ezekiel 28. On the other hand, as the father of mankind, he is a figure in between, siring both the evil killer and the innocent victim and a new beginning represented by Shem. The significance of this elaboration of the evil figure is deepened by the further development of the basic motifs in the patriarch biographies. Centred round situations of fraternal conflict and the local categories of relationship to the land/dwelling in exile in addition to relationship to the father, the motifs are developed into the final emotive scene of the contending brothers united in Egypt to be blessed by the dying father and to wait for liberation.[93]

Such an elaboration of the evil figure could of course be the result of some major reinterpretation of the religious concepts involved (cf. above to Isa. 1.10ff. and Jeremiah 7 and also to Numbers 16). But even so, it should be noted that the present composition of Genesis represents a parallel emphasis on the significance of the loser and the victor of the fraternal conflict. On the one hand, the composition prepares for the concluding reconciliation in Egypt. On the other hand, the description of the fate of the victor in the single biography both seen for itself and as a preparation for the Moses biography is decisive for the exposition. The subtlety of the composition and the vivid detail of each description of conflict in each biography demonstrates the theological importance attached both to the presence of the *ṣaddîq* as well as to the evil figure as religious hero. For the I-psalms, we have found both these categories relevant for the I-figure as a being in between.

The narrative and prophetic texts also strengthen the impression of the ideological function of the motif structure in the psalms. The basic motifs serve for an interpretative frame, giving a religious definition of states and stages of human being. This is the more interesting as at least some of these narrative and prophetic texts represent compilations of different types of given traditions, reshaped in the present compositions (cf. especially within Numbers 16–17 and 2 Chron. 26.16ff. related to 2 Kgs 15.5). For this reshaping, the basic motifs seems to provide a structural and connotative frame of a religious nature. The structural aspect is mainly expressed through local categories, the main figure

---

93. Hauge, 'The Struggles of the Blessed'.

described within a conceptual space of dwelling and movement in relationship to localities.

The connection to the motif structure of the I-psalms could deepen our understanding of the connotative frame of religious feeling inherent in these narrative and prophetic texts. The I-figure seems to reflect a tradition of religious practice connected with categories of inner integration of the religious ideal related to biographical experience and centred round 'sensory' experience of the divine presence. Such a background could provide an interesting angle for the understanding of the connotative impact of these texts as not confined to problems of purely priestly or prophetic or royal categories. As actualizations of the paradigmatic figures, the heroes of the single text would have the function of mirrors for the religious practice of everyone and applicable as paradigmatic illustrations with, for example, a didactic or exhortative function. And Genesis 2–3, given to a theme of acquisition of divine wisdom/ divine life, and ch. 4 to a theme of acquisition of divine acceptance, might even be comparable to Exod. 33.18ff. and 1 Kings 19 as critical evaluations of religious practice and experience.

e. *Temple and Anti-Temple: Exodus 32*
i. *Exodus 32 in the context.* So far, it seems possible to see a structure of basic motifs most easily recognized as reflections of some sacred topography, with temple and Sheol for contrast localities. A number of parallel or sub-motifs represent the concepts. Land of living, land, mythic mountain or garden, or the priestly localization of nearness, in addition to personal categories of a relationship before the divinity or the divine face or of a special experience of the divine presence, contrast with a fate of outside. Aside from the basic connotation of death, the character of the negative outside is expressed by contrast motifs which describe a state of no-stay in the positive place (e.g. earth opposed to divine mountain or heaven, cursed ground versus garden of trees, ground versus land of moving in addition to the contrasts of the I-psalms).

Human reality is defined by relationship to these localities, connected to basic movements of, for example, *'ālâ* and *yārad*, in their turn connected to basic religious qualifications of, for example, *ṣaddîq* and *rāšā'*. Dwelling in one of the localities is obviously bound to the corresponding qualification (e.g. in Psalm 5). But the application of this motif structure is dominated by the theological interest in human reality as a state 'in between', with the religious qualifications connected to the fundamental movements relative to temple and Sheol.

This interest is expressed both by the I-figure of the psalms and the theological significance attached to the evil figure in a number of texts. Thus, the texts where the evil is located to the temple—as lone usurper or in conflict with a contrast figure—could be seen as expressions of this interest. The addressed You of Isa. 1.10ff. and Jeremiah 7 together with the Adam of Genesis 2–3 are especially good illustrations of the significance of the I-figure in the psalms as given to or threatened by the negative fate.

But this interest in human reality as a state in between can also be expressed by additional motifs of locality. The fundamental movements of '*ālâ* and *yārad* can be connected to elaborations of some interjacent space between temple and Sheol.

Thus, the hero can be connected to motifs of way—defined as the miraculous journey of divine guidance or in volitional categories as a journey of trials and wholeness (for the latter aspect cf. above to Psalm 26). But we have also found indications of the evil located to a contrast place (cf. especially Pss. 84.11; 26.4-5; 42.7; Num. 16.12-15, 24ff.). As relevant localities for the dwelling of the positive figures in these texts, these localities of the evil obviously refer to volitional categories of human aspiration and choice. On the other hand, these localities are also closely connected with the fate of Sheol or death. The Numbers 16 story provides a good illustration of this connection, with the localities of the evil engulfed by Sheol (cf. above to Pss. 26.4-5 and 42.7).

In these psalms, the motifs of some contrast locality of revolt and alternative aspiration are not elaborated. But the references could allude to an important set of connotations. Aside from Numbers 16, the golden calf episode of Exodus 32 illustrates this possibility.

Exodus 32, both seen in itself[94] and related to the context, represents complex traditio-historical problems.[95] When we approach this text from

---

94. Lehming, 'Versuch zu Ex. XXXII', p. 50, claims to have identified 12 layers of tradition within ch. 32!

95. E.g. on the one hand, Aurelius, *Der Fürbitter Israels*, pp. 57-126 on ch. 32 as originally 'eine eigene Einheit', added to chs. 19–24 and later extended by 33–34 (p. 60). On the other hand Moberly, *At the Mountain of God: Story and Theology in Exodus 32–34* (JSOTSup 22; Sheffield: JSOT Press, 1983), pp. 185-86, on the final redaction of Exod. 32–34 as a literary unit by the 'Yahwist', identified with the 'level of pentateuchal redaction which is generally considered to be the earliest', tentatively dated to the tenth century. To Brichto, 'The Worship of the Golden Calf', Exod. 32–34 as a 'Fable' represents one integral narrative of succeeding 'episodes', to be analysed by 'the tools of literary criticism'. To P.J. Kearney, 'Creation and Liturgy: The

an interest based on the motif structure of the I-psalms, the significance of local categories of ritual localization is striking. This is underlined by the parallel version of the golden calf episode of 1 Kgs 12.26-30. Whatever the relationship between the two traditions,[96] the 1 Kings version connects the golden calf motif to categories of temple and anti-temple, expressed by the stark opposites of worship in Jerusalem and alternative sanctuaries. This provides a good illustration of the significance of the ritual localization in Exodus 32. On the other hand, the subtlety of the Exodus composition vastly transcends the other version.

Traditionally the literary context of ch. 32 has been sought in ch. 24, due to chs. 25–31 being understood as a later insertion. This context implies a basic contrast between the function of Moses and Aaron as well as between the worship of the people guided by Moses or by Aaron. Even when the present composition[97] is understood to include also chs. 25–31 as part of the context, this contrast of Moses and Aaron is striking. The worship of the golden calf depends on the absence of Moses (32.1; cf. the refusal in Num. 16.13 with a parallel repudiation connected to Moses as the leader of the people's *'ālâ*). The narrative frame juxtaposes the Moses of ch. 24 ascending the mountain to mediate the ritual instruction of chs. 25–31 and the Aaron of ch. 32 receiving a

P Redaction of Ex 25-40', *ZAW* 89 (1977), pp. 375-87, Exod. 25–40 is a special composition centred round a 'unifying framework' of creation- fall-restoration which corresponds to the structure of Gen. 1–9.17 (p. 383), seen as the product of the 'original P author' and related to similar cosmogonic ideas of Second Isaiah (p. 386).

96.   E.g. Coats, *Moses*, p. 174; Aurelius, *Der Fürbitter Israels*, pp. 75ff.; and in detail Lehming, 'Versuch zu Ex. XXXII', Moberly, *Mountain of God*, pp. 162ff.

97.   Maintained as relevant in spite of, for example, J.I. Durham, *Exodus* (Word Biblical Commentary 3; Waco: Word Books, 1987), p. 417 on 'recent assertions of a fundamental unity' as 'in some cases purely imaginary', related to among others Childs and 'above all Moberly'. Cf. also L.G. Perdue, 'The Making and Destruction of the Golden Calf—A Reply', *Bib* 54 (1973), pp. 237ff., related to S.E. Loewenstamm, 'The Making and Destruction of the Golden Calf', *Bib* 48 (1967), pp. 481-90, with the rejoinder of the latter 'The Making and the Destruction of the Golden Calf—a Rejoinder', *Bib* 56 (1975), pp. 330-43; and generally the references is Schmid, *Die Gestalt des Mose*, pp. 35ff. Durham's own sensitive treatment of the final form of Exod. 32–34 illustrates the possibilities of an approach which does not treat the present composition as a mindless compilation of revered traditions (the editor a 'monument of incompetence', according to Brichto, 'The Worship of the Golden Calf', p. 4), but as the work of, for example, some 'Ex' who based on collections of older traditions 'put the stamp of his theological outlook upon them', Knight, *Theology as Narration*, p. xi.

contrasting instruction from the people.

This contrast is connected to categories of localization. In the received composition of ch. 24, the significance of Moses on the mountain related to the divine presence is partly expressed by the awed descriptions of the mountain (vv. 16-17) framed by the repetitive vv. 15 and 18. It is also partly negatively underlined as something very special by the instruction in vv. 1-2 and its execution in vv. 12ff. Within this frame, the descriptions of the ritual events in vv. 4-8, 9-11 and the final ascent in vv. 12-18 suggest three basic[98] levels of local nearness, with the general worship at the foot of the mountain, the sacred meal/vision up in the mountain, and the ultimate summit on God's mountain. The significance of these categories is stressed by the general emphasis on ritual localization in the elaborations of the Sinai traditions.[99] In addition, a similar hierarchic order is presented in connection with the final descent from the mountain in ch. 34. Referred to the same categories of relationship to the divine presence (v. 30)—now radiated by the mediator[100]—the descending Moses is related to Aaron and the leaders, then to the people (vv. 31-32).

In this way, the connection between chs. 24 and 32 depicts a fundamental contrast of Aaron and the people ritually related to the calf at the foot of the mountain and the awesome situation of Moses on the mountain related to God.[101] Exodus 24.4ff. adds to this contrast by the description of a proper worship for the people at the mountain's foot when guided by Moses. Both stories describe events of two days, connected with ritual leaders, altar building and other motifs of ritual preparation and sacrifices. The contrast can also be linked to the motifs of sacred meal in Exod. 32.6 and 24.9-11.[102]

Either as related to the fundamental contrast to Moses or to the scenes of proper worship in ch. 24, the calf episode represents a mock

98. Cf. the ambiguity of v. 13. Connected to the events of Exod. 32.17 and 34.29ff., this ambiguity could reflect both an interest to separate Joshua from the apostasy of ch. 32 and to protect the exclusiveness of Moses.

99. E.g. Hauge, 'On the Sacred Spot', pp. 46ff.

100. Moberly, *The Mountain of God*, pp. 106-107.

101. Childs, *Exodus*, p. 562, on 'the simultaneous action going on between God and Moses on the top of the mountain and between Aaron and the people at the foot of the mountain'; Moberly, *The Mountain of God*, pp. 48-49.

102. Underlined by Durham, *Exodus*, p. 422, who finds a contrast of 'celebration of an obligating relationship' and 'an orgy of the desertion of responsibility'!

220   *Between Sheol and Temple*

version. The contrast between Moses and Aaron and the people represents stark opposites of religious hero and evil, with the contrast connected to the fundamental localities of mountain and a place separated from the summit. But, in addition, the connection between chs. 24 and 32 introduces a more subtle contrast, with the worship at the foot of the mountain related to two different scenes of worship. In relation to the same locality below, the same people are active in the two scenes, whether they are active in proper worship or anti-worship dependent on the presence or absence of Moses. The subtlety of this change of roles is also expressed by the identity of the worshipped divinity. In the connection between Exod. 32.1 and 4 it is defined as identical with the proper divinity,[103] with only the plural forms of vv. 1bα, 4b as a subtle[104] indication of something not right. Not only the worshipping people and the sanctuary qualified as below the mountain, but also the worshipped divinity are the same in the two scenes. The formal legitimacy of the mock version is given by the presence of Aaron the chosen priest and the rites defined as *ḥaḡ leYHWH*. These contrasts are comparable to the starker opposites of Jerusalem/alternative sanctuaries of 1 Kings 12, the latter also formally Yahwistic, but with parallel techniques qualified as really apostasy. They can also be compared to the implied scenery of Isa. 1.10ff. and Jeremiah 7, with the pious worshippers in the proper sanctuary, qualified as really evil.[105]

So far, we have related ch. 32 to the traditionally accepted context of ch. 24. But in the present context,[106] chs. 25–31 add more layers of connotation for the proper understanding of ch. 32.

In ch. 25, the introduction vv. 1-8 connects the production of the tabernacle and all its equipment to the voluntary gifts of the people (cf. also Exod. 28.36-38 and further 30.12-16). This corresponds to the emphasis on the people's gifts 32.2ff.[107] (cf. below to Exod. 35.1-29; 36.3-7; 38.21, 24-31). The emphasis on the divinely inspired craftsmanship in 31.1-11, 28.3 (cf. below to Exod. 35.30–36.2; 36.8-39) can be

103. Moberly, *The Mountain of God*, pp. 46-47.
104. 'Heavily ironic' according to Moberly, *The Mountain of God*, pp. 47-48; Coats, *Moses*, p. 174.
105. Cf. also the one locality 1 Kgs 18 as the sanctuary of Ba'al and Yahweh, the one people related to two succeeding events of contrasted worship.
106. Cf. Childs, *Exodus*, pp. 533ff., 542 and especially Kearney, 'Creation and Liturgy'.
107. Moberly, *The Mountain of God*, p. 47; Childs, *Exodus*, pp. 542-43.

compared to the details of the production of the golden calf from the people's gifts 32.2-4, 24, presented both as the result of craftsmanship and of magic. Further, the regulations on the production of the tabernacle and the sacred implements concluded by the regulations on the proper observance of the sabbath (31.13ff.; cf. the tent erected and filled by the glory on 'the first day of the first month', Exod. 40.2)[108] corresponds to the production of the golden calf ended by the proclamation of the *ḥag̱ leYHWH*.

The present composition suggests a contrast between the 'children of Israel' in chs. 25–31 and 'the people' in ch. 32. The first people are the object of divine instruction, mediated by Moses, related to the divine presence in the proper sanctuary revealed in vision (25.8-9 immediately connected to the instruction, vv. 1-8). The other people, in the absence of Moses ordering Aaron about, represent a mock version of worship.

In the same way, the composition contrasts two Aarons. In chs. 25–31, the sanctification of Aaron and his sons represents one of the central themes (Exod. 28.1–29.35; cf. further 30.18-21, 30-33). In the received composition, this divinely described Aaron differs from the Aaron described in 32.1-5, 21-25.[109] The concluding v. 35 could reflect this contrast. Verse 35b, with two final sentences and two originators of the golden calf, is usually seen to be the result of editorial insertions.[110] But the present version represents a neat summing up of the story as told in vv. 1-4 and of the two allocations of guilt in vv. 21 and 22-23. Alluding to the gifts of the people and to Aaron's function, v. 35b refers to the central themes of chs. 25–31 with an ironic contrast to the proper relationship as depicted in 28.36-38. The guilt of the people in connection with their gifts is taken for granted both in 32.35 and in 28.36ff. But while the Aaron of the divine regulations shall carry the guilt attached to the gifts of the people, the people of ch. 32 are smitten because of what was made out of their gifts not only by themselves, but also by Aaron.[111]

108. The concluding location of Exod. 31.13ff. within chs. 25–31 stressed by Kearney, 'Creation and Liturgy', pp. 375ff., as expression for the connection between Exod. 25–31 and Gen. 1–2.3.

109. The description of Aaron, vv. 21-24, confronted by Moses and putting the blame on the people, can be compared to the confrontation Gen. 3.9ff.

110. The final sentence seen as, for example, 'a clumsy, secondary addition' by Childs, *Exodus*, p. 557, defended by Moberly, *The Mountain of God*, p. 59, as an attempt to express the dual responsibility.

111. This would imply a concluding function for v. 35 as a whole within the

The contrast is also elaborated by the consecration of the Levites story in vv. 25-29. These verses are usually understood as a reflection of an original Levite tradition[112] with a problematical relationship to the context.[113] Within the present composition, the story of the faithful Levites contrasts with the role of Aaron and the people.[114] The significance of this contrast is best seen when related to chs. 25–31, where the consecration of Aaron is a central theme (cf. especially Exod. 28–29.35). Thus, the 'handfilling' motif of v. 29—as a so called *Levitenregel*, often seen as the kernel of the tradition[115]—corresponds to 28.41, 29.9, 29, 33, 35. While the designation of the priests in 28.1 is connected to categories of heritage, the designation of 32.26 is connected to volitional categories, the children of Levi separating themselves from the rest of the people as a response on the challenge 'who belongs to Yahweh?'[116] This can be compared to the separation scene in Num. 16.24ff., there also connected to a relationship to Moses. In this story, the serious character of the separation is underlined by the consecration effected by the blood of 'sons and brothers'.[117]

The contrast of the two Aarons of chs. 25–31 and ch. 32 is underlined by the sons of Levi as positive contrast figures. In addition, Moses with a function of atonement (32.30) can be related to the priestly function of intercession (28.38 and also 28.29-30).

The contrasts between two Aarons and two peoples in chs. 25–31 and ch. 32 is further elaborated in chs. 35–40 which recount how the divine regulations of chs. 25–31 were carried out. The regulations and the narration correspond closely to each other. The differences could reflect the

---

present composition of ch. 32; cf. also Moberly, *The Mountain of God*, p. 59.

112. E.g. Schmid, *Die Gestalt des Mose*, pp. 19, 52, 67.

113. According to, for example, Aurelius, *Der Fürbitter Israels*, pp. 66-67, originally 'zu Hause' in Num. 25. As a central expression for the assertion of Levitic priesthood, the tradition had to be connected, however badly, to the story of Israel's first apostasy at Sinai.

114. Childs, *Exodus*, pp. 570-71; Moberly, *The Mountain of God*, pp. 54-55.

115. Aurelius, *Der Fürbitter Israels*, p. 66.

116. Childs, *Exodus*, p. 571.

117. The Levites purging the fault of Aaron, according to Kearney, 'Creation and Liturgy', p. 383. In such a case, the function of the Levites related to Aaron would parallel the intercession of Moses related to the people. But while the story could allude to different sets of connotations, the 'handfilling' motif of v. 29 would primarily suggest the Levites as 'self-made' priests and substitutes for Aaron.

significance of the intermittent chs. 32–34.[118] In the received composition, the events are divided into two parts: chs. 35–39 and ch. 40. The first part is introduced by a summary repetition of the divine regulations, cited by Moses in 35.1-19, and given to the collection of the people's gifts and the elaboration of the gifts into sanctuary and sacred implements. It is ended by the concluding 39.32-43, the people finishing the effort and being blessed by Moses. The second part in ch. 40 describes how the work was finished by Moses (v. 33). This is introduced by divine regulations vv. 1-15, here addressed to Moses directly and not cited as repeated by Moses to the people. Parallel to the people's carrying out the instruction, vv. 16-33 describe how Moses erected and furnished the sanctuary with the sacred implements. Finally, the work finished, the sanctuary is filled by the divine presence (vv. 34-38).

When compared to chs. 25–31, this composition underlines the significance of the children of Israel (as 'people' only 36.3, 5-6) and Moses as the subjects of the sacred effort. Due to the ideological significance of the sanctuary, the description of Moses as temple-builder, described as performing a thousand and one menial tasks on the 'first day of the first month' without any help from either priests or Levites, must have been deeply meaningful to the author. But the role of the people is stressed too. Aside from the introductory 25.8-10, the production in chs. 25–31 is assigned to the addressed You, in 31.2-11 extended by the inspired craftsmen effecting the instruction of You (v. 11). But in chs. 35–39, the whole production, including the efforts of the craftsmen—who are considerately introduced to the children of Israel according to 35.30ff.—are qualified as the work of the people in the concluding 39.32ff., the people effecting the divine instructions mediated by Moses. In addition, the subjective categories of emotional attitude in the description of the people as cheerfully and exuberantly offering their gifts (35.21ff., 36.3-7), stress the significance of the people as actors.

Given the received version of the text, it is natural to relate this description to ch. 32. Contrasting with the negative worship by Aaron and the people, chs. 35–40 describe the right worship by Moses and the people. This suggests that in ch. 32, the theological significance of the evil figure is mainly connected to the role of the people, Aaron primarily having a subordinate role as the mediator of apostasy. This is expressed

118. Cf. especially Kearney, 'Creation and Liturgy', pp. 378ff., the differences related to the connection to the intermittent 32-34; and also Moberly, *The Mountain of God*, pp. 109-10.

by the divine verdict of Exod. 32.7 and the development of the guilt motif in connection with Moses as intercessor in vv. 30ff.[119]

The connection between chs. 32 and 35–40. in the present composition underlines the significance of temple categories for this theological interpretation of the Sinai traditions. Within chs. 25–40, the 'temple' is described in a threefold mode: as the object of the divine instructions with a shape given by the vision of a heavenly model in 25.9, 40; as man-made 'anti-temple' in ch. 32; and as rightfully created by human hands in chs. 35–40. To this exposition within chs. 25–40 must be added the relationship between chs. 32 and 24 (cf. above). That the mountain motifs of ch. 24 are interwoven with the present composition of chs. 25–40 is demonstrated by ch. 34. In all these expressions, the locality—as some place related to the mountain of God in ch. 24, or as an enclosed space connected to a building in chs. 25–31, 35–40, or as defined by the golden calf and altar in ch. 32—is connected to the idea of divine presence and relationship to this presence, contrasted to the mock presence of ch. 32. The significance of these categories[120] is also illustrated by the simple exposition of the 1 Kings version with the Zion temple juxtaposed to alternative temples.

The people, too, are described in three modes of being: as objects of divine instruction, as following their own inclinations due to the absence of the mediator, and as responding to the instruction mediated by Moses. In all the three cases, relationship to the temple describes their mode of being. In relation to the theological understanding expressed in this composition, the crass contradictions related to the same group of people must express a vital point. Dependent on the relationship to the mediator, the same group of people represent the 'children of Israel' or 'the people', with their gifts immediately ready and transformable into the true sanctuary or the golden calf. Parallel to the elaboration of the people motif, we also find the Aaron figure described in three modes. Within the received text, the same figure is seen as abruptly changing

119. According to Brichto, 'The Worship of the Golden Calf', p. 13, the function of 'Episode E' (vv. 21-24) with Moses accepting Aaron's story, is to make Aaron emerge from this story as 'hero, at best, or blameless, at the least', and thus preparing the role of Aaron as the consecrated priest of chs. 35–40.

120. Cf. also the laws, Exod. 34.11-26, which correspond to the present context, according to Moberly, *The Mountain of God*, pp. 132ff. a compilation of older laws assembled for this context; also Brichto, 'The Worship of the Golden Calf', pp. 32ff.; Childs, *Exodus*, p. 613, on the admonitions vv. 11-16.

from the ideological description in the instruction into an object for the people's wishes, and as transformed by the rituals of purification (40.30ff. as the expression for vv. 12ff.). In a normal story given to biographical verisimilitude such illogical changes would be impossible, and this is reflected in the usual critical allocation of these phenomena to different traditions and redactions. But as expression for a religious interest, the crass contradiction—especially when we pay attention also to the description in ch. 24—represents an elaborate expression of the theological application of the concept of the evil. While the fundamental motif structure juxtaposes the *ṣaddîq* and *rāšā'* figures as related to dwelling in the temple, both the I-figure of the Psalms and a number of other applications in different ways stress the significance of the religious hero as a figure in between. On the way and/or threatened by the nega-tive fate, the central figure is the potential actualization of the positive or the negative ideal. Both the Aaron figure and—as central for the interest of this composition—the 'people' could be understood as subtly elaborated expressions of this interest, as embodiments of the different roles of the motif structure.

Exodus 24–40 can add to our understanding of the relationship between the motif structure and religious practice. We have found it possible that the I-psalms could express a practice connected with the integration of a religious paradigm into biographical experience. The I-psalms suggest such an integration to have been related to psychic and emotional categories of inner experience, including choice and aspiration and development of inner wholeness (cf. above to especially Ps. 26).

The threefold description of the people in Exodus 25–40 can serve as a dramatic illustration of these categories. As instructed, as left to their own devices, and as effecting the instruction, the one set of actors repre-sents three stages of religious reality. The elaboration of the motif of the 'urging heart' (Exod. 25.2; 35.5, 29, as 'lifting heart'; 35.21, 26; 36.2) and 'urging spirit' (Exod. 35.21), ended by the scenes of 36.3ff., demon-strates the emphasis on total inner commitment for the realization of the instructions. This emphasis is the more striking as the total commitment seems completely unmotivated,[121] especially in a context of ch. 32 with

---

121. Cf. also Moberly, *The Mountain of God*, p. 110, connecting this change to the development within chs. 32–34. On the other hand, the understanding of Brichto, 'The Worship of the Golden Calf', of the story as a 'fable on idolatry' makes natural a 'finale which is a masterpiece of non-sequitur' (p. 3), the single 'episode' a literary illustration of some certain interest.

a contradicting description of the people's real character. Whatever the reason for this change, the crass contradictions in religious behaviour in chs. 32 and 35ff., related to the same group of people within a short time lapse, must reflect a definite theological understanding of humanity as manifesting different modes of religious being. What characterizes the different modes of being is the absence or presence of Moses mediating the divine instructions (Exod. 32.1; 35.1).

Compared to other applications of the motif structure, the peculiar concentration on temple motifs in Exodus 25–40 is rather special. To a certain degree Psalms 84 and also 42–43 represent parallel texts formally dominated by relationship to the temple as the central theme. But also in such a connection, the qualification of the people in Exodus 25–40. as negative or positive producers of gifts for temple building represents a remarkable theological definition.

One explanation for this special character could be found in the relationship to the version of 1 Kings 12. The points of contact, together with the independent literary elaboration of these points in the two texts, could suggest that they represent individual expressions of some given tradition characterized by a theme of temple building.

On the other hand, the description of Ezekiel's temple vision in chs. 40–47 represents a parallel expression of such a single-minded concentration on the religious significance of the temple as a building, here by the central motif of 'measuring the sanctuary'. The relationships between the actors correspond to Exodus 25–40. In Ezekiel 40–47 the right temple is seen in a vision and experienced by the prophet in a series of measurements demonstrated by the heavenly measurer. This experience is to be mediated to the people who in their turn shall measure the sanctuary (Ezek. 43.10-11). The MT of Ezek. 43.10-11—usually heavily emended—makes a peculiar connection between experience of the architecture of the temple and the people's shameful experience of their transgressions and a new measuring of the temple.[122] Obviously, here as in Exodus 25–40, relationship to the temple as a building—in the form of gifts or in measuring—serves for a total and emotive expression of religious behaviour. In both cases, the right relationship is contrasted with a past stage of negative relationship, the transition connected to mediation of the heavenly vision.

The two expressions for such a single-minded concentration on temple

---

122. Hauge, 'On the Sacred Spot', pp. 49ff.

relationship can be compared to Jeremiah 7 and Isa. 1.10ff. We have found it possible that the two prophetic texts represent applications of the motif structure connected to a reinterpretation of the religious paradigm, expressed by lists of positive characteristics presented as conditions for stay which contrast with some established popular practice. Exodus 25–40 and Ezekiel 40–47 could be seen as parallel expressions of such a need. The special background to such a need could be connected to the special fact that in all these texts, the 'people' represent the main figures, with the religious ideal presented by mediators.

The two types of text represent different sets of reinterpretation. In the prophetic texts, the temple motifs are somewhat weakened, with the evil in the temple juxtaposed to dwelling in the land and eating the goodness of the land, while religious behaviour is connected to social relationships. In Exodus 25–40 and Ezekiel 40–47, religious behaviour is connected solely to relationship to the temple as sacred architecture.

The significance of this application—both with regard to the concentration on temple motifs and to the 'people' as the main figure—can be illustrated by Exodus 25–40. In the present context, this composition links to ch. 24. The stark contrast of Moses as the religious hero on the mountain in an extraordinary communion with Yahweh and juxtaposed to the people at the foot of the mountain is dissolved in chs. 25–40 by the idea of a more sociable and lasting divine presence among the people, linked to concepts of institutional cult with sacred space, and sacred servants admitted into the sacred space. The emphasis on the sanctuary as created from the people's gifts and as humanly-produced corresponds to this idea of the divine presence transposed from the exclusiveness of the mountain to 'among the people' (Exod. 25.8; 29.45-46).[123] The whole of chs. 25–31 can be understood as a series of instructions on how the divine presence can be introduced into the midst of a human community without becoming the stupid travesty illustrated by ch. 32. In such a context, the episode of the golden calf, demonstrating the qualities of the people as temple-builders when left to themselves, stresses the miraculous character of such a divine condescension.

So, chs. 25–40 could reflect a theological interest of democratization,

---

123. Cf. Durham, *Exodus*, p. 353, on a connection between chs. 24 and 25–31 as a theological document extending 'that same Presence through a carefully presented and interlocked sequence of symbols', and also Childs, *Exodus*, p. 537, on a similar development from Sinai to Tabernacle and from the prophetic function of Moses to the perpetual priesthood of Aaron expressed in chs. 35–40.

with the motif structure connected to Moses as the embodiment of the religious ideal related to institutional cult. For this democratization, the concepts of relationship to the divine presence and the qualities of the persons admitted into relationship to the divine presence seem specially important. Similarly, Isa. 1.10ff. and Jeremiah 7 could reflect a parallel process of democratization, with the religious paradigm applied to a situation of ordinary religiosity, primarily connected to social categories.

ii. *Chapters 32–34.* Such a process of application must be related to the development in the subtle and seemingly haphazard compilation[124] of episodes in Exod. 32.21–34.35. Placed between chs. 25–31 and 35–40, the complex composition must somehow[125] describe the transformation of the evil worshippers of the golden calf into eager and accepted producers of materials for the sanctuary and an accepted environment for the divine dwelling.

From a context of the I-psalms, it is natural to stress the significance of the evil as central to the theological interest. At the same time it must be important for this interest that the transformation of the evil is connected to the role of Moses. Related to the categories of the motif structure in the I-psalms, Moses is the embodiment of the paradigm in Exod. 32.21–34.35. Corresponding to the basic contrasts of Moses on the mountain and the people/Aaron of the golden calf episode, Exod. 33.7-11, 33.18–34.7, 29-35 continue the description of Moses as especially related to the divine presence. In all three cases, the special relationship is connected to local categories.

The emphasis on Moses as the religious hero is especially strong in

124. E.g. Aurelius, *Der Fürbitter Israels*, pp. 91-126. To Childs, *Exodus*, pp. 349-50, the different traditions were already combined in the oral stage of transmission, both J and E sharing the same oral tradition. Thus, to Coats, *Moses*, p. 175, the core of Mosaic tradition lies embedded in this story, connected with Moses as identified with the people as intercessor, Moses as intimately related to God, Moses the authoritative leader of the people.

125. Aside from the preceding note cf. especially the different attempts to stress literary categories. Thus Kearney, 'Creation and Liturgy', argues for a function connected to an ideological pattern of creation–fall–restoration; to Brichto, 'The Worship of the Golden Calf', pp. 20ff., chs. 33–34 as 'Part Two: The Aftermath' is related to chs. 32–34 as 'an episodic narrative within a larger narrative framework' (p. 34), the episodic technique making every discrepancy deliberate; while Moberly, *The Mountain of God*, pp. 110, 186, finds chs. 32–34 to be an ancient literary composition of literary skill and theological depth.

Exod. 33.18–34.7 and 34.29-35. The latter episode concludes the development of chs. 32–34 and is followed by the story of Moses instructing the
people in 35.1ff. With this location, the description in 34.29ff. is parallel
to ch. 24 as the introductory frame for the instructions of chs. 25–31.
This corresponds to the motif development of the two descriptions. The
instruction delivered by Yahweh to Moses in 25.1ff. is mediated by
Moses to the people in 35.1ff. Exod. 24.1-2, 9ff. and 34.29ff. describe
the decisive ascent and descent of Moses to receive and mediate the
instructions. This correspondence is also seen by the parallel hierarchic
relationships to the divine presence in chs. 24 and 34.29ff. The three
levels of 24.4-8, 9-11, 12-18, with the general worship at the foot of the
mountain, the sacred meal/vision up in the mountain, and the ultimate
summit on God's mountain, correspond to the hierarchic order of
34.30ff, with the descending Moses related first to Aaron and the leaders
and then to the people. Given this background, it must be important that
while the hierarchic order in ch. 24 is related to the divine presence on
the mountain (cf. also the two different visual impressions in 24.10, 17),
in ch. 34 it is related to the radiance of Moses (v. 30) and to Moses as
'talking' (vv. 31, 32-33).[126] The special emphasis on the visual impression of Moses's face—as radiant or sprouting divine characteristics[127]—
is located in a context which includes an episode centred round the
impression of the divine face in Exod. 33.18ff. and an episode with the
golden calf for substitute. The extraordinary imagery states that for the
people, the relationship to the divine face[128] is mediated through the
shining face of Moses,[129] likewise unbearable to be seen unveiled.[130]

126. Moberly, *The Mountain of God*, pp. 106-107.

127. Moberly, *The Mountain of God*, pp. 107ff.; Coats, *Moses*, p. 174 on Moses
endowed with horns, in both cases related to the golden calf as substitute for Moses
(Exod. 32.1).

128. On the significance of this motif for ch. 33 as a whole (cf. also vv. 11, 14, 15),
see Moberly, *The Mountain of God*, p. 80.

129. The implications of the imagery could be deepened if categories of creation
are present for the composition as a whole, as argued by Kearney, 'Creation and
Liturgy', pp. 375ff.; cf. also Moberly, *The Mountain of God*, p. 108 referring to Gen.
1.26 for a parallel to Exod. 34.30ff.; and especially Brichto 'The Worship of the
Golden Calf', p. 44. The golden calf and Moses, described as contrasted mediators
for the divine presence among the people, the divine presence given concrete visual
expressions as mock image and 'real' radiation from a human face, could reflect the
connotations implied in the concept of humanity created in the divine 'image'.

130. While v. 33 is connected to the immediate episode of Moses' descent, the

The episode of Moses in relation to the divine face, 33.18ff., reflects a seemingly independent interest in Moses as the religious hero. In this case, this is felt due to the peculiar relationship between v. 17 and 34.1ff.[131] The transition from vv. 17 to 18 has caused particular concern among exegetes ancient and modern,[132] with Moses suddenly changing from compassionate intercessor to supplicant for individual favours of mystical character. The character of this special favour, connected to a special localization and expressed as visual experience of the divine presence, is comparable to the motif of beatific vision in the I-psalms.[133] The supplication of Moses corresponds to the prayers of the I-figure in the Psalms. The didactic repetition vv. 20, 23b—with the negated theophanies of 1 Kings 19 as expressions of a similar interest—must refer critically to an important tradition of sensory experience related to God (cf. above to Chapter 3).

In this context, the concern must be connected to the golden calf episode. Exodus 32 together with 1 Kgs 12.26ff. could be connected to a forbidden practice of representations of Yahweh by any image—often related to the special prescription in Exod. 34.17.[134] At some late date, the forbidden practice itself cannot have represented any actual aberration. But the fundamental character of the concepts involved—related to the idea and experience of divine reality—must have been of enormous significance for ideological interpretation.[135] This could be connected to 33.18ff. as a critical reference to an important religious practice demonstrated by the I-psalms and connected to the experience of divine reality

general character of vv. 34-35 could prepare for the transition from ch. 34 to the idea of the people's permanent relationship to God brought even closer down to earth by the erection of the tabernacle and the sanctification of the priests in chs. 35-40; cf. Childs, *Exodus*, p. 638, on 40.34-35 showing that an epoch is ended.

131. E.g. Aurelius, *Der Fürbitter Israels*, pp. 103-104 on vv. 18ff. as addenda called forth by the 'Theophaniebericht', Exod. 34.5-6.

132. Cf. the examples in Childs, *Exodus*, pp. 597ff.

133. Cf. Childs, *Exodus*, p. 596, on the story as originally given to a special individual revelation for Moses, changed to fit a context of sin and intercession and restoration of the covenant, the visible appearance of Yahweh changed into a revelation of Yahweh in terms of attributes relevant to the context.

134. Moberly, *The Mountain of God*, pp. 160-61, on 34.11-26 as a recapitulation of the earlier laws relevant to the situation; also Brichto 'The Worship of the Golden Calf', pp. 31ff.; Aurelius, *Der Fürbitter Israels*, pp. 119ff.

135. E.g. Brichto, 'The Worship of the Golden Calf', pp. 41ff. on the 'metaphoric usage' of 'idolatry'.

as the goal of the religious practice. In such a context, the golden calf episode could be seen as a subtle illustration of the dangers inherent to a religiosity of 'sensory experience'. At the same time, the elaboration of the divine face motif concluded by the radiating face of Moses demonstrates the proper experience of God. Parallel to the Elijah of 1 Kings 19, Moses is described as the embodiment of the traditional religious ideal. At the same time, the description negates certain expressions of this ideal, with the 'people' finally related to the institution of tabernacle and priestly mediators. God glimpsed 'from behind', resulting in the unbearable radiance from a human face, the 'stiffnecked' people lastingly related to the divine presence enshrined in the tabernacle, are emotive expressions for the proper experience of divine reality. The definition of God as 'merciful' in the story of the special revelation for Moses (Exod. 33.19; 34.6-7),[136] corresponds to this interpretation.

Underlying this interpretation, some considerable practice of religious experience must be involved. The central concepts expressed in some few basic motif groups are elaborated in a richly textured compilation of different traditions, their function subtly nuanced and constantly enhanced with added elaborations. Only some rather advanced tradition of practice and inner experience of mental-emotional character can explain such a compilation.

Exod. 33.7-11 is a third example of the special interest in Moses as the religious hero. In these verses, the character of Moses is described by motifs of separated locality connected to a special relationship to Yahweh. Here the separate locality is described as a tent—the Tent of Encounter—placed outside the camp. The remarkably detailed descriptions of the reactions of the people when the tent is used (vv. 8, 10), give a moving impression of the significance of the special encounter. The elaboration of the tent motifs—juxtaposing the tent of the encounter and the people's tents inside the camp[137]—must have a contrast function. The one locality inside is given for the people, the other outside for the specially qualified, being talked to 'face to face' by God (v. 11).

There is a basic contrast, met repeatedly and almost like a refrain, in these chapters, between different motif sets which express related aspects of religious being by local categories. The execution of this contrast in

136. Cf. Moberly, *The Mountain of God*, pp. 76-77, on the relationship between 33.18 and 19; also Childs, *Exodus*, p. 596; Aurelius, *Der Fürbitter Israels*, pp. 124-25.
137. Cf. a parallel use of tent motifs in Num. 16.26-27, with relationship to the 'tent- door' as a contrast to 'going up'.

Exod. 33.7-11, juxtaposing Moses and people as 'outside and inside the camp' is especially comparable to the relationship of localities in chs. 24–31 and 32. Moses on the summit and the people in their camp at the foot of the mountain correspond to the 'horizontal' nature of the following contrast.[138]

Verses 7-11 are usually seen as a separate tradition with a complicated relationship to the rest of ch. 33.[139] In the present context, vv. 7-11 are connected to vv. 4ff. and the description of the people's penitence. The motifs of guidance in vv. 12ff. link to the bad words of vv. 1-3 and thus suggest that a discourse on guidance is continued by vv. 12ff., vv. 4-11 describing intermittent scenes.[140] Related to the sin of the people and the intercession by Moses followed by the instructions on the tabernacle in ch. 35, the Tent of Encounter in this context must refer to an interim period.[141]

Due to the significance of the motifs, a wealth of connotations could be implied.[142] At the very least, the parallel of contrast localities in vv. 7-11 and in chs. 24–31 (cf. above) must be significant. This can be linked to the ornament motif (vv. 4-6), the importance of which is stressed by the repetitions.[143] In the present context, this motif is linked to the sorrow of the people and must function as an expression of penitence.[144] The connotation for its usage must be sought in relation to the golden calf episode.[145] And with this connection, the motif usage alludes to the

138. Aside from the contrast of Num. 16.26-27 and also 11.10 (as related to Deut. 1.27; Aurelius, *Der Fürbitter Israels*, p. 182) cf. the opposite application of 'outside and inside the camp' in Num. 12.

139. E.g. Durham, *Exodus*, p. 443, on these verses as 'completely out of place'.

140. Cf. Brichto, 'The Worship of the Golden Calf', p. 23, on vv. 7-11 as a 'digression', but even so an integral part of the story.

141. Brichto 'The Worship of the Golden Calf', p. 23; Moberly, *The Mountain of God*, pp. 63ff.

142. Cf. the preceding references to Brichto and Moberly in addition to Childs, *Exodus*, pp. 592-93, on the 'meaning' of this story, in different, but equally possible descriptions.

143. In a 'synoptic-resumptive narrative technique' according to Brichto, 'The Worship of the Golden Calf', p. 22, with v. 4 for bottom line, while vv. 5 and 6 go back in time, expanding the synopsis and explaining its meaning.

144. A 'sign of mourning' to Childs, *Exodus*, p. 589; to Brichto 'The Worship of the Golden Calf', p. 22, a metaphor for Israel 'still standing under judgment'.

145. Cf. Moberly, *The Mountain of God*, p. 60, who refers to Gen. 35.4 and rites of renunciation, the people removing the objects connected with the construction of the golden calf.

central gift motif in these stories, with the people related to some divine representation as producers of fine materials. The structure of ornament motifs followed by the description of the interim sanctuary in 33.4-11 corresponds to the connection of gifts related to the golden calf and the sanctuary in chs. 32 and 25ff., 35ff.

The relationship to ch. 32 is the most immediate. The non-use of the ornaments, connected to the people's sorrow and an imposed penitence, contrasts with both the offering of gifts and the festivities of ch. 32. The juxtaposition of the people's locality inside the camp and Moses related to the sanctuary outside the camp corresponds to the juxtapositions of mountain sanctuary and the people's sanctuary in in chs. 24–32. Such a connection is also reflected in the Joshua motifs in Exod. 33.11, corresponding to Exod. 24.13. This suggests some kind of parallelism between the sanctuaries of the two episodes. The people of penitence are now related to a sanctuary stressed as outside and distant, and in addition qualified as put up by Moses 'for himself' (v. 7). The interim character of this sanctuary apart is demonstrated by the erection of the tabernacle, the people very much active in the preparations, although this tent also is pitched by Moses (ch. 40), the new sanctuary qualified as an expression of the divine dwelling in the midst of the people (Exod. 25.8; 29.45).[146]

In this way, the actualization of the sanctuary as enshrining the divine presence is developed in successive stages:

1. The divine mountain which is connected to the vision of the heavenly model, contrasted by the mock sanctuary inside the camp;
2. the aberration resulting in the interim tent of encounter outside the camp and contrasted to the non-sanctuary inside the camp; and finally
3. the tabernacle inside the camp.

Within this development, the people are the central actors contrasting with Moses, the religious hero. Similar to the Aaron of Numbers 12 and the main part of the people who 'go up' in Numbers 16, the Aaron of ch. 32 is separated from the people as the really evil who has to pay for the golden calf (vv. 30-35). And, in chs. 33–34 the 'stiffneckedness' of

---

146. To the connection of the sanctuary as 'outside' and 'inside' cf. Brichto, 'The Worship of the Golden Calf', p. 24; Moberly, *The Mountain of God*, pp. 63-64; Childs, *Exodus*, pp. 592-93.

the people forms a central theme, while the 'children of Israel' are the central subjects for the instructions and the actualization of the instructions in chs. 35–40.

The contrast between Moses as positive figure and the people as the negative figures is especially expressed in Exod. 32.9-10, 32-33.[147] The initial divine verdict of 32.9-10 corresponds to the normal conclusion of the enemy situation in the I-psalms, with the people destroyed and Moses made into a great people in their stead (cf. above to the similar initial reaction Num. 16.21 with Moses and Aaron for positive contrast figures). Verses 32-33 allude to a confrontation of this kind, with Ps. 69.29 as a normal application of the book motif, connected with the concepts of righteousness and life/dwelling in the temple.[148] Seen in isolation, the episode in Exod. 32.26ff. can also be related to a normal type of confrontation. Similar to the 'going up' of Num. 16.24ff., a positive group separates itself from the evil. Here the representatives of the evil are killed, the killers elevated to a special status.[149]

But similarly to Numbers 12 and 16, the normal enemy situation is disrupted due to the intercession of Moses.[150] For the connection to the I-psalms, it is significant that the change in the people effected in chs. 32–34 is described according to the given categories of temple relationship. Corresponding to the qualification of Moses as the religious hero, the people are especially related to the divine presence,[151] in addition to

147. Usually seen as expressions for different late traditions, e.g. Aurelius, *Der Fürbitter Israels*, pp. 41ff., on vv. 7-14 as 'Einschub' dependent on the original kernel of Deut. 9–10, p. 89 on vv. 30ff. as dependent on Amos and Hosea traditions and the reconciliation scenes of the Jacob and Joseph-stories; on the other side Moberly, *The Mountain of God*, pp. 50-51, 57; Coats, *Moses*, p. 175. To Coats, Exod. 32 and the function of Moses as intercessor represents the kernel of the Moses tradition, also the suffering servant of Isa. 40–55 depicted within Moses categories as expressed Exod. 32.31-32 (p. 208).

148. Isa. 4.3-4; 56.5; Ezek. 13.9; Mal. 3.16ff.; Dan. 12.1ff.

149. Cf. also the Carmel scene of 1 Kgs 18, the plus figure and the 'evil' related to different gods within the 'same' sanctuary, the people 'in between' the two gods and their representatives, the story ended by the people confessing Yahweh for the true god and killing the negative representatives.

150. Cf. generally Moberly, *The Mountain of God* and Aurelius, *Der Fürbitter Israels* in addition to the emphasis on this function in Coats, *Moses*, pp. 175, 208-209.

151. Aside from the fundamental definition of the tabernacle in Exod. 25.8, 29.45-46, cf. 33.2-3, 5, 12-17, 34.9, 40.34ff. and especially the happy result of the intercession with the divine presence mediated by Moses, Exod. 34.29-35.

their role as 'urged by their hearts' to present gifts and to build the tabernacle.

The guidance and way motifs linked to the idea of divine presence in Exod. 32.34, 33.1-5, 12-17, 34.9 and 40.34ff. (cf. also 32.1, 23) can be related to the basic motifs of the I-psalms.[152] For the intercession, the question of divine guidance represents the main problem. On the one hand, this corresponds to the significance of guidance and way motifs in, for example, Pss. 5.8, 27.11, 43.4ff. On the other hand, it is peculiar in view of the composition chs. 25-40 as a whole, which primarily connects the golden calf episode to the significance of the building of the tabernacle. But the emphasis on the guidance motifs corresponds to the concluding qualification of the tabernacle in Exod. 40.36ff. with the divine dwelling and 'going up' as the sign for the departures of the people (cf. also Num. 9.15-23). This must be significant in view of the qualifications in Exod. 25.8 and 29.45 with the tabernacle as the place of Yahweh's dwelling in the midst of the people.

The two qualifications of the tabernacle could be connected to the discussion of the form of divine guidance in the intercession scenes in Exod. 32.34ff. In view of 23.20ff. (cf. also 'light' and 'truth' Ps. 43.3 and the messenger 1 Kgs 19.5ff.), the opposition of Moses to the messenger as guide is peculiar.[153] He evidently insists on something better, connected to the divine presence 'in the midst of' (Exod. 33.3, 5, 34.9) or 'with' (Exod. 33.16) the people, and as 'face' (Exod. 33.14-15). The divine face must be especially important in view of the significance of the motif in Exod. 33.11, 18ff. and as represented by the face of Moses in 34.29ff.[154]

These contrasts of special types of relationship could be connected to the idea of the special relationship to Yahweh in the I-psalms. The confession and prayer of the I certainly refer to some basic relationship to Yahweh in a situation of distress. The prayer for divine help links the relationship to some miraculous intervention, in the form of, for example, guidance on the way or salvation from the enemies. And the relationship to the divine face in the sanctuary obviously refers to experiences of a third kind. Thus, for example, Psalms 42–43 depict the I as related to God when 'in Sheol' (vv. 9ff. in addition to the refrain vv. 6, 12, 43.5),

152. Cf. further the motifs of 'separation from the evil', 34.12-16 corresponding to, for example, the obedient people of Num. 16.26ff. and to Ps. 26.4-5.

153. Moberly, *The Mountain of God*, pp. 61ff.

154. Moberly, *The Mountain of God*, p. 66.

his being led on the way refers to other sets of experiences (43.3), while
the special arrival before the divine face marks a special event in the
story of the I (vv. 1ff., 43.3-4). The narrative structure of 1 Kings 19 is
especially interesting in this respect, depicting Elijah as related to the
heavenly powers in the forms of the nourishing and sending angel and
of 'Yahweh's word', both clearly separated from the special experience
of Yahweh 'himself'.

Such a background is the more relevant for Exodus 32–34 as the
special vision in 33.18ff. refers to categories of extraordinary experience
of the divinity. The beatific vision of Moses—also as somewhat veiled by
the divine hand—not only contrasts with the extraordinary relationship
described in v. 11, but also alludes to the central theme of the composition in chs. 25–40, especially when introduced by ch. 24. For this composition, 'relationship to God' represents the main topic, expressed in
a scale of different actualizations related to the different actors as
juxtaposed and in their different modes of religious being. Against this
background, the audacity of Moses in asking for the beatific vision for
himself corresponds to his presumption in asking for the real divine
presence in the midst of the stiffnecked people! The introductory
contrast of Moses on the mountain and the evil people in their camp
around the golden calf is shifted into a parallel relationship of extraordinary experience of God. For the people, however, the experience is
linked to Yahweh as the extraordinary guide and 'co-walker'.

Related to the motif structure of the I-psalms, this indicates that the
categories of dwelling in the temple are transferred to way motifs: the
divine face of the beatific vision is connected to the idea of divine guidance on the way. This corresponds to the concluding interpretation of
the tabernacle in Exod. 40.36ff.: the sanctuary is now the place for the
divine dwelling extended by the act of 'going up' related to the departures and non-departures of the people.

A new emphasis on categories of way can be related to the I-figure of
the psalms as a figure in between—related to the fate of the *ṣaddîqîm*
and the *rešā'îm*. But the intercession scenes in chs. 33–34 suggests that
some special interest is expressed. Moreover, such an interest could also
be related to the critical attitude to the traditional religious practice and
expectations in Exod. 33.18ff. and the emphasis on Yahweh as the
merciful in the extraordinary experience of 34.5ff. Also the peculiar
ending of 40.35, with Moses unable to enter the new tent of encounter,
in a scene which contrasts with that of 33.9-10, can be connected to

a new application of the concepts.

This new application must also be connected to the emphasis on the people as 'evil' in chs. 32–34. The significance of the golden calf episode as an illustration of the character of the people is retained for the following scenes of intercession. The lasting 'stiff-neckedness' of the people is explicitly linked to the new forms of divine representation. Related to the categories of the I-psalms, the people of Exodus 25–40 are the embodiments both of the negative and the positive roles of the motif structure. Seen together, these factors could suggest that this interpretation reflects a democratization of the *ṣaddîq* paradigm.

In this case, chs. 25–40 could be seen as an expression of an interest which corresponds to the prophetic actualizations of the paradigm in Isa. 1.10ff. and Jeremiah 7. In both cases, 'the people' are related to the religious paradigm, the people cast in the role of the evil in the temple. The significance of the categories of dwelling in the temple is also reduced in these texts. But the material frames for the two types of applications differ: the evil in the prophetic texts is related to acts and attitudes of good behaviour connected to social categories; in Exodus 25–40 the evil is set in an environment of reinterpreted ritual reality. Moreover, Moses as a figure of transition who mediates the new relationship even to the point of erecting the new sanctuary all by himself, is central to the development in Exodus 25–40. Together with other expressions of the theme of the evil in the temple, these texts could witness to some considerable activity of theological reflection and reinterpretation at a certain period.

A process of transference and reinterpretation could also be expressed by the description of Moses in these chapters. The transition from Moses in intercession to his plea for seemingly egotistical aims in Exod. 33.18ff. represents a traditional exegetical crux. Isolated from the context and related to the I-psalms, the plea represents a normal expression of the goal of the I. But in the present context of Exodus 33, the plea's connection to the preceding intercession corresponds to its fulfilment in Exod. 34.8-9. At the summit of personal experience, the fleeting moment of the divine passing is exploited by Moses for a renewed intercession. In the new application, where Moses versus the people reflects the traditional contrast of positive and negative figures, the zenith of religious development is connected to the intercession on behalf of the losers.[155]

155. A similar transformation of the traditional 'élitist' figure related to the 'evil' could also be reflected in the epilogue of Job 42.9ff. The change of Job's fortunes is

f. *Conclusions*

An effort to pinpoint some basic findings within this fluid mass of rich
and subtly allusive materials feels rather distasteful, and must, given the
range of material and methodological questions involved, turn out as
woefully inadequate. But at the very least, these expressions of 'the evil
in the temple' open a considerable number of texts, representing different
literary genres, as possible applications of the motif structure. Also, the
subtlety of theological thought and the depth of feeling represented by
these texts add to the impression of the I-psalms as expressions of a
remarkable type of individual religiosity.

The significance of local categories for religious description is emphasized by these applications, especially in the Pentateuch stories. Events
which describe religious experiences and religious reality are projected
into some sacred space of sanctuary, holy mountain, Eden, places outside and inside the camp and so on, with contrast localities referring to
other levels of reality. Moreover, within the given context it is possible
to operate with a number of related localities which would seem to refer
to very different types of locality (e.g. Numbers 16, Exodus 24–40). In
the categories of sacred space, the religious description is expressed as
spatial relationships connected to the divine and human actors. This is
remarkable, as the motifs must refer to an inner reality of psychic and
mental-emotional character related to the biographical reality of normal
existence, and must reflect the significance and applicability of the basic
motifs of the structure.

In spite of the connection between the different text types, the relationship of the I-psalms to the narrative and prophetic texts seems to suggest
some fundamental difference between more original, or basic, and applied
actualizations. The different types of related texts stress the significance
of the I-psalms as the central expression of the given concepts and motif
sets. Compared to the comprehensive character of the psalms, the other
texts seem to express aspects of the motif structure as expositions of
some main concepts, often highly elaborate both with regard to literary
complexity and theological subtlety.

This also means that it is difficult to confine the motif structure to any
established socio-religious setting as the original *milieu*. The motif structure can be applied to a situation of priestly (Numbers 16–17, Exodus

---

not connected to the beatific vision of v. 5, but to his intercession on behalf of his
friends. Cf. also Coats, *Moses*, pp. 207-208 on the suffering servant of Isa. 40–55 as
a 'new Moses'.

25–31, 35–40) or prophetic (Numbers 12) categories, or to a situation of prophetic admonishment connected with ordinary worship (Isa. 1.10ff., Jer. 7). These texts also demonstrate that temple categories, which must be basic for this language, have a background in ritual reality. On the other hand, the application of the temple motifs in these texts transcends any confinements of literal use. Thus, the temple of, for example, Numbers 16 is contrasted to the negative tents of the evil, which are connected with the locality of Sheol. Compounded by the other applications of these texts, the possibilities of literary freedom and subtly allusive effects seem infinite.

Thus, these texts stress the basic ideological character of the motif structure as a vehicle of religious description. The literary figures are described not according to ordinary biographical data, but as embodiments of the paradigmatic roles of the motif structure. This also implies that the literary figures are presented as paradigmatic figures for the users of the texts.

While the function of the I-psalms is uncertain, some of the parallel texts could illustrate types of usage and application. Related to the different religious modes of the main figures described in Isa. 1.10ff. and Jeremiah 7, or in Numbers 16 and Exodus 32–34, Psalm 5 for example, could have the equally relevant functions of threatening admonishment, of promising exhortation, and of prayer and renewed commitment for those able to identify with the I-figure. In such a case, the I and the other actors of the text would represent literary figures, representing the possible modes of religious being to be actualized by the users. For the I-psalms as transmitted and used by posterity, this type of application could represent the characteristic usage.

The motif structure connected to such layers of religiosity presupposes psychic processes of internalization and identification. We have found such processes characteristic for the texts, which represent the theme 'the evil in the temple'. Related to these texts with the negative and positive paradigm applied to the same group of actors, the conflict of the I-psalms between the I and the enemies is internalized, referring primarily to inner commitment and choice between different modes of religious being for the individual actor.

Such processes correspond to characteristics we have found of some of the I-psalms. Thus, there are good reasons to see the I-psalms as expressions of—or at the very least closely related to—the same types of religiosity which are expressed in, for example, Isa. 1.10ff. or Exodus 25–40.

It is also possible that the differences between the applications of the I-psalms and some of the other texts could mirror more fundamental shifts of reinterpretation and reapplication of the motif structure. The relationship of, for example, Psalm 5 to the prophetic and narrative texts could demonstrate such a difference. The I-psalms seem to reflect some type of élitist religiosity centred round some special experience of intimate relationship to God, the I-figure being an expression of the positive paradigm. Applied to the people in, for example, Isa. 1.10ff., Jeremiah 7 and Exodus 25–40, the negative paradigm and the people as embodiment of the negative role form the central idea of the literary development. Thus, with the people for the religious actor, the application of the motif structure could reflect a process of extended application.

Such a process could also be related to the reduction of the significance of dwelling in the temple as connected to the mystical experience of God in these texts. Moreover, it could be significant that the religious qualification is different. In Isa. 1.10ff. and Jeremiah 7[156] lists of virtues describe the new ideal figure as qualified by acts and attitudes connected to social categories. In Exodus 25–40, at least on the superficial level, the new ideal is set in an environment of ritual reality, connected to priestly categories of mediation, with relationship to God depicted as relationship to a temple of sanctified priests passing from the outside to the inside.

This type of application couples the idea of ordinary people as expression for the religious paradigm with concepts of extraordinary relationship to Yahweh. Aside from the application of the motif structure on the priestly office (Numbers 16–17; Exodus 25–31, 35–40) and the function of the prophet in Isaiah 1, Jeremiah 7 and Ezekiel 18, it is above all the Moses figure in, for example, Numbers 16, 12 and Exodus 32–34 which demonstrates the significance of the extraordinary 'man of God' as necessary to the new application.

Thus, indirectly, the relationship between Moses and the people as parallel expressions of the religious paradigm in Exodus 25–40[157] is also an illustration of the difference between an original and a democratized

---

156. Cf. also the characteristics of the *ṣaddîq* Ezek. 18 with 3.18ff., 33.8ff. and further Ps. 15, 24 and Isa. 33.14-16.

157. Cf. also above to the prophet and the people as parallel 'measurers' in Ezek. 40–47.

application of the motif structure. In this story, Moses (and cf. Elijah as the parallel figure in 1 Kgs 19) is a perfected representative for the ideal figure of the I-psalms.

The texts do not give any clear indications of the background for what might represent a new type of application and reinterpretation of the religious paradigm. In Isa. 1.10ff. and Jeremiah 7, it is connected with a critical evaluation of ordinary religiosity, connected with new criteria of religious qualification. Exod. 33.18ff. and 1 Kgs 19.11ff., especially, could imply critical evaluations of the élitist religiosity. The elaboration of the conflict situation in the Moses stories—especially as prepared by the Genesis biographies connected to the theme of the contending brothers[158]—with the victor related to the evil as intercessor, could also reflect such an interest. The application of the Eden traditions in Genesis 2–4 could also be related to this interest as an expression of a general theological preoccupation with the religious significance of evilness.

In this way, the prophetic and narrative texts can represent a form of rupture with the past: the new applications are a reinterpretation determined by new interests. On the other hand, it is equally possible to stress the connection with the I-psalms: the new applications are an immediate extension of the traditional religiosity. Both the wealth of connotations and the possibilities for new literary expressions for the basic concepts illustrated by these texts warn against overly simple reconstructions of ideological development.

The I-psalms are fundamentally determined by the category of evil as relevant to the I-figure presented as the perfect confessor. In addition, the I-story can presuppose both a past history of lesser religious attainments (cf. above to Psalms 42–43) and a present of unperfected confession (e.g. Psalms 42–43, 36). With the I-psalms as expressions of religious development, the situation of the *ṣaddîqîm* is the ultimate goal and the I represents an unfinished story. This could also be related to the way motifs of the I-psalms. In Psalms 26 and also 84 especially, the application of the motif structure presents the I as a being of the way. Against this background, a situation in which the people as embodiments of the evil role is related to the religious paradigm might even represent the earlier phase of the story of the I. The relationship of Moses and the people as described in Numbers 16 and Exodus 32–34 could also be

158. Hauge, 'The Struggles of the Blessed', pp. 14-30.

relevant for the I-story. In Psalms 27 and 62 (cf. Chapter 6) the literary situation includes both an I as a paradigmatic figure and an admonished You related to the I. In this way, the relationship between élitist and democratized applications would merely reflect the different situations of religious address.

However this question is decided, it remains a remarkable fact that in the literary expressions for the evil in the temple, the representatives of the positive and the negative paradigm are described as human beings in a parallel striving towards or with a parallel dwelling in the temple. Compared to the literary possibilities for derogatory description of bad foreign kings, it is strange that the heroes of Isa. 14.4ff. and Ezek. 28.12ff. should be depicted in a movement of '*ālâ* or, as originally, 'on the mountain of Eden', given that the same motif types describe the strivings and the attainment of the positive figure. The significance of this parallelism is illustrated by Genesis 2–3, given to a theme of acquisition of divine wisdom or life and ch. 4 to a theme of acquisition of divine acceptance. The golden calf, produced as a substitute for Moses and representing the saviour from Egypt, must be an independent expression of the same theological understanding of evilness as somehow parallel to righteousness. In these texts, the negative ideal seems to be understood as a mock version or shadow-form of the positive. Only more or less subtle indications of usurpation or unproper attainment and application suggest the evilness of the hero.

Such a strange parallelism—added to by the elaboration of the evil hero as a tragic figure in, for example, Genesis 2–4 and the Genesis stories of the contending brothers—is remarkable. Its material implications suggest a foundation in some superior tradition of spiritual experience, referring to inner mental categories of striving and some subtle experience of religious striving gone wrong.

Such a definition of the negative figure could be connected to some crisis related both to an élitist (e.g. Exod. 33.18ff.; 1 Kgs 19) and an ordinary (e.g. Jer. 7) religiosity. In both cases, it reflects the profound religious character of the concepts involved. A religiosity of inner development and integration of the paradigm connected to personal biography can explain both the significance of the category of the evil and its definition as the shadow effort of the religious striving. Either in continuation of the religiosity of the I-psalms, or as expression of new types of reinterpretation and reapplication, these traditions of spirituality must have represented actual ways of reading the I-psalms.

Chapter 6

PSALM 62: THE CONFESSOR AS TEMPLE DWELLER

1. *Formal Character*

The psalm has proved rather resistant to any easy labels of genre. On the one hand, vv. 4-5 must refer to some kind of enemy situation with the enemies in the normal position of attack and persecution. This corresponds to the description of Yahweh as 'my rock', 'my refuge', 'my salvation' (vv. 2-3, 6-8), and points to the usual situation of the I in crisis. On the other hand, the forms of admonishment in vv. 9-13, usually related to forms of wisdom, must be important for the composition as a whole.

The dilemma can be illustrated by the solution of H. Schmidt. An original *Kern* in vv. 4-9 has been extended by vv. 2-3, the elements vv. 5-6 also used as introduction, and the cold *Lehre* in vv. 10ff.[1] When the significance of the first part in vv. 2-8 is stressed, the references to a situation of crisis and suffering are expressed by forms of confidence and trust.[2] There is no prayer,[3] and vv. 4-5 which correspond to the enemy description of the normal psalm,[4] have the form of a reproaching or accusing question. Seen as a whole, vv. 2-8 can be compared to the

---

1. Schmidt, *Psalmen*, p. 118; cf. also Gunkel, *Psalmen*, pp. 262-63 on vv. 4-8 as 'Vertrauenslied', added to by a series of 'Mahnungen' comparably to Pss. 130.7, 131.3.

2. Aside from the preceding references cf. Dahood, *Psalms II*, pp. 90; Taylor, *Psalms*, p. 322; and especially Beyerlin, *Die Rettung*, pp. 28-29 and F. Stolz, *Psalmen im nachkultischen Raum* (Theologische Studien 129; Zürich: Theologischer Verlag, 1983), pp. 51ff.

3. Cf. Gerstenberger, *Der bittende Mensch*, p. 124.

4. E.g. Kraus, *Psalmen*, p. 438, on vv. 4-5 as reflecting 'Stil der Klage', while Delekat, *Asylie*, p. 188, refutes such a connection. Due to vv. 4-5 as addressed to the enemies and the sufferer mentioned in the third person, the verses represent a citation of a formerly given oracle.

confessions of confidence in Ps. 27.1-6 and Psalm 23.

The motifs of this confession have been related to an institution of asylum. Some actual cultic situation for such a confession is suggested by the I as already accepted into the temple refuge by a divine oracle of admission.[5]

Related to a royal or representative I with national enemies, the expressions of crisis, confidence, and admonishment, all connected to a divine oracle, could reflect rites of protection.[6] Or with the royal I related to disloyalty within the people, vv. 4-5 could equally well represent forms of admonition addressed to the opponents, vv. 9ff. the exhortations to the people.[7]

The second part of the psalm can also be stressed. Verse 13 addressed to God[8] could represent the climax of the composition. Thus, to Eichhorn, vv. 12-13 mark the pivotal point. The I, with a cultic function as intercessionary mediator in a situation of national crisis, has received an oracle. The composition as a whole is given to the presentation of this oracle.[9]

These samples could at the very least demonstrate the connotative wealth of the text, as well as its flexibility for different types of application. If we put a greater emphasis on literary categories and relate the

---

5.   To Kraus, *Psalmen*, pp. 436-37, the expressions of confidence reflect the reception of the 'oracle of salvation', vv. 12b-13, which forms the basis both of vv. 2-8 and 9ff., the latter typical for a 'song of thanksgiving'. Related to the events of the ritual situation, the oracle represents an introductory 'Schutzerklärung', while the final divine verdict on the case is yet to come (p. 438). To Delekat, *Asylie*, pp. 188-89, vv. 4-5 represent the 'Aufnahmeorakel' related to a concrete situation of the enemies seeking to deceive the I into leaving the asylum and the city. This is refused by the I, who in vv. 9ff. demonstrate why the rich city-dwellers want him away. Such views are strongly opposed by Beyerlin, *Die Rettung*, pp. 28-29, to whom the text represents 'eine vergeistigt-verinnerliche Rettungshoffnung ohne den Rückhalt einer speziellen Kultinstitution'; cf. also Stolz, *Psalmen*, pp. 51ff.

6.   Birkeland, *Die Feinde*, pp. 257ff.; Mowinckel, *Psalms I*, pp. 219-20.

7.   Eaton, *Kingship*, p. 49; cf. also Croft, *The Identity of the Individual*, pp. 127-28, on vv. 9-11 as oracle of salvation delivered after vv. 2ff. understood as prayer, while vv. 12-13 reflects the king's response.

8.   M.E. Tate, *Psalms 51–100* (Word Biblical Commentary 20; Dallas: Word Books, 1990), p. 119.

9.   *Gott als Fels*, p. 38. While vv. 9-13 is usually seen as influenced by Wisdom, vv. 12b-13 is described as an oracle on God as the 'rock' of the people, vv. 9ff. understood 'in Strukturanalogie zur Gerichtsrede der vorexilischen Propheten' (p. 37).

text to the psalms analysed earlier, the confession vv. 2-3 and 6-8 stands out, both as repeated and as connected with Pss. 42.6, 12, 43.5.

a. *Verses 2-3, 6-8*

> Yes!—'towards' God is there 'silence'! my soul.
> From him is my salvation.
> Yes!—he is my rock and my salvation,
> my tower—I shall not totter much.
>
> Yes!—'before' God be 'still'! my soul.
> For from him is my hope.
> Yes!—he is my rock and my salvation,
> my tower—I shall not totter.
> 'Upon' God is my salvation and my glory,
> the rock of my stronghold, my refuge is 'on' God.

The small differences between vv. 2-3 and 6-7 are traditionally emended into a perfected refrain.[10] The commentators' assurance with regard to this rather evocative compilation of formulaic nominal constructions, applied with a subtle technique of repetition and variation, is probably a reflex of earlier ideas on the literary relationship of vv. 2-3 and 6-7 (cf. above). In its present form, v. 2a represents a statement, while 6a shifts the elements of this statement into an exhortation followed by a motivating *kî*—clause. Because of the parallel constructions of 2a and 6a, the concluding 'my soul' must have a parallel function as the addressee also in 2a.

In this way, vv. 2 and 6 express a situation with the I talking to and exhorting his soul. This corresponds to the literary frame of Psalm 42 where the psalm as a whole with its address to God is related to a situation of communication with the soul. An elaborate illustration of such a situation is represented by Ps. 131.2, where the I presents himself as one who has weaned the soul into a stage characterized by stillness.

Verses 2-8 are dominated by forms of confidence framed by the address to the soul and correspond to the composition of Psalms 42–43. The structure of confessing I-forms followed by exhortations in vv. 9ff. corresponds to Psalm 131 (cf. also 130, and further above to 27 concluded by the exhortation in v. 14).[11]

---

10. Kraus, *Psalmen*, p. 436, ponders whether the differences reflect 'eine Variation oder eine Variante'.

11. The connection between Pss. 131, 42–43, 62, and Lam. 3.21ff. is emphasized by Beyerlin, *Wider die Hybris*, pp. 63ff., with references also to Ps. 77.3.

The connection between these texts is also demonstrated by a common dependence on motifs related to the address to the soul. In 62.2a, 6a, the parallel location and the effect of alliteration suggest that *dûmiyyâ* and the imperative of *dāmam* reflect aspects of a common motif of stillness. While the other usages of *dûmiyyâ*[12] suggest that the statement in v. 2a refers to silence, *dāmam* in pol. form is connected with *šiwwâ*[13] for the instruction of the soul in 131.2. Further, forms of *yḥl* are found in the exhortations Pss. 42.6, 12, 43.5 and 131.3. This corresponds to the exhortation in Ps. 130.7, while the parallel I-forms in v. 5 add *qiwwâ* for the paradigmatic waiting. This usage connects to the concluding exhortation of Ps. 27.14.[14] The cluster of words and motifs obviously refers to a given background, centred round a concept of the still and waiting soul/person as an expression of the religious paradigm.

The motivating statements related to the address to the soul in 62.2-3, 6-8 and 42–43 suggest a special background in given forms. The motivations comprise sentences in the first person on the fate of the I as related to Yahweh: the repeated 'I shall not totter (much)' (62.3b, 7b) corresponds to 'I shall yet praise' of the refrain in Psalms 42–43. In both cases the divine 'salvation' is an important motif (62.2b, 3a, 7a, 8a and in the refrain in Pss. 42–43).[15] The Yahweh qualifications with suffixes in the first person dominate formally the motivations in Psalm 62.[16] This is comparable to the concluding elements of Pss. 42.12b, 43.5b. Aside from the unusual 'my face' added to 'my God', the significance of these forms is emphasized by the elements 'your God' in v. 11 and 'my God' in Ps. 43.4 which both conclude the preceding parts and prepare for the following address to the soul (cf. the introductory 'my God' in v. 7 immediately after v. 6). The function of these bridging elements in

12. Pss. 22.3; 39.3; 65.2.

13. Isa. 38.13; cf. the different usages Pss. 16.8, 18.34, 21.6, 89.20, 119.30 which suggest basic connotations of 'localization'.

14. Cf. also these words Lam. 3.21, 24, 25, 26 together with motifs of 'stillness', vv. 26 and 28, related to Yahweh's 'salvation', v. 26 and to 'hope', v. 29 corresponding to Ps. 62.2, 6. The significance of this series of statements in I-form in Lam. 3.21ff. is added to by v. 20, where the state of anguish is described by the Soul's *zakar* and *šîaḥ*, corresponding to Ps. 42.5ff.

15. Cf. Lam. 3.26 as a third type of combination of the given motifs.

16. In Lam. 3.24a a similar nominal sentence in the first-person form represent the confession of the soul. The relationship of the confession to the statement in Lam. 3.24b (cf. also v. 21 related to vv. 22ff.) corresponds to the relationship of exhortation and motivation in Pss. 62 and 42–43.

Pss. 42.7, 11, 43.4 can be compared to v. 8 in Psalm 62, which both connects formally to the preceding first-person statements and introduces the central Yahweh qualifications in the following exhortations.

b. *Verses 4-5*

> How long will you shout[17] against a man?
> all of you shall be killed!
> Like a wall bent down, a fence pushed in,
> Yes! from his exaltedness they counsel to thrust him.
> They favour falsehood,
> by the mouth they bless, by their inner they curse.

These verses framed by the address to the soul correspond to the main *corpus* of Psalms 42–43 as an expression for the I in crisis, connected with the enemy situation.[18] But for this expression of the crisis, we note not only the absence of the prayer forms, but also the consistent use of third-person forms for the sufferer. The vocalization of the second sentence of v. 4—usually emended into some form of complaint—even turns v. 4 into a threat.[19] Without the corresponding motifs of the context, vv. 4-5 could be seen as a relatively independent rhetorical address to the evil without any explicit connection to the I-forms, similarly to Ps. 52.3-7.

Thus, on the one hand, vv. 4-5 refer to the situation of normal crisis, a negative outcome fatal for the I as fallen and cast out and corresponding to the negative fate of Ps. 5.11. As usual, the enemies are characterized as evil, in a third-person description in the second line of v. 5.[20]

17. Cf. *BDB*, while the usual translation has been 'rush upon' with the following verb emended to a corresponding motif of *rûṣ*, e.g. Kraus, *Psalmen*, p. 435: 'bestürmen—anrennen'.

18. To Seybold, *Das Gebet*, p. 68, these verses refer to sickness.

19. With the second sentence of v. 4 vocalized according to MT, the comparisons of the second line of v. 4 could have a double function as equally related to the destruction of the enemies of v. 4 and the I of v. 5. This corresponds to the imagery of the comparisons. The implicit motif of falling is equally relevant for the killing of the enemies and the I removed from 'exaltedness'. Such a connection is also suggested by the motif of *ndḥ* in hiph. form v. 5 which corresponds to the enemies Ps. 5.11a as 'fallen' and 'cast out'. Connected to motifs of dwelling in the temple, the enemies obviously also here depicted as present in the sanctuary (cf. below), the motifs of defeat are equally relevant for the contenders.

20. Formally, the intermediate comparisons in the second line of v. 4 facilitate the transition from the enemies addressed in v. 4 and referred to in v. 5.

The contrast between the outer, connected to talking, and inner reality corresponds to, for example, Pss. 5.10 and 55.22. On the other hand, the elaboration of the normal situation marks a peculiarly de-tensed reference to the crisis.

When we see vv. 4-5 as an expression of the enemy crisis, introduced and followed by the address to the soul in vv. 6ff., the composition corresponds to the compositional pattern of Psalms 42–43. When we stress the special form of vv. 4-5 related to vv. 6ff. with confessions in I-form, the composition can be compared to a similar address to the evil in Ps. 52.3ff. Here, an introductory rhetorical question in v. 3a is contrasted with a declaratory statement of the divine 'grace' in v. 3b, followed by a description of the evilness of the You in vv. 4-6, concluded by stating imperfect forms on the destruction of the evil in v. 7.[21] Moreover, the motifs in the contrasting self-description in vv. 10-11, the I described with motifs of dwelling in the temple, as 'eternally' 'trusting' in the divine 'grace', and as 'waiting', can be related to the I-forms and admonishments of Psalm 62.[22]

In Psalm 52, the evil and the I are not related to each other as contenders, but function as contrasted expressions of the religious paradigm. A similar function can also explain the special form of the enemy situation in Psalm 62.

c. *Verses 9-13*

> Trust in him always! you people
> Pour out your hearts before him!
> God is our refuge.
> Yes! emptiness are the sons of man, falsehood the sons of men.
> In a pair of scales they rise. These are emptiness, all together.
> Do not trust in oppression! Do not become empty through robbery!
> Might—if it bears fruit—do not take it to heart!
> Once did God speak, twice this I heard:
> Strength belongs to God!
> To you, my Lord! belongs grace.
> For you recompense a man according to his doing.

The relationship of vv. 2-8 as a series of self-descriptive confessions in I-form and vv. 9ff. as a series of exhortations addressed to You

---

21. Cf. also the common motifs for the description of the evil v. 9 and in the admonishments Ps. 62.9a, 11.

22. Cf. also the confession v. 10b with God in the third person followed by God addressed in the concluding v. 11 corresponding to Ps. 62.12 and 13.

corresponds to the structure of Psalms 130–31. When we pay attention to the soul motifs of Psalms 62 and 131, emphasized by the refrain of Psalms 42–43, the connection is striking. Either in the form of a description addressed to Yahweh in Psalm 131 or as exhortations addressed to the soul in Psalms 42–43 and 62, the texts reflect a given situation of the spiritually more advanced I split from his soul and related to it in the role of admonishing teacher. The ideal of the soul's stillness represents the aim of the teacher in both Psalms 62 and 131.

The significance of these parallel texts is emphasized by the literary development in Psalm 62. The concluding localization and elaborate character of vv. 9ff. could suggest that these verses represent the central interest of the composition. Formally, the exhortations in vv. 9ff. are integrated into the text. This is seen by the final vv. 12-13 which revert to the first-person forms.[23] In this way, the exhortations are embedded in confessing forms. Within such a formal frame, the confessing I of vv. 2-6 and 12-13 represents the exhorter addressing the people in vv. 9ff.

Such a connection is also suggested by v. 8. This verse makes an extension to the refrain of vv. 2-3 and 6-7. Its formal character, with a series of short nominal constructions which describe God related to 'me', corresponds to the motivating statements of the refrain.[24] The slightly different rendering of the motifs 'rock' and 'my salvation' in v. 8 refers to the central vv. 3a, 7a.[25] On the other hand, the words 'strength' and 'refuge' in v. 8b are also used for the statements on God in vv. 9b and 12b. The central significance of these statements for the admonishments is seen by the elaborate introduction in v. 12a, while v. 9b motivates the positive admonishment in v. 9. Given this background, the application of these terms in v. 8b can hardly be coincidental, but must prepare for the application in the admonishments.[26]

23. To the significance of concluding I-forms cf. Ps. 92.16 and 52.10-11 related to the preceding third-person forms and 118.28 related to the preceding we-forms.

24. Concretely, the terms with suffixes in the first person related to 'God' with prepositions correspond to vv. 2b, 6b, and could reflect the significance of the soul's 'stillness' *'æl* and *le* God, vv. 2a, 6a.

25. With 'my hope' in v. 6b , differing from the parallel v. 2b, a too repetitive style is avoided.

26. Cf. the similar compositional technique, vv. 12b and 13 first line with the transition from third-person statements on God to second-person hymnic address expressed by two parallel nominal constructions in inverted order, bridged by the preposition *le*.

In this way, v. 8 as an extension to the refrain of vv. 6-7 seems to have a function of transition, linking the I-forms vv. 2-7 to the admonishments in vv. 9ff. With a parallel linkage expressed by the concluding I-forms in vv. 12-13, the composition suggests an important connection between the 'objective' forms of admonishment and the 'subjective' forms on the I as confessor.

Such a compositional interest is also reflected in the present form of the refrain in vv. 2-3 and 6-7. With v. 2a as a statement and v. 6a as an exhortation, the development of the refrain prepares for the exhortations in vv. 9ff. The situation of the I as confessor, addressing and admonishing his soul, is gradually extended into a wider scene of admonishment, with the I admonishing the people.

This connection is also suggested by the form of vv. 9-10. The first sentence of the address in vv. 2a, 6a, and 9a has a similar structure, with the addressee 'you people' in the final position corresponding to 'you my soul'. In all the three cases, the address is followed by a motivating statement on God in vv. 2b, 6b, 9b. In vv. 3 and 6, this is followed by a further motivation introduced by *'ak*. This corresponds to the similarly introduced v. 10 with a contrasting negative motivation, which prepares the negative admonishment in v. 11.

A connection between positive and negative motivations is also reflected in the motif usage. The context of the admonishments in vv. 9ff. suggests a contrast relationship between humanity as 'breath' in v. 10 (repeated, cf. also *hbl* in 11a) and human 'might' (11b) and God as 'refuge' in v. 9b and with 'strength' in v. 12b. At the same time, the sentence construction of vv. 3a, 7a and the first sentence of 10a express a contrast between the central qualification of God as 'rock' and humanity as weightless 'breath' (cf. the connection between the three qualifications of God in v. 8b).

In this way, vv. 9-10 can be seen as an application of the refrain, the confession of the I applied as admonishment to the people. The structure of the psalm as a whole can be described as a repeated structure of address (vv. 2a, 6a, 9a, 11) and motivation (vv. 2b-3, 6b-8, 9b-10, 12b with the conclusion v. 13).[27] Verses 4-5 formally represent an address to and description of the enemies, thus including the enemies as present in

---

27. With the structure added to by the submotivation, v. 13b, related to the statement of v. 13a. For the composition as a whole, this puts a special emphasis on the divine *hæsæd* here defined as retribution. This can be compared to the application of the term Ps. 52.3 related to the evil, 36.7-8 related to those seeking refuge.

the complex literary situation. But as to function, the verses form part of
vv. 2b-3, preparing the renewed address to the soul in 6a.

Within the series of motivations, the introduction v. 12a stresses the
significance of the concluding vv. 12b-13.[28] These verses—with 12b as
the oracle proper, due to v. 13 as addressed to God—correspond to the
dogmatic statements of religious truth found to be basic for the other
texts (cf. especially Pss. 5, 36, 84, and 140). The introduction in v. 12a
can be compared to the introduction 'I know' of Ps. 140.13.[29] Verse 13
formally changes the statement into a confession addressed to God. But
both the *le*-construction of v. 13a and the sentence type of v. 13b[30] give
the two statements in vv. 12-13 as closely related. The statement of
v. 12b is presented as the contents of a divine revelation, while v. 13 turns
the revealed truth into a confessing response. The relationship between a
general truth and confessing forms corresponds to the relationship
between the third-person statements and first-person forms of the other
texts.

Within the texts analysed above, such statements are usually juxtaposed to negative statements on the fate of the evil. In Psalm 62 a comparable negative saying is found in v. 10 on humanity as weightless
'breath'. The contrast between God and humanity in this psalm corresponds to the positive and negative application of *bāṭaḥ* in the admonishments vv. 9a and 11.

The admonishing interest is also reflected in the special expression of
the I in crisis in vv. 4-5. On the one hand, v. 5 especially represents a
traditional reference to the enemy situation. On the other hand, v. 4
greatly reduces the tension of the crisis. Verse 3b with the motif of
'tottering' corresponds to the motifs of v. 5, linking the description of
the crisis to the confession. In this way, vv. 4-5 prepare for the following
admonishment in v. 6a. Within this composition, the reference to the
enemy situation functions as an expression of confidence. This corresponds to the use of the enemy motifs in Ps. 27.1-6. In Psalm 27 the

28. Usually characterized as an oracle of promise or salvation. To its significance
in the composition cf. especially Eichhorn, *Gott als Fels*, p. 38, to its formal character
Beyerlin, *Die Rettung*, p. 28, who finds that its reflected character and the stylistic
influence of wisdom suggests a certain 'zeitliche Abstand' from the supposed
original 'Verkündigungsgeschehen'.

29. Cf. also the following statement, v. 14, introduced by *'ak*, which can
correspond to the application of this element in Ps. 62.

30. Cf. above to Pss. 5.12, 140.13, and also 36.11.

confessions with the I as the paradigmatic confessor are related to a situation of crisis (vv. 7-13) and a concluding exhortation addressed to a You in v. 14. This formal structure is comparable to Psalm 62, with vv. 4-5 followed by the exhortations to 'my soul' in vv. 6ff. and to the 'people' addressed as You in vv. 9ff.

In the texts analysed earlier, we have found descriptions of the enemies attacking the I related to general statements on the fate of the evil. Within this pattern, the enemies of the I are depicted as embodiments of the paradigmatic evil. In this psalm, v. 10 represents a similar general statement. But here this statement has a subordinate function, related to the exhortations of vv. 10 and 11. In addition, general negative qualifications are used in the exhortation of v. 11, with 'oppression' and 'robbery' corresponding to the description of the enemies in vv. 4-5. The use of *hbl* links the general statement in v. 10 and the exhortation in v. 11. By 'trusting' 'oppression' instead of 'God',[31] the people will 'become empty' like weightless humankind. Within this motif development, the evil are depicted as negative figures of imitation.

Against this background, the composition of the psalm as a whole is dominated by the exhortative interest of vv. 9ff. Moreover, the compositional development seems to express an interest in linking the two situations of the I addressing his soul and addressing the people. The admonishment of the people is an immediate extension of the I addressing his soul. In both cases, the I stands forth as the confessor.

This represents an interesting connection with Psalms 42–43 and 131. Common to Psalms 62 and 42–43 is a basic situation of the I talking to and admonishing his soul. While Psalms 42–43 confines the dialogue to man and soul in distress, Psalm 62 extends the dialogue to include the people as a second object of admonishment. This links to Psalm 131. But in the latter psalm, there is no formal link between the two situations of admonishment. Here, the I with a perfectly weaned soul is presented as an exemplary figure to be imitated by the addressed Israel.

The concept of the confessing I as an exemplary figure must also be expressed by the composition of Psalm 62, with a connection between I-forms and admonishments and between the two situations of admonishment. In this way, the I and his enemies are presented as embodiments of the negative and positive paradigms. This corresponds to the texts analysed above. In Psalm 62, however, the function of the I

31. Cf. also human 'might', v. 11a contrasted by the following statement on God's 'strength', v. 12b (in addition to v. 8b).

as paradigmatic figure presented as an ideal for imitation is much more striking. We have discussed this function for the I-figure above and especially in connection with Psalm 27. The relationship of Psalms 131, 62 and 42–43 to 'normal' prayer psalms more directly centred round the I in distress, could reflect important aspects of the function of the I-psalms. Given this background, Psalms 62 and 131 together with, for example, 27, 31, and 55 could be seen as reflections of a function of application and exhortation connected with a process of identification with the I-figure.

This could also explain the special form of Psalm 52. The structure of threatening address to the evil in vv. 3-7 followed by a parallel description by the righteous in vv. 8-9 and contrasting confessions in I-form in vv. 10-11 in Psalm 52 represent a rather special composition without any immediate relationship between the three sub-units. But related to Psalm 62, 52 could reflect an interest of admonishment connected to the evil and the I as contrasted paradigmatic figures. The composition represents a rhetorical compilation of certain stereotypes[32] which are meaningful as allusions to the given literary situation of the I-story. In this way, the special expressions of the I-story given in Psalms 52, 62 and 131 compared to, for example, Psalms 42/43, 27, 31, and 55 could reflect different degrees of the traditional literary shape influenced by the interest of application and function.

2. *The Application of the Motif Structure in Psalm 62: Dwelling in the Temple as a State of Religious Being*

Translated into a literary/fictional situation, the formal development of Psalm 62 reflects a complex drama of added sets of situations. The I is depicted in a situation of distress, under attack and addressing his enemies. But this situation of normal crisis is extended into a situation of the I addressing his soul with confession and exhortation. The address to the soul is further extended, the exhortation related to a new set of actors, with the people addressed.

The motif usage which describes the situation of the I is rather simple. Comparably to Ps. 27.1-6, it is centred round two basic motifs: the I is in crisis, related to the attack of the enemies (vv. 4-5); the I is related to a locality, described by motifs which refer to temple categories.

---

32. Cf. Ps. 52.3-7 compared to e.g. Ps. 62.4-5; the parallel qualification of the evil in Ps. 52.9 to 62.10; Ps. 52.10-11 to the I-forms of 62.

In Psalm 62, however, the motif usage does not separate between motifs on the temple and on the divine presence within the temple. Verses 3, 7, 9b imply God as a locality 'upon' which or 'in' which one stands oneself. Verse 8 refers to similar categories slightly mitigated, with 'my salvation' and 'my pride' located *'al* God (v. 8a), 'the rock of my stronghold' and 'my refuge' *be* God (v. 8b). On the other side, 'my salvation' 'from' God (vv. 2b, 6b) and the 'hearts poured out' 'before' him implies a directional relationship (cf. also the orientation of the soul in vv. 2a, 6a).

Parts of the imagery might reflect ancient concepts of some local divinity as originally identified with, for example, a certain sacred rock of the sanctuary, preserved through ritual practices. For such rites, the concepts connected with an act of standing oneself upon the rock could have been important.[33] But in the present usage, different types of motifs are added to each other. Related to the other texts, this usage seems to represent elliptical versions of more traditional types which separate between God and temple. Thus, for example, Pss. 43.3b-4, 5.8, 26.6-8, 27.4-6, 84.5, 8 convey more 'correct' impressions of relationship to God in the temple. On the other hand, Pss. 140.14, 5.5, 12, 42.2-3 and also 36.8-10 (with only v. 9b as direct reference to 'your house') represent stereotypical and elliptical allusions to dwelling in the temple. Parallel to the motif usage of Psalm 62, the latter examples stress the relationship to Yahweh as the essential characteristic of the temple motifs.

Whatever the background of the imagery, it stresses the importance of the religious being visualized by motifs of locality. Either in a posture of absolute stillness or as localized to a rock or some space of protection, the I as confessor is described by local categories.

The enemy situation of vv. 4-5 must refer to these categories. With the use of *dāḥâ* in v. 4b, the comparison 'Like a wall bent down, a fence pushed in' links to the situation of v. 5 with the enemies planning to *ndḥ* in hiph. form 'from his *śe'eṯ*'. The normal usage of *śe'eṯ*—aside from the technical use in Leviticus—refer to categories of position and dignity.[34] As linked to the comparison of v. 4, the expression could

33. E.g. Eichhorn, *Gott als Fels*, pp. 83ff., connected with the rock as 'Wohn- und Offenbarungsstätte Jahwes' reserved for the chosen intermediary; Delekat, *Asylie*, pp. 207ff., on 'standing on the rock' as the central act of the asylum seeker in search of divine protection.

34. Often emended in this text, but central to, for example, Croft, *Identity of the*

allude to some imagery of the man as elevated. This is supported by the context. The preceding formula 'I shall not totter' in v. 3b corresponds to the enemies trying to 'thrust' somebody from an elevated position. The formula of v. 3b is related to the preceding imagery of v. 3a with the I related to God as rock and tower. These motifs imply connotations of height, the I located to some elevated place. The motif usage of Ps. 27.5b related to vv. 5-6 and Ps. 61.3b related to vv. 3-5 stresses the traditional character of this imagery. The standing place of the I on the rock is a place of *rûm* (Ps. 61.3), Yahweh *rômēm* the I upon it (Ps. 27.5b; *nḥh* in hiph. form 61.3), his head *rûm* above the enemies around (Ps. 27.6).

These texts must be individual expressions of the same concepts. Details differ. Thus, in Pss. 27.5b and 61.3b Yahweh is not identified with the sacred rock. With the parallel terms of Pss. 27.5a and 61.5, 'rock' obviously is a comprehensive term for the temple as a whole, stressing certain aspects of its character as the elevated localization. But the insistence on Yahweh as subject for the movement of the I, 'elevating' onto the 'elevated place', is comparable to the categories of Ps. 62.3. With Yahweh either as 'my rock' or 'elevating' onto the rock, the imagery must allude to a common background in the miraculous aspects of the temple categories, usually expressed by motifs of divine intervention, guidance/admission, or of relationship to the presence.

This is related to the imagery of the immediately following vv. 4-5 in Psalm 62. In the present context, the 'thrusting' from 'exaltedness' connected to a comparison of 'walls bent down and thrust', continue the situation of the I related to God as 'my rock' and 'my tower', not given to 'totter'. Compared to Yahweh *nḥh* in hiph. form (Ps. 61.3) or *rômēm* (Ps. 27.5) the I unto the rock, *ndḥ* in hiph. form in Ps. 62.5, with the enemies for subject, must refer to the opposite movement.[35]

In this way, *ndḥ* in hiph. form related to the exalted position of dwelling in the temple, and with the enemies for subject, corresponds to its usage in the enemy prayer Ps. 5.11, with Yahweh for subject. To be removed from the temple signifies the negative fate. In Psalm 5, the negative fate is connected with the motif of falling (v. 11; cf. also the death motifs in v. 10), in Psalm 62 with the corresponding imagery of tottering in addition to the implied connotations of being brought down

Individual, p. 128, and Eaton, *Kingship*, p. 49 as referring to the royal eminence.

35. Cf. the expressions for the negative movement Ps. 26.9 with Yahweh for subject, and 36.12-13 with the enemies for subject.

from an exalted position. The conceptual connection between these motifs is seen in Pss. 36.12-13 and 26.9, with a parallel negative movement, contrasted with temple motifs and related to the locality of Sheol as the place of falling (36.13) or as togetherness with the evil.

The relationship of Pss. 62.4-5, 5.11, 36.12-13, and 26.9 demonstrates that the many singular motifs which describe the relationship between I and his enemies, could be abstracted to the idea of a struggle between life and death. The enemies seek to have the I killed, the I correspondingly prays for their death. The linkage to the categories of dwelling in the temple in Psalms 5 and 62, with removal from the temple as the expression of the negative fate, stresses this correspondence. In both texts, the motif development suggests that the confrontation takes place in the sanctuary. In Psalm 5, the enemies are even depicted as fellow aspirants to dwell in the temple, the I praying for their expulsion. In Psalm 62 only the negative part of the confrontation is expressed, in the form of the enemies' efforts to push the I away.

But the individual expressions of the concepts vary. In Psalm 62, the description of the enemy situation in vv. 4-5 linked to the confession to God as rock and tower and the formula 'I shall not totter' suggest an imagery comparable to Pss. 118.13a and 36.13: the I standing, the enemies around and 'pushing' so the stander shall 'fall'.

This rather special imagery also corresponds to the extension *rabbâ* added to the usual formula 'I shall not totter' in v. 3b. Seen isolated, the 'very much' seems a rather pedantic little modification of the exuberant confession, and has suffered accordingly in the hands of the commentators. But related to vv. 4-5, it corresponds well to a situation of the stander as 'bent and pushed' under the attack of the enemies. Also, it corresponds to the exhortation for 'stillness' addressed to the soul, both with regard to motif consistency[36] and as an encouraging motivation. This scene can be compared to the scenes of triumph in Pss. 27.5b-6 and 23.5, with dwelling in the temple related to the enemies. But as a scene of confrontation, it corresponds especially to the motif elaborations of Psalm 5 and Numbers 16.[37]

---

36. Cf. the corresponding imagery of Ps. 11.1 where taking refuge 'on' Yahweh contrasts the soul as a bird fleeing to the 'mountains'.

37. Cf. also the no-tottering as the rewards of dwelling in the temple, Ps. 15.5b and the implicit situation of permanent siege connected with dwelling in the temple, Isa. 33.16.

Compared to the other texts, Psalm 62 represents a radical contraction of the motif structure. The applications of the motif structure in other texts reflect a series of events, with dwelling in the temple related to miraculous categories of divine guidance and admission as the triumphant conclusion of the story of the I. Also in Psalm 62, the motif usage reflects that dwelling in the temple represents the *summum bonum* of the pattern. In addition, dwelling in the temple visualized as 'standing on the rock' is the pivotal point: the enemy crisis, the I as confessor extended into the exhortation of the soul, and the implicit divine intervention are connected to this situation. All is concentrated in the situation of the I in some delicate act of balancing upon the sacred rock, the enemies trying to unbalance the stander.[38] The main events of the motif structure take place in the temple, contracted into one scene of dwelling in the temple. Here, the important difference between outside and inside the temple has been dissolved. The outside events have been transposed into the temple, while the meaning of the inside events has been changed. With dwelling in the temple seen as an act of balancing upon the sacred rock, the formal significance of the temple motifs has been dissolved. Volitional aspects seem to dominate the motif application in Psalm 62. The motifs of dwelling in the temple and of the relationship to the divine presence represent a marked weakening of the miraculous categories. With the I as balancing stander, related to God as rock, and the soul exhorted to stillness, dwelling in the temple represents an act of trust and confession and single-minded concentration. It must be important that this volitional and exhortative function is closely connected with the miraculous categories. The act of confession and exhortation depends on the divine presence, the not-tottering connected to God as the 'rock' and 'tower'. For this application, dwelling in the temple seems to serve as comprehensive category for the motif structure as a whole and thus as a concentrated expression of religious being.

The motif contraction of Psalm 62 can be seen as a radical expression of similar operations in some other texts. Thus, both Pss. 26.6-7 and 5.8 use the motif entrance into the temple with a volitional function as qualification of the I as not-evil (cf. above to Ps. 84.6, 11). Together with Exodus 32 and also Isa. 1.10ff. and Jeremiah 7, these texts[39] witness to a

---

38. Cf. the similar application of way motifs in Ps. 26, with the miraculous categories of Ps. 43.3-4 expressed in volitional categories of non-tottering walking Ps. 26.1, 3, here related to a situation of ultimate standing, v. 12.

39. Cf. also the application of firmly standing in Ps. 112.6-8.

type of application where motifs of dwelling in the temple are used as a comprehensive category for a general description of religious being. In this way, Psalm 62 could provide a key to the other, more complicated applications of the motif structure.

3. *The Motif Structure as a Language of Religious Experience*

The character of the motif development in Psalm 62 can be added to what was found characteristic in Psalm 5. In the traditional form-historical operation of transposition, the literary situation of the I in Psalm 62 is directly transferred into some institutional situation of cultic character connected with a hypothetical biographical situation. This interpretation is absurd for this text.[40] On the other hand, it is natural to surmise that both the motifs as well as their basic relationship are derived from normal temple practice and ideology. The connection between the basic concepts of the psalm language and some normal cultic practice makes it possible to suppose constant interaction between psalm language and cult. For any prayer situation connected with ordinary life crises, as represented by, for example, the worshippers of Isa. 1.10ff. and Jeremiah 7, Psalm 62 as well as Psalm 5 would have been equally applicable. But the psalm language reflects an independent development of the connotations of temple practice in a language of conceptual character.

In the same way, it would be absurd to translate the psalm into some typical contemporary social reality, or to isolate single motifs as more biographical than others. Here as in the other psalms, the I-forms reflect some kind of autobiography. But the autobiography—especially when compared to the other I-stories cast in the same mould—is described by a set of motifs which transcends normal reality. For our perception of this difference, the motif development of Psalm 62 is especially helpful with an imagery so clearly separate from normality. With the connection between Psalm 62 and the other I-psalms analysed above,[41] this must

---

40. Cf. the commentators' reticence (with Delekat, *Asylie*, pp. 188-89, for exception) with regard to biographical conclusions drawn from Ps. 62.

41. Usually ignored by the separation of texts supposed to reflect different types of relationship to the surmised underlying rite, for example, Beyerlin, *Rettung*, pp. 9-10, with psalms 'mit Rettungsaussagen ohne Institutionsbezug' and 'mit institutions-bezogenen Rettungsaussagen' (cf. pp. 18ff. on the methodological problems involved); Seybold, *Das Gebet*, p. 8, on psalms with 'sicherem', 'sehr wahrscheinlichem' and

have consequences for our understanding of the other applications.

Compared to normal biographical reality, the I-psalms must refer to some sacred 'super-reality' of religious experience, with the I, the enemies, God, and temple/contrast localities for basic components. Nor can this other reality be confined to some physical dwelling in the temple precinct. In Psalm 62, the temple motifs express a special religious state of constant relationship to God, the threat of the enemies related to the state of relationship described as a kind of inner equilibrium. While normal biographical experience clearly is included, the language itself provides the categories for the religious description of this experience.

This could suggest that the I-figure really represents a fictional figure of literary character, created as a theological-religious construction. Earlier we have repeatedly been confronted by this possibility. As a fictional character, the I-figure could reflect both a background of mythic categories[42] and/or a presence of theological concern.[43]

The stereotypical character of the I-psalms, especially when seen as parallel applications of a common motif structure, stresses this possibility. Also, the I-figure presented as a religious paradigm, related to the evil as expression of the negative paradigm, could be connected to such a function. Connected to, for example, some didactic interest, the textual 'I' is presented to the reader/listener as a fictional I in connection with a process of identification, the reader identifying with the religious hero, rejecting the negative ideal. The narrative applications of the motif structure (cf. above Chapter 5) seem especially characterized by the motif structure applied as a conceptual frame for some theological concern.

On the other hand, this religious super-reality seems to be closely connected with the normal level of reality. Thus, while, for example,

---

'unsicherem Bezug zu Krankheit'; cf. also Stolz, *Psalmen*, pp. 21ff. on 'Kultpsalmen im nachkultischen Raum'.

42. Cf. the I-psalms seen as expressions for a mythic-cultic pattern connected to the role of the suffering king during the New Year Festival developed in the 'Myth and Ritual' tradition and the 'Uppsala-school', especially related to the idea of 'democratization', e.g. Widengren, *Sakrales Königtum*, p. 41. Connected to such a pattern of basic cosmic laws experienced as cultic drama, the individual subjective biography would be subordinated the 'objective' biography.

43. E.g. Brueggemann, 'Shape for Old Testament Theology I-II', with the I-psalms related to a bi-polar tension between 'structure legitimation' and 'embrace of pain'. Cf. also Collins, 'Decoding the Psalms', putting the emphasis on the I-psalms as sub-units with a function in the literary whole of the 'Book of Psalms'.

Exodus 32 in its context is given to a consistently sacred frame of ideological language, the description of the prophet in a sacred landscape in 1 Kings 19 is related to a biographical frame of the prophet's normal life. In Isa. 1.10ff. and Jeremiah 7, the concept of dwelling in the temple is connected to social behaviour outside the sanctuary. The linkage of everyday interests and the real problem as described in the sacred language is especially well illustrated by the story of Hezekiah's sickness in 2 Kings 20 (cf. above Chapter 2). In these applications two types of biography seem to be related to each other, the normal biography of everyday life and the sacred biography connected to temple categories. The interrelationship of the two levels of reality could be illustrated by the story of 1 Sam. 1-2. In the present context the ordinary Hannah of ch. 1 is identified with the I-figure of 2.1-10. The two biographies are linked by the *hitpallel* of Hannah related to the divine intervention (1 Sam. 1.10, 12, 26; 2.1).

In Psalm 62, the relationship to normal reality is especially clearly expressed by the I-situation extended into a situation of admonishment. As representatives of a very normal, non-sacred humanity, the people are related to the I-figure as the relevant paradigm, and thus invited to enter the same reality of sublime dwelling in the temple. The motifs of the evil are an expression of the difference and the connection between the two sets of reality. To the I, the evil represent active enemies. To the people, the evil are negative figures of identification. Impressed by the success of the evil, the people themselves can become evil.[44] Alternatively, the I represents a positive figure of identification. 'Trusting' God as 'refuge', the people can enter the same relationship to God. In this way, normal reality seems to be immediately linked to the sacred reality, the language referring to situations of religious orientation.

This can be illustrated, too, by the relationship of Psalm 62 to Psalm 26. The application of dwelling in the temple in Psalm 62 corresponds to the use of way motifs in Psalm 26, referring to comparable aspects of single-minded volition and religious orientation. Fundamentally, the function of the evil corresponds in the two texts. In Psalm 62, the threat of the enemies consists in pushing the I from his place of standing. In Psalm 26, the evil are visualized as tempting places of dwelling, leading the I from the way and ultimately to Sheol. On the other hand, the

---

44. To this connection between the evil as negative paradigms and as enemies cf. above to Ps. 36 and further Prov. 1.10-19 on the evil seducing the admonished You to enter a state defined as active enmity against 'the innocent'.

motifs on the evil in Psalm 26 also corresponds to the exhortations of Psalm 62. The people of Psalm 62 are related to two alternative objects of *bāṭaḥ*—'God' juxtaposed to 'oppression and robbery' linked to 'weightless' humanity. This corresponds to the contrasts of locality in Psalm 26, represented by the temple juxtaposed to the dwelling-places of the evil. For the people of Psalm 62 as for the I of Psalm 26, the evil represent negative figures of identification, leading to the 'emptiness' of Psalm 62, ultimately to Sheol in Psalm 26. In this way, the different figures of Psalms 26 and 62 seems to refer to different stages of religious choice and commitment, the I-figure of Psalm 62 presenting himself as a relevant paradigm for very normal and unperfected beings.

The connection between the reality of the paradigmatic I and the ordinary reality of the admonished people is stressed by the parallel situation of the I admonishing his soul. The significance of this situation is seen from the corresponding literary frame of Psalms 42–43 and the motif development of Psalm 131. The address to the soul presupposes an inner dichotomy of stronger and weaker parts. With this dichotomy of inner being related to the act of confession and trust and connected to the crisis, the address to the soul clearly refers to very ordinary reactions of emotional and mental nature, comparable to the reactions of the people confronted by the temptations of empty success in Ps. 62.9ff. Moreover, the motif development of Psalm 131 demonstrates that the situation of encouragement and admonishment refers to a definite situation, the soul in a position to become really 'still'. Psalm 131 presents a story of development, the soul gradually weaned into the perfect attitude. This could be deduced from a comparison between Psalms 131 and 42–43 seen together with Psalm 62 (cf. also the 'wholeness' of the walker in Psalm 26), the different types of the I's relationship to the soul suggesting different degrees of perfected confession.

The relationship of the I and his soul as admonisher and admonished refers to internalized psychic categories of humanity split in an inner confrontation between confessor and non-confession. Moreover, it must be important that this situation of inner dichotomy in Psalms 42–43, 62 and 131 is part of the I as paradigm presented for identification. This connection is especially urgent in Psalm 62, with the exhortation to the soul extended into the exhortation to the people. In these texts, not only the finished product of the perfect confession is relevant for the religious application, but also the inner struggle between confession and non-confession. In this way, the motif structure seems equally relevant for

the perfected I of Psalm 131 as well as for the very unperfected people
of Psalm 62, and for the more or less advanced figures of the other
texts. Moreover, both for Psalms 62 and 131, the relevance for ordinary
people dominates the application with the I-figure presented as paradigm
in religious address. This could be related to the corresponding theological interest in the figure of the evil (cf. above Chapter 5).

Given this background, the language of the motif structure seems to
refer to a level of reality closely connected with ordinary reality, the
stereotypical ideological motifs being a vehicle for the expression of real
autobiographic experience. What separates this autobiography from
other types of experience must be linked to the subject-matter, dealing
with a story of religious experience and development. Moreover, the
language describes a variety of experience, related to different levels of
religious being. The relationship of the admonishing I and admonished
people suggests that categories of hierarchy are important for the applications of this language. The hierarchic difference is connected to different levels of religious being expressed by the categories of the motif
structure, the actors of the different levels related to each other in a
parallel striving towards a given aim.

4. *Confession in Crisis*

We have found different expressions for the religious aim as presented in
the different texts. Usually the *summum bonum* of the motif structure is
connected to enemy or way motifs and/or of dwelling in the temple,
with the special relationship to Yahweh as the concentrated expression
of the crisis solved/dwelling in the temple. Usually the problem of the I is
negatively described as connected to some crisis, expressed in prayers
and descriptions of the crisis, dwelling in the temple more indirectly
expressed as the ultimate happy end.

The motif contraction of Psalm 62 (cf. above), supported by the motif
development of Psalm 131 and the literary frame of Psalms 42–43, puts
a special emphasis on the situation of the I as confessor in crisis. In
this psalm the confession is related to some future divine intervention
(vv. 12-13). Thus, also, this psalm reflects the motif structure as a series
of events, ending in some climax of miraculous intervention. On the
other hand, the composition concentrates the motif structure into the
imagery of the I-figure as confessor. Connected both to enemy and
temple motifs/relationship to God motifs, the expressions of confidence

and trust represent the interest of the composition. This could provide a key also to the other texts, as an indication of what it is all about.

Usually the I-psalms reflect a problem, with God for the ultimate problem solver. On the other hand, the prayer is connected to confessionary expressions of trust. This connection has posed a classical problem for form-historical analysis. The forms of confidence and trust in the prayer psalms correspond to similar forms in psalms of thanksgiving. For the prayers, the laments and prayers have been seen as central to the literary character, immediately translated into some biographical and ritual situation centred round the crisis and the interest of crisis solution. As a reflection of a ritual and life situation, the prayer can be separated from the genre of thanksgiving as a reflection of a completely different life/ritual situation. However, this understanding has, in some ways emphasized the problem. The prayer situation understood as a situation of despair and anguish is not immediately reconcilable with the situation of confidence expressed by the elements of confession.

This problem was seemingly solved by the assertion of oracular or other divinatory events as decisive for the literary structure of the prayer, by Mowinckel and Begrich especially. At least some of the expressions of confidence could be singled out and seen as the I's response to the divine promise. In this way, elements within the prayers could be related to similar elements in the thanksgiving genre without disturbing the criteria for formal and ritual classification.

But the problem represented by the forms of confidence in the prayers—and thus also the problem of the function of the prayer psalm in I-form[45]—has remained. This is demonstrated by the early discussion on the subgroup(s) of psalms of confidence or protection which formally links the two types of prayer and thanksgiving psalms.[46] Related to criteria of cult, this subgroup is understood to refer to other types of biographical and ritual situation.[47] But when textual categories are

---

45. Cf. especially Delekat, *Asylie*, pp. 11-12, on the differences between prayers in I-form and the concrete examples of prayers found elsewhere in the Old Testament. According to Delekat, 'private Klagegebete in poetischer Form' represent purely literary phenomena, while all 'im AT erhaltenen Gebete am Tempel sind Prosagebete', never 'sung' or 'played', but related to *qārâ*, *zā' aq*, etc.

46. Cf. also the difficulties of any precise application in the concrete materials of the idea of the 'Salvation oracle' or a similar form for divine intervention, here demonstrated in the introductory notes to Pss. 27 and 62.

47. E.g. H. Gunkel, *Einleitung in die Psalmen. Die Gattungen der religiösen*

emphasized, the all-important significance of the cultic principle is weakened in favour of literary or theological concerns. The linkage of confidence psalms to the two main types of I-psalm makes the function of the prayer psalm problematical.[48]

The understanding of the texts as expressions of a given motif structure of ideological nature would stress the connection between the different types of I-psalm. The different types—and indeed the great differences between individual texts traditionally understood to represent one type!—could reflect that they represent different parts or aspects of the motif structure. As such, they would be related to each other not only as representing different events of an ideologically given pattern, but also as linked by a basic common ideological interest. With the confessions of confidence and trust as the most impressive common elements, it is natural to stress these elements as the basic expression of this interest. Thus, they could also be central to the application of the motif structure in the prayer psalms.

This can be concretely illustrated by Psalms 27 and 62. In the two texts, the confessions are elaborated into relatively independent

Lyrik Israels, Zu Ende geführt von Joachim Begrich, II (Göttingen: Vandenhoeck & Ruprecht, 1966), pp. 254ff., on confidence psalms as derived from the 'Vertrauensäüsserung' of the laments as 'Keimzelle', and Mowinckel, *Psalmenstudien 1*, pp. 125-26, on whether confidence psalms should be related to the genre of lament or thanksgiving. Later, Mowinckel stressed psalms of confidence as in some cases indistinguishable from thanksgiving psalms (*Psalms II*, p. 41), in other cases as a subgroup of 'protection psalms' from laments (*Psalms I*, p. 20). The ' "mixing" of eulogy and thanksgiving and confident prayers "reflect" earlier times, when the different kinds of psalms had not yet been distinguished from each other and separately cultivated according to their special uses in the cult'. These deliberations clearly demonstrate that it is not the literary categories, but the application of the cultic principle which is decisive for the classification of the different genres. The recalcitrance of both the problem and the methodological model is demonstrated by Gerstenberger, *Der bittende Mensch*. On the one hand, the prayer is understood as the characteristic element for the prayer psalms connected to a setting of 'Bittzeremonie' (pp. 119ff. 134ff.). On the other hand, Ps. 62 can be classified as a prayer psalm 'ohne Bittformulierung' (p. 124).

48. The possible significance of the co-existence of prayers and laments together with expressions of confidence is illustrated by Brueggemann, 'Shape for Old Testament Theology I-II'. The laments are used as the prime expressions for the 'structure legitimation' and protest seen as basic principles for the development of an Old Testament theology. Cf. similar criteria applied for a differentiation of types of prayer psalms in Broyles, *Conflict of Faith*.

subunits. Pss. 27.1-6 and 62.2-8 are seen as individual compositions (cf. the introductory notes to Chapters 4 and 6) and could be related to, for example, Psalm 23 as three parallel psalms of confidence. It is natural to suppose that the function of the three expressions—also with two of them as sub-units within contexts—must be rather closely related. The independent function of Psalm 23 as expression of the I's confession must correspond to the function of Pss. 62.2-8 and 27.1-6 within their respective contexts. The function of Pss. 27.1-6 and 62.2-8 must be related, the first connected to prayers, the other to admonishments. Similarly to Pss. 62.2-8 and 23, the I as described in 27.1-6 must reflect a special emphasis on the I as confessor.

Above, we found that the prayers of Ps. 27.7ff. represent a particular application of the I as confessor. While the self-description in vv. 1ff. is of general character, the parallel connection of crisis and prayer in vv. 7ff. connects the situation to some determinate crisis. In this way, the connection of terrible suffering and the turning to Yahweh in prayer could represent the sublime expression of the confession (cf. above to the refrain of Psalms 42–43 and further Pss. 36.2-5, 6-10, 84.2-8). This would correspond to the motif application of Psalm 62, with the motif structure contracted into the imagery of the I as confessor related to ordinary people as paradigm and admonisher. Such an interest could be linked to the use of a special type of statement in these texts, usually in the third person, which expresses general religious truths of dogmatic character. They are given to the fate of the evil (cf. above to Pss. 5.5b, 6a; 36.13; 62.10; 140.12) and the positive contrast figures (cf. above to Pss. 5.12; 84.5-8, 13; 140.14). Often these statements are related to similar statements on Yahweh (cf. above to Pss. 5.5a, 6b, 7, the last sentence of 12a, 13; 84.12; 140.13; and 62.12-13).

We found these statements central to the composition of the individual text, related to the descriptions of the enemies as evil, to the contrasting self-descriptions, and also to the prayers. In relation to the I-forms, these statements represent the religious paradigm, the I-forms an application of parts of the paradigm. Dominated by the prayers, the I-forms can be said to represent the paradigmatic story in subjunctive form.

The importance of these statements is also stressed by their compilations in Psalms 34 and 37. The connection to an I story in Ps. 34.2-7 (cf. also the I-forms Ps. 37.25, 35-36) formally links these compilations to the literary situation of the I-psalms. Connected to a frame of admonishment, the applications of these statements in Psalms 34 and 37 correspond to Psalm 62. Both the general proverbial form of these statements and their use in Psalms 34 and 37 demonstrate that they must represent some special religious knowledge. This can also be seen from their introduction 'I know' in Ps. 140.13-14 and by the special introduction of 62.12 as divine speech, responded to in v. 13.[49]

For our understanding of the special character of this 'knowledge', its connection with religious experience must be important. The significance of the expressions on the special relationship to Yahweh of, for example, Ps. 27.4 and further vv. 8-9, 36.8-10, 42.2-3, 43.3-4, 84.3, 11, 140.14 together with 5.9, 27.11 are usually ignored.[50] Exod. 33.18ff. and the parallel 1 Kings 19 suggest that the expressions could refer to experiences of a rather exclusive character (cf. above Chapter 3). The modifications of especially Exod. 33.20, 22-23 demonstrate the significance of such expressions understood in the literal sense, and presuppose reflection on their validity. In a context of the Sinai revelation where the special relationship to Yahweh is consistently described in categories of sacred locality, Exod. 33.20, 22-23 link the experiences of Moses to a traditional background of what we could label 'mystical experience'. Indirectly, these critical modifications stress the extraordinary character of such events, both with regard to their contents of relationship with Yahweh and to the stature of the people involved. Either, usually, presented in a series of events leading to the ultimate mystical experience or contracted into one situation of relationship as in Psalm 62, the

49. Stressed as a 'real' oracle by Eichhorn, *Gott als Fels*, p. 38, connected to a general understanding of the I as oracular intermediary in psalms with 'Fels, Burg und Zuflucht' for Yahweh-designations. The supposed character of v. 12 as a concrete message in a concrete situation of crisis corresponds badly to the general character of this 'oracle', e.g. Beyerlin, *Die Rettung*, p. 28.

50. Probably due to the usual transcription of the texts into methodological models which stress categories of 'normal' socio-historical reality and some ritual practice orientated towards the solution of problems of political/national or private character. Cf. on the other hand Eichhorn, *Gott als Fels*, and also the intimations of an 'inneren Kreis von Riten, Weihen und Erlebnissen' reserved for special cult servants by von Rad, '"Gerechtigkeit" und "Leben"', pp. 239-40. It should also be noted that to Mowinckel the very concept of cult was linked to categories of 'feeling' and 'religious experience'. Properly executed, certain types of rite would lead to strong experiences of 'ecstatic' character for the participants, *Psalms I*, p. 15 and especially 'Det kultiske synspunkt som forskningsprincip', p. 25; cf. Hauge, 'Sigmund Mowinckel and the Psalms', pp. 69ff.

significance of the confession must be seen in the light of this extraordinary experience.

For this reason, the application of the special statements of religious knowledge in the I-psalms must be important. Seen for themselves, the statements seem rather bland and self-evident. But as confession of the truth of the paradigm in a situation of crisis, they could have a much more significant function. Stated by the I in a context of suffering and impending death, they represent concentrated expressions of the I as confessor and thus also as potentially related to the experience of divine intervention. Confession in crisis implies the ultimate confrontation between two sets of reality, with biographical reality opened for the divine intervention. Thus, the application of the religious paradigm in the I-psalms, stated as really true, could represent an extraordinary event.

This could be linked to the categories of paradigm and actualization which seems to characterize the I-psalms. With the I-story as actualization of the paradigm and the I the embodiment of the paradigmatic fate, confession in crisis would represent the sublime expression of the qualified biography. The image of the I as the ultimate confessor in Pss. 27.1-6, 62.2-8 together with Psalm 23 on the one hand, and the development of the soul motifs in Psalms 42–43, 62, and 131 on the other hand, stresses the significance of the connection between autobiographic experience and the ideological definition of religious reality.

These implications, both for the general statements of religious truth and for the expressions of confession in I-form, could be illustrated by the development of the I-story in Psalm 73.

5. *The Way to Confession (Psalm 73)*

The formal structure of this psalm[51] is characterized by introductory and

---

51. Characterized as a 'Wisdom Psalm' by Gunkel, its history of classification demonstrates the lack of criteria for a proper labelling as well as the elusive character of 'wisdom' when applied outside certain established genres, e.g. Murphy, 'The Classification "Wisdom Psalms"', and especially Gerstenberger, *Der bittende Mensch*, p. 126. Gerstenberger solves the dilemma of conflicting data by separating between criteria of form and function. The materials reflect wisdom, while the function of the texts is cultic. A corresponding separation is traditional for the understanding of Ps. 73. Although the influence of wisdom is generally acknowledged, the psalm has been held to represent the typical genres of the I-psalm. Often labelled a psalm of thanksgiving (Mowinckel, *Psalms II*, pp. 35ff.; Schmidt, *Psalmen*, p. 140; Kraus, *Psalmen*, p. 504; Murphy, 'The Classification "Wisdom Psalms"', p. 164), it has

concluding statements of general nature in vv. 1[52] and 27:

> Yes! good for Israel is God, for the pure of heart!
>
> For behold! those distant from you shall perish.
> You annihilate everyone whoring himself away from you!

These statements represent simple sentence constructions, based on qualifying terms in a subject position (v. 27a) or as objects related to the divine acts (vv. 1, 27b), thematically given to the fate of the qualified. This corresponds to the other statements of religious truth. Also in this text (cf. especially Pss. 5 and 140), the two statements form a contrast saying. In this psalm their formal connection is stressed by the following statements vv. 2 and 28,[53] in the first person and introduced by *wa'anî*.

---

also been seen as a psalm of trust (McCullough, *Psalms*, p. 390) and even as a lament (Gerstenberger, *Der bittende Mensch*, p. 118, with v. 24 for the prayer, vv. 18 and 27 for 'Feindverwünschungen', p. 126). And such classifications have been related to the typical form-historical settings of, for example, sickness (Mowinckel and Schmidt, further Seybold, *Das Gebet*, p. 68), the royal sufferer surrounded by national enemies (Eaton, *Kingship*, p. 76; E. Würthwein, 'Erwägungen zu Psalm 73', in W. Baumgartner (ed.), *Festschrift für Alfred Bertholet zum 80. Geburtstag gewidmet von Kollegen und Freunden* (Tübingen: Mohr, 1950), pp. 543ff.; cf. also Birkeland, *Die Feinde*, p. 272) or in ritual humiliation during the New Year Festival (H. Ringgren, 'Einige Bemerkungen zum LXXIII Psalm', *VT* 3 [1953], pp. 270-71). Or the I is seen as 'ein levitischer Kultprophet am Zionsheiligtum' by Eichhorn, *Gott als Fels*, p. 43 or related to the asylum institution with the psalm as 'Asylflüchtlingstheodizee' by Delekat, *Asylie*, pp. 250ff. Recently, however, the sapiential aspects are stressed as decisive for the character of the psalm, L.G. Perdue, *Wisdom and Cult. A Critical Analysis of the Views of Cult in the Wisdom Literatures of Israel and the Ancient Near East* (SBLDS 30; Missoula: Scholars Press, 1977), pp. 290-91; Stolz, *Psalmen*, pp. 47ff.; Croft, *The Identity of the Individual*, pp. 161ff.; K. Spronk, *Beatific Afterlife in Ancient Israel and in the Ancient Near East* (AOAT 219; Neukirchen Vluyn: Neukirchener Verlag, 1986), pp. 315-16; and essentially also J.F. Ross, 'Psalm 73', in J.G. Gammie *et al.* (eds.), *Israelite Wisdom. Theological and Literary Essays in Honor of Samuel Terrien* (Missoula: Scholars Press, 1978), p. 170; J.C. McCann Jr 'Psalm 73: A Microcosm of Old Testament Theology', in K.G. Hoglund *et al.* (eds.), *The Listening Heart. Essays in Wisdom and the Psalms in Honor of Roland E. Murphy* (JSOTSup 58; Sheffield: JSOT Press, 1987), pp. 248-49.

52. Stressed as 'the basis for the structure', Perdue, *Wisdom*, p. 288 and by Stolz, *Psalmen*, p. 47 as a 'Verallgemeinerung' of what 'das Vertrauensbekenntnis im Ich-Stil formuliert'; cf. also McCann, ' 'Ps 73', p. 249 on vv. 1, 15, 28.

53. The contrast relationship between the two verses as 'inclusion of the whole poem' stressed by Spronk, *Beatific Afterlife*, p. 319.

The first-person statements of vv. 2 and 28 have a contrast function related to the preceding confessions. In v. 28, the qualification of 'nearness' contrasts the I to those 'distant' and 'moving away' from God in v. 27 (cf. the similar relationship for Ps. 5.8 within vv. 5-7).[54] Similarly, v. 2 describes the I as 'almost' a contrast figure to the 'pure of heart' of v. 1. This is followed by a description of the 'almost' event of falling, ended with the rhetorical anti-confession of vv. 12-14. Corresponding to vv. 1-2 and 27-28, vv. 12-14 consist of a general statement (v. 12), contrasted by I-forms (vv. 13-14). Verses 13-14 are linked to the fundamental confession of v. 1 by the motifs of purification and the introductory '*ak*-element (cf. this element introducing the real truth on the evil in vv. 18-20). The introductory *hinnê* of v. 12 corresponds to the concluding statement on the fate of the evil in v. 27.[55]

This structure stresses the significance of the general statements of religious truth for the composition as a whole. Verses 1 and 27 together with vv. 12-14 and 18-20 form central elements of the literary development, the statement on the fate of the positive paradigm, v. 1, connected to the anti-confessional I-forms, vv. 13-14, the contrast statement on the fate of the evil, v. 27, to the anti-confession, v. 12, and the concrete insight of vv. 18-20.

The development of the general statements is connected to a special application of the stereotyped elements of the lament. Isolated from the context, vv. 6-11 represent a normal description of the evilness of the evil. As usual, the I is described as a contrast figure (v. 13; cf. the similar contrast in Ps. 26.4-6). But the introductory 'in vain' in v. 13 continued by v. 14 together with the introductory narrative in vv. 2-3 and the statements vv. 4-5 turn the stereotypes upside-down. Verse 12, which concludes the description of the evil, is in this context made into a statement on the positive fate of the evil, while the pious I represents the negative fate.

The rhetorical anti-confessions of vv. 12-14 resulted from experience of what took place 'in reality'. The observations 'seen' (v. 3b), are abstracted into the dogmatic statement of v. 12 together with vv. 13-14

54. Cf. also the similar relationship signalled by the *wa'anî*-element vv. 22-23, with two statements contrasting the I as animal 'with you' and as the confessor 'with you'.

55. According to Spronk, *Beatific Afterlife*, p. 319, these elements function as compositional markers, '*ak* vv. 1, 13, 18 introducing the three 'stanzas', *hinnê* of vv. 12 and 27 at the end of the first and last 'stanza'.

as the given truth on the fate of the evil. Not totally overwhelmed by his observations from real life[56] however, the I's anti-confession was not uttered (v. 15). But the mental and emotional anguish and the efforts to understand (v. 16) witness the continued crisis.

The description of the crisis conforms to the motif structure of the other I-psalms. Verse 2 represents an imagery which corresponds to, especially, Ps. 62.4-5 and further Pss. 36.12-13, 118.13. The I is 'almost bent down with regard to my feet', while the 'foot-steps' of the parallel v. 2b link the imagery to the concept of way. Reflecting motifs of standing/ falling, v. 2 related to v. 1 describes the I as 'almost' suffering the negative fate of the evil, contrasted to the 'goodness' of the fate of the pure.

In v. 18 the same type of motif describes the fate of the evil,[57] connected with motifs of death and annihilation in vv. 19-20 and also 27. Thus, as in the other texts, the I and the evil are related to the same negative fate in some kind of either/or relationship. Usually this relationship is expressed by the situation of enmity, the evil enemies seeking the life of the I. Thus in, for example, Ps. 118.13, the imagery of Ps. 73.2 is connected to a scene of the enemy 'pushing' the I. In Psalm 73 the threat of the evil as provoking the 'bentness' is of purely mental-emotional nature, connected to the reactions of the I on the success of the evil (vv. 3ff.). But in Psalm 62, the two types of motif application are combined. The description of the enemies is given to the imagery of 'pushing', while the admonitions of vv. 9ff. reflect experiences similar to Psalm 73, with the evil as negative figures of identification connected with their success in life. But even with these differences, the types of motif application correspond. Both for Psalm 73 and the admonishments of Psalm 62, the evil represent the threat of failure to the I within the categories of the motif structure.

As usual for the other applications of the motif structure, the solution of the crisis is linked to two sets of motifs: the local categories of dwelling in the temple and the destruction of the evil. In this text, local motifs on the good place are found within three types of application. The I 'coming to the temple' of v. 17a (cf. especially Pss. 42.3, 43.3-4) represents the central event. Here this event is simply stated without any

---

56. On this background, the admonishment of Ps. 62.11 must carry a heavy load of meaning as a compressed result of the confrontation between two sets of truth.

57. The motif connection between vv. 2 and 18 is pointed out by Kraus, *Psalmen*, p. 508; Stolz, *Psalmen*, p. 49; McCann, 'Psalm 73', p. 249.

implication of miraculous categories of divine intervention comparably
to, for example, Ps. 43.3-4 with motifs of guidance and admission. Temple
entrance in this type of usage can be connected to the volitional applications of Ps. 26.6 within vv. 4-8, Ps. 5.8 within vv. 5-8 and also Ps. 84.11.
But in v. 24 we find motifs of guidance and admission connected to
miraculous categories. Here the divine 'taking' probably represents an
extension of the series of events with a future elevation unto the 'good
place'.[58] Thirdly, God as 'rock' v. 26 and further v. 28 on 'nearness' to
God as 'my refuge' represents an application of dwelling in the temple
similarly to 62.3, 7. As in Psalm 62, this type of usage represents contracted types of application, which transcend ritual categories. Here,
motifs of locality are mixed with motifs of other categories to describe a
certain state of being. God as, for example, 'rock of my heart' (v. 26),
'on' whom 'my refuge is put' (v. 28) connects the local categories to
mental-emotional attitudes. But as to function, the confessions of vv. 23-
26, 28 can be compared to the volitional applications in Psalms 5, 26
and 84, where the local categories are more consistently used.

The significance of these categories as the fundamental expressions of
religious experience of the I is also demonstrated by the structure of the

58. Verse 24b is traditionally understood to refer to categories of the hereafter, cf.
especially Dahood, *Psalms II*, pp. 194-95, who also finds vv. 17-18 as an expression
for experiences in the heavenly sanctuary; Spronk, *Beatific Afterlife*, pp. 321ff.,
finding a number of references to the afterlife; cf. Ross. 'Psalm 73', p. 175 for a
sceptical approach. In our context it is natural to relate *nāḥâ* and *lāqaḥ* with divine
subject and the I for object to the motifs of guidance and admission into the temple
(cf. especially Pss. 27.5-6, 61.3 and 62.5 in addition to 43.3-4). Ps. 5 (cf. also 26) is
of special significance in this connection, combining the idea of a present dwelling in
the temple with the usual orientation towards future events of a special dwelling. This
connection would suggest Ps. 73.24 as an individual application of temple motifs
comparable to the other I-psalms. On the other hand, the traditional understanding of
Ps. 73.24 provides a good illustration of the extraordinary, 'transcendent' character
of dwelling in the temple for this and the other psalms, separate from the 'non-
miraculous' dwelling, with implications of a special relationship to the divine
presence. It is of course also possible that the motifs, centred round the contrast
localities of Sheol and temple, could refer to categories of 'beatific afterlife'—or at
the very least immediately be applicable for such categories. But with Moses and
Elijah for the most concrete figures of realization, it seems reasonable to stress the
significance of the experience of the 'beatific vision' or 'audition' as the central event
of dwelling in the temple. But with direct relationship to God as the contents of the
ecstatic experience, it would be rather pointless to try to limit this experience of
ultimate life!

story. The I 'coming to the temple' in v. 17a is presented as the decisive event which turns the 'almost-fallen' into someone permanently localized 'with' Yahweh. The introductory 'until' separates between the time of crisis outside and a new situation dependent on dwelling in the temple. Moreover, the description retains some aspects of miraculous categories. While the coming is stated as a fact, it is connected to some extraordinary event which caused the new understanding.

The dependence on the traditional language is expressed by the link-age of temple motifs with the destruction of the evil. Here the two sets are combined into one imagery: in the temple the I *bîn* their fate of falling and death.

'*ābînâ* could refer to different types of experience. Subordinated to the parallel '*ābô* of a, it could have a function similar to the infinitives with *le* in 27.4b:

Until I came into the sanctuary of God to consider their end.

Such an understanding could be related to the mental-emotional char-acter of the crisis, the anguished pondering transferred to the more suit-able locality.[59] But the similar combination in Neh. 13.7 and further in Ezra 8.15 and Prov. 7.7 demonstrate the formal independence of '*ābînâ* in 27.4b and even suggests that the verb in this combination refers to actual observation:

until I came into the sanctuary of God and observed their end.[60]

59. E.g. Kraus, *Psalmen*, p. 501, who renders the verb of v. 17b as a cohortative 'Erkennen will ich (dort) ihr Ende'. Related to an oracle or a theophany, the experi-ence transcends empirical categories as 'prophetisch durchleuchtet', referring to cate-gories of eschatology and 'eine letzte, nicht mehr anschaubare Gewissheit' (pp. 507-508). For further examples of 'spiritualizing' interpretations of what really happened in the sanctuary, cf. Ross, 'Psalm 73', pp. 165-66. The rather elusive character of such descriptions, related to the robust concreteness of most of the alternative descriptions referred to in the following note, suggests a lamentable lack of categories and concepts for a precise description of religious experiences in the Old Testament.

60. This represents the usual understanding of v. 17. While, for example, Schmidt, *Psalmen*, pp. 138-39, and Delekat, *Asylle*, p. 252, find references to somebody 'evil' concretely dying, the experience is usually related to ritual categories of oracular or theophanic nature (e.g. Würthwein, Eaton, Perdue and Eichhorn, cf. the references above); to some festival experience of God's great mercies in the past (McCullough) or of the enemies destroyed in some mock battle (Ringgren). Mowinckel, *Salmeboken*, pp. 156-57, combines ritual events with personal categories of inner

While the nature of this 'observation' is rather uncertain, it must be stressed that the linkage of motifs on the destruction of the enemies and temple motifs corresponds to the other texts. But the type of linkage differs from text to text, and even within the individual text. The imagery of Psalm 73 with the fall of the evil observed in the temple would correspond most immediately to Psalm 5 and comparable texts. But while Psalm 5 and, for example, Numbers 16 have representatives for the evil present as enemies, the I of Psalm 73 seems to perceive the end of the evil *en masse*.

Thus, while aspects of the narrative v. 17 are uncertain, it can be seen as an individual expression of central components of the motif structure common to the other I-psalms. The I entering the temple, this event somehow connected to the destruction of the evil and thus with the categories of divine intervention implied, forms the decisive event of the I-story. Its very vagueness as to detail can even be seen as typical for the very allusive and stereotypical references to the inside experiences in these texts (cf. above to, for example, Pss. 5.12; 140.14; 43.3-4; 84.5; further 84.8; 42.2-3; 36.8ff.; 27.4).

In the other texts, the inside experience seems to express the climactic event of the motif structure. In this text, it is connected to a new kind of understanding contrasted to the prior non-*yāda'* of a stupid animal (vv. 21-22). The new understanding is based on the insight into the fate of the evil vv. 18-20, related to the anti-confession in v. 12 and the final statement on the fate of the evil in v. 27. The consequences of this insight are expressed in a series of confessions in I-form (vv. 23-26) which can be compared especially to Pss. 62.2-8 and 27.1-6. They are concluded by the general statement on the evil in v. 27 and the self-descriptive v. 28 which contrasts the I to the negative figures of v. 27.

In this way, the I as confessor represents the happy ending of the crisis. The new position of the I is expressed by the citation of the

conflict and experience, the new understanding connected to some deep insight obtained in the ritual of healing. Ross, 'Psalm 73', pp. 167ff., finds cultic experiences, however intense, inadequate to provide 'new knowledge' and 'inspiration', preferring the 'deliberations of the wisdom schools' (p. 167) as a more plausible source. This is connected to the plural 'sanctuaries' of v. 17a, held to refer not only to the temple proper, but also to the buildings of the sacred compound where 'wisdom teachers discussed the problem of good and evil' (p. 169)! To McCann, 'Psalm 73', p. 250, v. 15 represents the central verse. It expresses the psalmist's decision to remain faithful, which sets the stage for the reversal of perspective, vv. 18ff.

dogmatic statements in vv. 1 and 27 connected to first-person statements of confession. The biographical data of the past are presented as the story on how the I became confessor.

As related to categories of Wisdom, Psalm 73 is usually seen as a reflection of a theologically critical approach to the given religious tradition, younger than the normal I-psalm. While the normal psalm reverently repeats the sacred forms of the ancient ritual tradition, Psalm 73 represents the sapiential critical examination of the tradition.[61] This model of religious development is, of course, possible.[62] But in our context, it is natural to stress the connection to the other I-psalms as parallel applications of the given motif structure. And as an expression for how the I became confessor, with the composition centred round general statements of religious truth connected to confessing I-forms, the theological interest of the psalm can be related to the other texts. Psalm 62 together with 27.1-6 related to 23 are especially relevant as comparable expressions of comprehensive compositions on the I as confessor (cf. above to Pss. 84, 36, and 26).

What is special for Psalm 73 compared to the normal expression of this interest is the emphasis on the conflict between two sets of biographical reality perceived by the I as 'animal' and as a man of 'knowledge', with the motif structure given to the solution of the conflict. In this way, the traditional language is related to the experiences of the pre-confessioner.

61. Connected to this model, Ps. 73 would at the very least be an expression for a given stratum of religious thought, representing not only itself and other texts related to this stratum, but also the 'older' texts as interpreted and used at a certain period.

62. A reversed model is just as possible: compared to the other I-psalms analysed in this study, it is above all Pss. 34 and 37 which explicitly stand out from the rest, with reduced significance of the I-forms and a marked swelling of the statements of religious truth. If Ps. 73 represents a critical interest with regard to some tradition, it could be related to some kind of tradition exemplified by these two psalms. Thus, Ps. 73 related to Pss. 34 and 37 on the one hand, to the other I-psalms on the other, could reflect that the critical interest is due to the influence of the religiosity of the 'normal' I-psalms. Ps. 73 as also the book of Job could be concrete expressions for the reinterpretation of sapiential traditions related to the 'mystical' and 'miraculous' categories of the I-psalms. On the other hand, the convergence of traditions in these texts, especially if we also take the elaboration of the narrative material in the Pentateuch into consideration, seems too complicated for any easy models of development. Thus, also Pss. 34 and 37 as a compilation of I-story, admonishment and general statements of religious truth can primarily be seen as developed applications of the motif structure, expressing a theological interest which correspond to tendencies in other I-psalms.

The psychological interest, centred round an internalized conflict, differs from the usual application. Even as a language of religious experience, the motif structure is given to outer categories of description. The inner world of experience and commitment is described by a man located in a sacred landscape of localities, related to God and to enemies. Emotional aspects of, for example, anguish or longing are connected to the relationship to phenomena of this outer world. While we find allusions to and hints of inner conflict, the normal expression is given to the description of the I as the perfect confessor completely trusting in God (e.g. Pss. 26.4-5; 84.11; 27.2-3, 5; 23.4; and 73.26).

To a certain degree, the internalized application of Psalm 73 can be compared to the compositional frame of soul address for Psalms 42–43 and 62 (cf. Ps. 27.14). It also corresponds to the compositional development of Psalm 36 and to the motif development of Psalm 131. But in these texts, both the material and formal repercussions of this interest are more indirect, at least when compared to Psalm 73. By the separation of the self into I and soul, the I fills the role of the paradigmatic confessor, only the address to the soul is an allusion to the inner turmoil. With the address to the soul confined to the refrain, the formal significance of the address for the literary development of the motif structure is reduced.

With the motif structure centred round the I as confessor, it is above all Psalm 62 which represents the closest parallel. But while 62 represents a contracted version of the motif structure, the ultimate event of dwelling in the temple identified with the I as confessor, the application of the motif structure in Psalm 73 is more complicated. On the one hand, Psalm 73 reflects the motif structure as a whole subordinated to the situation of confession. Entrance into the temple (v. 17) and the implied miraculous categories are applied to describe the inner transformation of the I—the happy ending of the story ended by the confessions of vv. 23ff. This is also reflected by the concluding deflection into forms of thanksgiving v. 28b (cf. the first-person forms in Ps. 26.12 together with Pss. 52.11; 92.16; in the third person 5.12; 140.14). On the other hand, the motifs of the confession, vv. 26, 28, underlined by the negative v. 27 depicts the idea of permanent dwelling, now related to Yahweh as rock and refuge. The imagery is further disturbed by vv. 23-24, with the permanent relationship 'with' Yahweh coupled with the guidance motif and the future elevation into 'the good place'. Thus, the application of the motif structure in Psalm 73 reflects the dissolution of the temple motif found especially in Psalms 5 and 26 and also expressed by the double application in Ps. 27.1-6, 7ff.

In this way, Psalm 73 can provide a dramatic illustration of the religious significance of the confession in the other texts, especially when connected to a situation of prayer. Turning to Yahweh in a situation of crisis is an expression of the I as embodiment of the paradigm actualized in the personal biography. According to Psalm 73, this position is the result of the religious truths experienced as true, due to miraculous illumination after an anguished inner confrontation nearly leading to non-confession.

This also means that Psalm 73 is important in connecting the literary I-form to categories of autobiography. The narrative forms vv. 2-3, 15-17 together with vv. 13-14 reflect experiences of the 'narrator's' efforts to reconcile the fundamental religious truths with real-life observations. The miraculous insight leading to true knowledge and the exuberant description of the new relationship to Yahweh in vv. 23ff. are presented as equally autobiographical. This must have repercussions for our understanding of the corresponding I-forms of the other psalms. The literary form of the I-story in Psalm 73, evidently autobiographical, reflects both the objective pattern of the motif structure and the individual literary adaptation of this pattern. This corresponds to what we have found characteristic of the other I-psalms as individual expressions of a literary tradition connected to the motif structure. It is natural to conclude that the other applications in I-form represent a corresponding amalgam of the objective ideal-figure of proper religious behaviour, individual literary elaboration, and subjective categories of individual biography.

The categories of *paradigm* and *actualization*—connected with religious practice—could explain this riddle of objective subjectivity in the I-psalms. Such categories imply a religious practice directed towards inner integration and internalization of the paradigm. This corresponds to the I-story of Psalm 73, centred round the I's mental-emotional reactions in connection with the conflict between the dogmatic truths and observations from real life. Similarly, the categories of divine intervention are related to this inner conflict transforming the I from animal into a person of knowledge. The animal-I and the confessor obviously represent different levels of religious being connected to inner categories of perception of reality. The new understanding is expressed by the citation of the truths in vv. 1 and 27, connected to the I-forms of vv. 23ff., contrasted by the animal anti-confession of vv. 12-14.

This also includes a religious practice connected to categories of development and inner change. We have repeatedly discussed the relevance of such categories (cf. e.g. Chapter 5, and discussion on Ps. 62). Thus, the main characteristic of the I in the prayer psalms analysed above seems to be the position in between—identifying with the positive paradigm, in threat of suffering the fate of defeat save for divine intervention. The hero of Psalms 42–43 illustrates the dramatic character of the religious mobility of the I-figure, with a past relationship to the temple, now located to Sheol, praying for guidance to the temple. While the categories of change and development in this psalm are expressed by motifs of locality, the relationship of Psalms 62 to 73 can illustrate their significance as connected to mental-emotional aspects.

In Psalm 62 we find two types of religious figure, aside from the evil. The confessing I and the admonished people represent two types of religious being. The difference between the two types is seen by the different relationship to the evil. To the I, the evil represent active enemies. To the addressed people the evil are negative figures of identification. Impressed by the success of the evil, the people themselves can become evil. On the other hand—with the admonished soul linking the experiences of I and the people—the I represents the positive figure of identification. 'Trusting' God as 'refuge' (v. 9), the people can enter the same type of relationship to God. In this way, Psalm 62 suggests an immediate connection between the evil as negative figures of identification and as enemies, between the evil and the people, and between the I and the people as representing successive stages of religious stature.

This can be compared to the development of the I-figure in Psalm 73. The I of vv. 2-14 as 'almost' becoming evil himself corresponds to the people of Psalm 62 facing two contrasted types of 'trust'. Moreover, the danger of evilness is in both cases connected with the impression of the success of the evil. And the I of Ps. 73.1, 23ff. corresponds to the stature of the I in Psalm 62.

But in Psalm 73, the two types of religious being are linked to one figure, here referring to two successive levels of religious understanding. The observer of reality on the animal level without any understanding was transformed into confessor, with coming to the temple marking the transition from one level to the other.

The two levels are depicted as strangely parallel. The I and the evil represent the main actors. Both the anti-confessions of vv. 12-14 and the proper confessions are linked to perceptions of reality. In both cases, the fate of the evil is the object of perception, as 'seen' (v. 3) from the animal level and as observed from within the temple (v. 17). Moreover, the animal level was connected with religious observance (v. 13).

In this way, the biography of Psalm 73 illustrates categories of inner change. The religious reality of the different figures in Psalm 62 is bridged within one individual biography of development from animal to person of knowledge (cf. the applications touched upon in Chapter 3, and Chapter 5). A very ordinary state of religious being and the exalted stature of the I as confessor represent successive stages of individual development.

The close relationship between the positive and negative figures, the I 'almost' becoming evil, also illustrates the possibility of negative development. This provides a background for the theological interest in the figure of the evil (cf. Chapter 5), in Psalm 73 developed in personal and psychological categories. With the mobility of the I-figures in the sacred landscape of Sheol and temple, and the self split into confessing I and admonished soul in Psalms 42–43 and 62 for parallel illustrations of changes in being, the contrasts of Psalm 73 expressed in a series of succeeding events in one biography must be important for the other texts (cf. the implications of inner development in Ps. 131).

The difference of religious stature between the I and the people in Psalm 62 demonstrates the real significance of the inner change which has taken place in the biography of the I in Psalm 73. The miraculous story of inner transformation in Psalm 73—connected to a story of crisis and anguish—should be taken literally as an expression of events of special character, the I as confessor presented as an extraordinary being. In both cases, the psychological aspects of the I-story in Psalm 73 could provide a key to the understanding of the applications of the motif structure in the other I-psalms.

Finally, Psalm 73 is important in demonstrating that the categories of paradigm and actualization connected to ideas of individual development and change of being are related to some special experience of the divine reality. The realization of the objective truths of vv. 1 and 27 seen in isolation could refer primarily to experiences limited to psychic processes of mental-emotional nature, naturally related to, for example, ponderings and learned deliberations of sapiential character.[63] Whereas psychic

63. Such categories seem intransigently connected to texts deemed influenced by Wisdom, e.g. Ross, 'Psalm 73', pp. 167ff., and especially Beyerlin, *Wider die Hybris*, pp. 83ff. where the confluence of sapiential and psalmic traditions in Ps. 131 is

processes of opposition and acceptance—probably connected to ponderings and deliberations!—seem real enough, the context relates them closely to categories of religious experience and non-experience. This is expressed by the connection of the dogmatic statements and confessionary I-forms of vv. 1-2 and vv. 27-28, in addition to vv. 23ff. The new understanding is obtained by the divine intervention (cf. the confession Job 42.2-6). It leads to the new relationship to Yahweh as described vv. 23ff.

This corresponds to the miraculous categories of the other I-psalms. What is special for Psalm 73—similarly to Psalm 62—is the emphasis on the state of confessor in the application of the motif structure. Usually the literary present is presented as a situation of confession, while the categories of dwelling in the temple/special relationship to God represent the ultimate event of the motif structure. Thus, the ultimate event of the positive fate is the object of confession. In Psalms 73 and 62, the two situations are identified, the bliss of permanent dwelling in the temple in the divine presence contracted into the situation of the confessor 'upon' or 'together with' God. The special character of this contraction is illustrated by the attack of the enemies 'in the temple' in Ps. 62.4-5 (cf. also 73.26). The inside situation of permanent bliss is connected to the outside situation of suffering. Thus, the central ideas of dwelling in the temple seem to have been transferred into a situation of religious devotion in life, with trust for the main characteristic. This seems to include conflict and suffering as a permanent aspect of the religious life.

It is possible that this application represents a reinterpretation of the

explained by the I as a professional teacher of wisdom with tenure at the temple school of Zion, the occupation of 'Schreiberschulung' thus also connected with professional intercourse with psalmic texts. In addition, the author 'war auch ein Leidender', adding depth to the professorial attainments (p. 86). A third example is represented by the attempt to identify the theological impact of Ps. 73 by McCann, 'Psalm 73', by the application of Brueggemann's categories of 'structure legitimation' and 'embrace of pain'. According to Brueggemann, 'Shape for Old Testament Theology I-II', Old Testament theology should be understood from a bi-polar tension between these phenomena. 'Faith' 'reflects the ambiguity of our experiences about structure and pain caused by structure' (p. 31). McCann finds this tension also decisive for Ps. 73. The psalmist legitimates 'structure by professing his loyalty to the community and its institutions', and on the other hand acknowledges his experience of pain by challenging 'the common theology'. In this way, 'the theological richness of Ps. 73 consists of its holding in tension the legitimation of structure and the embrace of pain' ('Psalm 73', pp. 252-53).

motif structure, when compared with the normal I-psalm. The definition
of the tabernacle in Exod. 40.36ff. as a sanctuary for the people of the
way, the divine presence the signal for departure, may represent a parallel
expression of such an understanding (cf. below to Lam. 3.27ff.).

Given the richness and variety of individual application demonstrated
by the different texts, Psalms 62 and 73 can as well express a special
emphasis on certain aspects, parallel to other applications. Both psalms
contain elliptical allusions (62.12-13 and 73.24) to an ultimate happy
ending which transcends the present bliss. Moreover, the concepts of
suffering and crisis—mostly described in the categories of the enemy
situation—represent an integral part of the I-story. Connected to confession and prayer and related to the divine intervention, suffering seems
given as an ingredient of the human biography opened to the divine
reality. From the very number of I-psalms, the significance of crisis to
the religious story seems, if not a theological, a statistical and practical
fact.

The various descriptions of the crisis obviously do not prescribe suffering, as a religious virtue to be embraced[64] willingly and eagerly, as a
prerequisite of dwelling in the temple. Lam. 3.27ff. represents an example
of a prescription of suffering, clearly a reflection of the same tradition as
in, for example, Psalms 62 and 131.[65] Here the experience of suffering
common to the I-psalms is set in proverbial form, proclaimed as a good
religious exercise for a young man. On the other hand, this proverb
reflects that *confession* in crisis (vv. 28ff.) represents the paradigmatic
attitude. In the I-psalms, a state of crisis and suffering by itself represents
an intolerable situation, met with revolt and sought to be overcome.

Conflicts are clearly presented as a normal phenomenon of the religious biography, in the form of outer crisis and—usually implied—inner
conflict. This could be connected to the basic understanding of reality
expressed by the motif structure. The crisis is usually connected to categories of death—the I defined as a being in movement between Sheol
and temple. With divine intervention necessary to avoid the negative
fate, death and agents of death represent the basic fact of human reality.
Even with reality extended by the concepts of way and temple, the positive fate represents miraculous events.

---

64. Cf. Brueggemann's expression 'embrace of pain' 'Shape for Old Testament
Theology II'.
65. Beyerlin, *Wider die Hybris*, pp. 63ff.

SUMMARY

In the analysis of individual texts we have repeatedly faced the same basic questions. Again and again there has been reason to stress the conceptual and ideological character of the language of the I-psalms, which make the traditional deductions of ritual and biographical character rather questionable. Fundamentally, the language seems to refer to itself as a religious language, expressing an interpretative symbol-system of conceptual character. This seems to be connected with the basic motifs and concepts as expressions of a paradigm of religious reality.

It is possible that this language can be expressed in parallel concepts and motif sets. But the connection to categories of locality seems the basic expression—at the very least the most accessible for observation and analysis. In the religious description of humanity being related to God, humanity is set in a sacred topography of contrast localities connected to the idea of movement between the contrast localities. 'Temple', 'Sheol' and 'way' seem to represent the basic conceptual structure of this description.

On the other hand, the individual psalm seems to be a reflection of biographical experience. The biographical character is directly connected with the ideological aspects, the given truths of the religious tradition connected to first-person forms. The background to this connection of religious stereotype and intense personal application could be related to categories of paradigm and actualization. The I-psalm reflects an effort to integrate the paradigm with personal experience. The I represents an embodiment of aspects of the paradigm.

This implies that it is difficult to find satisfactory categories for the type of language involved. It could be transcribed as a symbol system or perhaps better as metaphorical language, centred round stereotypical root metaphors and secondary expressions. This would certainly reflect important aspects of this language system. Thus, the I localized on God, only tottering a bit while the enemies are pushing, clearly represents an indirect visualization of any life situation. The temple motifs represent traditional literary stereotypes for the description of such a situation.

The language seems to serve as the vehicle for intense personal experience centred round an experience of God, connected with ideas of the development of inner wholeness and personal integration of the paradigm. To a certain degree, individual reflections of such an interest can be observed. But related to this interest, the austerity of the language with regard to psychological categories is remarkable. While Psalm 73 is an expression of the I-story as internalized, the normal I-psalm seems to express an individual application of the traditional stereotypes. This sobriety of expression is illustrated by Psalms 42–43 in relation to 62. While the psalm obviously is dominated by a psychological interest, this aspect is expressed by the refrain of address to the soul and the rest of the psalm is a normal composition.

Thus, it might be even more precise to stress the literal aspects of the language, primarily referring to an autobiography of inner mental-emotional experience which results from the confrontation with the normal conditions of life. The vibrancy of, for example, Psalms 42–43 must reflect that the symbols or metaphors of a sacred topography are applied as the precise description of biographical experience. The incredibly rich and flexible application of the basic motifs in the individual text is an expression of the intensity of this experience, the paradigmatic stereotypes embodied by the flesh and blood of an I.

Thus, the most important fact of the language of these texts could be their character as expressions of an intensely personal type of religiosity centred round defined experiences of the divine reality in the individual biography.

The experience of the divine reality is most directly connected to the divine intervention in crisis. The crisis is actual or expected as a given fact of existence. It is usually connected to categories of death, with death and agents of death as the basic fact of human reality. In this way, the I-psalm represents an expression of the human reality, obviously perceived as critical if not tragic, opened to the divine reality as manifested in active intervention. The individual I represents an actualization of the relevance of divine manifestation, presented as biographical experience. The concentrated expression of this interest is found in the emphasis on the I as confessor.

This means that the relationship between human and divine transcends the limits of the immediate crisis. This is most clearly seen by the application of temple motifs. The crisis of the I is related to categories of permanent dwelling in the temple connected with some special experience of the divine presence. The connection between crisis and dwelling in the temple differs from text to text. There are even indications that the texts could reflect different stages and levels of relationship to God, with, for example, the successive scenes of nearness in Exodus 24 as a picture of this process. Whatever the particular expression, dwelling in the temple/nearness to God represent the decisive event of the religious biography. This can be connected to basic categories of outside and inside as an expression of two contrasted levels of being. By the idea of dwelling in the temple, the fundamental duality between sets of reality actualized by the crisis is dissolved. By the religious hero dwelling in the temple/related to the divine presence, human and divine reality is united as 'eternal' togetherness.

However, the single composition being given to certain interests connected to aspects of the motif structure tends to blur the difference between the motifs as expression of a series of successive events or parallel levels. With the emphasis on the I as confessor, the I of the single text—however subjectively perfected—embodies the paradigmatic situation of submission and devotion. Certain applications of the way motifs (Pss. 26 and 84, Exod. 25–40) express this tendency. A picture of the theological significance of such an understanding is given by Psalm 62. Here the characteristics of outside and inside realities are presented as one, relationship to enemies and to God united in one situation of 'almost non-tottering standing'.

This implies that the applications of the motif structure reflect a fundamental understanding of humans as the potential embodiment of very different levels of being. The mobility of the I as outside and inside and on the way is given a parallel expression by references to emotional and mental experience. This can be connected to the categories of paradigm and actualization. They entail psychological and mental aspects of inner integration, centred round ideas of religious development and transformation. The inner integration should not be confined to aspects of emotion and religious feeling connected with the experience of the divine. Thus, for example, Psalm 26 renders motifs which usually refer to miraculous events in volitional categories, with a hero totally committed to the way. Related to more modern and better documented experience of spiritual development, the attainments of the hero of Psalm 26 would be the result of a long process of faithful discipline. Similarly, Psalm 131 together with Psalm 62 illustrate the perfect confession as the result of some discipline of stillness in crisis.

The applications of the evil motifs are a radical expression for these ideas of inner change. The paradigmatic sentences in the third person, and the compositional development of the normal I-psalm, seemingly operate with an absolute separation of humanity into, for example, *ṣaddîqîm* and *rešā'îm*. But a number of applications blur the difference, with the actors as past or present or potential evil and the evil as potential heroes. The absolutes of the paradigm have been applied to a practical reality of human endeavour.

This is also seen in some actualizations of the religious paradigm. As far as we know from more modern types of religiosity, a religious practice connected to the concepts of the motif structure would represent an élite type of spiritual effort. The heroes of, for example, Pss. 27.1-6 and 62, not to mention Moses and Elijah, stand forth as extraordinary figures of religious attainment. Nevertheless, the addressed You of Psalm 62 and, for example, the addressees of Isa. 1.10ff. and Jeremiah 7 demonstrate that the religious paradigm was applied as relevant to people of very modest attainments.

It is possible that in certain texts (cf. below) the I represents 'later' efforts of reinterpretation and democratization of the religious ideal. Even so, this would represent an extension of a traditional practice connected to categories of paradigm and actualization, with the heroes of, for example, Psalms 42–43 and 73 as illustrations of radical transformation. Thus, Moses leading Israel from Egypt to the land could represent an emotive picture both of the applicability of the paradigm as well as of the type of élitism implied.

The human as confessor seems to represent the immediate aim of the religious interest of these applications. This interest could also be the background to the production and transmission of the I-psalms. As a manifestation of the paradigmatic story, the experience of the I—told in terms of autobiography—would be of central significance in a *milieu* characterized by an interest in experience of God connected to categories of paradigm and actualization.

The I-form of these texts could directly reflect this interest. As expression of a biography, the I is presented as living proof of the relevance of the paradigm, separate from the We of Psalm 118 or the You of Psalm 62. But with the I as embodiment of a super-personal experience, the I-form shares the experience with listeners or readers of the same religious practice, inviting them into an inner process of identification. This could mean that a number of I-psalms apply the I-form as a literary device, as a direct expression of an interest of religious address and indirect admonishment. But, basically, the I-form must reflect a tradition of biographical experience, centred round the categories of paradigm and actualization.

The number of I-psalms together with the very facts of transmission and inclusion in the book of Psalms point to an established *milieu* of considerable size and, probably, duration. Its theological significance is demonstrated by its influence upon the elaboration of the pentateuchal and other historiographical traditions and the sapiential tradition.

The characteristics of the religious practice deduced from the I-psalms suggests the existence of a *milieu* as a prerequisite. It must have included people very differently stationed 'on the way', probably connected in some type of hierarchic relationship. The importance attached to the presentation of the different heroes in the I-psalms, especially when related to a wider set of actors, such as the We-group in Psalm 118 or the admonished You in Psalms 31, 62 and 131, could illustrate both such a relationship and the function of the paradigmatic figure for a wider group.

A more precise description of the character of such a *milieu* must be highly speculative. Important characteristics of the religious practice—an established literary *milieu* centred round individual experience of reality and ideas of élitism—would naturally point to a background of sapiential practice as this is traditionally described.[1] On the other hand, a religious practice orientated towards a special experience of God—the expression of which invites labels like 'ecstatic' or 'mystical'—would be connected to the prophetic tradition. Especially when understood as institutionalized cult prophecy, this tradition might offer a satisfactory setting both for the underlying religious practice and also for its literary expressions.[2] Moreover, recent models which presuppose some type of confluence of traditions, with special emphasis on the sapiential influence,[3] seem to provide relevant categories for some institutionalized setting for the language of the I-psalms.

Whereas the religious practice could be related to different types of

1. E.g. Beyerlin, *Wider die Hybris*, pp. 83ff. and further the preceding chapter.
2. Mowinckel, *Psalms II*, pp. 55ff., 92ff. and especially Eichhorn, *Gott als Fels*, cf. above Chapter 3.
3. Aside from the implications of Eichhorn's *Gott als Fels* e.g. Kaiser, *Jesaja 1–12*, pp. 27-28, Beyerlin, *Weisheitlich-kultische Heilsordnung*.

milieu, the language itself points to a basic significance of ritual concepts. The relationship of Psalm 5 to Jeremiah 7 and Isa. 1.10ff., emphasized by the story of Hezekiah's healing in 2 Kings 20/Isaiah 38, demonstrates that the main components of the motif structure as well as the structure itself reflect the given temple ideology and the usual order of events connected with rites of crisis. The present composition of Exodus 25–40 with the paradigm set in an environment of reinterpreted ritual reality reflects the connection between the language of the I-psalms and ritual language. This is also demonstrated by the relationship of Numbers 16 to 17, the former connected to the interest of Psalm 5, the latter an expression of priestly categories. So far as we can make deductions from language type to background, it is natural to stress a background of normal religiosity connected with normal temple practice. This is also suggested by Psalm 112 and 2 Kings 20, which apply aspects of the motif structure as a relevant religious frame for situations of non-élitist, normal biography and normal religiosity.

So, if we had to choose between the generally accepted institutionalized settings of religious activity, the language of the I-psalms would point to a theological development of concepts connected to temple ideology and normal practice. But, such a choice is confounded by the relationship between Psalm 118 and the Babylonian 'I will praise the Lord of Wisdom', suggesting the I-psalms to be expressions of an ancient literary tradition. Also, the special character of the I-psalms makes it impossible to identify their religiosity with normal religiosity and with priestly interests as expressed in, for example, Numbers 17. When we pay attention to the great number of I-psalms, this would suggest the, at least originally, independent character of this tradition as related to the usual understanding of 'Priestly', 'Sapiential' and 'Prophetic' settings. Compared to such applications, the motif structure with the I-psalms as prime literary expression seems to represent a language *sui generis*; on the other hand it is malleable to different types of actualization and interest. Thus, the literary and theological connections to genres traditionally understood to refer to different institutionalized settings, could be seen primarily as an expression of the theological and spiritual impact of the *milieu* represented by the I-psalms.

This could be illustrated by the applications in Numbers 16–17 compared to Numbers 12. The situations of the two stories correspond, with the same set of actors connected to a parallel situation of contention and a parallel relationship to the divine intervention. But in the one version the contention is related to priestly categories of 'nearness', in the other to prophetic.

A further illustration of the relatively independent character of the motif structure is represented by the applications of Exod. 33.18ff. and 1 Kings 19 (cf. the relationship of Num. 16 and 17, Chapter 5, above). In both stories the experience of God is set in a frame of professional function, but at the same time—and in different ways—the literary elaboration sets this experience apart from the context. The special experience of God, and the events surrounding this experience, clearly reflect events of a special character. In both cases the professional context of mediation and renewed prophetic mission is broken by intensely personal categories and a special interest in ecstatic experience.

With regard to questions of dating and change in time, the analysis has provided few indications. At the very least, the previous discussion on possible background suggests the *milieu* of the I-psalms to be of considerable age and duration. Given the uncertainty of dating any type of Old Testament phenomenon these days, 'considerable age' might tentatively be rendered as pre-exilic. Thus, perhaps the best indication of development and re-application can be connected to the categories of Torah as significant to the description of the paradigmatic figure. Ezek. 3.18ff., 18, 33.8ff. related to Isa. 1.10ff. and Jeremiah 7, with Psalms 15, 24 and Isa. 33.14ff. as the perfected results of this interest, could suggest that at a certain time the paradigm was expressed in a new definition of *zaddiq*hood, with the qualification of the religious hero connected to specific criteria of observance. The bourgeois ideal of the application in Psalm 112 could represent a parallel interest in social actualization, the soaring hero of the sacred landscape changed into confident householder. This may have been connected to an extended form of application, the paradigm of élite practice extended to the normal religious observance of everyone. Exodus 25–40 can represent an important expression of such an extension. The transition from Moses to people as the heroes of the sacred story and the corresponding divine movement from mountain to tent 'in the midst of the people' as the new place of extraordinary meeting, represents a remarkable application of the motif structure. On the other hand, the transmission of the texts and the lasting influence of the religious tradition expressed by the I-figures of the psalms have infused a radical challenge into the ordinary reality of ever new generations as potential embodiments of 'I'.

BIBLIOGRAPHY

Aletti, J.N., 'Séduction et Parole en Proverbes I-IX', *VT* 27 (1977), pp. 129-44.

Alonso Schökel, L., 'The Poetic Structure of Psalm 42–43', *JSOT* 1 (1976), pp. 4-11.

—'Psalm 42–43. A Response to Ridderbos and Kessler (JSOT 1 [1976] 12-21)', *JSOT* 3 (1977), pp. 61-65.

Alter, R., *The Art of Biblical Narrative* (New York: Basic Books, 1981).

—*The Art of Biblical Poetry* (New York: Basic Books, 1985).

Aurelius, E., *Der Fürbitter Israels. Eine Studie zum Mosebild im Alten Testament* (ConBOT 27; Stockholm: Almquist & Wiksell, 1988).

Barr, J., 'The Literal, the Allegorical, and Modern Biblical Scholarship', *JSOT* 44 (1989), pp. 3-17.

Barstad, H.M., *The Religious Polemics of Amos. Studies in the Preaching of Amos 2,7B-8; 4,1-13; 5,1-27; 6,4-7; 8,14* (VTSup 34; Leiden: Brill, 1984).

—*A Way in the Wilderness. The 'Second Exodus' in the Message of Second Isaiah* (JSS Monograph 12; Manchester: Manchester University Press, 1989).

Barton, J., *Reading the Old Testament. Method in Biblical Study* (London: Darton, Longman & Todd, 1984).

Becker, J.,*Wege der Psalmenexegese* (SBS 78; Stuttgart: KBW Verlag, 1975).

Begrich, J., 'Das priesterliche Heilsorakel', *ZAW* 52 (1934); repr. in *Gesammelte Studien zum Alten Testament* (TBü 21; Munich: C. Kaiser, 1964), pp. 217-31.

—'Die priesterliche Tora', *BZAW* 66 (1936); repr. in *Gesammelte Studien zum Alten Testament* (TBü 21; Munich: C. Kaiser, 1964), pp. 232-60.

—*Studien zu Deuterojesaja* (TBü 20; Munich: C. Kaiser, repr. 1963 [1938]).

Bellinger, W.H., Jr, *Psalmody and Prophecy* (JSOTSup 27; Sheffield: JSOT Press, 1984).

Bentzen, A., *Jahves Gæst. Studier i israelittisk salmedigtning* (Copenhagen: P. Haase, 1926).

Beyerlin, W., 'Die *tôdā* der Heilsvergegenwärtigung in den Klageliedern des Einzelnen', *ZAW* 79 (1967), pp. 208-24.

—*Die Rettung der Bedrängten in den Feindpsalmen der Einzelnen auf institutionelle Zusammenhänge untersucht* (FRLANT 99; Göttingen: Vandenhoeck & Ruprecht, 1970).

—*Der 52.Psalm. Studien zu seiner Einordnung* (BWANT 111; Stuttgart: Kohlhammer, 1980).

—*Wider die Hybris des Geistes. Studien zum 131.Psalm* (SBS 108; Stuttgart: Katholisches Bibelwerk, 1982).

—*Weisheitlicher Vergewisserung mit Bezug auf den Zionskult. Studien zum 125.Psalm* (OBO 68; Göttingen: Vandenhoeck & Ruprecht, 1985).

—*Weisheitlich-kultische Heilsordnung. Studien zum 15.Psalm* (Biblisch-Theologische Studien 9; Neukirchen-Vluyn: Neukirchener Verlag, 1985).

Birkeland, H., *Die Feinde des Individuums in der israelitischen Psalmenliteratur. Ein Beitrag zur Kenntnis der semitischen Literatur- und Religionsgeschichte* (Oslo: Grøndahl, 1933).

Brichto, H.C., 'The Worship of the Golden Calf: A Literary Analysis of a Fable on Idolatry', *HUCA* 54 (1983), pp. 1-44.

Broström, G., *Proverbiastudien: die Weisheit und das fremde Weib in Sprüche 1-9* (LUÅ NF Avd.1, Bd 30 Nr 3; Lund: Gleerup, 1935).

Brownlee, W.H., *Ezekiel 1–19* (Word Biblical Commentary 28; Waco, TX: Word Books 1986).

—'Ezekiel's Parable of the Watchman and the Editing of Ezekiel', *VT* 28 (1978), pp. 392-408.

Broyles, C.C., *The Conflict of Faith and Experience in the Psalms. A Form-Critical and Theological Study* (JSOTSup 52; Sheffield: JSOT Press, 1989).

Brueggemann, W., 'From Hurt to Joy, From Death to Life', *Int* 28 (1974), pp. 3-19.

—'Psalms and the Life of Faith: A Suggested Typology of Function' *JSOT* 17 (1980), pp. 3-32.

—*The Message of the Psalms. A Theological Commentary* (Minneapolis: Augsburg, 1984).

—'Shape for Old Testament Theology I: Structure Legitimation', *CBQ* 47 (1985), pp. 28-46.

—'Shape for Old Testament Theology II: Embrace of Pain', *CBQ* 47 (1985), pp. 395-415.

—'A Response to "The Song of Miriam" by Bernhard Anderson', in E.R. Follis (ed.), *Directions in Biblical Hebrew Poetry* (JSOTSup 40; Sheffield: JSOT Press, 1987), pp. 297-302.

Budd, P.J., *Numbers* (Word Biblical Commentary 5; Waco, TX: Word Books, 1984).

Bühlmann, W., *Von Rechten Reden und Schweigen. Studien zu Proverbia 10–31* (OBO 12; Freiburg: Universitätsverlag, 1976).

Camp, C.V., *Wisdom and the Feminine in the Book of Proverbs* (Bible and Literature Series, 11; Decatur: Almond Press, 1985).

—'Woman Wisdom as Root Metaphor: A Theological Consideration', in K.G. Hoglund *et al.* (eds.), *The Listening Heart. Essays in Wisdom and the Psalms in Honor of Roland E. Murphy* (JSOTSup 58; Sheffield: JSOT Press, 1987), pp. 45-76.

Carroll, R.P., *The Book of Jeremiah* (OTL; London: SCM, 1986).

Childs, B.S., 'A Traditio-historical Study of the Reed Sea Tradition', *VT* 20 (1970), pp. 406-18.

—*Exodus. A Critical, Theological Commentary* (OTL; Philadelphia: Westminster Press, 1974).

—'The Sensus Literalis of Scripture; an Ancient and Modern Problem', in H. Donner, R. Hanhart, R. Smend (eds.), *Beiträge zur Alttestamentlichen Theologie. Festschrift für Walther Zimmerli zum 70.Geburtstag* (Göttingen: Vandenhoeck & Ruprecht, 1977), pp. 80-93.

—'On Reading the Elijah Narratives', *Int* 34 (1980), pp. 128-37.

Christensen, D.L., 'Narrative Poetics and the Interpretation of The Book of Jonah', in E.R. Follis (ed.), *Directions in Biblical Hebrew Poetry* (JSOTSup 40; Sheffield: JSOT Press, 1987), pp. 29-48.

Clifford, R.J., *The Cosmic Mountain in Canaan and the Old Testament* (HSM 4; Cambridge MA: Harvard University Press, 1972).

Clines, D.J.A., *The Theme of the Pentateuch* (JSOTSup 10; Sheffield: JSOT Press, 1982).

Coats, G.W., 'The Traditio-historical Character of the Reed Sea Motif', *VT* 17 (1967), pp. 253-65.

—*Rebellion in the Wilderness. The Murmuring Motif in the Wilderness Tradition of the Old Testament* (Nashville: Abingdon Press, 1968).

—'An Exposition of the Wilderness Traditions', *VT* 22 (1972), pp. 288-95.

—'A Structural Transition in Exodus', *VT* 22 (1972), pp. 129-42.

—'History and Theology in the Sea Tradition', *ST* 29 (1975), pp. 53-62.

—'Humility and Honor: A Moses Legend in Numbers 12', in D.J.A. Clines, D.M. Gunn and A.J. Hauser (eds.), *Art and Meaning: Rhetoric in Biblical Literature* (JSOTSup 19; Sheffield: JSOT Press, 1982), pp. 97-107.

—*Moses. Heroic Man, Man of God* (JSOTSup 57; Sheffield: JSOT Press, 1988).

Cody, A., *A History of Old Testament Priesthood* (AnBib 35; Rome: Pontifical Biblical Institute, 1969).

Collins, T., 'Decoding the Psalms: A Structural Approach to the Psalter', *JSOT* 37 (1987), pp. 41-60.

Conrad, E.W., *Fear Not Warrior: A Study of 'al tira' Pericopes in the Hebrew Scriptures* (Brown Judaic Studies 75; Chico, CA: Scholars Press, 1985).

Craigie, P.C., *Psalms 1–50* (Word Biblical Commentary 19; Waco, TX: Word Books, 1983).

Croft, S.J.L., *The Identity of the Individual in the Psalms* (JSOTSup 44; Sheffield: JSOT Press, 1987).

Crüsemann, F., *Studien zur Formgeschichte von Hymnus und Danklied in Israel* (WMANT 32; Neukirchen-Vluyn: Neukirchener Verlag, 1969).

Culley, R.C., *Oral Formulaic Language in the Biblical Psalms* (Near and Middle East Series 4; Toronto: University of Toronto Press, 1967).

Curtis, A.H.W., 'Subjugation of the Waters Motif in the Psalms: Imagery or Polemic?', *JSS* 23 (1978), pp. 245-56.

Dahood, M., *Psalms I. 1–50* (AB; New York: Doubleday, 1966).

—*Psalms II. 51–100* (AB; New York: Doubleday, 1968).

—*Psalms III. 101–150* (AB; New York: Doubleday, 1970).

Davies, E.W., *Prophecy and Ethics. Isaiah and the Ethical Tradition of Israel* (JSOTSup 16; Sheffield: JSOT Press, 1981).

Delekat, L., *Asylie und Schutzorakel am Zionheiligtum. Eine Untersuchung zu den privaten Feindpsalmen* (Leiden: Brill, 1967).

Dillard, R.B., *2.Chronicles* (Word Biblical Commentary 15; Waco, TX: Word Books, 1987).

Durham, J.I., *Exodus* (Word Biblical Commentary 3; Waco, TX: Word Books 1987).

Eaton, J.H., *Kingship and the Psalms* (Sheffield: JSOT Press, 1986).

Eichhorn, D., *Gott als Fels, Burg und Zuflucht. Eine Untersuchung zum Gebet des Mittlers in den Psalmen* (Europäische Hochschulschriften, XXIII/4; Frankfurt: Lang, 1972).

Engnell, I., 'Lidande', in I. Engnell and A. Fridrichsen (eds.), *Svenskt Bibliskt Uppslagsverk. Andra bandet* (Gävle: Skolförlaget, 1952), pp. 69-78.

Eriksson, L.O., *'Come, children, listen to me!' Ps 34 in the Hebrew Bible and in Early Christian Writings* (ConBOT 32; Stockholm: Almqvist & Wiksell, 1991).

Fohrer, G., *Überlieferung und Geschichte des Exodus* (BZAW 91; Berlin: A. Topelmann, 1964).

—*Elia* (ATANT 53; Zürich: Zwingli Verlag, 1968).

Freedman, D.N., 'The Twenty-Third Psalm', in *Pottery, Poetry and Prophecy. Collected Essays on Hebrew Poetry* (Winona Lake: Eisenbrauns, 1980), pp. 275-302.

Geertz, C., *The Interpretation of Cultures. Selected Essays* (New York: Basic Books, 1973).

Gerstenberger, E.S., *Der bittende Mensch. Bittritual und Klagelied des Einzelnen im Alten Testament* (WMANT 51; Neukirchen-Vluyn: Neukirchener Verlag, 1980).

—*Psalms Part I with an Introduction to Cultic Poetry* (The Forms of Old Testament Literature 14; Grand Rapids: Eerdmans, 1988).

Girard, R., *La route antique des hommes pervers* (Paris: Grasset, 1985).

Gitay, Y., 'The Study of the Prophetic Discourse', *VT* 33 (1983), pp. 207-21.

Goulder, M.D., *The Psalms of the Sons of Korah* (JSOTSup 20; Sheffield: JSOT Press, 1982).

Graupner, A., *Auftrag und Geschichte des Propheten Jeremia. Literarische Eigenart, Herkunft und Intention vordeuteronomistischer Prosa im Jeremiabuch* (Biblisch-Theologische Studien 15; Neukirchen-Vluyn: Neukirchener Verlag, 1991).

Greenberg, M., *Ezekiel 1–20* (AB 22; New York: Doubleday, 1983).

Gunkel, H., *Die Psalmen* (Göttingen: Vandenhoeck & Ruprecht, 5th edn, 1968).

—*Einleitung in die Psalmen. Die Gattungen der religiösen Lyrik Israels, Zu Ende geführt von Joachim Begrich* (Göttingen: Vandenhoeck & Ruprecht, 2nd edn, 1966).

Gunneweg, A.H.J., *Leviten und Priester. Hauptlinien der Traditionsbildung und Geschichte des israelitisch-jüdischen Kultpersonals* (FRLANT 89; Göttingen: Vandenhoeck & Ruprecht, 1965).

Haag, E., 'Die Sehnsucht nach dem lebendigen Gott im Zeugnis des Psalms 42/43', *Geist und Leben* 49 (1976), pp. 167-77.

Haran, M., *Temples and Temple-Service in Ancient Israel. An Inquiry into the Character of Cult Phenomena and the Historical Setting of the Priestly School* (Oxford: Clarendon Press, 1978).

—'Divine Presence in the Israelite Cult and the Cultic Institutions', *Bib* 50 (1969), pp. 251-67.

—'Priestertum, Tempeldienst und Gebet' in G. Strecker (ed.), *Das Land Israel in biblischer Zeit* (Göttingen: Vandenhoeck & Ruprecht, 1983), pp. 141-53.

Hauge, M.R., 'The Struggles of the Blessed in Estrangement', *ST* 29 (1975), pp. 1-30, 113-46.

—'Salme 118—initiasjon av en Rettferdig', *NTT* 82 (1983), pp. 101-117.

—'Some Aspects of the Motif "The City facing Death" of Ps 68,21', *SJOT* 1 (1988), pp. 1-29.

—'Sigmund Mowinckel and the Psalms—a Query into his Concern', *SJOT* 2 (1988), pp. 56-71.

—'On the Sacred Spot. The Concept of the Proper Localization before God', *SJOT* 1 (1990), pp. 30-60.

Hauser, A.J., 'Genesis 2–3: The Theme of Intimacy and Alienation', in D.J.A. Clines, D.M. Gunn and A. Hauser (eds.), *Art and Meaning: Rhetoric in Biblical Literature* (JSOTSup 19; Sheffield: JSOT Press, 1982), pp. 20-36.

Hermisson, H.J., *Sprache und Ritus im altisraelitischen Kult. Zur 'Spiritualisierung' der Kultbegriffe im Alten Testament* (WMANT 19; Neukirchen-Vluyn: Neukirchener Verlag, 1965).

Hoffmann, H.W., *Die Intention der Verkündigung Jesajas* (BZAW 136; Berlin: de Gruyter, 1974).

Holladay, W.L., *Jeremiah 1. A Commentary on the Book of the Prophet Jeremiah Chapters 1–25* (Hermeneia; Philadelphia: Fortress Press, 1986).

Jensen, J., *The Use of tôrâ by Isaiah. His Debate with the Wisdom Tradition* (CBQMS 3; Washington DC: Catholic Biblical Association of America, 1973).

Jeremias, J., *Theophanie. Die Geschichte einer alttestamentlichen Gattung* (WMANT 10; Neukirchen-Vluyn: Neukirchener Verlag, 1965).

Johnson, A.R., *Sacral Kingship in Ancient Israel* (Cardiff: University of Wales Press, 1967).

—*The Cultic Prophet and Israel's Psalmody* (Cardiff: University of Wales Press, 1979).

Joyce, P., *Divine Initiative and Human Response in Ezekiel* (JSOTSup 51; Sheffield: JSOT Press, 1989).

Kaiser, O., *Die mythische Bedeutung des Meeres in Ägypten, Ugarit und Israel* (BZAW 78; Berlin: A. Topelmann, 1959).

—*Isaiah 1–12* (OTL; London: SCM Press, 1972).

—*Isaiah 13–39* (OTL; London: SCM Press, 1980).

Käser, W., 'Beobachtungen zum alttestamentlichen Makarismus', *ZAW* 82 (1970), pp. 225-50.

Kearney, P.J., 'Creation and Liturgy: The P Redaction of Ex 25-40', *ZAW* 89 (1977), pp. 375-87.

Keel, O., *Feinde und Gottesleugner. Studien zum Image der Widersacher in den Individualpsalmen* (SBM 7; Stuttgart: Katholisches Bibelwerk, 1969).

Kessler, M., 'Response', *JSOT* 1 (1976), pp. 12-15.

Knibb, M.A., 'Life and Death in the Old Testament', in R.E. Clements (ed.), *The World of Ancient Israel* (Cambridge: Cambridge University Press, 1989), pp. 395-415.

Knierim, R., 'Old Testament Form Criticism Reconsidered', *Int* 27 (1973), pp. 435-68.

Knight, D.A., 'The Understanding of "Sitz im Leben" in Form Criticism', in G. MacRae (ed.), *SBL 1974 Seminar Papers I* (Missoula: Scholars Press, 1974), pp. 105-25.

Knight, G.A.F., *Theology as Narration. A Commentary on the Book of Exodus* (Edinburgh: Handsel Press, 1976).

Koch, K., 'Gibt es ein Vergeltungsdogma im AT?', *ZTK* 52 (1955), pp. 1-42.

—'Tempeleinlassliturgien und Dekaloge', in R. Rendtorff and K. Koch (eds.), *Studien zur Theologie der alttestamentlichen Überlieferungen. Gerhard von Rad zum 60. Geburtstag* (Neukirchen: Neukirchener Verlag, 1961), pp. 45-60.

Kraus, H.-J., *Psalmen* (BKAT XV/1 and 2; Neukirchen-Vluyn: Neukirchener Verlag, 1961).

Kselman, J.S., 'A Note on Numbers XII 6-8', *VT* 26 (1976), pp. 500-505.

Kuntz, J.K., 'The Canonical Wisdom Psalms of Ancient Israel—Their Rhetorical, Thematic and Formal Dimensions', in J.J. Jackson and M. Kessler (eds.), *Rhetorical Criticism. Essays in Honor of J.M. Muilenburg* (Pittsburgh Theological Monograph Series 1; Pittsburgh: Pickwick Press, 1974), pp. 186-222.

—'The Retribution Motif in Psalmic Wisdom', *ZAW* 89 (1977), pp. 223-33.

Lang, B., 'Street Theater, Raising the Dead, and the Zoroastrian Connection in Ezekiel's Prophecy', in J. Lust (ed.), *Ezekiel and his Book. Textual and Literary Criticism and their Interrelation* (BETL 74; Leuven: Leuven University Press, 1986), pp. 297-316.

Lehming, S., 'Versuch zu Ex. XXXII', *VT 10* (1960), pp. 16-50.

—'Versuch zu Num 16', *ZAW* 77 (1962), pp. 291-321.

Lemche, N.P., *The Canaanites and Their Land. The Tradition of the Canaanites* (JSOTSup 110; Sheffield: JSOT Press, 1991).

Lescow, T., 'Die dreistufige Tora. Beobachtungen zu einer Form', *ZAW* 82 (1970), pp. 362-79.

Lindars, B., 'Ezekiel and Individual Responsibility', *VT* 15 (1965), pp. 52-67.

Lindblom, J., *Prophecy in Ancient Israel* (Oxford: Basil Blackwell, 1963).

Ljung, I., *Tradition and Interpretation. A Study of the Use and Application of Formulaic Language in the so-called Ebed YHWH-psalms* (ConBOT 12; Lund: Liber Läromedel/Gleerup, 1978).

Lohfink, N., '"Gewalt" als Thema alttestamentlicher Forschung', in N. Lohfink (ed.), *Gewalt und Gewaltlosigkeit im Alten Testament* (Quaestiones Disputatae 96; Freiburg: Herder, 1983), pp. 15-50.

Loewenstamm, S.E., 'The Making and Destruction of the Golden Calf', *Bib* 48 (1967), pp. 481-90.

—'The Making and the Destruction of the Golden Calf—a Rejoinder', *Bib* 56 (1975), pp. 330-43.

Lundager Jensen, H.J., 'Efterskrift', in R. Girard, *Job—Idol og syndebuk* (Fredriksberg: Forlaget ANIS, 1990), pp. 171-84.

Lundblom, J.R., 'Psalm 23: Song of Passage', *Int* 40 (1986), pp. 6-16.

McAlpine, T.H., *Sleep, Divine and Human, in the Old Testament* (JSOTSup 38; Sheffield: JSOT Press, 1987).

McCann, J.C., Jr, 'Psalm 73: A Microcosm of Old Testament Theology', in K.G. Hoglund *et al.* (eds.), *The Listening Heart. Essays in Wisdom and the Psalms in Honor of Roland E. Murphy* (JSOTSup 58; Sheffield: JSOT Press 1987), pp. 247-57.

McCarthy, D., 'Plagues and Sea of Reeds: Exodus 5-14', *JBL* 85 (1966), pp. 137-58.

McCullough, W.S., and W.R. Taylor, *The Book of Psalms* (IB 4; New York; Abingdon Press, 1955).

McKane, W., *Proverbs. A New Approach* (OTL; London: SCM Press, 1970).

McKay, J.W., and J.W. Rogerson, *Psalms 1–50, Psalms 51–100, Psalms 101–150* (The Cambridge Bible Commentary; Cambridge: Cambridge University Press, 1977).

Miller, P.D., 'Trouble and Woe (Interpreting the Biblical Laments)', *Int* 37 (1983), pp. 32-45.

—*Interpreting the Psalms* (Philadelphia: Fortress Press, 1986).

Moberly, R.W.L., *At the Mountain of God: Story and Theology in Exodus 32–34* (JSOTSup 22; Sheffield: JSOT Press, 1983).

Mowinckel, S., *Psalmenstudien 1: Åwæn und die individuellen Klagepsalmen* (Videnskapsselskapets skrifter. II, Hist.-filos. klasse; Kristiania: Jacob Dybwad, 1921).

—*Psalmenstudien 3: Kultprophetie und prophetische Psalmen* (Videnskapsselskapets skrifter. II, Hist.-filos. klasse; Kristiania: Jacob Dybwad, 1923).

—*Le décalogue* (Études d'histoire et de philosophie religieuse 16; Paris: Alcan, 1927).

—*The Psalms in Israel's Worship I–II* (Oxford: Basil Blackwell, 1962).

—*Salmeboken* (Skriftene 1.Del, Det gamle testamente oversatt av Michelet, Mowinckel og Messel, IV; Oslo: H. Aschehoug, 1955).

—'Det kultiske synspunkt som forskningsprincip i den gammeltestamentlige videnskap', *NTT* 25 (1924), pp. 1-23.

Murphy, R.E., 'A Consideration of the Classification "Wisdom Psalms"', *VTS* 9 (1963), pp. 156-67.

Niditch, S., 'The Composition of Isaiah 1', *Bib* 61 (1980), pp. 509-29.

Noth, M., *Das zweite Buch Mose. Exodus* (ATD 5; Göttingen: Vandenhoeck & Ruprecht, 1959).

—*Numbers: A Commentary* (OTL; London: SCM Press, 1966).

Ollenburger, B.C., *Zion the City of the Great King. A Theological Symbol of the Jerusalem Cult* (JSOTSup 41; Sheffield: JSOT Press, 1987).

Pedersen, J., *Israel, Its Life and Culture III–IV* (London: Oxford University Press, 1940).

Perdue, L.G., 'The Making and Destruction of the Golden Calf—A Reply', *Bib* 54 (1973), pp. 237-46.

—*Wisdom and Cult. A Critical Analysis of the Views of Cult in the Wisdom Literatures of Israel and the Ancient Near East* (SBLDS 30; Missoula: Scholars Press, 1977).

Plöger, O., *Sprüche Salomos (Proverbia)* (BKAT 17; Neukirchen-Vluyn: Neukirchener Verlag, 1984).

von Rad, G., 'Die Anrechnung des Glaubens zur Gerechtigkeit', *TLZ* 76 (1951); repr. in *Gesammelte Studien zum Alten Testament* (TBü 8; Munich 1971: C. Kaiser, 1971), pp. 130-35.

—'"Gerechtigkeit" und "Leben" in der Kultsprache der Psalmen', *Festschrift für Alfred Bertholet* (1950); repr. in *Gesammelte Studien* (TBü 8; München: C. Kaiser, 1971), pp. 225-47.

—'Die Vorgeschichte der Gattung vom 1.Kor 13,4-7', *Geschichte und Altes Testament* (Beiträge zur historischen Theologie 16) 1953; repr. in *Gesammelte Studien* (TBü 8; Munich: C. Kaiser, 1971), pp. 281-96.

—*Theologie des Alten Testaments I. Die Theologie der geschichtlichen Überlieferungen Israels* (Munich: C. Kaiser, 1961).

—*Weisheit in Israel* (Neukirchen-Vluyn: Neukirchener Verlag, 1970).

Rendtorff, R., *Die Gesetze in der Priesterschrift* (FRLANT 44; Göttingen: Vandenhoeck & Ruprecht, 1954).

—*Das überlieferungsgeschichtliche Problem des Pentateuch* (BZAW 147; Berlin: de Gruyter, 1977).

Reventlow, H.G., *Liturgie und prophetisches Ich bei Jeremia* (Gütersloh: Mohn, 1963).

—'Gattung und Überlieferung in der "Tempelrede Jeremias", Jer 7 und 26', *ZAW* 81 (1969), pp. 315-52.

Richter, G., 'Die Einheitlichkeit der Geschichte von der Rotte Korach (Num 16)', *ZAW* 39 (1921), pp. 128-37.

Ridderbos, N.H., *Die Psalmen. Stilistische Verfahren und Aufbau. Mit besonderer Berucksichtigung von Ps.1–41* (BZAW 117; Berlin: de Gruyter, 1972).

—'Response', *JSOT* 1 (1976), pp. 16-21.

Ringgren, H., 'Einige Bemerkungen zum LXXIII Psalm', *VT* 3 (1953), pp. 265-72.

—*Sprüche* (ATD 16/1; Göttingen: Vandenhoeck & Ruprecht, 1980).

Rogerson, J.W., and J.W. McKay, *Psalms 1–50, Psalms 51–100, Psalms 101–150* (The Cambridge Bible Commentary; Cambridge: Cambridge University Press, 1977).

Ross, J.F., 'Psalm 73', in J.G. Gammie *et al.* (eds.), *Israelite Wisdom. Theological and Literary Essays in Honor of Samuel Terrien* (Missoula: Scholars Press, 1978), pp. 161-75.

Rudolph, W., *Jeremia* (HAT 12; Tübingen: Mohr, 1947).

—'Ussias "Haus der Freiheit"', *ZAW* 89 (1977), p. 418.

Ruppert, L., *Der leidende Gerechte. Eine motiv-geschichtliche Untersuchung zum Alten Testament und zwischentestamentlichen Judentum* (FB 5; Würzburg: Echter Verlag, 1972).

—'Klagelieder in Israel und Babylonien—verschiedene Deutungen der Gewalt', in N. Lohfink (ed.), *Gewalt und Gewaltlosigkeit im Alten Testament* (Quaestiones Disputatae 96; Freiburg: Herder, 1983), pp. 111-58.

Schmid, H.H., *Der sogenannte Jahwist. Beobachtungen und Fragen zur Pentateuchforschung* (Zürich: Theologischer Verlag, 1976).

Schmid, H., *Die Gestalt des Mose. Probleme alttestamentlicher Forschung unter Berücksichtigung der Pentateuchkrise* (EdF 237; Darmstadt: Wissentschaftliche Buchgesellschaft, 1986).

Schmidt, H., *Die Psalmen* (HAT 15; Tübingen: Mohr, 1934).

Schwager, R., *Brauchen wir einen Sündenbock? Gewalt und Erlösung in den biblischen Schriften* (Munich: Kösel Verlag, 1978).

—'Eindrücke, von einer Begegnung', in N. Lohfink (ed.), *Gewalt und Gewaltlosigkeit im Alten Testament* (Quaestiones Disputatae 96; Freiburg: Herder, 1983), pp. 214-24.

Scott, R.B.Y., *The Way of Wisdom in the Old Testament* (New York: Macmillan, 1971).

Van Seters, J., *In Search of History. Historiography in the Ancient World and the Origins of Biblical History* (New Haven: Yale University Press, 1983).

Seybold, K., *Das Gebet des Kranken im Alten Testament. Untersuchungen zur Bestimmung und Zuordnung der Krankheits- und Heiligungspsalmen* (BWANT 5.19; Stuttgart: Kohlhammer, 1973).

Smith, M.S., 'Setting and Rhetoric in Psalm 23', *JSOT* 41 (1988), pp. 61-66.

Snaith, N.H., *The First and Second Books of Kings* (IB 3; New York: Abingdon Press, 1954).

Soggin, J.A., 'Tod und Auferstehung des leidenden Gottesknechtes', *ZAW* 87 (1975), pp. 346-55.

Spronk, K., *Beatific Afterlife in Ancient Israel and in the Ancient Near East* (AOAT 219; Neukirchen Vluyn: Neukirchener Verlag, 1986).

Stolz, F., *Psalmen im nachkultischen Raum* (Theologische Studien 129; Zürich: Theologischer Verlag, 1983).

Tate, M.E., *Psalms 51–100* (Word Biblical Commentary 20; Dallas: Word Books, 1990).

Taylor, W.R., and W. Stewart McCullough, *The Book of Psalms* (IB 4; New York: Abingdon Press, 1955).

Thiel, W., *Die devteronomistische Redaktion von Jeremia 1–25* (WMANT 41; Neukirchen-Vluyn: Neukirchener Verlag, 1973).

Thompson, T.L., *The Historicity of the Patriarchal Narratives. The Quest for the Historical Abraham* (BZAW 133; Berlin: de Gruyter, 1974).

—*The Origin Tradition of Ancient Israel. I. The Literary Formation of Genesis and Exodus 1–23* (JSOTSup 55; Sheffield: JSOT Press, 1987).

Tromp, N.J., *Primitive Conceptions of Death and the Nether World in the Old Testament* (Biblica et Orientalia 21; Rome: Pontifical Biblical Institute, 1969).

Vogt, E., 'Psalm 26, ein Pilgergebet', *Bib* 43 (1962), pp. 328-37.

—*Untersuchungen zum Buch Ezechiel* (AnBib 95; Rome: Pontifical Biblical Institute, 1981).

Vorländer, H., *Die Entstehungszeit des jehowistischen Geschichtswerkes* (Europäische Hochschulschriften XIII/109; Frankfurt: Lang, 1978).

Wanke, G., *Die Zionstheologie der Korachiten* (BZAW 97; Berlin: Topelmann, 1966).

Watson, W., 'Archaic Elements in the Language of Chronicles', *Bib* 53 (1972), pp. 191-207.

Watters, W.R., *Formula Criticism and the Poetry of the Old Testament* (BZAW 138; Berlin: de Gruyter, 1976).

Watts, J.D.W., *Isaiah 1–33* (Word Biblical Commentary 24; Waco, TX: Word Books, 1985).

Weippert, H., *Die Prosareden des Jeremiabuches* (BZAW 132; Berlin: de Gruyter, 1973).

Weiser, A., *Die Psalmen* (ATD 14/15; Göttingen: Vandenhoeck & Ruprecht, 1955).

Weiss, M., 'Wege der neuen Dichtungswissenschaft in ihrer Anwendung auf die Psalmenforschung', *Bib* 42 (1961), pp. 255-302.

—'Die Methode der "Total-Interpretation"', in *Uppsala Congress Volume 1971* (VTSup 22; Leiden: Brill, 1972), pp. 88-112.

Wenham, G.J., 'Aaron's Rod (Numbers 17:16-28)', *ZAW* 93 (1981), pp. 280-81.

Westermann, C., 'Struktur und Geschichte der Klage im Alten Testament', *ZAW* 66 (1954), pp. 44-80.

—*Genesis 1–11* (BKAT 1/1; Neukirchen-Vluyn: Neukirchener Verlag, 1974).

—*Wurzeln der Weisheit. Die ältesten Sprüche Israels und anderer Völker* (Göttingen: Vandenhoeck & Ruprecht, 1990).

Whybray, R.N., *The Making of the Pentateuch. A Methodological Study* (JSOTSup 53; Sheffield: JSOT Press, 1987).

Widengren, G., *Sakrales Königtum im Alten Testament und im Judentum* (Stuttgart: Kohlhammer, 1955).

Wildberger, H., *Jesaja. I. Jesaja 1–12* (BKAT X/1; Neukirchen-Vluyn: Neukirchener Verlag, 1972).

—*Jesaja. II. Jesaja 13–27* (BKAT X/2; Neukirchen-Vluyn: Neukirchener Verlag, 1978).

—*Jesaja. III. Jesaja 28–39* (BKAT X/3; Neukirchen-Vluyn: Neukirchener Verlag, 1982).

Willi, T., 'Die Freiheit Israels. Philologische Notizen zu den Wurzeln *ḥpš*, *'zb* and *drr*', in H. Donner, R. Hanhart and R. Smend (eds.), *Beiträge zur alttestamentlichen Theologie. Festschrift für Walther Zimmerli zum 70. Geburtstag* (Göttingen: Vandenhoeck & Ruprecht, 1977), pp. 531-46.

Willis, J.T., 'The First Pericope in the Book of Isaiah', *VT* 34 (1984), pp. 63-77.

Wilson, R.R., 'An Interpretation of Ezekiel's Dumbness', *VT* 22 (1972), pp. 91-104.

Würthwein, E., 'Erwägungen zu Psalm 73', in W. Baumgartner (ed.), *Festschrift für Alfred Bertholet zum 80. Geburtstag gewidmet von Kollegen und Freunden* (Tübingen: Mohr, 1950), pp. 532-49.

—'Der Ursprung der prophetischen Gerichtsrede', *ZTK* 49 (1952), pp. 1-16.

Zeron, A., 'Die Anmassung des Königs Usias im Lichte von Jesajas Berufung. Zu 2.Chr. 26,16-22 und Jes. 6,1ff', *TZ* 33 (1977), pp. 65-68.

Zimmerli, W., 'Die Eigenart der prophetischen Rede des Ezechiel', *ZAW* 66 (1954), pp. 1-26.

—'"Leben" und "Tod" im Buche des Propheten Ezechiel', *TZ* 13 (1957), pp. 494-508.

—*Ezekiel 1. A Commentary on the Book of the Prophet Ezekiel, Ch. 1–24* (Hermeneia; Philadelphia: Fortress Press, 1979).

—*Ezekiel 2. A Commentary on the Book of the Prophet Ezekiel, Ch 25–48* (Hermeneia; Philadelphia: Fortress Press, 1983).

INDEXES

INDEX OF REFERENCES

INDEX OF AUTHORS

JOURNAL FOR THE STUDY OF THE OLD TESTAMENT

Supplement Series